The Methodist Revolution

THE
METHODIST
REVOLUTION

BY

BERNARD SEMMEL

Basic Books, Inc., Publishers

NEW YORK

Library of Congress Catalog Card Number: 72-89282
SBN 465-04570-7
Manufactured in the United States of America
DESIGNED BY VINCENT TORRE
73 74 75 76 10 9 8 7 6 5 4 3 2 1

FOR STUART

Preface

In this book, I have argued that the Methodist Revolution might have been the English counterpart to the "democratic revolution of the eighteenth century" which, in the view of a number of recent historians, erupted in many parts of the Atlantic world. I have suggested further that the special form which this English Revolution took may have had a decisive impact in the shaping of what foreign observers considered the unique qualities of nineteenth-century England, with its blending of liberty and order, and its special sense of national mission. It is too big a subject for such an essay, and can only be justified as an hypothesis or a set of hypotheses, with all the tentativeness which that term suggests, accompanied, I hope, by the reader's indulgence for its abstractions (and hence, inevitable simplifications).

Over a very long period, though more heatedly during the course of the last two decades, there has been a debate among historians concerning the social role played by Methodism and evangelical religion generally in British development. This book—which may at least have the merit of bringing theological questions more decidedly into the forefront of the discussion—is offered as a contribution to this debate. There are a number of historians in both England and the United States who are now making intensive studies of local religious developments, attempting to discover what actually happened in the various communities and congregations, to see what relationship these local events, so much closer to the largely inarticulate individual Methodists who occupied the pews, have to those larger questions historians have long discussed. Relying on the views of the leaders of the denomination as these appeared in their sermons, tracts, letters, etc., I have attempted to extend the range of questions being asked and to present a new synthesis.

Much of the early research for this study was made possible by a Guggenheim Fellowship, in 1967–1968. I have also enjoyed summer research fellowships of the State University of New York. I am especially appreciative for released time from teaching duties made possible by my department, to all of whose members I owe a debt of gratitude, and by my university. There are many people with whom I have discussed the book over the years, or who have read the manuscript, in whole or in part. I should particularly like to thank Professors Gertrude Himmelfarb of the City University of New York, William Lamont of the University of Sussex, and my colleagues at Stony Brook, Karl S Bottigheimer, John W. Pratt, David F. Trask, Fred Weinstein, Ruben Weltsch, and John A. Williams. I am especially grateful for the advice given to me by John D. Walsh of Jesus College, Oxford.

I have used the collections of the British Museum, the New York Public Library, and the libraries of Columbia University and of the Union Theological Seminary, and in all cases I have found reason to feel indebted to their staffs. I am most especially in the debt of the Methodist Church Archives, the City Road, London, and its knowledgeable director, Dr. J. C. Bowmer, who was my guide to its rich collection of pamphlets and manuscripts. The manuscript collection of the Wesleyan Methodist Missionary Society Archives was also useful to me, as was the help of its director. I wish to thank Sonia Sbarge for the typing of a first draft, and my wife Maxine for typing all the others, and for checking most of the references. My wife has also been a most willing audience for exhortations concerning the Methodist Revolution, as has my son, Stuart. This book is dedicated to him.

BERNARD SEMMEL

Stony Brook, N.Y.
March 1972

Contents

The Methodist Revolution

I

The Methodist Revolution

About this time, the sect of the Methodists . . . began to spread into most parts of the nation: though . . . I know of few novel opinions which they maintain, except that of the lawfulness of preaching without a legal call; and of assembling in conventicles or in the open fields in direct opposition to the laws of the land. . . . Mr. Wesley however, I am convinced, had no thoughts, at that time, of separating from the Established Church . . . much less of robbing the community of so many useful mechanics: who, with a view of raising themselves above their fellow plebeians . . . forsake their lawful callings, and commence reformers and teachers of their brethren. But 'the beginning of strife is as the letting out of water': and if one man may break through the established order of society, another has the same right to do it; which must end at last in utter confusion. . . . But our modern itinerant reformers, by the mere force of the imagination, have conjured up the powers of darkness in an enlightened age. They are acting in defiance of human laws, without any apparent necessity, or any divine commission. They are planting the Gospel in a Christian country.

Richard Graves, The Spiritual Quixote or the
Summer's Ramble of Mr. Geoffrey Wildgoose, *1773*

In recent years, historians have once again turned their attention to the evangelical Revival and, more particularly, to Wesleyan Methodism, and this more or less in the context of the well-known Halévy thesis. For over a century and a half, historians have intuited—given the lack of "hard" evidence, no other word can be used—that England was spared a violent counterpart to the French Revolution by the widespread effects of the evangelical Revival which Wesley and Whitefield initiated in 1739.[1] For most of these historians as well as for some who for one reason or other doubted such a view, Methodism has been pictured as a regressive, repressive religion, in both doctrine and practice. It is an image common to Leslie Stephen, to the Hammonds, to E. J. Hobsbawm, and to E. P. Thompson, among others.[2] Thompson's book has been especially influential during the past decade in depicting Methodism as designed to crush rather than to elevate the spirit of the new proletariat.

In none of the works of these authors does Methodist theology play a significant role, as Calvinist doctrine does, for example, in studies of seventeenth-century Puritanism. Where Methodist doctrine has been discussed, it has been presented in a highly unfavorable light, generally ac-

3

companied by the view that Wesley and his associates were hardly systematic theologians—they were guilty of "promiscuous opportunism," wrote Thompson [3]—were hopelessly confused and intellectually inadequate. The historians who have compared Methodism to Calvinism have found the latter much more satisfying: Calvin had a "system" and systems have always been congenial to intellectuals. Leslie Stephen, for example, nearly a century ago saw a Methodism which had shed "all the most powerful intellectual elements" and was therefore but "a faint reflection of the grander Puritanism of the seventeenth century." Wesley, Stephen continued, in opposing Calvinism, "was not able to distinguish the philosophic core of the doctrine from the perversions to which it is liable." [4] In the same spirit, E. P. Thompson has suggested that in his theology, "Wesley appears to have dispensed with the best and selected unhesitatingly the worst elements of Puritanism." Like so many of Wesley's far from friendly contemporaries, Thompson, quite mistakenly, has even understood Wesley to have shared the view of his Calvinist associate Whitefield in totally dismissing good works in favor of faith.[5]

Thus, most liberal, secular-minded historians have judged Methodism to be a reactionary movement, a protest against the Enlightenment and reason, and have seen its discipline, polity, and doctrine in this spirit; denominational historians, while stressing the comforting qualities which Methodism brought to its followers, have appeared, if only implicitly, more or less to accept this assessment. Even so, both groups of historians have been somewhat troubled by such a one-sided view and have, though only peripherally, offered another. Though they have seen the Revival as fanaticism burying reason, of religion once again proving itself the opiate of the people, some have conceded that Methodism may also have helped the workingmen to face the challenges of the burgeoning industrial order and, others have added, may even have prepared them for a later socialism.[6] If the Hammonds, for example, saw Wilberforce as a villain and Evangelicalism as an opiate, they were nonetheless prepared to grant that Methodism had made many men "better rebels." [7] E. J. Hobsbawm insisted in one essay that Methodists, especially Primitive Methodists, were very much involved in radical activities in the early decades of the nineteenth century, observing that it was "too easily assumed" that industrial workers turned toward religious sects *as an alternative* to revolution or radical politics," rather than that workers became Methodists or Radicals for the same reasons; [8] in another essay, however, Hobsbawm took a very different view.[9] Halévy—anticipated by Taine—seems to have understood that Methodism had something quite positive to offer, and proved so successful an obstacle to revolution because it was itself a "popular revolution." [10] This seeming confusion is a consequence of the real ambiguities and contradictions at the very heart of the Revival and its doctrines. It originates, I shall suggest, in the failure to see the Revival as both a spiritual Revolution of a

progressive and liberal character and as a counter to revolutionary violence, a circumstance growing out of the ideology and structure of Methodism, as well as the conditions under which it rose and developed.

Certainly Methodist theology deserves the kind of attention which
seventeenth-century Calvinism has received. If the accepted view of Methodist theology as a regressive and repressive doctrine were correct, it is
unlikely that Methodism could have played such a "revolutionary" role. I
will argue that Methodist doctrine, as set forward by the leading spokesmen of the movement, was essentially a liberal and "progressive" (in the
sense of both confirming and helping to advance the movement from a traditional to a modern society) ideology, much more decidedly liberal and
progressive than that of Calvinism, whose liberal and "modern" character
has received so much attention from social scientists and historians. The
Revival was, indeed, a revolution—undeniably on a spiritual and in all
likelihood on a social level as well—and was so understood by both Methodists and their opponents. Both the Establishment in Church and state
and the Methodist leadership, conservative and Tory by predisposition,
feared the translation of a liberal and egalitarian Methodist religious doctrine to the political sphere, and made strenuous efforts to inhibit such a
development. The enemy was Disorder. Wesley and his associates and successors declaimed against the "speculative" Antinomianism (opposition to
both the restraints of scriptural law and to the necessity of good works)
which they found in the traditional doctrines of Reformation Protestantism
lest it lead to the practical Antinomianism of those seeking violent revolution. They worked to contain the Enthusiasm which was indispensable to
their own evangelization within the bounds of order. They discouraged political activity, enjoined the Biblical commands of obedience to the King as
to God, and attempted, after Wesley's death, to divert evangelical Enthusiasm to the missionary movement. These efforts appeared to be successful:
there seemed to be no direct or obvious translation of Methodist Enthusiasm and spiritual egalitarianism to the political realm. It was their apparent success which gave rise to the Halévy thesis, in both the relatively positive terms in which they were couched by its formulator and in its
subsequent reduction to depicting Methodism as a popular opiate.

This study will describe the development and dissemination of Methodist doctrine, and will suggest that the nature of this doctrine, together with
the circumstances which led to efforts to prevent its political translation,
may have helped to form the special character of nineteenth-century England. To understand the Methodist Revolution in all its dimensions would
of course require volumes: we would, for example, want to know who
those converted to Methodism were and where they came from; we would
want to know what questions they were anxious about and what kinds of
consolation and reassurance they sought. We do know that the adherents
of Methodism took their religion so seriously that they could not help but

attempt to translate it to other parts of their lives, but we do not yet know enough about the ways in which such translations could have been accomplished. These questions cannot be answered by a discussion of the conduct or the doctrine of the leading spokesmen for Methodism. However, the danger is that these immensely important questions may be closed off by the prevailing view that Methodism was thoroughly repressive. A study that portrays Wesleyan Methodism as a profoundly "liberal" and "modern" ideology may thus serve some purpose if it persuades scholars to reexamine these problems from a fresh standpoint.

The eighteenth century in Europe, from its middle decades onward, was a time of spiritual turmoil, perhaps not too unlike the ferment we are now experiencing. " [We] live in curious times and amid astonishing contrasts," Voltaire said; "reason on the one hand, the most absurd fanaticism on the other . . . a civil war in every soul. *Sauve qui peut*." [11] This "civil war in every soul" which afflicted Europe erupted with sudden violence in France in 1789. Reason—by which Voltaire meant the ideals of liberty and equality which were to be enshrined by the Revolution—strove to bury fanaticism, the religious superstition and obscurantism of the old order.

Writing half a century later, however, Alexis de Tocqueville saw the issue somewhat differently. He was convinced that the French Revolution was fundamentally a religious revolution. The institutions of Western Europe were breaking down, he observed, and the "stirrings" of revolution "were perceptible in almost all European countries." Yet even while the Church was under attack as representing a rich and privileged order, and "skepticism was in fashion in the royal courts and among the intellectuals," Tocqueville argued that the "religious instinct" continued to have "its most abiding home in the hearts of the common people." The common people needed a faith, and they turned to the Revolution, which "developed into a species of religion," and "created an atmosphere of missionary fervor and, indeed, assumed all the aspects of a religious revival." The Revolution's "approach" to the problems of man's terrestrial existence was in Tocqueville's view "exactly similar to that of the religious revolutions as regards his after life." Like the revealed religions, the French Revolution concerned itself with producing "new men": "No previous political upheaval, however violent, had aroused such passionate enthusiasm," for its ideal was "nothing short of a regeneration of the whole human race." Tocqueville was convinced that "when we seek to study the French Revolution in the light of similar movements" elsewhere and at other times, it was "to the great religious revolutions we should turn." [12]

In the eighteenth and early nineteenth centuries, England underwent a powerful and pervasive experience—equally devoted to the "regeneration" of the race and the producing of 'new men"—which I call the Methodist

Revolution. There are three principal reasons why this term seems useful. First of all, I wish to consider the Methodist Revival in its dominant Wesleyan aspect as the culmination of a Protestant Counter-Reformation, a revolt against certain leading views of Luther and Calvin which had long dominated Protestantism, particularly sectarian Protestantism. Secondly, and overlapping the latter, I am persuaded by historians who see the period between 1760 and 1815 as an "Age of the Democratic Revolution" in the West, a time when the traditional, hierarchical society which had characterized Europe for many centuries was eroding and a recognizably modern society was taking its place. This was a time when the entire Atlantic world, moved by the desire for greater personal autonomy and roused by the slogans of liberty and equality, rose to overturn the privileged, governing classes, bringing the long-suppressed, inarticulate lower classes onto the stage of events.[13] I will suggest that the Methodist Revival may have been the English version of the "Democratic Revolution," and that Wesleyan doctrine was the theological form taken by the liberal ideology of the time. Lastly, in terms of the well-known debate concerning Methodism and revolution, I shall suggest that Methodism may have helped to block a violent English counterpart to the French Revolution by preempting the critical appeal and objective of that Revolution. Indeed, it might be said that only because of what the Methodist Revolution was accomplishing could the Methodist counter to revolutionary violence be effective.

The lower ranks in eighteenth-century France and England were exposed to great social and economic dislocations, accompanied by a disorientation of the traditional family structure. Such changes produced widespread and profound anxiety, and, one may argue with Tocqueville, religious revolutions. Certainly it was to the anxious—the dislocated, the rootless, the disturbed—that the Methodist preachers came with their doctrine of reassurance. Though you are covered in sin, they said, though there is nothing in you which merits God's goodness, yet God is ready to welcome you—*all* of you—as His children, should you strive to attain His grace and live the holy life which will enable you to enter into His Kingdom. This was a message of hope for men in despair. It was accompanied by an offer to enlist those regenerated by God's grace into a brotherhood of the newly reborn in which all would watch over the spiritual welfare of each. The Methodist preachers broadcast a liberal and egalitarian religious doctrine, and endeavored to quell the anxieties of their adherents by initiating them into the new families of Methodist bands and societies.

The origins, character, and, insofar as possible, the consequences of the apparently ambiguous roles of Methodism need to be explored, because the resolution of the contradictory forces within the Revival, forces emerging from the religious and political struggles of the sixteenth and seventeenth century, was to affect forcefully, and possibly critically, the evolution of perhaps the most characteristic qualities of nineteenth-century England—its relative stability, its ordered freedom, and its sense of world mission.

Modern society requires the transformation of large masses of men from the relatively inert passivity which characterizes their state in a traditional society to one in which their personalities are sufficiently strong to enable them to emerge from a state of subordination to one of relative independence. Masses of men were obliged to come of age. Anthropologists tell us that the rites of passage by means of which adulthood is attained among primitive peoples vary considerably. The purgative shedding of blood is frequently encountered in societies on such occasions, and it has been argued that the revolt against dependence requires a similar bloodletting, as a people moves from dependence to a quasi-autonomy.[14] In the eighteenth century, England proved able to make this transformation relatively peacefully, despite the great pressures which seemed to be pushing her toward violent revolution. I shall examine how the special character of the "new man" envisioned and to some extent created by Wesley's evangelical Arminianism *might* have helped—that is all we can safely say—to bridge the gap between the traditional and the modern orders without tumultuous upheaval, while at the same time promoting the ideals which would be most useful to the new society.

It was Arminianism, particularly in its Wesleyan, evangelical form, which bore the revolutionary message of liberty and equality—of free will and universal salvation—in the shape best able to appeal to masses of men who aspired to personal autonomy but who were still rooted in a strong dependence, a deep internal attachment to traditional values. The move toward liberty and equality, as Tocqueville was to observe, was the most powerful one of the eighteenth and nineteenth centuries, and the hierarchical principle, bound up with a system of restrictive privileges, was a negation of liberal egalitarianism. Europe was moving from the quasi-feudal dependence of a static, agrarian, traditional society to the new individualism of a competitive, progressive industrialism. In the new industrial society the traditional paternalism of master and man was no more. Large numbers of men found themselves alienated from their patrimonies and expected vocations; the evangelists of the day proclaimed them "alienated from God" as well. The lower classes, stumblingly aware of their presumed equality in law and in the eyes of their Savior, began the long move from the old dependence upon paternal favor to a growing demand for autonomy, which had early repercussions in politics. The Calvinist sects, it has been argued by Max Weber and others, had helped to produce "modern" men fitted to the purposes of emerging seventeenth-century commercial society. I suggest that evangelical religion in the eighteenth century probably accomplished for masses of men what sixteenth- and seventeenth-century Calvinism could only confirm for a relative few. Particularly in its Wesleyan, Arminian Methodist form, in seeking to reconcile God and the masses "alienated from God," it may have performed the service of mediating between the ideals of the old society and those of the new.

FROM THE TRADITIONAL TO THE MODERN

The particular circumstances which saw Wesley preaching to the miners outside of Bristol in 1739 may have been fortuitous, as were, no doubt, the special talents which Wesley brought to his mission, but it is noteworthy that Wesley scored his initial successes among the proletariat in the mining districts and in the manufacturing towns which, being marginal in the still largely traditional society of mid-eighteenth-century England, had been neglected by the Established Church. The enclosures, which destroyed the tribal society of the Highlands and rocked the traditional order of England, loosened the ties of dependence which bound the different ranks, and sent tens of thousands of discontented laborers not only to the commercial towns but to the villages of the north and west where the new industry was establishing itself. These sectors of society were to expand considerably in the following three-quarters of a century, and a religious awakening appeared, district by district, to accompany industrial growth. In both England and France, the traditional order had been undermined for some time because of the growth of commerce. Commercial expansion —spurred largely by the growth of trade with the colonial world—was striking on both sides of the Channel in the middle decades of the eighteenth century, making the traditional assumptions concerning both the relatively static character of an economy of scarcity and those of a hierarchical society appear outmoded. Associated with this commercial growth was a great increase in population: the population of France, which had been approximately 19 million in 1715, rose to some 26 million in 1789; in England and Wales, a population estimated at about 5,826,000 at the beginning of the century increased to about 9,156,000 by the century's end.[15] The ideals of this new society of increasing numbers burst forth upon Europe in the revolutionary slogan of *liberté, egalité, fraternité,* sentiments not new in themselves, but now cast in the pervasive and powerful forms which prefigured the advent of modern society—that is, a commercial and industrial society governed by a liberal, national state based upon the principles of political equality and popular sovereignty, on a rational, contractual basis.

Very roughly, I mean to invoke the dichotomy between the "modern" and the "traditional" as one, in Tönnies' terminology, between *Gessellschaft* and *Gemeinschaft*. Following the example of the classic sociological thinkers, I will not assume the necessary primacy of economic forces in this transformation of society, but will examine the subtle interplay between ideological, socio-political, and economic forces. Nor do I believe that there was a specific moment in the early modern period when the unambiguously "modern" emerged with a mechanical uniformity, or even that elements of the "modern" constellation work as necessary allies against the "traditional." It might be argued that the history of industrial society can be understood as one of a continuing struggle between the "modern" and the "traditional," and there is good reason to acknowledge the persistent strength of the latter. All this is useful in the effort to understand the role a number of important theological formulations may have played in reflecting, and, at the same time, helping to bring about the European transition from the "traditional" to the "modern."

FROM GRACE TO CONTRACT

Before the Protestant Revolt, there had been a good deal of confusion in Catholic theology on such questions as election, free will, works, etc., and within the Church opinions on both sides of each issue were more or less tolerated. After the Revolt, the forces of the Counter-Reformation insisted upon conformity in opposition to a Protestantism which, in the hands of Luther, Calvin and their followers, had constructed an unrelenting, self-conscious ideology in an effort to return to the purity of primitive Christianity. Although the "modern" was certainly present in its individualistic (and egalitarian) view of the priesthood of all believers, and in its rejection of clerical thaumaturgical gifts, on other questions Protestant theology— with its belief in salvation by faith rather than works; in election, with its attendant view of the inability of man to be saved by his own efforts; and in determinism—can only be seen as belonging to a "traditional" order.

Nor is this too surprising when we consider that the Reformation may be regarded as a deliberate return to an earlier Christianity by the most socially and economically backward parts of Christendom against a foreign prince-bishop who had permitted the wealth of the Church and the commercial standards of its most economically advanced territories to subvert its primitive purity. We must recollect that the immediate cause of Luther's revolt was the sale of indulgences: to purchase exemption from the punishment of one's sins seemed a corruption of the Biblical doctrine of salvation by works, especially when the sale was made by a time-serving cleric, with the Church acting as a middleman banker transferring Christ's merit by sale in the most sordid commercial fashion. Had the Church not been tainted by its association with usurious Italian bankers who in pursuit of private interests or as the agents of the Church were fleecing all Europe? Was this not the time to reassert that salvation could not be purchased from such worldlings, but was the sole gift of God, at his pleasure, by his unpurchased will? Luther, an Augustinian monk, was in later years to return to the principles of absolute, unconditional election and irresistible grace of the founder of his order, also accepting the deterministic outlook which underlay these principles; and Calvin elaborated upon these views in his *Institutes,* seeing justification as bestowed by Christ alone, and declaring it vain and sinful for degenerate man to regard any action on his part as helping to secure God's grace.

Erasmus and Melanchthon, as well as Cranmer and other English Protestant divines, raised the banner of free will against Luther and Calvin, unable to accept this reversion to the theology of a primitive Augustinian Christianity. Protestants working in the Erasmian tradition in the commercial cities of Holland, primarily in Amsterdam, joined together under the leadership of the Dutch theologian Arminius in the early years of the seventeenth century to offer still another view of the relationship of God and man—one which because of its character we must view in the light of Holland's commercial pre-eminence. The views of the Arminians, it might be noted, did not penetrate deeply into the rural hinterland of the Netherlands, where the Calvinistic return to Augustinian Christianity went relatively unchallenged.

The Remonstrance of 1610, enunciated by Episcopius and other followers of Arminius a year after the latter's death, put forward the exhilarating view that because of Christ's sacrifice and atonement, *all* men *might* be saved, not merely a preordained elect as Calvin had stipulated. The Reformation Protestantism of Calvin and Luther had stressed justification by faith alone; the Arminian scheme had an important place for works as well: though all men might take up the Gospel offer of salvation by faith through their acceptance of God's freely offered grace, after this conversion and regeneration by the Holy Ghost, the men who had experienced this New Birth, if they were to attain final salvation, were obliged to strive conscientiously to lead a Godly life, unlike the Calvinist saved for whom election was sufficient. If election was not preordained, neither was sin: departing from the determinism, the doctrine of predestination of Calvin and Luther, the Arminians saw man as endowed with free will, capable of choice and morally responsible for his conduct. Thus, a man had first of all to choose to seek justification, to avail himself of God's grace, for it was not irresistible as the Calvinists held and without its regenerating power all good works would prove ineffectual. If a man made this indispensable choice, he became justified, "reborn," a "new man." However, unlike Calvin's "elect," whom the Calvinist doctrine of final perseverance declared incapable of falling, the Arminian justified might by evil conduct fall from grace. Election hence was not absolute but conditional. If the conduct of one who had been justified continued to be righteous until the time of his death and judgment, he was sanctified by the joining of his good works to his earlier justification by faith, and he would enter into the kingdom of the saints.

As good Protestants, Arminians could not accept the middleman role of the Church as an Italian banker selling Christ's merit, nor, as citizens of an advanced, commercial republic, could they accept the seeming whimsicality of the award of Christ's merit to a preordained elect, who would, regardless of conduct, maintain elect status (the doctrine of irresistible grace). The individual had to strive directly, without any intermediary, to obtain God's grace. The Arminians, moreover, saw the relationship between Christ and his worshippers as akin to a commercial contract. While continuing to insist that Christ was the author of all salvation, they held that this salvation was to be accomplished not by the wilful imputation of Christ's righteousness to individual Christians, in the manner of a despot arbitrarily disposing favors. Rather Arminians saw Christ as having, by his sacrifice, both *purchased* favorable *terms* or *conditions* for men, and also as having restored to men a great part of their ability to fulfill these conditions of which they had been deprived by Adam's sin. God seemed as much bound by the contract, which offered a *quid pro quo,* as was the individual worshipper. This was at the heart of the Arminian doctrine of "conditional justification" which saw Christians as seeking, by good works, to attain holiness, and as striving to retain holiness in order to fulfill their part of the contract with God—whose terms, the Arminians insisted, were clear in the Gospels—in exchange for which God, because of Christ's sacrifice, had agreed to grant eternal salvation.

Certainly, such a contractual view of man's relationship with God conformed to the commercial, and increasingly, the political principles of "modern" society in a much more decided fashion than did the ethos of Reformation Christianity. Of course, the classical Protestantism of Luther and Calvin probably helped to ease the transition from the "traditional" to the "modern" by stressing the continuing security of the traditional religious patterns of authority even as unsettling social patterns were making their initial appearance. Yet, before long, the more advanced sections of Northern Europe returned, albeit in a more sophisticated form, to the gospel of works. In thus stipulating that salvation was dependent upon man's rational, responsible behavior, the Arminians were asking for the kind of conduct which "modern" political and economic life would find essential, and which, especially so far as the lower classes were concerned, was almost nonexistent in the traditional order.

John Wesley was to be the mediator between the "traditional" Protestantism of the Reformation which had flowered in England during the seventeenth century and was still the prized possession of tens of thousands of the devout, and the "modern" Arminian Protestantism which had become characteristic of both Laudian and Latitudinarian Anglicanism, as we shall see. Wesley appealed to both the Puritan sense of man's degenerate state, with its passionate plea for God's grace so essential to salvation, as well as to the Arminian insistence on personal responsibility, on free will and good works. We must stress that while the essential Arminian principles cannot be viewed as a crude product of commercial development—the core of Arminian theology might be found in fifth-century Pelagianism which also espoused universal salvation and free will—it would be difficult to see their adoption, in Holland and England, as independent of the superior economic development of those countries. Similarly, we cannot fail to see in Grotius' views on natural rights (Grotius was one of the leaders of the Arminian party in Holland) and in Locke's liberalism and in his ideas of social contract (Locke also came under the direct influence of Dutch Arminianism) the interplay of similar theological, political, and economic forces. It was to be Wesley's role not only to unite Puritanism and Arminianism into an instrument for the evangelization of England's new and growing industrial proletariat, but also to inspire a similar fusion by both Anglican Evangelicals and Dissenters.

FROM ENTHUSIASM TO ORDER

The eighteenth century, like our own, was a time when rioting, apparently beyond the power of the law to control, was endemic. There were riots against the Gin Acts and the Scottish malt tax, in opposition to the preaching of evangelists and the granting of citizenship to Jews, riots directed against the employment of Irish weavers in Spitalfields and French actors at the Haymarket, riots against the Militia Acts and the new turnpike trusts. A chronic cause of disturbance was high corn prices, and there was frequent rioting against millers or merchants who sought to send corn, at times of shortage, to far-off cities or to foreign markets. These disturbances occurred particularly at times of poor harvests. The years 1739 and 1740, when Methodism erupted, were especially bad years, but there were intermittent food riots throughout the century. High corn prices were usually the spark, but meat, butter, and cheese prices were also frequently at issue, and there were often riots for higher wages. The records of these uprisings reveal that they were most frequent where Methodism was most active: the Kingswood miners, for example, to whom Wesley addressed his first open-air sermon in 1739, were regularly a source of difficulty. During the wage riots in the 1760s—1766 was a very bad year—which accompanied the corn riots, workingmen broke open the houses of masters, and burned and destroyed looms; there were also demonstrations against enclosures. The year 1768 coincided with the Wilkes agitation and proved an especially bad year for London; it was marked by mob actions against high corn prices and low wages. The early seventies were also troublesome years. In 1779, marking a new era, mobs of workingmen destroyed Arkwright's recently installed machinery. The traditional method of coping with the rioting was repression: the arming of "respectable" householders, and the hiring of mercenary toughs, as well as the call for the militia. There were a host of minor Peterloos, and a summary justice executed, jailed, or banished the rioters.

This rioting provoked intermittent but largely unsubstantial fears of revolution. On occasions, of course, there were clear threats to the ruling dynasty, as in the alarms preceding the Stuart efforts to reclaim the throne in 1715 and 1745, and there were occasional flurries about the possibilities of invasion during the French wars. There was some fear of revolution in the seventies during the course of the troubles with America, a time also of economic difficulties, when a substantial number of Dissenters, Whigs, and London artisans were sufficiently sympathetic to the American cause to give concern. The ever-loyal John Wesley was to attribute this discontent to Antinomian Calvinism yearning for the restoration of the Commonwealth, supported by distorted Lockean principles and serviced by French gold. The Gordon Riots in 1780, directed against Catholics, cut a path of disorder from the Bank of England in the City of London to the Spaniards' Inn at Hampstead. This had more of the smell of revolution but not the reality. A similar pattern of rioting was apparent in contemporary France where it did indeed prove a prelude to full scale upheaval. In France, revolution had been long and even eagerly anticipated: not only the radical *philosophes* who were urging its program, but substantial sections of the upper classes who had accepted their critique had lost all faith in the old order, and in cheering Figaro's triumphs over the Comte de Almaviva were welcoming a revolution which, they believed, could not but improve a hopeless situation. On the other hand, it was widely believed that England had already experienced such a salutary revolution. The English government, after all, was already based on a concern for liberty, and for a subordination of all, including the monarch, to the law. Consequently, what had England to fear?

During most of the century, despite these grounds for confidence, the governing classes of England nonetheless continued to dread Enthusiasm, that sense of certainty which made the enthusiast convinced not only of his own salvation but often of his role as God's chosen instrument. Religious Enthusiasm had figured prominently in virtually every civil conflict in Europe for over two centuries, and might again, as in the Civil Wars, be the means of stimulating discontented masses to concerted revolutionary action. The Puritan saints who had successfully stoked the fires of revolt had been ideologists in the modern mold, doctrinaire enthusiasts whose religious principles had impelled them to act to impose their understanding of the divine purpose by violent means upon the nation. Toward the end of the seventeenth century, tolerance triumphed over Enthusiasm, and the Glorious Revolution of 1688 confirmed the chief constitutional changes which it had been the original purpose of the Country party to effect. Yet there seems to have been, on the one hand, a persistent fear of a Tory and royalist "conspiracy" which would undo the beneficent consequences of the events of 1688 and again make resistance to tyranny a necessity; on the other hand, many of those who governed the state and the Church appeared similarly obsessed with the threat of a renewal of revolutionary ardor among the descendants of their ancient enemies, and among the populace generally. The democratic political aspirations of the Puritan Revolution continued to maintain the allegiance of circles of eighteenth-century Commonwealthmen, and frequently such circles overlapped those of religious Dissent.

For David Hume, writing in the 1740s, the "true sources of ENTHUSI-ASM" were "hope, pride, presumption, a warm imagination, together with ignorance"; from these arose "raptures, transports, and surprising flights of fancy; and confidence and presumption still increasing, these raptures, being altogether unaccountable, and seeming quite beyond the reach of our ordinary faculties, are attributed to the immediate inspiration of that Divine Being, who is the object of devotion." Indeed,

in a little time, the inspired person comes to regard himself as a distinguished favourite of the Divinity; and when this frenzy once takes place, which is the summit of enthusiasm, every whimsy is consecrated: Human reason, and even morality are rejected as fallacious guides; And the fanatic madman delivers himself over, blindly, and without reserve, to the supposed illapses of the spirit, and to inspiration from above.

In this way, did Enthusiasm lead to Antinomianism, the denial of all constraints, and governance solely by divine impulse. *"Religions, which partake of enthusiasm,"* were *"furious and violent."* "The violence of this species of religion, when excited by novelty, and animated by opposition," was clear in the examples of "the *anabaptists* in GERMANY, the *camisars* in FRANCE, the *levellers* and other fanatics in ENGLAND, and the *covenanters* in SCOTLAND." The victim of Enthusiasm, regarding himself a "favourite of the Divinity," was anxious to throw over "the yoke of the ecclesiastics." Hume called religion "superstition," where priestly power and elaborate ceremonials predominated, and he suggested that the followers of this sort of faith were attached to political principles of nonresistance and divine right. On the other hand, Enthusiasm provoked resistance to authority, and though ready to acknowledge that the "fury" of Enthusiasm might be quickly spent, that the Dissenters, the descendants of the "fanatical sects" of the seventeenth century who "were formerly such dangerous bigots, are now becoming very free reasoners," Hume did not doubt that the intensity of enthusiastic religion could, as in the preceding century, bring about revolutions and civil wars. "It is thus Enthusiasm," Hume concluded, "produces the most cruel disorders in human society." [16] On this matter the prelates of the Established Church were in complete agreement with the Scottish agnostic.

It was the charge of Enthusiasm and Antinomianism which was the principal one directed against the Methodists in the middle decades of the eighteenth century. The best known of the anti-Methodist tracts [17] was Bishop Lavington's *The Enthusiasm of Methodists and Papists Compared,* written in the forties. Like the Catholic enthusiasts, Lavington argued, the Methodists were field preachers, fanatical opponents of diversion, superstitious proponents of the casting of lots, prophesying, cures and miracles, practitioners of private confession, pretenders to visions, trances, and ecstasies, who believed themselves to be continually contending with the Devil. The Methodist New Birth, moreover, resembled the pagan mysteries. These excesses of the Methodists led them to a "wild and pernicious *Enthusiasm*" which undermined the bases of *"true Religion."* The result of this laying aside of *"cool Reason and plain Scripture"* was that the Methodists had arrived at "that *Summit of Arrogance,"* a claim of "absolute Freedom from Corruption" which was the privilege of Christ alone. Their turn to Faith instead of Works (here again the views of George Whitefield were taken to be those of the entire movement) had the inevitable result of encouraging every form of vice and immorality. The Methodists were "hair-brained (*sic*) Enthusiasts, and crafty Impostors" who worked upon the "Passions of weak, credulous, or distempered People." [18]

Warburton, the Bishop of Gloucester, who wrote his almost equally well-known tract against the Methodists over a decade later, insisted that he was not so much attacking Methodist doctrine as the methods by which that doctrine was propagated. Methodist claims to a "high degree of divine communications" and to "supernatural powers," their exposition of the New Birth, and their mysticism must, he was convinced, "soon degenerate into Superstition or Fanaticism." Indeed, the Bishop continued, "a FANATIC MANNER of preaching tho' it were the doctrine of an Apostle, may do more harm, to Society at least," than the "modest" preaching of heresies, since it "tends to bewilder the imaginations of some, to inflame the passions of others," and "to spread disorder and disturbance throughout the whole community." "The *Zeal* and the *Faith* of a Fanatic," Warburton proclaimed, "came into the world together to disturb Society and dishonour Christianity"; "sectaries must either kick or be kicked," they must "either persecute, or they must provoke persecution." The issue as Warburton saw it was between Fanaticism on the one hand, and the Erasmian temper as it had appeared in "the divine Genius of those Masters of Reason, a GROTIUS, or an EPISCOPIUS, a HOOKER, or a CHILLINGWORTH," on the other. Methodist fanaticism, like that of the Puritans, would carry "the doctrine of *Justification by Faith alone* into a dangerous and impure Antinomianism." [19]

Sharing this general view of Enthusiasm held by Hume and the Anglican Bishops was John Wesley, a loyal clergyman of the Church of England. Yet Wesley's role was to be that of the preacher of a new Enthusiasm, one whose appeal and fervor recalled that of the revolutionary frenzy of the seventeenth century. But Wesley was no revolutionary. It was a curious paradox that Wesley was a loyal churchman who leaned to the ritual and doctrine of the High Church, and who was a believer in the far-from-fashionable principle of the divine right of kings. In his early life he had been a supporter of the exiled Stuarts, and consequently possessed all the insignia which Hume had assigned to followers of "Superstition"; but he became convinced of the essential truth of the religion of Protestant "Enthusiasm." Cleaving to this spiritual truth, and acknowledging it as his vocation to bring the good news of salvation to those of his countrymen beyond the reach of the Establishment—the "dangerous classes" of early industrial Britain—the loyal clergyman, out of conviction and necessity, took up the methods and the central message of the Protestant enthusiasts—the call to salvation by faith, though not only for the preordained "elect" of Reformation doctrine, but for all who were ready to accept the divine offer. From the earliest days of his mission, Wesley was faced by the problem of separating the methods and message of the seventeenth-century enthusiasts from their revolutionary venom.

The concepts of Christian Perfection and Assurance were perhaps the most characteristic Wesleyan doctrines, and were most subject to attack as Enthusiasm. It was not by mere opinions, which were relative trifles, Wesleyan preachers often proclaimed, but by their conduct that Methodists were to be distinguished from other men: they were to be known because of their continual striving to drive sin from their hearts. Nor was this an impossible task, as the Reformation Protestants had held. While the followers of Luther and Calvin—some of whom came to call themselves "true Protestants" to distinguish themselves from Wesley—saw man as inherently and irredeemably corrupt, incapable of being made holy except by borrowing from God's holiness, by the "imputation of the Righteousness" of Christ, the Wesleyans saw men as having sufficient righteousness within themselves to attain (with God's help) by their individual efforts (supplemented by the support of the bands, orders, and societies), a state of sinless perfection. Although it would more frequently be achieved at the moment of death, for an increasing number of people, thanks in good part to the mutual efforts of the societies of regenerated men, Christian Perfection was possible *in this life* (though, of course, Wesleyans never doubted the indispensability of God's grace to the process). Methodism, moreover, stressed experience and saw itself as an "experimental" religion. By a profound emotional and mystical experience achieved by methods not requiring learning or analysis, by an experience more accessible to the humble and unsophisticated than to their better situated or better educated fellows, large numbers of men might attain the certainty—the Assurance—that though they had been sinners, their sins had been forgiven and they had been accepted by God and could by their own efforts, reinforced by the fraternal spirit of the societies, find ultimate sanctification, that is, salvation. It was their sense of Assurance and belief in the possibility of Perfection which the enemies of the Methodists reviled as Enthusiasm, doctrines that the Methodists felt were indispensable to their mission.

A more systematic view of our problem is possible through a formal scheme put forward by Parsons and Shils to describe the transition from the traditional to the modern.[20] Their first category concerns the movement from "affectivity" to "affective neutrality," that is, to the essentially modern effort to keep emotion in check, to strive for rational control. In this, both Calvinism and Methodism (in contrast to a traditional Catholicism) were essentially modern, despite their initial recourse to a highly emotional conversion. It was this determination to keep rational control, as we will see, which helped to induce Methodism to act against the doctrines of "speculative" Antinomianism, which it associated with Reformation Protestantism. Secondly, Parsons and Shils have distinguished between the "collectivity-orientation" of the traditional society—where the Church played the essential mediating role between God and man—to the modern "self-orientation": here, again, both Calvinism and Methodism were on the side of the modern, while traditional Catholicism—in which individual conscience did not play a critical role—fell short. (It was Wesley's "modern" temper, to offer an example from another realm, which caused him to condemn Moravian communitarianism in favor of economic individualism.) In Parsons' and Shils' third distinction—"particularism" *vs* "universalism"—we have Calvinism in the realm of a traditional particularism in its insistence upon the doctrine of the elect, a theological mirror-image of the traditional political structure. Methodism, on the other hand, in the modern manner, wished to include *all* in the expectation of salvation. In the case of Parsons' and Shils' fourth distinction as well, Methodism opted for a modern "achievement" in its doctrine of works, while Calvinism, again mirroring traditional social structure, turned to "ascription," to a grace that was bestowed rather than earned. Thus, so far as these four criteria are concerned (a fifth concerning the division of labor may be put aside for our present purposes), Methodism was "modern" by all four tests, while Calvinist doctrine remained fixed at an earlier stage of development in two of the four cases.

So we find Wesley—on a religious level at any rate, though there were ramifications in socioeconomic if not, as yet, political life—as the advocate of all the chief modern values in this scheme, while Calvinism, although it had certain discernibly modern features, was determinedly traditional in others. The Wesleyan leaders were, as we shall see, able to turn

Calvinism's ambiguous heritage against itself by arguing that the Calvinist doctrines of "particularism" and "ascription," in Parsons' and Shils' terminology, undermined even the undeniable Calvinist devotion to "affective neutrality," i.e., that such doctrines as election and the imputation of Christ's righteousness led to Antinomianism. Moreover Calvinism was illiberal in both its deterministic position and in its view of man's unregenerate nature, while Methodism opted for free will, and although accepting the Augustinian view of fallen man, saw sufficient good in man to envision the possibility of his attaining Christian Perfection in this life. It might be said, therefore, that Wesley extended the "modern" values introduced by Calvinism in a decidedly liberal direction, contrary to the views on this question of Leslie Stephen, E. P. Thompson, and others.*

SECT AND CHURCH

Methodism, following the pattern of the Protestant sects of the sixteenth and seventeenth centuries, had to appeal to the passions, the inclination to emotional self-indulgence of the masses of the people, if it was to rouse them to the considerable effort required to overcome their spiritual passivity and bring them to a position where they might take up their Creator's offer of salvation. Certainly, the rational skepticism of the governing elite which presented itself as the "enlightened" Latitudinarianism of the Established Church could not rouse them. Smollett, a child of the Enlightenment, writing in the middle decades of the eighteenth century, had vaunted the "progress of reason, and free cultivation of the human mind" which characterized his time, while bemoaning that "imposture and fanaticism still hang upon the skirts of religion" and that those "ridiculous sects and schisms of which the kingdom had been formerly so productive" still survived to seduce "weak minds." Foremost among these, he declared, was "a superstition styled Methodism," raised by preachers who "propagated their doctrines to the most remote corners of the British dominions, and found means to lay the whole kingdom under contribution." "Many thousands in the lower ranks of life were infected with this species of enthusiasm,"

---

* Catholicism was apparently modern in its acceptance of the ideas of universality and its stress on achievement rather than a Calvinist ascription, yet these values have a somewhat different meaning in the context of Catholic "affectivity" and "collectivity-orientation"; more particularly, Catholicism depended on a mediating priesthood to enforce morality, while Methodism, like Calvinism, sought the internalization of values under the supervision of the individual conscience. Most important, while a traditional Catholicism might accept such doctrines on the level of ideas, Methodism defended these values in the increasingly "modern" social context of eighteenth-century England, out of which they in part grew, and into which they were in part translated.

Smollett observed, and Methodist ranters "bitterly inveighed against Newton as an ignorant pretender who had presumed to set up his own ridiculous chimaeras in opposition to the sacred philosophy of the
Pentateuch." [21] Wesleyans and Anglican Latitudinarians apparently shared
a common Arminian doctrine, yet as Oliver Goldsmith's Chinese traveller
observed in 1762, the two camps "hate each other" and "quarrel for opinions they both equally defend." [22] For what the Anglican minister accepted
as ornamental platitude—free will or universal salvation—and placed
amid the periphera of scholarly exegesis, the plebeian Methodist preacher
made the soul of his creed. Moreover, unlike their Anglican counterparts,
Methodist preachers were able to express themselves, as Dr. Johnson observed, "in a plain and familiar manner, which is the only way to do good
to the common people." The difference was one of class, between the
masses always in the need of satisfaction of their religious impulses, and a
skeptical elite. Dr. Johnson suggested that all clergymen ought to preach
similarly to the Methodists, "from a principle of duty, when it is suited to
their congregations." [23] By the end of the century, Methodist Enthusiasm
was to triumph even among congregations which Dr. Johnson would not
have thought precisely suitable. William Hazlitt, a Radical of the Enlightenment, writing in the early nineteenth century, surveyed the spread of
evangelicalism and declared with contempt that its "vital Christianity" was
"no other than an attempt to lower all religion to the level of the capacities of the lowest of the people." [24]

Methodism thus began as a sect within a Church (as John Wesley's
"Connection") but, even before Wesley's death in 1791, it was to become,
in parts of the nation at least, virtually a second National Church, a proselytizing arm of the Establishment which undertook first the conversion of
the lower classes in England, and then the missionizing of the heathen
abroad. It has been persuasively suggested that Methodism may best be regarded as a "denomination" midway between sect and church, and sharing
characteristics of both. Certainly, unlike the conventional sect, Methodism
did not think of itself as *exclusively* in possession of religious truth, making it possible, as we shall see, for the Connection later to participate in
"interdenominational" activities.[25] The ideal-types of sect and church
described by the German sociologists, particularly Weber and Troeltsch,
can nonetheless be very useful in understanding the Methodist role. While
membership in the church, stemming from birth, is, more or less, obliga-
tory for all those in a given territory, or those whose parents are members
of the church, the sect is a voluntary association which insists upon scrutinizing the purity and religious qualifications of those admitted to the communion table. In a traditional society, sectarianism was the only means by
which an ethos different from the dominant one transmitted by the family
could be effectively disseminated. As we know, while the Protestant sects
tended to subscribe to certain ascetic, almost monastic, values required by

the new society, the church, frowning on asceticism, was very much of the world as it was. The church makes room for the greatest possible number of adherents and comprises widely differing views in matters of theology or ritual, while sects tend to restrict their members to those in complete agreement with their views. The church is an institution which administers grace, and aims, if it can, to monopolize this function, excluding sectarian interlopers who proclaim themselves possessed of a spiritual charisma. For a churchman, or for anyone steeped in the traditional outlook, a sectarian was *ipso facto* a rebel. A great deal of the religious history of the last four centuries may be understood as belonging to the conflict between church and sect. The Anglican hierarchy saw Methodism as a threat akin to that posed by the Puritans of the preceding century, and, intermittently, sought to arouse relatively tolerant and complacent state authorities against the Methodist peril. The Methodists, in the ambiguous position of seeming to be a sect within a church and possessing certain of the characteristics of both, resembled the associations and Conventicles of the Puritan Richard Baxter and of German pietism in the seventeenth century. The Methodists saw themselves not as a danger to the established order, but as a catalyst for evangelizing and revitalizing what was widely regarded as a sluggish church, more and more given to the preaching of a flat "enlightened" religion, while at the same time shielding the state from the unsettling effects emanating from the preaching of religious Enthusiasm. That they were largely successful in this was in good part a consequence of their ability to make the appeal and wield the discipline of both sect and church.

In addition to the basic contradiction stemming from the sect-church dichotomy—what I will call, somewhat simplifying a more complex phenomenon, the paradox of a Laudian Enthusiasm—there was another, related contradiction: there was a conflict within Methodism of political tendencies which can be associated with the two principal forms of seventeenth-century Arminianism—that of Archbishop Laud, the enemy of Puritanism who headed the Church of England at the time of Charles I, with its reputed churchly attachment to the divine right of kings, and that of the Remonstrants of seventeenth-century Holland, the defenders of the doctrines of the Arminian Remonstrance of 1610, with its sectarian leanings toward natural rights and liberal equality.* In his poli-

---

* Although Wesley, in his early years, felt a special tie to the memory of the Archbishop, it would be a mistake to exaggerate the direct influence of Laud's ideas upon Wesley's thinking; no more, indeed, would I wish to suggest that Wesley was exclusively dependent on the Dutch Remonstrants for his notions of liberty and equality. Both sets of ideas were rather common currency in Wesley's England, and were derived from many sources. When I speak of them as "Laudian" or as those of the Remonstrants, this is a species of shorthand which has a special usefulness for the subject of this essay. For my purposes, furthermore, it is unnecessary to go into the question of whether Laud or the Remonstrants fully held many of the doctrines which became associated with their names.

tics, as in his theology, Wesley was obliged to play the role of mediator between the "traditional" and the "modern." Wesley began as a high Tory, and it was an analogue of the "Laudian" politics of divine right which can be said to have formed the basis for Wesley's virtually absolute control of the Methodist Connection. However, in the middle and last decades of his mission, Wesley found it increasingly congenial, and perhaps even necessary, to appeal to the "Whiggish Arminianism" of the Remonstrancers as well. The internal tension resulting from the contrary pulls of the two Arminianisms—a Church Arminianism and a sectarian Arminianism—was also a problem for Wesley's successors, and they, like Wesley, were to endeavor to resolve this tension in a period of revolution, which made the conflict more acute and its solution more difficult.

Moreover, confronted by a hostile Established Church, and constantly fearful, with reason, of suppression, Methodism was obliged to defend itself against the charge, reiterated for over three-quarters of a century, that it sought the overthrow of Church and State. Out of the efforts to resolve this "civil war" in the soul, growing out of the revolutionary character of a developing Methodist doctrine, accompanied by the strenuous efforts to prevent the translation of its liberal and egalitarian elements into political life, and the contradictions and ambiguities emerging from the conflict of the two Arminianisms and of the related and simultaneous paradox of a Laudian Enthusiasm, emerged the special role of Methodism. The travails undergone by the Connection from the beginning of the Revival into the early decades of the nineteenth century, I will argue, traumatized it and fixed its form, and with it, helped to fix the form of nineteenth-century English society.

II

The Battle Against
"Speculative" Antinomianism

John Wesley defined his doctrinal position in the course of a series of quarrels with his evangelistic allies. Among the scores of preachers who spread the gospel of salvation to almost every part of Great Britain and Ireland, the best known in the forties, fifties, and sixties of the eighteenth century was George Whitefield. Whitefield's substantially Calvinist message, that of election and the nothingness of mere works compared to the efficacy of Christ's grace and righteousness, was popularly considered to be the central doctrine of the Revival; variations of these views were offered by Whitefield's disciples, by William Cudworth, James Relly, and others. Less prominent were the Moravians whose message of universal salvation, as opposed to Whitefield's election, was, however, also accompanied by the more distinctively Reformation view which stressed the imputation of Christ's righteousness. Cennick and Ingham (who preached with success in Yorkshire, founding many societies) were intermittently allied to the Moravian movement. Wesley, a loyal son of the High Church of the Establishment and devoted to its doctrine, felt it especially necessary to distinguish his views from those of a Calvinist Whitefield, whose preeminence had given the entire movement the appearance of a revival of seventeenth-century Puritanism, as well as from those of the Moravians who had secured Wesley's own conversion.

Drawing upon a number of theological formulations and trying to avoid their pitfalls and extremes, Wesley constructed a synthesis which was well suited to the requirements of the newly-reborn of the eighteenth century. He frequently enlisted in his ranks persons who had been awakened to sin and had experienced regeneration because of the preachings of Whitefield and his disciples, who were never able to match Wesley's powers of organization. Wesley formed societies to keep the newly-reborn from backsliding, and by the end of the century, Wesleyan Methodism had societies everywhere, with its bulwarks in the "holy cities" of Bristol, Newcastle, and London. On a popular level, as we shall see, Wesleyanism was to become riddled by what came to be called the "true Protestantism" of his evangelical opponents, but Wesley did succeed in filling out the doctrinal implications of the great evangelistic crusade on which he had embarked on his own lines, making the entire revival more clearly an instrument for the transition to a modern, liberal society.

We must understand Wesley's doctrinal controversies, then, as in good part the means by which he hoped to create a distinctive position by a new synthesis, a new balance of many elements. The two doctrines which set all wings of the Methodist Revolution into motion were those of justification by faith and the New Birth. Allegiance to these by all the evangelists seemed more important, until perhaps the 1770s, than various theological differences. But from the earliest years of the movement Wesley never ceased his efforts to define his position more precisely by stressing those parts of his views which differed from those of his evangelical comrades, a circumstance which tended to disguise their more essential agreement.

The growth and consolidation of Wesleyan Arminianism was, indeed, to lead to a vituperative revival of the seventeenth-century disputes between Calvinists and Arminians. But while these ideological divisions continued to have real meaning in a number of quarters, on the whole the old Dissenters and the Church Evangelicals clung to the doctrinal slogans of Calvinism largely out of loyalty to the past. In truth, with some important exceptions, the Calvinism of the eighteenth century had followed more on the moderate lines charted by Richard Baxter—the seventeenth-century Puritan whose theology was an attempt at compromise between Calvinism and Arminianism—and others, and the doctrines of "Calvinistic" Church Evangelicals and their Wesleyan colleagues and competitors were to appear increasingly similar by the end of the century.

It may be useful to note that the Calvinistic Methodists who followed George Whitefield and the Countess of Huntingdon, as well as the Evangelicals of the Church of England, many of whose doctrines tended toward Calvinism, seem to have achieved results very similar to Wesley's. Despite a more "traditional" theology, for all practical purposes they helped to forward the Methodist Revolution. For the very act of evangelization—the dissemination of the divine offer of salvation to all—implied a doctrine rather different from that of a rigid Calvinism, and it was this process of evangelism and conversion which had the deepest effect on men. The work of Methodist evangelization was, for its time, a huge and enormously successful campaign of mass indoctrination. Yet the continuation of the doctrinal disputes between Calvinism and Arminianism did more than simply validate the existence of rival evangelist organizations. The elaboration of Wesleyan Arminianism, as it strove to distinguish itself from its "Calvinistic" rivals, made clear the full implications of the Methodist Revolution, to which the evangelicals and all shades of Methodists were to contribute. It was Arminian doctrine which was ultimately to triumph. The Wesleyan leadership was more conscious of the almost inevitable theological basis of the spiritual revolution, and must consequently receive our systematic attention.

In order to understand the clusters of ideas which were to be the causes of dispute between Wesley and his evangelist colleagues and rivals, it is necessary to say something more about the early history of Protestantism. When Martin Luther raised the flag of revolt in 1517, he proclaimed the underground doctrines expressed a century earlier by the Hussites, which called for the liberation of the believer from subordination to clerical authority. Luther demoted the doctrine of justification by works which had placed the levers of control in the hands of the Church, and preached that salvation was a freely offered gift of God's grace and divine love available to those who had faith in His saving power. This was the great Protestant doctrine of justification by faith. Luther, moreover, proclaimed every man a priest. In the elevation of the doctrine of justification by faith, so necessary for the initial revolt against the Church, there were the seeds of other revolutions. If salvation were the gift of God, freely given to the faithful, did not any effort to lead a virtuous life smack of a papish hankering for good works? Were not such efforts inherently sinful, since men were saved not on their own account but through the merits of Christ who proclaimed that he had freed believers from the severities of the law? To the pure in heart all things were pure. This view was *antinomianism* (*nomos*, Gr., law), and it represented the limit to which the doctrine of justification by faith might be extended. Not long after Luther's revolt, the city of Münster was turned into an Antinomian utopia: the law was set aside, and, according to contemporary accounts, murder, free love, polygamy, and collective ownership became the rule of the Antinomian Anabaptists of that city. Münster was destroyed by combined Catholic and Protestant armies, and the name of Anabaptist, for well over a century, became associated with its reputed excesses. Again and again, amid the splintering Protestant sects, the Antinomian heresy arose to plague the authorities, civil and ecclesiastical. Not surprisingly, this was the case during the turmoils of the civil war and interregnum period of seventeenth-century England. Churchmen had come to fear enthusiastic sectarianism as having powerful leanings toward anarchy, promiscuous copulation, and communism.

Calvin placed special emphasis upon one of the parts of Luther's program, the doctrine of election. If salvation were the free gift of God, it was for God to determine which of his children were to receive that gift. A man gained assurance of his favored status by his impulses to lead a godly life—sober, chaste, frugal, God-fearing—and by the earthly rewards of God's favor, a foretoken of future heavenly rewards. This consciousness of election may have helped lead to the development of a capitalist ethic; it may also have endowed those who experienced it with a special confidence which made them ready to rend the political fabric, if necessary, to remove the godless from the seats of power, and install, in accordance with God's evident wishes, the Elect of the Lord. While Luther and Calvin had followed the Catholic Church in recommending the antirevolutionary political passivity enjoined by the New Testament, though both felt strong contrary impulses, their followers in the sixteenth and seventeenth centuries, agreeing in this matter with contemporary Jesuit enthusiasts, were ready to advocate revolution when this seemed necessary, rather than permit the rule of false religion. In this spirit, Calvin's disciples helped to move the northern Netherlands to rebel against their temporal masters who owed spiritual allegiance to the whore of Babylon; at the same time, other Calvinists brought Scotland into the hands of the godly, banishing the recalcitrant head of the ruling dynasty and bending a younger member of it to their purpose. In the middle of the seventeenth century, later followers of the Geneva prophet succeeded in overthrowing the ruling dynasty of England, beheading a king, and establishing a republic which became a dictatorship of the Elect. The political fruits of Calvinism seemed to be revolution, regicide, republicanism, and repression.

John Wesley was an heir to the Protestant tradition, the grandson, on both sides of his family, of Puritan Dissenters of the preceding century, whose parents had joined the Church in reaction against this heritage of Puritan rebellion. While remaining loyal to the Establishment, Wesley worked to bring the masses of both Anglicanism and Dissent back to a Bible Christianity congenial to the Protestant spirit. There were, however, two other wings of the evangelical movement, equally aware of the inadequacies of the Establishment in meeting the religious needs of Englishmen, but not so heedful of the dangers inherent in sectarian Enthusiasm: there were the Moravians, as well as groups of Calvinistic Methodists in Wales under the leadership of Howell Harris, a Welsh preacher who had begun his evangelical efforts before Wesley, and in England following George Whitefield and the Countess of Huntingdon.[1] The Protestantism of the Moravians and of Whitefield was more in the "classic" mould of Luther and Calvin, and of the Puritan sectarians of the seventeenth century. Within the evangelical movement, there was sporadic conflict as Wesley fought the Calvinism of Whitefield and his followers, as well as the quietism and "speculative" Antinomianism of the English followers of the German Moravian leader, Count Zinzendorf.

Wesleyanism, establishing itself mid-way between the Establishment and Dissent, sought to purge evangelical Protestantism of those doctrinal elements of "speculative" Antinomianism which had helped, many believed, to inspire nearly two centuries of rebellion and disorder throughout Western Europe. (We may, of course, also see in the move from "speculative" Antinomianism to Arminianism, from grace to contract—to the importance of works, free will, universal salvation, reason—as providing the theological foundation for the advance from a traditional to a modern society.) If the pietist movement of the eighteenth century can be called a second Protestant Reformation, then it may be argued that Wesleyanism, embodying so much of the doctrinal outlook of the Tridentine Counter-Reformation, may be described as continuing and successfully concluding the Protestant Counter-Reformation begun by the seventeenth-century Arminians. By combatting "speculative" Antinomianism and the "practical" Antinomianism to which it led, the Wesleyans hoped to insure that the Methodist Revolution to which they were devoting themselves would be a nonviolent one.

WESLEY'S "CIVIL WAR" IN THE SOUL

These conflicts, both theological and political, appeared *in nuce* in the earliest years of the movement, and were even foreshadowed in the early life and thought of its founder.[2] Wesley's parents, Samuel and Susanna Wesley, were loyal to the High Church, that part of the Establishment today called Anglo-Catholic, whose theology, and liturgy, and politics (those of divine right and nonresistance) were those associated with Archbishop Laud. The grandparents of John Wesley, on both his mother's and father's sides, had been Puritan Dissenters during the time of Laud and the Interregnum; indeed, both Wesley's grandfathers had, after the Restoration, been deprived of their livings as clergymen because of their views. Wesley's father, in whom an undeniable strain of opportunism can be observed,[3] and his mother had broken with the religious opinions of their parents to rejoin the national church. During the reign of William and Mary, Samuel was a supporter of the Revolution of 1688 while Susanna was irreconcilably Jacobite;[4] in later years, perhaps disappointed with his lack of preferment, Samuel too became a bit of a Jacobite.

A number of reasons—political, economic, personal—made the Reverend Samuel Wesley rather unpopular in Epworth: he was an active Tory in a Whig countryside, a friend and supporter of the local collector of the unpopular tax on reclaimed fenland, and a frequent absentee from his parish to pursue his own self-interest at church convocations, who, when in his pulpit, intemperately berated his parishioners. Samuel Wesley found his house and the adjoining flax crop set afire in 1702 and in 1704 in the tradition of a resentful countryside. On the night of February 9, 1709, a third fire, again apparently deliberately set, entirely consumed the Wesley home. In the excitement, though the other children were led to safety, six-year-old John Wesley, remembered too late, was left sleeping in his bed, but awoke at the last moment and was rescued. Susanna saw the incident as demonstrating the special interest of Divine Providence in her son, and resolved to be, as she wrote, *"more particularly* careful of the soul of this child, which God had so mercifully provided for." [5]

The incident was pregnant with meaning for the entire family, and for John in particular. He was first rescued by a miracle, and then, although he was neither the oldest nor the youngest, chosen by his mother for special favor. Was it a wonder that John Wesley should believe that individuals might be "chosen" for certain tasks? Wesley regularly celebrated the anniversary of his rescue, and had a house in flames engraved under one of his portraits, with the motto, "Is not this a brand plucked out of the burning?," [6] the last phrase of which he also used in 1749 when he was ill and believed himself dying as a self-composed epitaph. Nor could the supposed cause of the fire be forgotten: a populace, among whom there were not a few who still cherished a heritage of hatred for Church and monarchy, had been so antagonistic to their High Church Rector and his Tory opinions that some from among them had on three separate occasions attempted to burn down his house. Was it surprising that, in response to such vituperative displays of disloyalty and lawlessness, the sons of the family should espouse the unwavering Tory and Jacobite principles of their mother? Was it extraordinary that John Wesley should have come to believe—and the later events of his lifetime would only confirm such an opinion—that disrespect for law and order was a besetting English vice which had already brought violence and revolution and might do so again? Nor was it surprising that John Wesley should have endeavored to combat those parts of the theology of the Dissenters—"speculative" Antinomianism, even where no direct "practical" Antinomian conclusions of any sort were drawn from doctrines designed to elevate the grace and righteousness of Christ—which had in the past served, and might serve again, as seeming justification for such behavior. The violent hostility of the mobs to Methodist preaching—Wesley, himself, was more than once threatened with stoning or dismemberment—confirmed his feelings that lawless behavior was a great and everpresent threat. [7] When "speculative" Antinomianism gave way to "practical" Antinomianism in the 1770s when the American colonists rose in revolt and Wesley feared that Englishmen might seek to re-enact the events of the 1640s, Wesley repeatedly returned, as we shall see, to the metaphor of "raging fires"—so like the fires of Satan's domain—which had to be extinguished.

John Wesley was at first educated by his mother, then sent to Charterhouse in 1714, and to Christ Church, Oxford, in 1720. Wesley was ordained a deacon in 1725, elected a Fellow of Lincoln in 1726, and ordained a priest of the Church of England in 1728. In 1729, he became a member, and soon the leader, of a religious society at Oxford whose members came together to read the Greek Testament; other members included Wesley's brother Charles, John Gambold, who later became a Moravian bishop, Benjamin Ingham, the future evangelist of Yorkshire, James Hervey, who became famous as the author of *Meditations among the Tombs,* and, joining the society in 1735, George Whitefield, the son of a Gloucester innkeeper who was to rival Wesley as an evangelist. The regularity with which these gentlemen pursued their studies and performed their religious observances brought them the sobriquet of "Methodists." In the manner of other religious societies—many had come into existence in the preceding half-century—the "Methodists" of Oxford not only cultivated personal piety but undertook a regimen of visits to the poor, to the sick, and to the prisoners in the Oxford jail. Their inspiration came from the writings of Bishop Taylor and from those of the mystic William Law, whose tract on *Christian Perfection* and whose *Serious Call* were among the most influential works of the eighteenth century, bringing many to a new conception of Christian duty.

In liturgy and doctrine, the Oxford "Methodists" were of the Arminian High Church; in politics, their sympathies were Jacobite. It was in June 1734 that John Wesley himself preached at Oxford what his brother Charles called "his Jacobite sermon," for which he was "much mauled and threatened," but, since he had been sufficiently farsighted to secure the earlier approval of its text by the vice-chancellor, there were no serious repercussions.[8] These Oxford "Methodists" were strongly opposed to the Calvinist doctrines of predestination and election. As early as 1725, John Wesley wrote to his mother his view that these doctrines consigned "a vast majority of the world" to "eternal death, without so much as a possibility of avoiding it." "How is this," he asked, "consistent with either the Divine Justice or Mercy?" Was it "merciful to ordain a creature to everlasting misery?" Was it just to "punish man for crimes which he could not but commit?" These doctrines would make God "the author of sin and injustice." "To lie under either a physical or a moral necessity is entirely repugnant to human liberty," Wesley, a good churchman, declared. Wesley was convinced of the usefulness of reason as the best means of understanding scripture; he called "faith an assent upon rational grounds." [9] Another of the Arminian predispositions of the High Church which the Oxford "Methodists" shared was—as is demonstrated by their insistence upon attending weekly communion, rigorous observance of university statutes, and their visits to the poor and sick—a sympathy for the doctrine of justification by works. The Church of England, like that of Rome, asserted the need for both faith and works. In practice, however, both distrusted "faith" and stressed works in contrast to the predisposition of the Dissenters to elevate faith to the point where works were not only overshadowed, but in some cases obliterated.

It was, however, the doctrine of justification by faith, so overwhelmingly a part of that "Protestant" feeling to be found among great numbers of Englishmen, which was to possess the emotional force required to convert

England. "In 1729," Wesley was to declare subsequently, "two young men, reading the Bible, saw they could not be saved without holiness, followed after it, and incited others so to do." "In 1737," Wesley continued, "they saw holiness comes by faith." [10]

This lesson had come from the German Moravians, whom John and Charles Wesley had met for the first time in 1735 on board ship on their way to become missionaries in Georgia. John had declined, earlier that year, to succeed to his father's living at Epworth after the old man's death, and had determined, rather, to go to Georgia to minister to the spiritual needs of the colonists and to attempt to convert the Indians, and by undergoing privations to come nearer to the holiness he sought. The Moravians, too, were on their way to Georgia to convert the Indians. Wesley was much impressed by their spiritual serenity, which he hoped to attain, and by his discovery that their quest for holiness seemed fulfilled. The Moravian Brethren, a sect whose members regarded themselves as the heirs to the medieval Hussites, Protestant before the birth of Luther, had been welcomed, after their expulsion from Moravia, to build their community at Herrnhut, in Saxony, in the domain of Count Zinzendorf. The Count, eccentric and authoritarian, was under the influence of Spener and the German pietists, and conceived of the Moravians, whose unchallenged leader he was, as the means of infiltrating all the Protestant churches and inspiring a Protestant ecumenicism which would push back the incursions of "rational" religion. As a persecuted Protestant and a German nobleman, Zinzendorf had succeeded in securing recognition of himself as Bishop of the Moravian Church by the Archbishop of Canterbury. From this position, he hoped to instill an evangelical fervor into the Church of England. John Wesley learned German and sought every opportunity to converse with the Moravians, both on shipboard and during the two years he spent in Georgia.

John Wesley returned from Georgia in February 1738 after a difficult sojourn. There had been a scandal in the colony: Wesley had evidently fallen in love with a young woman, and had then declined to marry her on the advice of the Moravian missionaries; after she had married another, Wesley, for what he regarded as substantial grounds though some suggested he was moved by jealousy, banned her from the communion table, and was consequently sued by her husband for defamation of her character. Wesley thus came back to London somewhat under a cloud and with the mark of failure, both worldly and spiritual. He had not achieved holiness, and had come to the painful conclusion that he himself had never been truly converted.[11] It was in a mood of depression, indeed of incipient breakdown, that four days after his arrival in London, Wesley met Peter Böhler, a minister of the Moravian Church ordained a year earlier by Count Zinzendorf, who persuaded him of the truth of the doctrine of salvation by faith. Following Böhler's urgings, he preached salvation by faith before he himself believed. Wesley and a number of others organized themselves into a religious society meeting in Fetter Lane, linking themselves with the Moravians. On the evening of May 24, 1738, while attending a meeting of another religious society in Aldersgate Street, Wesley heard a reading of Luther's Preface to the Epistle to the Romans, during the course of which, he later declared, "I felt my heart strangely warmed": "I felt I did trust in Christ alone, for salvation; and an assurance was given me, that he had taken away my sins, even mine, and saved me from the law of sin and death." [12] Charles Wesley was also converted by a combination of Böhler and Luther, this time by Luther's Comment on the Epistle to the Galatians. "Who would believe cur Church had been founded on this important article of justification by faith alone," Charles inquired in his *Journal*. "I am astonished I should ever think this a new doctrine." "I spent some hours this evening," Charles wrote on May 17, 1738, "in private with Martin Luther, who was greatly blessed to me." [13]

At St. Mary's, Oxford, on June 18, 1738, less than a month after his conversion, John Wesley, the former High Churchman and a Fellow of Lincoln College, preached a sermon on "Salvation by Faith," a eulogy of Reformation doctrine of which he was later to be so critical. "All the blessings which God hath bestowed upon man, are of his mere grace, bounty, or favour; his free, undeserved favour; favour altogether undeserved; man having no claim to the least of his mercies," Wesley declared. "For there is nothing we are, or have, or do, which can deserve the least thing at God's hand." How can "a sinful man atone for any the least of his sins?" By "his own works?" Never. "Were they ever so many, or holy, they are not his own, but God's." Indeed, "they are all unholy and sinful themselves, so that every one of them needs a fresh atonement," for "only corrupt fruit grows on a corrupt tree." "Grace is the source, faith the condition, of salvation." What of the High Church's objections to the doctrine of salvation by faith? "But does not preaching this faith lead men into pride?" Wesley asked. "Accidentally," that might be the case. However, "if a man were justified by his works, he would have whereof to glory." "For all our works, all our righteousness, which were before our believing, merited nothing of God but condemnation." Will not speaking of salvation by faith "encourage men in sin?" "Indeed it may and will," Wesley replied, "but their blood is upon their own head." There was another, "quite contrary," objection: "If a man can not be saved by all that he can do, this will drive men to despair." "True," declared Wesley, "to despair of being saved by their own works, their own merits, or righteousness." And this was good, "for one can trust in the merits of Christ, till he has utterly renounced his own." It was "endless to attack, one by one, all the errors" of Rome; "but salvation by faith strikes at the root, and all fall at once where this is established." "For this reason [did] the adversary. . . . call forth all his forces . . . to affright Martin Luther from reviving it."

But if Wesley abandoned the High Church in preaching justification by faith, he nonetheless rejected Luther's and Calvin's doctrine of election, preaching "mercy for all," observing that the doctrine of "whosoever believeth in him shall be saved" must be "the foundation of all our preaching." The poor had "a peculiar right to have the gospel preached unto them," as did "the unlearned," since "God hath revealed these things unto unlearned and ignorant men from the beginning." It was only by preaching to all that "the increase of the Romish delusion among us" could be prevented.

Was not this a revival of Enthusiasm, embedded in the renewal of the sectarian appeal to justification by faith, and highly dangerous? Might not the effort to secure universal salvation by these means lead to rampant Antinomianism? There seemed a hint of Antinomianism in Wesley's assertion, in this sermon, that "the righteousness which is of faith cannot be given him while he trusteth in that which is of the law"; moreover in 1738 Wesley even appeared to have accepted the doctrine of salvation by the imputation of Christ's righteousness, which he was later to denounce. Here, too, however, even in the moment of the exaltation of conversion, the High Churchman in Wesley retained much of its hold. Even while excoriating salvation by mere works, Wesley carefully avoided the doctrine of Protestant extremists. He did not, he insisted, "preach against holiness and good works." On the contrary, "we speak of a faith" which is "productive of all good works." Nor do we make void the law through faith. The saved, "while they trust in the blood of Christ alone, use all the ordinances which he hath appointed, do all the 'good works which he had before prepared that they should walk therein,' and enjoy and manifest all holy and heavenly tempers, even the same mind that was in Christ Jesus." [14] The Reformation Protestantism to which Wesley had become converted, while losing none of its ability to appeal to great masses of Englishmen (which the High Church never could), was thus shorn of those extreme doctrines which, as the experience of the preceding century seemed to have proved, possessed the greatest revolutionary potential.

After his conversion at the hands of the Moravians in the summer of 1738, Wesley, accompanied by Ingham, one of his Oxford friends, undertook a pilgrimage to Herrnhut, the model community which Zinzendorf had established on the continent. (Ingham later became persuaded that God called for the imitation of the Moravian Utopia, and he helped to establish some forty societies in Yorkshire. At Lamb's Hill, subsequently called Fulneck, Moravians, with some financial help by Ingham, set up an English Herrnhut, which, like its German model, anticipated the "socialist" phalanxes of the nineteenth century.[15]) Wesley, however, was not particularly attracted to propagating the communitarian message of Herrnhut. His mission was not to be a monastic one, but one in and of the world, the rather bustling world of an increasingly commercial and industrial England. What impressed Wesley most about Herrnhut was the system of bands and societies into which the believers were organized as a means of watching over each other's morals, as well as making for their more orderly supervision by the leaders of the Church, particularly Count Zinzendorf. It has often been said that Wesley had a genius for organization. Certainly, he frequently reiterated the importance of the proper organization of those who had been saved by Methodist evangelism. Preaching alone might produce "conversions," but these souls would "backslide" and be lost unless the newly saved could be systematically brought together to exhort and to encourage each other, and to guard each other against the sinfulness of the world. Wesley's genius, in part, consisted in applying a pattern constructed to serve a monastic community to men and women who lived within the sinful world.

Wesley returned from Germany in October 1738, and continued his preaching, much to the growing unhappiness of the priests and the hierarchy of the established Church, who, mindful of what the ranting of religious enthusiasts had led to in the preceding century, were concerned when a Fellow of Lincoln College began to preach justification by faith to crowded congregations.[16] In the autumn of 1738, John and Charles Wesley had an interview with the Bishop of London during which the Wesleys informed the Bishop that they understood they had "been charged as Antinomians, for preaching justification by faith only." They found themselves thoroughly comprehending the fears of those who had made the accusation: "Indeed," the Wesleys declared, "by preaching it strongly, and not inculcating good works, many have been made Antinomians in theory, though not in practice: especially in King Charles's time." Their keen awareness of the peril, with the implication that the Wesleys would not preach faith "strongly" or omit the preaching of good works may have reassured the Bishop. Another complaint lodged against the Wesleys was that they preached "an absolute assurance of salvation." [17] In a later interview with the Wesleys in February 1739, however, the Bishop again found it necessary to warn the Wesleys "against Antinomianism," as Charles wrote in his *Journal*.[18] The fear of Antinomianism was a fixation of the High Church, which Wesley not only shared but had confirmed and deepened by his personal history. Yet Wesley was convinced of the scriptural truth of salvation by faith, and was determined to preach that doctrine (as he had understood it in his St. Mary's sermon earlier that year) despite the efforts of the Church to discourage him. And in parish after parish, in London and elsewhere, the churches closed their doors upon him and his message.

It was about this time, in the early months of 1739, that George Whitefield, who had returned to London from America in December 1738 (having gone to join the Wesleys in Georgia before he discovered their intention to return), set off for the West-country, and preached particularly in and about the city of Bristol. There was considerable distress in the West-country generally, as well as in Cornwall, in Yorkshire, and in Newcastle; mining regions—both tin and coal—and the areas of the old woolen industry were the ones most severely struck. There was rioting and even instances of petty rebellions.[19] It was to the rioting Kingswood colliers, near Bristol, that Whitefield came with his message of salvation. "It was but natural," as Elie Halévy observed, "that Christian enthusiasm should endeavor to turn this popular ferment to its own profit." [20] Denied the use of the churches, Whitefield, following the example of Griffith Jones and Howell Harris, Welsh preachers who had already mounted a revival in their home principality, preached in the open air. Two hundred heard him at Kingswood on February 17, 1739, two thousand, when he returned four days later.

Whitefield called on Wesley for assistance, and Wesley set off from London to Bristol where he witnessed an open-air sermon by Whitefield. The High Churchman in Wesley was at first disturbed at such an irregular proceeding. "I could scarce reconcile myself at first to this strange way of preaching in the fields," he noted in his *Journal,* "having been all my life (till very lately) so tenacious of every point relating to decency and order, that I should have thought the saving of souls almost a sin if it had not been done in a church." Yet it was just such a disorderly—indeed revolutionary—conclusion to which John Wesley had been led by his acceptance of the doctrine of salvation by faith. On Sunday, April 1, 1739, Whitefield not being present, Wesley, in the open air, began "expounding our Lord's Sermon on the Mount," observing that that constituted "one pretty remarkable precedent of field-preaching, though I suppose there were churches at that time also." [21] A remarkable, and, from the standpoint of the established Church, a not reassuring analogy. Wesley's message was that of salvation by God's grace, a New Birth, love, and Christian Perfection. The result, Wesley was happy to report in his *Journal* in November 1739, was a remarkable transformation. "Kingswood does not now, as a year ago, resound with cursing and blasphemy," he declared; "it is no more filled with drunkenness and uncleanness . . . wars and fightings." On the contrary, "peace and love are there"; "great numbers of the people are mild, gentle, and easy to be entreated." [22]

Were Wesley and his fellow evangelists Antinomian enthusiasts like the Anabaptists and the Puritans, or was a Jacobite Wesley a popish apologist preparing for a restoration of the Stuarts? Both charges were made, and Wesley denied them both. "Oh, ye fools," Wesley declared, "when will ye understand that the preaching of justification by faith alone, the allowing no meritorious cause of justification but the death and righteousness of Christ, and no conditional or instrumental cause but faith, is overturning

Popery from the foundation?" [23] While Wesley's Protestant friends might find satisfaction in this conversion from High Church popery, they could not help worrying about the persistence of a predilection for good works, a High Church antidote for the Antinomian excesses of Protestant Enthusiasm. The Protestant credentials of George Whitefield and the Welsh Methodists were more genuine, made almost unimpeachable by their adherence to the Calvinistic doctrines of election and predestination, while Wesley was so far embedded in High Church Arminianism that, as he inscribed in his *Journal* for April 26, 1739, "While I was preaching at Newgate on these words, 'He that believeth hath everlasting life,' I was insensibly led, without any previous design, to declare strongly and explicitly that God willeth 'all men to be' thus 'saved.' " [24]

What could Wesley do to rescue himself from the entanglements of his doctrinal and practical positions? He was determined to reconcile his continued attachment to the Church of England with highly irregular activities which smacked of the Puritan sectarians of the seventeenth century: open-air preaching, the acceptance of lay preachers, the raising up of a body of followers organized into societies independent of the Church. While determined to avoid unnecessary controversy with his Methodist, evangelist allies—the Moravians, the Calvinist followers of Whitefield, the Rellyean Perfectionists—he was even more determined to distinguish his own views and those of his immediate followers from confusion with views, originating in the doctrines of Luther and Calvin, adopted by others, particularly the Moravians and the Whitefield Methodists. In Wesley's opinion, one of which he became increasingly certain in 1740 and 1741, there were in the doctrines of both Moravians and Calvinists the germs of that Antinomianism which others had seen implicit in his own opinions and actions. If Wesley were to attempt to resolve the seeming paradox of a Laudian Enthusiasm, he had to wage war against those doctrines of his evangelistic allies which, he believed, led inexorably to speculative, and threatened to lead to practical Antinomianism as well.

WESLEY VS. ZINZENDORF AND LUTHER (1739–1742)

At Oxford, all the Methodists regarded themselves as the disciples of William Law, perhaps the most influential writer on religious matters in the early eighteenth century, and Law's theological system, a mix of both Calvinist and Arminian elements—Law's later writings revealed a turn to mysticism—was the stock from which both Wesley and Whitefield shaped their views.[25] Wesley, of course, was to acknowledge the influence of other writers—among them Jeremy Taylor, a seventeenth-century prelate, a one-time favorite of Laud's whose later sermons were denounced as Pelagian, as well as Thomas à Kempis, and the German mystics Behmen and Spener; for, as Bishop Lavington understood, Methodism had substantial ties with mysticism in relying—as in its doctrine of Assurance—on spiritual experience. Yet Wesley, in the course of still another inner struggle, felt compelled to turn against the more mystical doctrines of the Moravians which he was to denounce as abhorrent to reason and as leading to Antinomianism.

Josiah Tucker, the future Dean of Gloucester and an Arminian theologian as well as an economist, wrote a tract in 1742 when he was Vicar of All Saints, Bristol, in which he observed that both Wesley and Whitefield were relatively unversed in theology; when more learned men heard Whitefield preach the New Birth, they described him as a Calvinist, and Whitefield, from that point onward, Tucker noted, had turned to Calvinist argument to fill in yawning theological gaps; Wesley, similarly, tried to make the medley of views he had borrowed from Law and from the Moravians into a coherent system, which became increasingly, and not surprisingly for a Churchman, a species of Arminianism. At first, Wesley had accepted the Moravian doctrine of "Imputative Righteousness," Tucker noted, as we have already observed in his sermon on "Justification by Faith." This was a doctrine borrowed from Calvinism which declared that man's only hope of salvation lay not in his own merits, not in his own righteousness, but in his being admitted to a share in the righteousness of Christ. Wesley continued, nonetheless, to oppose, as the Moravians did, Calvinist election in favor of universal redemption.

As a good Churchman, however, Wesley soon disagreed with the Moravians on the means of grace (prayer, reading of scripture, participation in communion, etc.). On this last question, Tucker observed, the logic of the Moravians was unexceptionable: for, if no conditions or qualifications were required prior to justification, there was no advantage in attending to the means of grace, since holiness was not a condition but a consequence of justification; a man, consequently, need only wait for the imputation of Christ's righteousness. Either Wesley "must give up the Doctrine of *Imputed Righteousness,* and make Gospel Holiness to be a necessary Qualification antecedent to Justification," Tucker argued, "or else, if he holds to Imputation, he must strike off the *Necessity* of any Religious Performances as *previous* or requisite to attain it." Tucker predicted a schism within Methodist ranks, led by Wesley, who, he thought, would come over to the view that works were a condition of justification.[26] Indeed, this was to be the case. Tucker's prediction, in fact, was already partially fulfilled at the time he made it.

"The true gospel," Wesley later declared at his seventeenth annual conference with Methodist preachers, "touches the very edge both of Calvinism and Antinomianism, so that nothing but the mighty power of God can prevent our sliding either into the one or the other." [27] In separating himself from his allies in the evangelical crusade to reform England during the early forties, Wesley believed that, with God's help, he had managed to avoid these slippery slopes. At first, the Moravians appeared the more dangerous threat to Wesley's effort to raise a holy people, for, in the earliest years of his mission, Wesley and his followers were almost a part of the Moravian movement in England. It was, consequently, to prove necessary for Wesley to win adherents away from Moravian societies that he himself had helped to found. For over two years, Wesley struggled for the leadership of the London societies. But the issue was cloudy, for if Wesley was beginning, in 1738, 1739, and 1740, to feel an increasing hostility to Zinzendorf and to the Moravians generally, many of Wesley's chief associates, including his brother Charles, continued to feel that they were the best of men and of Christians.[28]

In Germany, the Reformers of the sixteenth century, the followers of Luther and Melanchthon, had divided during the period of the Thirty Years War into Lutherans (sometimes called Evangelicals) and the Reformed. The Lutherans had become a church, neglecting their former sectarian emphasis upon Scripture and the ideal of the priesthood of all believers in favor of theological formularies handed down by an authoritarian, and, in the course of time, indifferent pastorate. If in the Reformed Church, on the other hand, the people did have a share in a church government organized on presbyterian principles, its Calvinist theology made for a narrow, restrictive puritanism. A pietist movement, designed to remedy the faults of the German churches, particularly of the Lutherans, had been got underway by Philip Jacob Spener in the last decades of the seventeenth century. Spener, a mystic who wished to return to the Lutheran emphasis on the Bible, and, following the example of the Reformed Church, to foster a meaningful Christian life for the people, organized religious societies for prayer and discussion, thus endeavoring to give a greater share to the laity in the government of the Church; he stressed the importance of works, of practical Christianity as a sign of salvation, and, following decades of religious wars, urged sympathetic treatment of theological opponents. Spener's views deeply offended most of the Lutheran pastorate, but convinced men like August Hermann Francke, "converted" in 1688, whose lectures at the University of Halle spread the pietist view that not the holding of correct doctrine but the necessity of a New Birth and the leading of a holy life of a puritanical cast were the hallmarks of the good Christian. The influence of Spener and Francke was present in the outlook of Count von Zinzendorf, a godson of Spener and a pupil of the Halle Orphanage established by Francke. In 1727, the year of Francke's death, Zinzendorf organized the Moravian church to propagate the views of the German pietists. These views, of course, were largely to become those of the early Methodists who followed John Wesley, as we have observed.

But almost as soon as he had returned from Herrnhut, in September 1738, Wesley began to have doubts about Moravianism, doubts which he set down in a letter written, but never completed or sent, to his Moravian hosts. "Is not the Count all in all?" he asked. "Is there not something of levity in your behaviour? Are you, in general, serious enough? Are you zealous and watchful to redeem time? Do you not sometimes fall into trifling conversation?" [29] Concerning the position of the Count, Wesley was in later years to declare that "I must still insist on the right of private judgement," and "I dare call no man Rabbi." [30] It seems clear that Wesley was not only defending an abstract "right to private judgement": it was not to fill a position subordinate to Zinzendorf that he had been plucked from the burning.[31] The failure of continental pietism to come up to the sober standard of English puritanism—the brunt of Wesley's other questions—was a matter to which Wesley would refer, again and again.[32] Zinzendorf and the German Moravians were foreigners, subject to all the well-known faults of foreigners: [33] in 1740, for example, Wesley protested at the systematic, un-English habit of lying on the part of the Moravians; [34] in all this, Wesley compared them to the Jesuits, and Zinzendorf to Loyola.[35] Wesley attacked the Moravians for their presumption: "you greatly, yea, above measure, exalt yourselves and despise others," he declared; the Moravians spoke of their Church as "infallible," and asserted that there was "no true Church on earth," but theirs and "no true Christians out of it." Wesley condemned Moravian mysticism, and found the damage compounded because the Moravians "receive not the ancient but the modern mystics as the best interpreters of Scripture." [36] Wesley, a loyal son of the Establishment, was especially disturbed by a report, in late 1739, that the English Moravian leadership had determined "to *raise a church,* as they term it; and I suppose above half our brethren are on their side." [37]

Many of the doctrines with which Wesley found the greatest fault, although readily derivable from Moravian beliefs, were not so much those of Zinzendorf himself but of certain of the Moravian leaders in England, particularly a German named Molther, then newly arrived from the continent. Others, however, were at the very core of the Protestant experience. Wesley was upset when he heard many German Moravians—"particularly Mr. Molther"—suggest that "a man may have justifying faith and not know it." On the other hand, other Moravians insisted that there was "no such thing as weak faith," and that there was "no justifying faith where there is ever any doubt," that, indeed, those who had not an undoubted faith and "a new or clean heart" were "only awakened, not justified." (This had not been Wesley's own experience, and it seemed that these Moravians were all too ready to concede that Wesley had merely been "awakened," and not "justified"! In view of this, it is especially surprising how close these latter views were to the later Methodist doctrine of Assurance, as we shall see.) Moravian preachers, moreover, had instructed their followers, Wesley charged, to ignore the means of grace, "not to search the Scriptures, not to pray, not to communicate; and have often affirmed that to do these things is seeking salvation by works"; indeed they had suggested that "till these works are laid aside, no man can receive faith.' This was reprehensible quietism. Wesley charged the Moravians with undervaluing "good works (especially works of outward mercy), never publicly insisting on the necessity of them, nor declaring their weight and excellency." By such neglect, Moravians "wholly avoid the taking up your cross in order to do good." "I have heard some of you affirm," Wesley further observed, that Christian salvation "does not imply the proper taking away our sins, the cleansing our souls from all sin, but only the tearing the system of sin in pieces." That, furthermore, such salvation implied "liberty from the commandments of God, so that one who is saved through faith is not obliged or bound to obey them," that "to a believer there is no commandment at all." This was brazen Antinomianism. "Thus have I declared," Wesley concluded, "and in the plainest manner I can, the real controversy between us and the Moravian Brethren." [38]

Count Zinzendorf made every effort to settle the divisions within the ranks of his English followers and sympathizers but was unsuccessful. In early September 1741, the Count came to England to speak with Wesley. Zinzendorf, charging Wesley with ingratitude and betrayal, accused him of having changed his religion when he preached that "true Christians are not miserable sinners": "The best of men are miserable sinners up until their death," Zinzendorf insisted; "those who say otherwise, are either gross deceivers, or have been seduced by the devil." Wesley, who had begun to develop the doctrine of Christian Perfection which he had found in William Law, as well as in à Kempis, Taylor, and others, replied that "the Spirit of Christ worked perfection in true Christians," and that holiness might be achieved by a justified Christian. The Count thundered that "all our perfection is in Christ," that "Christian perfection is all imputed, not inherent," that "we are perfect in Christ, in ourselves never perfect." To say otherwise was the *"error errorum,"* which Zinzendorf was determined to "pursue everywhere with fire and with sword"; "he who follows the doctrine of inherent perfection," the Count declared, "denies Christ." Zinzendorf distinguished between a *sanctitas legalis* and a *sanctitas evangelica.* To the Count, the view of an inherent holiness smacked of the doctrine of good works: this was what he meant by *sanctitas legalis,* a mere "legal" holiness which came from conforming to commandments and ordinances rather than the *sanctitas evangelica,* which came from faith. "These are mere words," Wesley retorted: "You concede that the whole heart and life of the believer is holy, that he loves God with all his heart and serves him with all his powers; I ask nothing more in the way of Christian perfection and holiness." Wesley concluded the interview by praising self-denial, through which, he told the Count, "we live more and more in God." Zinzendorf, in the best Protestant manner, insisted that "we reject and despise all denials. Believers do what they wish and no more. We laugh at all mortifications. No purification is necessary to perfect love." [39] Such a declaration affected Wesley as it would have many Anglican divines of the time: the view that "believers do what they wish and no more" was Antinomianism.

The issue between Wesley and the Moravians, indeed, seemed unbridgeable. James Hutton, a friend of both Wesleys and a member of the Fetter Lane Society of the Moravians, had, in 1737, denounced the Anglican clergy as "so Pharisaic, so Pelagian, and more than Papistically merit-earning," because of their stress on good works, and the influence upon them of the "Pelagian" views on Christian Perfection of such divines as Jeremy Taylor and William Law; by 1744, Hutton was describing Wesley, similarly, as "the Fanatical Pelagian Pharisaic." [40] For his part, Wesley could only regard Zinzendorf and Hutton as Antinomians, and, consequently, as dangerous to the souls of Christians, as well as to the polity.

Wesley, at this time, discovered the source of the Antinomian doctrine of the Moravians: the culprit was Martin Luther. Wesley turned upon Luther, one of whose sermons, we recall, had helped to bring to him a sense of personal salvation, with a Laudian, or even Tridentine, horror. In his *Journal,* in June 1741, after reading Luther's Comment on the Epistle to the Galatians, Wesley confessed himself "ashamed" at having "esteemed this book" on the testimony of others or because of quotations from it. "Now I see with my own eyes" that Luther was "quite shallow," "muddy and confused"; that "he is deeply tinctured with mysticism throughout, and hence often dangerously wrong." "How does he (almost in the words of Tauler)," Wesley asked, "decry reason, right or wrong, as an irreconcilable enemy to the gospel of Christ!" "Whereas, what is reason (the faculty so called) but the power of apprehending, judging, and discoursing? Which power is no more to be condemned in the gross than seeing, hearing, or feeling." "How blasphemously" did Luther "speak of good works and of the law of God—constantly coupling the law with sin, death, hell, or the devil; and teaching that Christ delivers us from all alike."

"It can no more be proved by Scripture that Christ delivers us from the law of God," Wesley declared, "than that He delivers us from holiness or from heaven." "Here [I apprehend]," Wesley concluded, "is the real spring of the grand error of the Moravians," for "they follow Luther, for better, for worse." It was from Luther, the source and core of Protestant doctrine, that came their doctrine of "No works; no law; no commandments," [41] and Wesley thought it his "bounden duty openly to warn the congregation" against Luther's "dangerous treatise." [42]

WESLEY VS. WHITEFIELD AND
CALVIN (1740–1770)

By this time, Wesley had already felt himself obliged to warn his congregation against the baleful doctrines of Calvin. Wesley, when a High Churchman, had rejected predestination and election, those doctrinal hallmarks of English Dissent. The Moravians had rejected them as well. Whitefield, increasingly committed to the Calvinism of the Dissenters, had indeed, as early as July 1739, begun to worry that the Moravians were gaining too much of an ascendancy over Wesley. When Wesley decided to set up a school at Kingswood, Whitefield inquired whether "the house at Kingswood is intended hereafter for the brethren to dwell in, as at Herrnhuth," and took the occasion to remind Wesley that the Moravians had not lived together in communities like Herrnhut "til they were obliged by persecution." Whitefield need not have worried, for Wesley had no monastic vocation. What troubled Whitefield more profoundly was that Wesley shared the Moravian view of universal redemption. "How," he asked, "shall I tell the Dissenters I do not approve of their doctrines, without wronging my own soul? How shall I tell them I do, without contradicting my honoured friend, whom I desire to love as my own soul?" [43]

A break between Whitefield and Wesley seemed inevitable. In March 1740, writing from Georgia, Whitefield told Wesley. "I am ten thousand times more convinced of the doctrine of *election,* and the *final* perseverance," that is, the impossibility of the elect falling from grace, "of those that are truly in Christ, than when I saw you last," even while he cautioned him that they must not follow the example of Luther, the last part of whose life "was so much taken up in disputing with Zuinglius and others." [44] Two months later, in May 1740, Whitefield, apparently forgetting his resolve, declared that the more he examined "the experiences of the most established Christians," the more he disagreed with Wesley on the issues of Christian Perfection, election, and final perseverance. "I dread coming to England," Whitefield wrote, "unless you are resolved to oppose these truths with less warmth than when I was there last"; Whitefield was tempted to remain in America, because Americans held so tenaciously to the doctrine of election.[45] In August 1740, writing from Charleston, he urged upon Wesley that the doctrines of election and of final perseverance may have been "abused," but "they are children's bread, and ought not to be withheld from them." Whitefield had earlier been dismayed when he heard Charles Wesley declare that his purpose was "to drive John Calvin out of Bristol." [46] In September 1740, writing from Boston, Whitefield attacked a recent sermon of Wesley's on Christian Perfection, and returned to the defense of final perseverance and even of reprobation, i.e., the damnation of the nonelect. "What then is there in *reprobation* so horrid? . . . If God might have passed by all, He may pass by some." "If you think so meanly of Bunyan and the Puritan writers," Whitefield concluded, "I do not wonder that you think me wrong." [47]

In December 1740, Whitefield penned an impassioned plea urging Wesley to "consider how you dishonour God by denying election": "You plainly make man's salvation depend not on God's *free grace,* but on man's *free will*." [48] When, early in 1741, Whitefield returned from Georgia, he informed Wesley, as the latter recorded in his *Journal,* that "he and I preached two different gospels, and therefore he not only would not join with, or give me the right hand of fellowship, but was resolved publicly to preach against me and my brother, wheresoever he preached at all." [49] Wesley, who in a reply to one of Whitefield's letters had noted, "there are bigots both for predestination and against it," [50] declared the existence of "an open (and probably irreparable) breach between him and me." [51]

During this period, there were local disturbances of a similar character within the societies. In June 1740, for example, a man named Acourt complained that, by Charles Wesley's order, he had been ejected from one of Wesley's societies because of his belief in election. John Wesley, denying that Acourt had been excluded for his opinions but only because he had insisted on troubling "others by disputing" about them,[52] urged his followers "not to 'receive one another to doubtful disputations,' but simply to follow after holiness, and the things that make for peace." [53]

A more serious business was the defection and then expulsion of John Cennick, a land surveyor and writing master, the first of the men whom John Wesley, at first reluctantly, and to the great discomfort of his brother, encouraged to become a lay preacher. In mid-December of 1740, Cennick, preaching at Kingswood in Wesley's absence, accused Wesley of not preaching "the truth" concerning election.[54] A week later, on Boxing Day, on his return to Kingswood, Wesley discovered that "my congregation was gone to hear Mr. C [ennick], so that (except a few from Bristol) I had not above two or three men and as many women." [55] There was a confrontation between Wesley and Cennick and their supporters on February 22, 1741, in which Wesley protested at Cennick's having "supplanted me in my own house, stealing the hearts of the people." The followers of Cennick retorted that Wesley "did preach up man's faithfulness, and not the faithfulness of God," and did preach that "there is righteousness in man." Wesley produced a letter which Cennick had written to Whitefield the previous January, in which Cennick had urged Whitefield to "come quickly" to block "Satan" who was "now making war with the saints": "I believe no atheist can more preach against Predestination" than the brothers Wesley, Cennick had observed, "and all who believe Election are counted enemies to God." [56] The following week, on February 28, John Wesley read a manifesto of expulsion of Cennick and his followers to the much-surprised members of the Kingswood bands, "not for their opinions" but for having "studiously endeavoured to prejudice other members of that society" against the Wesleys.[57] Cennick, who later became famous as an evangelist and the author of many hymns, was no doctrinaire Calvinist—though believing in election for the "first fruits," he favored an ultimate universal redemption,[58] in the fashion becoming more and more common, and he soon moved from the camp of Whitefield to that of the Moravians, actually embarking for Herrnhut in 1745.[59]

The personal breach between Whitefield and Wesley was not to last. Whitefield, an open-hearted man, was dismayed at the break, and Wesley saw the harm which would come of a split, especially since it was Wesley's better-organized Connection which secured the bulk of the English converts won over by Whitefield's preaching. In May 1742, Wesley and Whitefield made their peace, agreeing to stress doctrines held in common and to continue their evangelization of England in fellowship. (What helped to preserve friendly relations was Whitefield's determination to devote his principal energies to the New World.) Although never relinquishing the suspicion that Whitefield might once more be persuaded to denounce him, Wesley kept the peace, at least with Whitefield personally. In August 1743, to solidify the peaceful understanding with Whitefield, Wesley set down his sentiments on the issues under dispute in terms of apparent compromise, which was later to make him regret—though without substantial grounds—that he had, on this occasion, leaned too much toward Calvinism.[60] Subsequent entries in Wesley's *Journal* speak of increasingly warm feelings for Whitefield, though there continued, for a time, to be occasional signs of hostility.[61] Despite his truce with Whitefield personally, Wesley continued to strike out against other predestinarians, and against Antinomianism, which seemed in Wesley's eyes more and more associated with the doctrines and the persons of certain Calvinist evangelical preachers, during this time (the forties, fifties, and sixties) of the great expansion of the Methodist societies. It was the followers of Whitefield who restrained their fire until, approximately, the time of the latter's death.

In 1769, Whitefield set off again for America where he died, in Newburyport, Massachusetts, in 1770. Wesley, in a funeral sermon preached at Whitefield's wish at the Tottenham Court Road Chapel in November 1770, alluded to the peace between Whitefield and himself, acknowledging that though they had disagreed concerning "many doctrines of a less essential nature," mere opinions, they were as one in clinging "to the grand scriptural doctrines" of the New Birth, i.e. the making of a "new man," cleansed of sin and conscious of his personal salvation, and, consequently, striving toward holiness, and of justification by faith.[62] The doctrine of justification by faith was not only scripturally true, but "experimentally" true, for Wesley had seen men almost on the level of brutes, "saved," transformed, sometimes instantaneously, by the freely bestowed grace of Christ; in a letter to a friend in 1765, Wesley declared that "I think on Justification just as I have done any time these seven-and-twenty years, and just as Mr. Calvin does," not differing from Calvin in this matter by "an hair's breadth." [63] Still, Wesley had to admit that "the doctrines of Justification and Salvation by Faith are grievously abused by many Methodists," [64] and might be the source of pernicious Antinomianism, along with the doctrines of election and predestination.

But since belief in predestination and election was "opinion," distinct from "essential doctrine," and therefore "compatible with love of Christ, and a genuine work of grace," Wesley wrote in 1765—and Wesley had known men with "real Christian experience" who believed in predestination [65]—Wesley would regard himself as a "bigot," if he were to attack a man for a mere "opinion." [66] Bigotry was a Catholic vice, which the Reformation Protestants had taken up (Wesley more than once bemoaned the fate of Servetus at the hands of Calvin [67]), a vice which had brought disorder and bloodletting for two centuries. Thirty years earlier, Wesley acknowledged, both he and his brother had thought it "our duty to oppose Predestination with our whole strength; not as an opinion but as a dangerous mistake, which appears to be subversive of the very foundation of Christian experience." [68] But in the first generation of the Revival, it was as an "opinion," and not as a point of "essential doctrine," that Wesley continued to denounce predestination and election.

In the thirty years of personal truce, Wesley reiterated the sum of his views on election and on free grace, which had so disturbed Whitefield, in numerous tracts and sermons. He took special issue with the Calvinist view of the "Perseverance of the Saints," that a true believer, once he had achieved grace, would everlastingly retain it: "God is the Father of them that Believe, so long as they Believe," Wesley proclaimed, "but the Devil is the Father of them that Believe not, whether they did once Believe or no." [69] He insisted that the Calvinist view that God's grace, when it was bestowed, was "irresistible," made man "a mere machine." "How is it more for the glory of God to save man irresistibly," Wesley inquired, "than to save him as a free agent, by such grace as he may either concur with or resist?" Indeed, Wesley declared, Calvinism was not only a totally unscriptural error, "it is an error of so pernicious consequence to the souls of men," since "it directly and naturally tends to hinder the inward work of God in every stage of it." A man, if he believes himself to be one of the elect, will think he need do nothing but wait for "irresistible grace"; he grows "slacker," and "so he sins on, and sleeps on, till he awakes in hell." [70]

The predestinarians, in contentiously putting forth their opinions, continually raised havoc among those whom Methodist preaching had helped to free from sin. With their "doubtful disputations," Wesley noted in his *Journal* in 1751, the predestinarians had "thrown back those who had begun to run well"—some had returned to "the world," others had joined the Baptists, and still others had joined the "endless disputes concerning the secret counsels of God!" Still others "broke out into the wildest enthusiasm." [71] In the spring of 1753, Wesley observed that the Society at Alnwick had been "harassed" by a few "violent Predestinarians," who had, at last, left the Society. "I can have no connexion with those who will be contentious," Wesley declared at this time. "These I reject, not for their opinion, but for their sin; for their unchristian temper and unchristian practice; for being haters of reproof, haters of peace, haters of their brethren, and, consequently, of God." [72] In these ways, also, did Calvinist opinions lead to Antinomianism.

WESLEY VS. CUDWORTH AND HERVEY ON IMPUTED RIGHTEOUSNESS (1745–1758)

If Wesley, at least intermittently during this period, felt he could not reject predestinarians merely for their "opinions," and if he felt some restraint in denouncing predestinarian doctrine as "fundamental error," he did combat, without any qualms, the more straightforward doctrines of "speculative" Antinomianism, which he feared were readily convertible into "practical" Antinomianism. While Bishop Browne, Wesley wrote in a letter in 1774, might think that various forms of deistic unitarianism were "the flood which the dragon is in this age pouring out of his mouth to swallow up the woman," Wesley held that "the main flood in England seems to be Antinomianism," which had been "a greater hindrance to the work of God than any or all others put together." [73] At the first conference with his lay preachers in June 1744, he pictured speculative Antinomianism as "the doctrine which makes void the law through faith," which held that "Christ abolished the moral law," and that consequently "Christian liberty" was a "liberty from obeying the commandments of God," that "a believer is not obliged to use the ordinances of God, or to do good works." Wesley, on the other hand, asserted that Christ had abolished merely "the ritual law of Moses," and that Christian liberty meant freedom from that law and from sin. [74]

Wesley denounced the Antinomianism of several evangelists, particularly William Cudworth. Cudworth, with James Relly, a former follower of Whitefield, had separated from Whitefield because they were offended at the idea of reprobation: while believers in election, they held the elect to be merely the first fruits, for Christ had died so *all* men would be saved. (The sect of Rellyean Universalists emerged from the followers of Relly and Cudworth.) Cudworth and Relly also believed that to continue in sin was punishment sufficient in itself and required no further punishment in the hereafter, almost in the manner of the Cambridge Platonist Whichcote or the deist Shaftesbury. This was what troubled Wesley, who detested the two universalists who would save all sinners without first requiring them to achieve holiness. Both Cudworth and Relly, turning to Luther for support, steadfastly denied they were Antinomians.[75] Relly and Cudworth were "properly Antinomians," Wesley observed in later years, "absolute, avowed enemies to the law of God," who "termed all legalists" who preached that law; they were men who "would 'preach Christ,' as they called it, but without one word either of holiness or good works." It especially irritated Wesley that such men were "still denominated Methodists" by the public.[76]

Wesley constructed a stereotypical Antinomian by weaving together quotations from Cudworth's writings. This Antinomian held that "to believe certainly, that Christ suffered death for us, is enough"; "one must do nothing, but quietly attend the voice of the Lord," for "works are not only not required, but forbidden." Like Count Zinzendorf, the Antinomian denied that a believer could possess "inherent righteousness," and insisted that "our righteousness is nothing but the imputation of the righteousness of Christ," and that therefore the "very moment" a believer is justified, "he is wholly sanctified." To Wesley, this was "a heap of broad absurdities," contradictory to reason, Scripture, and common sense.[77] In 1762, Wesley observed that the phrase "imputing the Righteousness of Christ"— which was "so dreadfully abused" by Antinomians "to justify the grossest Abominations"—was not to be found in the Bible.[78]

Wesley, at times, seemed aware that certain of his doctrinal differences with Cudworth were not substantial, but rather "a strife of words," but he nonetheless found Cudworth's "confused," "insincere," and "unscriptural" phrases "a dangerous way of speaking." Speculative Antinomianism had "a peculiar tendency" to "puff" up the speaker, "to engender pride," and "to make him exalt himself (under pretence of exalting the grace of God,) and despise others." Its effect upon those who heard such preaching was even more injurious, for it "plunges not a few into all the wretchedness of unclean living."[79]

Wesley had a number of encounters with groups of Antinomians, who wished "to rest contented with what was done for us seventeen hundred years ago," who believed that Christ had "done *all* for us"; and that "we have nothing to do but to *believe*."[80] He railed at these "fierce, unclean, brutish, blasphemous Antinomians."[81] In 1746, Wesley met at Wednesbury the Antinomian preacher Stephen Timmins, whom he believed "pride" had made mad: "an uncommon wildness and fierceness in his air, his words and the whole manner of his behaviour, almost induced me to think God had for a season given him up into the hands of Satan." At Birmingham, Wesley cross-questioned another Antinomian, setting down the conversation so that all "may know what these men mean by their favourite phrase of being 'perfect in Christ, not in themselves' ":

"Do you believe you have nothing to do with the law of God?"
"I have not; I am not under the law: I live by faith."
"Have you, as living by faith, a right to everything in the world?"
"I have; all is mine, since Christ is mine."
"May you, then, take anything . . . without consent or knowledge of the owner?"
"I may, if I want it; for it is mine. Only I will not give offence."
"Have you also a right to all the women in the world?"
"Yes, if they consent."
"And is that not a sin?"
"Yes, to him that thinks it is a sin; but not to those whose *hearts are free*." [82]

In 1750, Wesley denounced the preacher Roger Ball who believed, in classic Antinomian fashion, that, in Wesley's words, "a believer had a right to all women," Wesley adding suggestively that "I marvel he has turned only three persons out of the way." [83] Wesley could only conclude that "surely these [Antinomians] are the first born children of Satan!" [84]

Wesley could not really have believed that Zinzendorf and Cudworth, in preaching in favor of the imputation of Christ's righteousness, were Johns of Leyden, urging the faithful toward communism of goods and women. However, he did fear that their words might be extended by others to include such ends, and therefore he struck out vigorously against evangelistic leaders who maintained themselves "Preachers of God's Righteousness," which was, after all, a proper Reformation position for which Cudworth had quite properly invoked Luther's support. Methodism itself had been accused of speculative Antinomianism, as we know, a charge which the Church almost automatically levelled against all enthusiasts. To battle against speculative Antinomianism was for Wesley to reassert his loyalty to the Church of England. [85]

In the fifties and sixties, Wesley found himself quarreling openly with long-time associates, now his evangelical rivals, on this issue. For example, Wesley denounced Thomas Maxfield, for a time his favorite among the lay preachers, for having pushed the doctrine of "justification by faith alone" to its final Antinomian limits and for having become a preacher of the imputation of Christ's righteousness. Following Satan, such preachers held that "all is in Christ, nothing in man"; this was "a blow at the root"— such a doctrine "makes men afraid of personal holiness," and good works become "a stink in their nostrils." "Come back to Christ," Wesley urged his errant disciples, "who died to make you an holy people, 'zealous of good works.' " [86]

In the fifties, also, there began a dispute concerning these questions which led to a violent schism in the ranks of the evangelical forces, and to open warfare between the "Arminians," a label the Wesleyans at last embraced, and the Calvinists. James Hervey, a former member of the society of Oxford "Methodists," had published in 1755 a series of letters entitled *Theron and Aspasio,* containing views which revealed their author to be, by Wesley's lights, an Antinomian and a Calvinist. In 1756, Wesley wrote to Hervey protesting the uses to which Hervey had put the phrase "the imputed righteousness of Christ"; he was also disturbed to find Hervey so much a Calvinist as to be oblivious of the fate of the nonelect, "the bulk of mankind." How could Hervey write, "the grand end which God proposes in all His favourable dispensations to fallen man is to demonstrate the sovereignty of His grace"? Wesley preferred to think that "to impart happiness to His creatures is His grand end herein," for "barely to demonstrate His sovereignty is a principle of action fit for the great Turk, not the Most High God." Wesley took pains to display for Hervey "the central point wherein Calvinism and Antinomianism meet." [87]

The following year, writing to Samuel Furly, one of his lay preachers, Wesley called Hervey "a deeply-rooted Antinomian—that is, a Calvinist consistent with himself," which, he added, "Mr. Whitefield is not." [88] By 1758, ill, and no longer capable of seeing his replies to Wesley through the press, Hervey turned for help and advice to William Cudworth, whom Wesley regarded as an "insolent, scurrilous, virulent libeller" who was provoking a dying Hervey to controversy. [89] Wesley even suspected Cudworth of introducing offensive changes into Hervey's manuscript. [90] Hervey was much admired by the Countess of Huntingdon, a Calvinist evangelical to whom Whitefield served as chaplain, who, although declining the dedication of *Theron and Aspasio,* had taken Hervey under her protection. After Hervey's death in December 1758, Lady Huntingdon's circle, who thought themselves "true Protestants," and Romaine, one of the leading evangelical clergymen in that circle, urged Christians to read Hervey's work so as to convince themselves that a believer might say, "In the Lord have I righteousness and salvation." Only then, Romaine concluded, in a clear reference to Wesley's views, would a believer "be delivered from those dangerous errors which are now propagated." [91]

WESLEY'S WAR ON CALVINIST ANTINOMIANISM (1770–1780)

In the sixties, ostensibly provoked by the Hervey controversy, forces were assembled to see whether Wesley's Arminianism or the Calvinism of Lady Huntingdon and her ministers would dominate the Methodist movement. After Hervey's death, it seemed that John Fletcher, the Vicar of Madely, might be groomed by Lady Huntingdon as Wesley's doctrinal opponent, but Fletcher, though a worried Wesley had felt obliged to warn him against the dangers of too close association with Calvinism,[92] was not tempted to fill this role. The man who did aspire, successfully, to be the theological champion of Calvinist evangelicalism was Augustus Montague Toplady. Toplady had begun his career as a free-willer who had agreed with Wesley on the question of the imputation of Christ's righteousness,[93] but his views changed,[94] and in 1769 he published a translation from the sixteenth-century predestinarian divine Zanchius,[95] and a few years later a long tract "vindicating the Church of England from the charge of Arminianism." [96] In 1770, Wesley replied with a quasi-satiric "abridgement" of Toplady's translation, the final lines of which stated that "the sum of all is this: One in twenty [suppose] of mankind are elected; nineteen in twenty are reprobated. The elect shall be saved, do what they will: The reprobate shall be damned, do what they can." [97] Wesley did not fail to declare that such doctrines encouraged extreme Antinomianism. Toplady proclaimed Wesley a forger, and began a stream of vituperation, to be answered in the same coin by Wesley and his followers, which prompted Wesley to call him "too dirty a writer for me to meddle with." [98] Toplady suggested that if Wesley were really searching for Antinomians, those "truly and justly so called," he "must look for them, not among those whom you term Calvinists, but among your own hair-brained (sic) perfectionists." [99]

The war fully began in August 1770 when Wesley presented "Doctrinal Minutes" to his annual conference of Methodist preachers, asserting once more the doctrine of salvation "not by the *merit* of works, but by works as a *condition*." Wesley was repeating his view that while justification required only faith, though we might have earnestly to seek grace, sanctification or final salvation—possible, of course, only after justifying faith had brought about a rebirth—was dependent on works as a condition. The "new man" had to strive to maintain holiness if he were to achieve sanctification at the time of judgment. To the Calvinist, this seemed too much like justification by works.[100] Urging all men to rally to "true Protestantism," the Reverend Walter Shirley, a relative and associate of the Countess of Huntingdon, sent out a circular letter to all evangelical clergymen, who he believed could only disapprove of Wesley's "Doctrinal Minutes," urging they demand a recantation.[101] The Countess of Huntingdon, who had become the patroness of a school at Trevecca for the training of evangelical clergymen, called upon all those associated with that school either to disown Wesley's minutes or to resign: Joseph Benson, recommended to Lady Huntingdon by Wesley as principal of Trevecca, resigned, and John Fletcher, whom the Countess had been carefully cultivating, withdrew as superintendent of the school in support of both Benson and Wesley.[102]

The battle between Arminianism and Calvinism, simmering for over thirty years within the evangelical ranks, was now in full blaze. Shirley and others associated with the Countess of Huntingdon, no doubt to explain their own intimate past association with such a heretic, accused Wesley of having changed the gospel he had previously preached. Wesley, quite correctly, denied the charge; in a letter to the Countess dated June 19, 1771, Wesley declared the steadfastness of the view he had formed at Oxford that "without holiness no man shall see the Lord." Although a decade later he had become convinced that only by "faith in the Son of God" could man be saved from sin, he nonetheless believed that "through faith, one might attain holiness." For believing this, Wesley continued, "all the religious world," following "the example of one of my eldest sons, Mr. Whitefield," had "set themselves in array against me," and had accused him of being "unsound in the faith," and of preaching "another gospel." Wesley noted a number of his earlier sermons in which he had set forth the doctrines of his 1770 Minutes, and declared that "whether it be the same which they preach or not, it is the same which I have preached for above thirty years." [103] In another letter, in 1771, addressed to a number of evangelical preachers, Wesley noted once more that his minutes were "no heresy, but the words of truth and soberness." "By salvation I here mean final salvation," Wesley declared; "and who can deny that both inward good works (loving God and our neighbour) and outward good works (keeping His commandments) are a condition of this?" [104]

John Fletcher produced a tract—his *First Check to Antinomianism*—to support Wesley. At Wesley's 1771 Conference, to which Shirley and a few of his supporters came, an understanding was apparently reached, and Shirley declared himself satisfied that Wesley was not truly preaching justification by works, that "most perilous and abominable doctrine." Fletcher thereupon asked, in the interests of peace, that his *First Check,* not yet in print, be suppressed. Wesley, however, determined that his opponents not be given the opportunity of claiming victory, insisted on publication, and set about to extirpate the heresy of Calvinist Antinomianism,[105] which was threatening to turn the Revival away from the Arminian program. Toplady had observed that in the sixties, Wesley had complained that "the evangelical clergy are leaving no stone unturned 'to raise John Calvin's ghost, in all quarters of the land.' " Under these circumstances, Toplady suggested, Wesley "never had a fairer opportunity of trying your strength upon John Calvin, than at present." [106] Wesley was seizing this opportunity.

This struggle for "true Protestantism," on the one hand, and the full Arminian critique, on the other, which accompanied the competition for the leadership of the evangelical movement after Whitefield's death, was carried on, like later political struggles of a similarly strong ideological character, in a fiercely "sectarian" spirit. Both Wesleyans and Calvinists saw their quarrel as war to the death. Wesley had given up all earlier hopes of a "coalition with Calvinism." [107] "O beware of Calvinism and everything that has the least tendency thereto," he wrote in a letter in 1777; "let a burnt child dread the fire!" [108] In 1778, he observed that "fire and water cannot well dwell together, nor warm Calvinists and Arminians." [109] Wesley saw Calvinism as "the very antidote of Methodism, the most deadly and successful enemy which it ever had." [110] In 1778, he condemned Calvinism as being "anti-evangelical," for while few Methodists were in any danger of "imbibing error" from the ministers of the Church of England, they were in great danger of "imbibing the grand error—Calvinism" [111]—not only from the Old Dissent, but from "evangelical" clergymen like Shirley, Madan, and Romaine, who were allied with the Countess of Huntingdon. These men were "wholly swallowed up in that detestable doctrine of Predestination." [112] Wesley had written of Romaine's writings in 1771, that they were "brimful of Antinomianism." [113] Wesley might have been ready to grant that the Calvinists "do not intend Antinomianism," but, he insisted, "they preach it continually." [114]

As always, Antinomianism was the great enemy for Wesley: it was, he wrote in 1789, "the great hindrance to the inward work of God." [115] It was the absolute identification of Calvinism and Antinomianism which the Wesleyans made in the seventies—although there were evidences of this earlier—that underlay Wesleyan ferocity. The evangelical Calvinists, on the other hand, believed that they fought for "true Protestantism" against popery, that they fought to defend the omnipotence of God against what they regarded as Wesley's efforts to humble the Deity. How could such causes fail to call forth vigorous sentiments?

This debate between Calvinism and its opponents, while far from the most subtle in theological argument, must be ranked among the most vituperative and prolific. On the Wesleyan side was Walter Sellon, a baker become first lay and then ordained preacher, whose violent attack on Hervey and Cudworth in 1767,[116] and whose reply to Toplady's vindication of the Church of England from the charge of Arminianism a few years afterward,[117] had helped to set the scurrilous tone of the controversy. Thomas Olivers, a Welsh artisan and lay preacher, a favorite of Wesley who became the first editor of the *Arminian Magazine* in 1778, took a no more elevated tone than had Sellon, and he also set about to rebut Toplady in 1770; [118] Olivers also replied to the writings of the Calvinist evangelists, the brothers Richard and Rowland Hill.[119] Even the respectable Charles Perronet, signing himself "a Legalist belonging to Mr Wesley's Society," thus parodied the Calvinism of his opponents: "I believe I may deny *Christ,* worship *Ashtaroth,* murder, rob, commit Adultery and Incest. Who shall lay anything to the charge of a Believer?" [120] Fletcher's *Checks,* embodying the most dignified and least vituperative contributions to the controversy, were written in answer not only to Toplady and Shirley, but, primarily, to the brothers Richard and Rowland Hill, whose Calvinist tracts were roughly on the same polemical level as those of Olivers and Sellon. The brothers Hill entered the dispute in 1771, at which time Richard wrote Wesley off as a Pelagian and therefore considerably worse than a papist.[121] Sellon and Olivers were dismissed as controversialists not worth disputing with because of their plebeian origins, as objects of "absolute insignificance." [122]

The chief pamphleteer on the Arminian side was, of course, Wesley himself. Although he repeatedly declared that he would leave others to bear the brunt of the controversy,[123] again and again Wesley joined the debate. He confronted Toplady once more in 1771, attacking the scheme of predestination.[124] In 1772, Wesley issued a call to battle, urging his fellow Arminians no longer "to remain only on the defensive," but rather to "chase the fiend, Reprobation, to his own hell, and every doctrine connected with it." Calvinism inspired "pride" and "haughtiness," presumption of the worst kind. "Let none pity or spare one limb of either speculative or practical Antinomianism," he thundered, "or of any doctrine that naturally tends thereto," disguised "under the specious name of free grace." [125] (Wesley regretted that he had for so long, "from a well-meant, but ill-judged, tenderness," permitted "the reprobation Preachers . . . to spread their poison, almost without opposition"; noting his relationship to the Countess of Huntingdon and her highborn associates, he declared that "I have humbled myself to them for these thirty years," but "it is all lost labour." [126]) In 1773, there was another tract by Wesley against Hill,[127] and in 1777, in an answer to Rowland Hill's "Imposture Detected," Wesley referred to his more specifically political differences with Antinomian Calvinism declaring "I will have no fellowship with those who rail at their governors." [128] There were a number of lesser contributors on the Wesleyan side.[129]

It may have been the Swiss-born Fletcher, the best theologian on the Wesleyan side, who helped to persuade Wesley to adapt in more open fashion the continental Arminianism of the Dutch Remonstrancers to the needs of the evangelical movement, that is, to set Wesleyanism in a wider Arminian system and to make that system serve Wesley's overriding passion, the fight against Antinomianism. (Fletcher's thirteen tracts, contributed between 1771 and 1775 to the debate with the Calvinists, were even called *Checks to Antinomianism.* Wesley regarded Fletcher's tracts as breathing "the very spirit of the gospel"—having an "inimitable sweetness and gentleness.") [130] John William Fletcher,[131] born Jean Guillaume de la Fléchière at Nyon, Switzerland, in 1729, the son of a professional soldier of high rank, was converted by Methodist preaching while on a visit to England in 1752. After his ordination in 1757, he assisted Wesley in carrying the gospel to French refugees in London before accepting, in 1760, the living of Madely, in Shropshire, a parish with a rapidly growing population working in extensive coal mines and iron works, where he became a popular preacher. Wesley was delighted by the support of this cultivated man of good family, whose learning and talents stood in sharp contrast to the shoemaker or carpenter lay preachers who his enemies charged were Wesley's only supporters: he found Fletcher "better qualified," in personality, learning, and communion with God, than "Mr. Whitefield himself," and better able to "sound an alarm through all the nation"; indeed, for Wesley, Fletcher seemed not inferior to Wesley's much admired Christian mystics, Gregory Lopez and M. de Renty.[132] Wesley had seen "the charms of Calvinism" steal away his choicest disciples—Whitefield, Cennick, Maxfield, Toplady.[133] Why was Calvinism so attractive to the well born or talented? Wesley beseeched Fletcher not to seek the company of Lady Huntingdon and her set, but to associate only with persons "vigorously working out their salvation, persons athirst for full redemption," who would "commonly be poor and mean; seldom possessed of either riches or learning." [134] Fletcher remained faithful. In 1773, Wesley was worried that without an able successor, "*one* to preside over *all*," the "work will indeed come to an end," and he implored Fletcher, as best qualified to preside over "preachers and people," and as knowing "the whole plan of Methodism," [135] to be his heir, but Fletcher declined, modestly doubting his ability to lead.[136]

Joseph Benson, in 1770, while still principal at Trevecca, wrote that "Mr. Fletcher thought the Churches throughout Christendom to be verging very fast toward Antinomianism," and had consequently wished Wesley's doctrinal minutes "confirmed [rather] than revoked." [137] Certainly Fletcher's *Checks to Antinomianism* constituted a full defense of Wesley's position on both speculative, and, as we shall see, practical Antinomianism. Fearful of the advancing tide of revolution, Fletcher's reply to the question of whether there was not "as much danger from overdoing in Pharisaic *works,* as in Antinomian *faith,*" was "not at present," since "the stream runs too rapidly on the side of lawless faith." [138] For Fletcher, as for Wesley, "speculative Antinomianism and bare-faced Calvinism" were "one and the same thing," [139] and Fletcher warned Britons who had "unhappily fallen in love with the Genevan Delilah" to restore "the balance between St. Paul's and St. James' justification" now "lost among pious Protestants." [140] In accepting Wesley's doctrine of Christian Perfection, Fletcher came to the "alarming" conclusion that "there is no medium between pleading for the continuance of indwelling sin, and pleading for the continuance of heart Antinomianism." Fletcher, a stalwart of the Methodist Revolution, was fighting "for the most precious liberty in the world, heart liberty," for "liberty from the most galling of all yokes, the yoke of heart corruption," *in this life,* and not in a purgatory after death. He urged Christians that "instead of shouting Indwelling sin and death purgatory," they might "fulfill the law of liberty" and shout "Christ and Christian liberty forever!" If we exaggerated "the difficulties of keeping Christ's laws," Fletcher declared, we have "Calvinistically traduced the equity of our gracious God, and inadvertently encouraged the Antinomian delusions." [141]

So, events from the 1740s through the 1770s more or less took the turn which Dean Tucker had predicted as early as 1742. Wesley denounced both the Moravian and Calvinist use of the Reformation doctrine of the imputation of Christ's righteousness as leading to Antinomianism, and turned his energies to opposing election and predestination as well. It may be that Wesley was persuaded by Tucker's argument, with which he was familiar,[142] and which may have helped to provide for Wesley the more systematic theological base he required. In any event, Wesley more and more described himself as an Arminian,[143] and just as he had taken up and proudly worn the name of Methodist, which had originally been derisively bestowed, so, from 1770 onward, supported by Fletcher, he bore with similar pride the name of Arminian as he understood it, which was for Calvinists virtually synonymous with Papist. It might be argued, given the general acceptance by most Dissenters of Baxter's compromise position between Calvinism and Arminianism, that true Calvinism had long been dead, and that Wesley had sounded its requiem in his sermon on Free Grace in 1741. Certainly this moderate Calvinism, as we shall later observe, was an ambiguous doctrine; on the other hand, a rigid, hyper-Calvinism did persist well into the eighteenth century.[144]

Wesley had undertaken the exposure of rigid Calvinist doctrines, so discordant with the commercial society of eighteenth-century England, in good part because he believed that they led to a speculative Antinomianism. This effort was the theological companion of what was becoming the leading principle of the High Church, to which Wesley wholeheartedly subscribed; for Anglicanism seemed to be making passive obedience and nonresistance its most essential spiritual doctrine in the hope of assuring peace, order, and the stability of the dynasty. By striking at "Antinomian" doctrines held by the evangelical sects, masses of enthusiasts that had posed such a danger to state and church in the past, Wesley was seeking to counter the ideological forces that had helped lead to the practical Antinomianism of civil war in the preceding century, and which, he feared, might be leading in the same direction in his own lifetime. In so doing, he was, as we shall see, more and more consciously setting forth a libertarian and egalitarian doctrine couched in constitutional (i.e., rational and contractual) forms suitable for a modern society.

In the seventies, the grand moment for which Wesley might be said to have prepared himself and his followers seemed at hand. As Wesley and his followers saw it, speculative Antinomianism had at last erupted into practical Antinomianism, as they had always known it would. The seventies were a time of revolution—actual in the colonies, potential at home —and the need to prevent such a revolution had become, for Wesley, a predominant consideration. Practical Antinomianism was one of the bitter fruits of Reformation Protestantism which the Arminian Counter-Reformation might extirpate. It was, no doubt, with some satisfaction that Wesley observed in a letter in 1775 that "those who are the avowed enemies of Christian Perfection are in general the warmest enemies of King George and of all that are in authority under him." [145]

III

Confrontation with "Practical" Antinomianism

Do you honour and obey all in authority? All your governors, spiritual pastors, and masters? Do you behave lowly and reverently to all your betters? Do you hurt nobody by word or deed? Are you true and just in all your dealings? Do you take care to pay whatever you owe? Do you feel no malice, or envy, or revenge, no hatred or bitterness to any man? If you do, it is plain you are not of God; for all these are the tempers of the devil. . . . Have you learned, in every state wherein you are, therewith to be content? Do you labour to get your own living, abhorring idleness as you abhor hell-fire? . . . Whatever your hand finds to do, do you do it with your might? And do you do all as unto the Lord, as a sacrifice unto God, acceptable in Christ Jesus?

This, and this alone, is the old religion. This is true, primitive Christianity. Oh, when shall it spread over all the earth? when shall it be found both in us and you? Without waiting for others, let each of us by the grace of God amend one.

John Wesley, 1749

> *The silent laws have lost their force,*
> *Where rebels arm'd obstruct their course,*
> *And grasp at sovereign power,*
> *Their law their own despotic will*
> *Their whole delight to slay and kill. . . .*
>
> *March through a land that is not theirs,*
> *Impatient to demand their shares,*
> *And seize the whole at last.*

[Charles Wesley]
From "Hymns for the National Fast,
February 8, 1782"

In 1782, Wesley declared that it was the "main and constant business" of a Christian minister to "preach Jesus Christ, and him crucified," rather than become immersed in matters political. That a concern for politics would endanger personal salvation had been the message of the gospels, reflecting the Pharisaic abhorrence of the political fanaticism of the Zealots. The injunction to political passivity had been repeated by Luther, horrified by the Peasant Wars, and later by Calvin—though not by all of their followers. Wesley joined in this call, and urged obedience. He insisted that his only motive for speaking out on political questions was to restore the people to obedience, to counter the false religion of sectarians who, following the Puritan example, were acting to undermine the authority of those whom God had set up to rule. There was "a plain command in the Bible, 'thou shalt not speak evil of the ruler of thy people,' " Wesley observed, yet many who called themselves "religious" did "speak evil of him continually," and spoke "many things that are palpably false." Under these circumstances, it was the "bounden duty" of every Christian minister "to refute these vile aspersions, in public as well as in private." [1] Wesley saw politics, as he had observed in 1768, as lying "quite out of my province." He ridiculed the prevailing notion that "every Englishman is a politician," and despaired that "every cobbler, tinker, porter, and hackney-coachman" felt able to "point out every blunder" of the Ministry. Yet he saw a general discontent in the nation "which now rises to an higher degree than it has done in the memory of man"; he had "heard it affirmed with my own ears, 'King George ought to be treated as King Charles was!'," [2] and he felt it his duty to defend his King.

THE POLITICS OF DIVINE RIGHT

Wesley's early politics, the counterpart to his Laudian theological outlook, were, as we have observed, Tory and Jacobite, and like his mentor William Law, he had even been a nonjuror. These were the politics of the entire Wesley family. Wesley distinguished nonjurors from "the members of the episcopal church" in that the former believed *"that it is never lawful for the people, under any provocation or pretext whatever to resist the sovereign,"* i.e., *"passive obedience,"* and that *"the hereditary succession to the throne is of divine institution, and therefore, can never be interrupted, suspended, or annulled, on any pretext."* [3] Augustin Léger has described the divine-right, patriarchal theories of Wesley's father, and his great hostility to the republicanism of the previous century. "The memory of the Civil War hung over him as a specter," Léger wrote of Samuel, and he suggested that this was the most potent reason for Samuel's having left the ranks of Dissent.[4] Wesley, in later life, boasted that his father had written Sacheverell's speech extolling divine right and passive obedience to the House of Lords at the time of the latter's impeachment in 1710.[5] Susanna's Jacobitism was clear in an observation she had made in 1709 that "whether they did well in driving a Prince from his hereditary throne, I leave to their consciences to determine; though I cannot tell how to think that a King of England can ever be accountable to his subjects for any mal-administration or abuse of power: but as he derives his power from God, so to Him only must he answer for using it." [6] As late as 1734, we have noted, Wesley had preached a Jacobite sermon at Oxford.

During the early years of the Revival, with the threat of the Pretender mounting, Wesley began to preach absolute loyalty to George II. In this he followed the path of other Jacobites, who, as the usurper became better established, extended the principles of nonresistance and passive obedience to him, and, as a final gesture, gave him divine right as well. Since a restoration of the Stuarts could occur only as a result of a violent upheaval, Wesley could not continue to be a Jacobite. Nevertheless, the loyalty of Methodist preachers was often challenged in 1744 and 1745, when the dynasty felt itself in particular danger; [7] at Wesley's instructions, the preachers had recourse to the courts where they were, albeit reluctantly, cleared. Wesley, in a display of loyalty, published in 1745 a tract in which he warned that the victory of the Pretender would mean the French conquest of England, and bemoaned that English liberties would be destroyed and Englishmen compelled to "copy after the French rules of government." If the Pretender and the French "prevail, what but Popery and slavery?" [8] In late September of 1745, Wesley was in Newcastle at the time when the army of the Pretender was marching on the city. In a letter to the Mayor of Newcastle, whose loyal efforts to organize the defense of the city brought his commendation, Wesley proclaimed that "I cry unto God, day by day, in public and in private, to put all his [the King's] enemies to confusion: and I exhort all that hear me to do the same; and, in their several stations, to exert themselves as loyal subjects; who so long as they fear God, cannot but honour the King." Earlier in this letter, Wesley wrote of the King, ' whom I honour and love," and of whom, he declared, "I think not less than I did my own father." [9] In 1749, Wesley observed that the Methodists preached the "firmest loyalty to our Prince," and were the "faithful, loyal subjects to their Prince, His sacred Majesty King George." [10]

From the earliest years of the Revival, Wesley urged Methodists who possessed the franchise to exercise it in behalf of God and the King. At a time when it was not uncommon to accept a gratuity in some form from candidates, Wesley denounced such practices. "Will you sell your own soul?" he asked. The freeholder, Wesley declared, must "act as if the whole election depended on your single vote, and as if the whole Parliament depended (and therein the whole nation) on that single person whom you now choose to be a member of it." For whom ought a believer to vote? "For the man that loves God," Wesley asserted, and if there were none such in contention, "then vote for him that loves the King, King George, whom the wise providence of God has appointed to reign over us." Was "not the interest of the King of England, and of the country of England, one and the same?" "A King is a lovely, sacred name," Wesley exclaimed; "he is a Minister of God unto thee for good." If a man "does not love the King, he cannot love God." [11]

Before the accession of George III, a Methodist would vote for those whom they believed to be earnest supporters of the Hanoverians. In 1756, for example, Wesley, who regarded Bristol with its many Methodists as a city in which he ought to take an active political role, declared himself in favor of the King's candidate—as he regarded him—in opposition to the "Jacobite" candidate, in Wesley's words, in a closely contested election. When the "Jacobite"—a man whom Wesley *suspected* of favoring a restoration of the Stuarts—won by a narrow margin, Wesley declared unhappily that the whole city was "in confusion"; "oh what a pity there could not be some way of managing elections of every sort, without this embittering of Englishmen against Englishmen, and kindling fires which cannot be quenched in many years!" [12] In 1760, George II—whom Wesley regarded as the very best of kings—died, and Wesley transferred his loyalty to George III and his favorites.

It is probable that well into the eighteenth century the arguments for divine right based on the blood royal and the political injunctions of the New Testament appeared more substantial to many, perhaps to most Englishmen, than those which spoke of a social contract. (Indeed, the patriarchal theory of kingship had a solid, psychological base in the relatively unchallenged position of the father in traditional society.) Like his mother, Wesley had faith in such "tangibles" as the blood royal, and although utilitarian grounds no doubt predominated in his transferring his loyalties from the Stuarts to the Hanoverians in the forties, he was sufficiently his mother's son to wish to satisfy his scruples by discovering some genealogical flaw as grounds for his new position—which he managed to do in the seventies. [13] Of overwhelming importance for Wesley and his associates and followers, however, was that divine right and nonresistance had been commanded by the Bible. "Let every soul be subject unto the higher powers," were the words of Romans xiii, 1, 2, 5, which added that "there is no power but of God: the powers that be are ordained of God," and "they that resist, shall receive to themselves damnation"; and believers were further admonished to "be subject, not only for wrath, but also for conscience sake." "Submit yourself to every ordinance of man for the Lord's sake," was the injunction of 1 Peter ii, 13, 14, "whether it be to the King, as supreme; or unto governors"; these commands had been summed up in 1 Peter ii, 17, as "Fear God. Honour the King." These were impressive grounds for Christians, and present-day historians may seriously underestimate the numbers of persons influenced by them. Jeremy Bentham, for example, in his *Fragment on Government,* observed that as a young man "I saw strong countenance lent in the sacred writings to monarchic government: and none to any other"; "I saw *passive obedience* deep stamped with the seal of the Christian Virtues of humility and self-denial"; as for the lawyers with "their Original Contract," Bentham continued, "I bid them open to me that page of history in which the solemnization of this important contract was recorded." [14]

Yet, as impressive as these biblical injunctions might have been, support for divine right was sharply modified even by Tories in the course of the eighteenth century. Bentham was soon to reject the divine right of kings, along with original contracts and natural law, in favor of utility. It is possible to argue that John Wesley, in the last decades of his life, moved in a similar direction. Though never fully yielding his conviction that God had enjoined Tory principles, principles which he felt had a peculiar usefulness in obstructing practical Antinomianism, Wesley—whether yielding to the Whiggish implications of Arminianism or responding to the precarious position of Methodism—appeared to modify his views, in this instance mediating between the "traditional" politics of divine right and constitutionalism. It may have been for this reason that Wesley later recommended to his followers in an abridgement he himself made, a religio-political novel by Henry Brooke, *The Fool of Quality,* which he described as "the most excellent in its kind of any that I have seen." (If it were not for Brooke's political views, it is difficult to see the virtues Wesley perceived in the novel, since he proclaimed Brooke's "Mystic Divinity" to be "more philosophical than scriptural.") Long sections of the novel discussed the feudal constitution in the approved Whig manner, and though Wesley saw fit to eliminate much of this as "of little use to the generality of readers," he did include Brooke's lengthy eulogy of Whig constitutional theory, which began with the declaration that "thus, as all others owe allegiance to the King, the King himself oweth allegiance to the Constitution." [15] This view, although Wesley might on occasion push it aside if he believed practical Antinomianism might be encouraged by its espousal, was to become, increasingly, the Methodist position.

Thus it was not as an unreconstructed Tory that Wesley was to encounter, in the sixties, seventies, and eighties, the threats of revolution. In 1785, Wesley defended his eldest brother, Samuel, against posthumous charges of Jacobitism, of seeking a Stuart restoration, and, in process, tried to exculpate himself. Those who had called Samuel a Jacobite, he wrote, "did not distinguish between a Jacobite and a Tory." A Tory was "one that believes God, not the people, to be the origin of all civil power." "In this sense," Wesley acknowledged, Samuel "was a Tory," adding "so was my father," and "so am I. But I am no more a Jacobite than I am a Turk." [16] It was as a Tory, "in this sense," that he was to view the Wilkes agitation and the American revolt. Moreover, during the late sixties, seventies, and eighties, Wesley was to connect such agitations to the speculative Antinomianism of the evangelists of the Countess of Huntingdon's Connection and of the leaders of Dissent, whose theology bred presumption, and whose organization—or lack of it—had resulted in backsliding, compounding the evils of presumption. Political differences were becoming sharper, and by the late sixties a crisis was at hand which would reawaken Wesley's long-held fears concerning the imminence of revolution.

QUENCHING THE FIRES OF REVOLUTION

The attacks upon the Court made by an anonymous follower of Pitt, writing in *The North Briton* in 1763, had resulted in the issue of a General Warrant, and the arrest of John Wilkes for seditious libel. The Whigs, by and large, were to maintain that Wilkes, an M.P., was not subject to arrest because of parliamentary privilege, and to insist that General Warrants were illegal. In 1764 Wilkes was expelled from parliament and he fled to Paris. His return to London in 1768 brought turmoil to the country. Wilkes was again and again elected to parliament and as often expelled at the Court's insistence. Finally, he was excluded from parliament when the Commons declared a candidate with a lower poll elected. London mobs shouted "Wilkes and Liberty." Rioting artisans, disturbed by unemployment and high bread prices, made Wilkes the focus of their discontent; demonstrators, proclaiming that the Court was violating the liberties of Englishmen, turned their venom against the King, who was threatened with the fate of Charles I. Wesley was enormously disturbed at this revival of the revolutionary fervor of the previous century.

What was the cause of "this amazing ferment" among the people? The character of the King was good, and his ministers were "not one jot worse" than in the past. While Wesley would not defend General Warrants, he saw them as "no extraordinary measure," and of "little importance to the nation in general"; and, furthermore, he was persuaded that if the Commons had the right to expel a member, it had the right to exclude him. The "violent outcry" that the nation was "oppressed" and "deprived" of its former liberty was "the highest infatuation." England, "from the time of William the Conqueror, yea, of Julius Caesar, never enjoyed such liberty, civil and religious, as it does at this day," Wesley declared; nor did any other state enjoy as much liberty. The people had been inflamed by men stirred by selfish motives: "Covetousness"—"do not many hunger after the lucrative employments which their neighbours enjoy?"; "ambition"—"how many desire honour, perhaps more than they do money itself?"; "pride," "envy," and "resentment" because they have been "disappointed" in their expectation of office. (Wesley also spoke ominously of a nefarious role played in all this by "French gold.") Animated by such motives, these men "talk largely and vehemently," "write abundantly," and "publish addresses, petitions, remonstrances"; "their orators make use of all the powers of rhetoric." In consequence, "the flame spreads wider and wider." It "runs as fire among the stubble." The end was "easy to fore-see": just as in the preceding century, the nation had become "inflamed" by the "most effectual libels" against King and government, even as the perpetrators professed the "highest regard" for the King, professions which continued "till within a short time of the cutting off his head." The people would be "inflamed more and more"; the "torrent will swell higher and higher, till at length it burst through all opposition, and overflows the land." The consequences, "unless an higher hand interpose," would be "exactly the same as those of the like commotions in the last century": the land would become "a field of blood"; "thousands of poor Englishmen will sheathe their swords in each other's bowels." The result of all this must be "either a commonwealth" or "a second Cromwell." The choice was be-tween "King W [ilkes] or King Mob."

The preoccupation which we have so far traced in Wesley's theological controversies had received full, direct, almost hysterical expression in a political tract. Wesley's mission had become the reformation of England so as to extinguish—once again, we note the repeated metaphor—the fires of revolution. Like a prophet of old, Wesley called his countrymen, seduced either by irreligion or Deism on the one hand, or by the false theological doctrines which engendered Antinomianism and bred presumption (covet-ousness, ambition, pride, envy and resentment) on the other, back to the true God. Perhaps "general humiliation and repentance may prevent gen-eral destruction," were Wesley's concluding words in this pamphlet; if Eng-land could be turned back to God, she might prove "a brand plucked from the burning." [17] But, in 1770, Wesley judged that "a Sacheverell madness has spread far and wide," [18] and in that year, when visiting an Abbey which had been burnt down by the Puritan reformers of the Civil Wars, Wesley could only exclaim "God deliver us from reforming mobs!" [19]

The aftermath of the Wilkes agitation brought repeated harangues on the part of the Opposition on the need for Englishmen to reclaim their vanishing liberties, and early in 1772 Wesley took up the question from the position of a natural-rights Arminianism. "The love of liberty," Wes-ley proclaimed, was "the glory of rational beings," and of "Britons in par-ticular." There were two principal forms of liberty—civil and religious. Religious liberty was the "liberty to choose our own religion, to worship God according to our own conscience," and, he continued, employing the natural rights allusions of the time, "every man living, as man, has a right to this, as he is a rational creature"; on religious questions, every man had to "judge for himself, because every man must give an account of himself to God," and, "consequently, this is an indefensible right" which was "in-separable from humanity." But the religious liberties of Englishmen were not in jeopardy; indeed, no other nation "enjoys such liberty of con-science." Nor was civil liberty, the liberty "to enjoy our lives and fortunes in our own way," in any jeopardy. The horse guards, in protecting Wesley against the mob which had wished to do him injury for not having illuminated his windows in honor of Wilkes, "instead of anyway abridging it, plainly preserved my liberty and property," he declared. Yet that " 'many-headed beast,' the people, roars for liberty." This "general infatuation," this "epidemic madness," this making a Caligula or Nero of "one of the best of Princes," was making the people "perfectly intoxicated." Increasingly in some European countries, and "indeed in England," the right to call "a Monarch to account," and, if necessary, "taking off his head" if "he did not behave in a dutiful manner to our sovereign lords the people," was called liberty. Wilkes and his supporters were really contending for the liberty of "King Mob," which Wesley defined as the "liberty of taking our neighbors' wives and daughters." [20]

Wesley, haunted by the specter of a popular revolution, could only reject and denounce the theories of social contract and popular sovereignty which he saw as facilitating such a revolution. No original, creative political theorist like Burke, Wesley's only recourse was to the theory of divine right, the theory of the politics of stability of his youth, combined with the faith of a defender of the Glorious Revolution (which he had become) in the usefulness of a limited monarchy in defending both civil and religious liberty. In a tract on the origin of power, Wesley derived all power from God, denouncing the opinion "now generally espoused by men of understanding and education" not only in England "but almost in every civilized nation," the view based on equality and the "original compact," that the people were the source of power. This was nonsense, and "is every way indefensible." Why was the franchise reserved only for adult, male freeholders? Not even the most advanced Whig wished to extend it "to every individual of the human species." The people had never chosen their own governors. The "power of the sword" [21] was of God, and He had given that power to the King. Therefore, for our real liberties, "let us be thankful . . . to God and the King!" Let Englishmen not "by our vile unthankfulness, yea, our denial that we enjoy it at all, provoke the King of kings to take it away." [22]

When troubles with the American colonists erupted, Wesley, fearful of revolution at home, came down so firmly against the colonists as to give rise to a view of him as being among the most bigoted of the defenders of the royal authority. The facts are more ambiguous. As early as 1758, Wesley had declined to defend the government's American policy, indicating doubts as to whether "any man can defend them, either on the foot of law, equity, or prudence." [23] In June 1775, when the difficulties with the colonies had come to a violent head and he was preparing an intransigent tract against the colonists, Wesley began a private correspondence with Lord North, the prime minister whose integrity he much admired, and with Lord Dartmouth, the colonial secretary and a leading Evangelical (the capitalized form will mean an Anglican "evangelical") layman, in which he urged concessions, and defended the arguments of the Opposition, the "full force" of which, Wesley observed, North and Dartmouth might have missed because of their tainted source. As "a High Churchman, the son of a High Churchman, bred up from my childhood in the highest notions of passive obedience and non-resistance," all his "prejudices," Wesley confessed, "are against the Americans." Yet, despite such "rooted prejudices," Wesley could not but believe that the colonists, "an oppressed people," were asking "for nothing more than their legal rights," and "in the most modest and inoffensive manner which the nature of the thing would allow." Wesley warned North that it would not be easy to defeat the Americans in the light of the conditions in which the war would be waged, and since the Americans were "calm, deliberate enthusiasts," "enthusiasts for liberty" fighting "for their wives, children, liberty!" England's European enemies would take advantage of her preoccupation, Wesley warned; and at home there were "thousands of enemies, perhaps more dangerous than French or Spaniards," for "an huge majority" of the people were "exasperated almost to madness," and "ripe for open rebellion." Just as in 1640, revolutionary sentiments were intensified by "a general decay of trade," and by "an uncommon dearness of provisions." Such a revolution, Wesley wrote, might be God's punishment for "the astonishing *luxury* of the rich, and the *profaneness* of rich and poor." Wesley concluded by urging the Ministers to "remember Rehoboam! Remember Philip the Second! Remember King Charles the First!" [24] On August 23, 1775, this time writing only to Lord Dartmouth, Wesley repeated these views.[25]

While in private, writing to ministers of the Crown, Wesley urged concessions, in public he presented a full defense of the ministry's position. In a letter to one of his followers, in late 1775, while insisting that "the Supreme Power" maintain its right to tax, he nonetheless urged Josiah Tucker's view that Britain ought to abandon her ungrateful colonies: "I say, as Dean Tucker, 'Let them drop' ": the colonies had cost Britain many millions of pounds, Wesley observed, and now "let them have their desire and support themselves," cutting "off all other connexion with them than we have with Holland or Germany." [26] In his well-known *Calm Address* Wesley argued the undoubted right of the metropolis to tax the colonies, and defended the theory of virtual representation. The colonists, he asserted, "had *ceded*" to King and parliament, *"the power of disposing without their consent,* of both *their lives, liberties and properties,"* he declared. America was in an "uproar," because of the plottings of "a few men in England" who were "determined enemies to Monarchy" and lived "in hopes of erecting their grand idol, their dear Commonwealth upon its ruins." These conspirators hoped that the "total defection" of the colonies would make the English "so irreconciliably disgusted" that the Commonwealth men would be able, perhaps with foreign help, to "overturn" the government.

Wesley warned the Americans that "no governments under heaven are so despotic as the Republican," and declared that "no subjects are governed in so arbitrary a manner as those of a Commonwealth." [27]

Later that year, in November 1775, Wesley preached a sermon in which he described Englishmen as "deprived of our senses," "mad with party zeal," "foaming with rage," "ready to tear out one another's throats, and to plunge their swords into each other's bowels," and "ripe" for "treason and rebellion." [28] Wesley returned to this theme in 1776 when he wrote of England as "a kingdom divided against itself," and threatened with "the most dreadful" of evils, Civil War. All good men must do "the utmost, that either human or divine prudence can suggest, to prevent it." If we saw our house or that of a neighbor on fire, we would bring "ro combustible material to increase the flame, but water and a helping hand to extinguish it." This was what Wesley saw himself doing when he publicly rejected arguments of the colonists that he had privately found acceptable. [29]

In 1776 as well, Wesley replied to a pamphlet of the Unitarian minister, Dr. Price, whose recently published *Observations on the Nature of Civil Liberty* had been a defense of the Americans. Wesley's position had hardened as he had become convinced that the colonies did not really wish compromise but were determined on independence. Once again, Wesley denounced the view (which was Price's), based on "original compact," which derived government from the people. In this, he described himself as pleading the cause "of every country under heaven, where there is any regular Government," since Price's principles tended "to unhinge all government, and overturn it from the foundation," and to "plunge every nation into total anarchy." Price, in appealing to these ideas of the seventeenth century, was seeking to foment rebellion, to revive the Civil War which had "made the land a field of blood," and had "set every man's sword against his brother." In his closest anticipation of Burke, Wesley vaunted laws, charters, and traditions in opposition to Price's wish to see the determination of political questions by the general principles of liberty. Wesley had no doubt that there was more liberty "under a limited monarchy" than under a democracy, and urged the "millions in England" who "have no more voice in the Parliament" than the Americans that "they must needs be subject" and "that not only for wrath, for fear of punishment, but for conscience sake." [30]

Wesley's views on the revolution in America were to arouse a storm of opposition. Caleb Evans, a Baptist clergyman with strong Calvinist leanings and the leader of nonconformist Radicalism in Bristol as Price was in London, and Augustus Toplady were Wesley's principal political antagonists. Evans wrote an impassioned tract which charged Wesley with having gone back upon his original position and with having published a "most palpable forgery" since the principal arguments of the *Calm Address* had been taken from Dr. Samuel Johnson's *Taxation No Tyranny*. There was a point-by-point refutation of Wesley in terms of the political principles of "the immortal Locke." Evans accused Wesley of having, in his writings, "revived the good old Jacobite doctrines of hereditary, indefeasible, divine right, and of passive obedience and non-resistance." Since this was so, Evans urged Wesley to "come boldly forth and avow the old jure-divino doctrine." [31] Toplady published his reply to Wesley under the pseudonym of "Hanoverian," a plain reference to Wesley's old Jacobite leanings. Although clearly sympathetic to the colonial position, Toplady devoted his tract primarily to proving the case of plagiarism against Wesley, that "puny Tadpole in divinity, which proudly seeks to disembowel a high and mighty whale in politics [i.e. Price]." Was it possible, Toplady inquired, that Wesley wished to be made a bishop? [32] There were other tracts making similar charges. [33]

Wesley, plainly disturbed, admitted that he had changed his view of colonial affairs, and that, indeed, he had been converted by Dr. Johnson's pamphlet, [34] but asserted that he had not written to gain favor. "England is in a flame!" he declared in his *Journal,* "a flame of malice and rage against the King, and almost all that are in authority under him." "I labour to put out this flame," he observed; "ought not every true patriot to do the same?" [35] In a letter to a newspaper in November 1775, Wesley had observed how many were "pouring oil into the flame, by crying out, 'How unjustly, how cruelly, the King is using the poor Americans, who are only contending for their liberty and for their legal privileges!' " This Wesley was determined not to do. [36] Wesley's *Journal* for February 3, 1777, noted "some disturbance at Bristol," stirred up by "men whose tongues were set on fire against the Government." Wesley hurried to that city, which he regarded as peculiarly his own, to dampen the flames, preaching on the text "put them in mind to be subject to principalities and powers, to speak evil of no man." Though Wesley was content, after his preaching, that God had "convinced many that they had been out of their way," there were, nevertheless, in the days following, "repeated attempts to set fire to the city" which had caused a "general consternation."

In response to these outbreaks in Bristol, indeed in the week of their occurrence early in 1777, Wesley wrote another tract which he asked God to consecrate "to the quenching of that evil fire which is still among us!" [37] In this tract, Wesley once more denounced the Americans who, in seeking independence, had "diligently" cultivated "the republican notion, which they received from their forefathers"; no longer depicted as dupes, the Americans were seen as resurrected Roundheads. King Mob reigned in America, whereas in England it was "impossible to conceive a fuller Liberty than we enjoy," a liberty which had begun in 1638 and was not "derived from our forefathers" who had never enjoyed it. Wesley urged all Christians to "be cheerfully *subject to the higher powers"* since these were *"of God."*

In this 1777 tract, Wesley addressed himself particularly to the Dissen-

ters, who were as a group, he believed, sympathetic to the American rebels. Wesley warned the Dissenters that there were High Churchmen
enough, restrained only by the King, who wished to suppress or even to
expel them. Did they not see that their sympathy for the King's enemies
would give occasion for offense? Remember, he warned them, your "present behaviour" would not be forgotten: when matters of "greater moment" were finally settled, "our Governors" would "find a time for you."
Wesley cautioned the Dissenters that if they were to fulfill their purpose to
"unhinge the present Government, and set up another in its stead," they
would most probably forfeit their goods and lives to King Mob. Wesley
concluded his tract with the hope that none "in connexion with me" did
"blaspheme God or the King" as did others who called themselves
Methodists—clearly a reference to the Countess of Huntingdon's Connection. These had "no connexion with *us*"; indeed they "corcially hate us as
dreadful heretics, for believing, *That God willeth all men to be saved:* who
hate the King and all his Ministers, only less than they do—an
Arminian." [38]

The controversy between Arminian and Calvinist, to which Wesley alluded, had already been translated to the political sphere by John Fletcher
the previous year. In a *Vindication* of Wesley's *Calm Address,* couched as
a reply to Caleb Evans, Fletcher had proclaimed the American controversy "closely connected with Christianity in general, and with Protestantism in particular"; it was "a *religious,* as well as of a civil matter," since
"strict morality" compelled us to "submit ourselves to all our governors."
Fletcher defended Wesley's views on colonial taxation as "rational, scriptural and constitutional," vaunted the English constitution as the best protection against "that many-headed monster, a *Mob,*" and praised the King
and his ministers for "making a constitutional stand against the boisterous
overflowings of civil antinomianism." Power came from God, not the people, Fletcher declared; "you may call this a 'Jacobite doctrine' " but it was
nonetheless true. Fletcher was hopeful that the Ministry would, in the future, consult the colonies about taxation, but only after the latter had submitted to lawful authority, for although loving the English constitution as a
"happy medium," if he must choose between an "arbitrary King" and an
"arbitrary mob," Fletcher preferred the former and thought "all our danger is, at present from King *Mob.*"

Fletcher was especially unhappy about the Antinomian "levelling
scheme" implicit in Evans' and Price's "doctrine of a right to equal representation": it had been "against this very rock" that *"many* of the first,
over-doing Protestants steered their course, and dashed their ark in
pieces." Luther, "in his zeal for salvation without works, had been ready
to burn the epistle of St. James," making the passage from "ecclesiastical
to civil antinomianism" both "easy and obvious," and this "republican,
mobbing spirit" had passed from Germany to England. The early "over-

doing Protestants"—such Antinomian Anabaptists and levellers as Ket and John of Leyden—had overthrown their governors, had constructed republics, and had arranged for all their goods to be held in common. A "seed of the error of the republican Anabaptists" had continued to grow in England "ever since the Reformation"; indeed, "the fiery zeal of some Independents, and later Anabaptists," "the injudicious zeal of sectaries, especially of the Anabaptists and Antinomians," was the "chief ladder by which artful Cromwell climbed to the height of supreme power." Were not the Whig "patriots" preparing the ground similarly? Were not their goddesses, like those of the rebellious mobs of Boston and London, *"Licentiousness,* and *Antinomian Liberty"*? Did not these so-called patriots hope that a colonial uprising "would be naturally productive of a revolution in England," and toward this end were not *"some* dissenters" guilty of "openly" supporting "their dissatisfied brethren in America"? [39] Fletcher's *Vindication* was well regarded by the Ministry, which offered him, according to one report, any preferment he would choose. Fletcher was reported to have requested "more grace." [40]

Caleb Evans, to whom the *Vindication* had been addressed, hastened to deny that he had spoken in behalf of *"lawless* liberty," insisting that, as a good Whig, he had defended "British Constitutional Liberty," and that he desired neither revolution nor a "levelling scheme." Evans suggested that Fletcher's and Wesley's theory would have demonstrated the rule by "divine right" of Oliver Cromwell or John of Leyden, since it defended *"the powers* that are" as *"ordained of* God." The Bristol Baptist declared that no "Tory or Jacobite, anyone who espouses the principles for which you plead" could be as loyal a supporter of George III as he himself was. Fletcher's doctrines, "long-exploded," would "overturn" the "superb, I had almost said, the divine edifice" which was the British Constitution. Evans admitted to the charge of being both a Calvinist and an Anabaptist, but asked, "in the name of common sense what has this to do with my dispute about Mr. W.?" Was Blackstone, with whose constitutional principles Evans agreed, "a *Calvinist,* an *Anabaptist,* an *Antinomian patriot?"* Why had not Fletcher attacked the Antinomianism of *"high church* rioters," whose "attachment to the principles of slavery most precisely resembled yourself." Evans worried lest "the present race of high-churchmen, whether methodists or anti-methodists" might not be "as great persecutors in their hearts as their forefathers," and were not attempting to exalt "arbitrary power" so they might use it to crush the Dissenters.[41]

Rowland Hill, one of the brothers who were upholding Calvinism in the theological controversy with Fletcher and Wesley, in defending Evans, strenuously objected to Wesley's view that Calvinist Methodists were "traitors, Antinomians," and so on.[42] (His brother, Sir Richard Hill, was later to become seriously disturbed when an opponent, in similar fashion, was to declare that he "favoured too much the enthusiasm of the last century." [43]) Rowland further observed that he had been told that Wesley's remarks on this subject had persuaded "a large circle of magistrates" that "there must be some horrid plot actually forming amongst Calvinists and Dissenters . . . to dethrone the King and establish a republic." [44]

While a Whig country gentleman similarly denounced Wesley's followers as having "sworn to the creed of Archbishop Laud, and the doctrine of Sacheverell," [45] Wesley's friends rushed to repeat the arguments of their master and of Fletcher. W. Mason, a Wesleyan lay preacher, called the nation back to passive obedience and nonresistance, urging that "the Bible is our best rule in politics." [46] Thomas Taylor, another Methodist lay preacher, was to add that "the design of the Gospel is to turn men from rebellion to obedience." [47] In more polemical fashion, Thomas Olivers, replying to Evans and other "hot-headed Antinomians," advised the Dissenters to be grateful for the protection and toleration of the State "which you and your forefathers have received from the governors of this land." [48]

Later in 1776, Fletcher published another political tract in which he defended himself against the charge of a Calvinist weekly that he was "a mere Sacheverell." Sacheverell "ran as fiercely in the *high-monarchical* extreme, as Dr. Price does into the *high-republican* extreme," Fletcher observed, and if Sacheverell were alive and "his erroneous, enthusiastical, mobbing politics endangered the public tranquility" as the doctrines of Evans and Price did at present, Fletcher would oppose "the *nigh* churchman, as much as I now do the *high dissenters.*" The politics of Evans and Price were those of "republican levellers," who were attempting to undermine the royal government by contrasting "appearances" of irreligion in the King's party, with the supposed religiosity of the Americans. Fletcher, however, concluded by urging the Ministry to make concessions, as "indulgent Parents," to the Americans, even to the extent of granting them representation: this might be necessary "to stem the torrent of political enthusiasm, which deluges America, and threatens to overflow Great Britain itself." [49] In his reply to Fletcher, Evans described his own politics as "those of every Whig in the Kingdom," and denounced those of his Methodist opponent as entirely Jacobite. [50]

The debates between Wesley, Fletcher, Price, and Evans brought up in the sharpest fashion the question of whether Calvinism was, as Wesley and Fletcher charged, a force for revolutionary instability in the 1770s and 1780s. The Americans had had, through the middle decades of the eighteenth century, their own Revival, but it had been Jonathan Edwards followed by Whitefield, not Wesley, who had been the great Awakeners of the New World. It was thus a Calvinist evangelicalism which had permeated virtually all the denominations in the colonies, and it was to these

Calvinist auspices, as well as to the ties between the colonists and their seventeenth-century Puritan ancestors, that Wesley attributed the revolutionary spirit of the Americans.

"From the beginning," Wesley observed in 1778, the New England colonists had "an hankering after Independency"; how could it be otherwise "considering their Families, their Education, their Relations, and the Connexions they had formed before they left their native Country." This was the "Spirit they communicated to their Children, from whom it descended to the present Generation." The plenty of the colonies which almost all enjoyed, "nourished" pride and luxury, idleness and wantonness, as it confirmed the "Spirit of Independency." Although the Awakening in America had seemed successful, "a vast majority" of those who had been awakened had *"turned back,"* since those "more or less affected" by Whitefield's preaching "had no Discipline at all," had not been organized into "Societies," had "no Christian connexion with each other, nor were ever taught to watch over each other's souls." The lack of discipline of Whitefield's Awakening proceeded, as it must have seemed to Wesley, from a Calvinism which stipulated irresistible grace and the perseverance of the saints.[51] Recently an American scholar has presented an opinion very similar to Wesley's concerning the respective roles of Calvinism and Arminianism during the American Revolution, though this view has been seriously questioned.[52]

Was English Calvinism, however, like its American counterpart? In a man like Evans, we may perhaps, like Fletcher, see the influences of both Calvinism and Anabaptism, and, perhaps, speak of the theological *propensities* of the Protestantism of Calvin and Luther to lead from speculative to practical Antinomianism. Yet, as we have observed, the cluster of views surrounding the doctrine of election were a theological reflection of the traditional socio-political structure; while loyal to this theology, the dissenting middle classes, in the eighteenth century, were Whig liberals, even as Wesleyans struggled to keep their politics free of the translation of Arminian theological principles. As often as not, genuine political radicalism was the province of Unitarians and Quakers: both Price and Priestley, for example, were Unitarians, believers in universal salvation, and Price, at least, was a believer in free will; Tom Paine was a Deist of Quaker background. Among the Calvinist Methodists who had gathered about George Whitefield and Lady Huntingdon, Calvinist "rigidities" were still taken seriously, but the special sympathy with the colonies (where their religious views found a more ready acceptance than in the metropolis) which they—and the Dissenters—possessed, can be readily explained on the same grounds as those which made other Whigs sympathetic to the colonial cause. Chatham and Burke, the parliamentary defenders of the colonists, were neither Dissenters nor Calvinists. Augustus Toplady—like Evans—was a Whig, and the Whigs in the eighteenth century were hardly revolutionaries. On the day of the General Fast, on which the Almighty was asked to bring the colonies back into submission, December 13, 1776, Toplady delivered a sermon expressing indirect and discrete sympathy for the colonists when he observed that "were liberty to perish irretrievably, from any part of the English world, the whole would soon be deluged, by the black sea of arbitrary power." A good English Whig, Toplady was proud to proclaim that "next to the gospel of Christ, I love and revere the constitution of my country." [53] He strenuously denied the imputation that Calvinist doctrines were "unfavourable to loyalty," and reminded his readers, as he had on other occasions, of the contrast in the preceding century between "the loyalty of the Calvinistic archbishop Usher, with that of the Arminian ranter and fifth monarchy man John Goodwin." [54] (There was, however, one point of faith which the Calvinists and Fifth Monarchy men —though there is evidence that Goodwin did not belong to this group— had in common, and which had a revolutionary potential: their common apocalyptic view of world history, the banner of historic inevitability; in this, of course, many Unitarians who accepted Priestley's determinism resembled them.[55]) English evangelical Calvinism, however, practically speaking, had no more stomach for revolution than did the Dissenters.

MEDIATING BETWEEN AQUINAS AND ADAM SMITH

There has been no adequate treatment of the full range of John Wesley's economic views. Was he merely a spokesman for the traditional Aquinian ethic, an advocate of the just price, and an opponent of usury, forestalling, engrossing, and the monopoly of enclosures, as some have suggested? [56] Were his economics those of the later preachers of the social gospel, as others have argued? [57] Or was Max Weber correct in placing him with those Protestants who helped to formulate the capitalist ethic? [58] There is some evidence for all these positions, but those who have addressed themselves to the problem have attempted, with one or two exceptions, to fit Wesley rather too firmly into one or another stereotype, sometimes because they have been familiar with only a small part of the evidence.[59] The question is an important one, for if Methodism may be seen as having helped to facilitate the relatively nonviolent rites of passage of many tens of thousands of Englishmen from a traditional to a modern, industrial nation, Wesley's economic message to the growing industrial proletariat which was his principal audience must be understood if its impact is to be properly weighed. England, in the middle decades of the eighteenth century, was preparing for the "take-off" which would make her the foremost industrial nation, as she already was the foremost commercial country. I will argue that, without having adopted the precise views of contemporary political economy, the predominant thrust of Wesley's economics was not Aquinian, nor was it directed along the communitarian lines of the Moravians. Wesley's economics were, on the other hand, clearly in line with the individualistic, entrepreneurial mood of a commercial England, and the nostalgic echo of the Aquinian economics which Wesley never fully abandoned was suppressed lest its restatement, even as traditional ethic, provide an occasion for popular discontent.

It was the poor of the nascent proletariat of England's growing factory towns to whom Wesley's message was primarily directed,[60] and who were, in the middle decades of the century, to respond to it with the greatest enthusiasm. "If riches had been their [the Methodists'] aim," Wesley wrote in 1749, "they would have sought out the rich, not the poor; not the tinners in Cornwall, the colliers of Kingswood, the keelmen in Newcastle-upon-Tyne."[61] "But I love the poor," Wesley declared on another occasion; "in many of them I find pure genuine grace, unmixed with paint, folly, and affectation."[62] Though hardly an economist, possessing none of the sophistication of even the second-rate thinkers in the field, Wesley appears to have been a reasonably reliable observer whose half-a-century of circuit riding throughout Great Britain and Ireland had given him ample opportunities to observe. While more sophisticated theorists— Richard Price, for example—were convinced that England's population was relatively stable, or, because of such factors as colonization, was actually in decline, Wesley had no doubt that there had been "a very large and swift increase."

"One sign of this," Wesley noted, was "the swarms of little children which we see in every place." (How great, then, must be the "ignorance" and the "confidence" of "those that affirm population decreases in England" [!], was Wesley's opinion of Price's observations.)[63] In the newer industrial towns, especially, Wesley found the growth of population to have been phenomenal. When he revisited Burslem in the potteries district in 1781, Wesley could only be amazed at how "the whole face of this country [has] changed in about twenty years!" Since the start of large scale pottery production, "inhabitants have continually flowed in from every side"; the "wilderness is literally become a fruitful field"; "houses, villages, towns have sprung up"; and the countryside "is not more improved than the people," Wesley concluded with satisfaction: "Sinners are daily awakened and converted to God."[64] Since it was here, among the poor—miners and factory workers of the growing industrial districts— that Methodism found its unique vocation, it might be argued that Wesley, from the beginning, had a vested interest—albeit philanthropic and divinely sanctioned—in the new industrial system.

The English Moravians, following the example of Herrnhut, had called for a restatement of a quasi-monastic, "communitarian" ethic among the

new proletariat, recently dispossessed from the land. After seeing Herrnhut, Wesley was disposed to imitate particular communitarian features—
for example, the organization of bands and societies—which would provide a more secure social fabric for the floundering, alienated poor of the
English towns, certainly a defense against the practical Antinomianism he
dreaded. Wesley's followers would attempt to overcome feelings of uproot-
edness by bringing the newly converted into a broader family, whose members would address each other as "brother" and "sister," and would watch
over each other's morals in fraternal fashion. The utopian economics of
Herrnhut or Lamb's Hill, later Fulneck, however, were another matter.
Wesley was affronted by a Moravian collectivism which he saw as exploit-
ing the humbler members of the commune. "Most of the English who are
with them, that are of any trade," he wrote in his *Journal* in 1753, "now
trade for the Saviour; that is, they work for the Germans, who take all the
profits and use them as their journeymen"; they were obliged to "punc-
tually give in their accounts and cash," and "if they want a coat, or anything, ask it of the Brethren." If such proceedings smacked of Anabaptist,
Antinomian communism, their "marriage economy" was worse: "the particulars are too shocking to relate," Wesley asserted; "I believe no such
things were ever practised before" not even "among the most barbarous
heathens." [65] Later in his life, in the eighties, Wesley had sufficiently mel-
lowed to view the Moravian communes as business enterprises, seeing
their leaders in the position of employers. Seen in this light, he could regard them more favorably, admiring their industry and frugality. [66] "I cannot see how it is possible for this community," he wrote in 1783 upon visiting a Moravian commune, "to avoid growing immensely rich." [67] Nor
was this said entirely in a spirit of disapproval.

Wesley, indeed, despite inevitable backward glances toward the traditional outlook, might appear a complete exponent of what has been called
"the Calvinist ethic," the "modern" ethic which Wesleyan societies endeavored to preach to the "new men." "I exhorted the little society," Wesley
recorded in 1765, "to avoid sloth, prodigality, and sluttishness, and, on the
contrary, to be patterns of diligence, frugality, and cleanliness." [68] The
same advice was repeated in the rules to guide the members of band societies. In a letter to an adherent in 1769, Wesley enjoined the young man to
"fly from every degree, every appearance" of "laziness, sloth, indolence"
or "else you will never be more than half a Christian," to "be cleanly," refrain from wearing torn clothing ("mend your clothes, or I shall never expect you to mend your lives"; "let none ever see a ragged Methodist"), and
to "touch no dram," for it was "liquid fire," "a sure though slow
poison." [69] Wesley urged his followers to "lose no time," to "never leave
anything till to-morrow, which you can do to-day," and to "do it as well as
possible." It was startling, Wesley observed, how few used "common
sense"—"all the understanding which God has given you"—in their busi-

ness; a man ought to be "continually learning" to do "better to-day than you did yesterday," yet it was "amazing to observe," Wesley wrote, "how few do this" in their enterprises, "how men run on in the same dull track with their forefathers." Certainly "it is a shame for a Christian not to improve upon" those ones "who know not God," in "whatever he takes in hand." [70]

Wesley cautioned his followers that these injunctions to enterprise were subject to necessary restraints: "to gain money, we must not lose our souls." [71] Methodists were not permitted to steal, or to engage in smuggling, since a smuggler was "no honester than an highwayman," who robs the King, who "is a good father." Indeed, a smuggler was "a thief-general" who not only robbed the King, but "every honest man in the nation," for "the more the King's duties are diminished, the more the taxes must be increased." [72] Wesley waged war against smuggling, and acted to enforce the expulsion of Methodists in communities along the coast, particularly in Cornwall, who were parties to smuggling. There were echoes of the traditional ethic in Wesley's denunciation of those who gained "by over-grown bills . . . on account of physic, or law, or any thing else"; by pawn-broking, which was illegal in England; by selling goods "below the market price," thus ruining another man's trade; or by "taking such interest as even the laws of our country forbid." (However, it must be observed that it was the taking not of interest but of an *illegal* interest which Wesley specifically condemned.) Of course, those who sold "that liquid fire," or who operated immoral opera or playhouses were risking their souls.[73]

Wesley was faced with a dilemma which made it impossible for him to be a simple-minded advocate of accumulation. He saw that "Religion must necessarily produce both Industry and Frugality," and that these qualities "cannot but produce Riches." "But as Riches increase, so will Pride, Anger, and Love of the world in all its branches." [74] Wesley declared that he knew "a hundred tradesmen in London who began to be industrious since they began to fear God, and their circumstances, low enough till then, are now easy and affluent." [75] Riches, Wesley proclaimed, were "the trap Satan has laid for you, that is ready to break your bones in pieces," and "to crush your soul to death." The richest of men were, "in general, the most discontented, the most miserable." [76] On another occasion, he marvelled at "how great is the temptation to Atheism which naturally flows from riches." [77] In still another sermon, he asked "if the danger of barely having them [riches] is so great, how much greater is the danger of *increasing* them!" [78] "How then," Wesley fearfully asked, "is it possible that Methodism, that is, the Religion of the heart, though it flourishes now as a green bay tree, should continue in this state?" Was this why, "in the nature of things," that no "revival of true Religion" can "continue long"? [79] Yet, "we ought not to forbid people to be diligent and frugal," Wesley wrote. On the contrary, "we *must* exhort all Christians, to gain all they can, and to save all they can: that is, in effect, to grow rich!" However, in order that "our money may not sink us to the nethermost hell," those "who *gain all they can,* and *save all they can,* will likewise *give all they can."* In this way, "the more they gain, the more they will grow in grace, and the more treasure they will lay up in heaven." [80] It was this call to charity which softened the sharp edges of an ethic, which when set in a predestinarian context, might lead to the hard social consequences depicted in Wesley's sermon on "Free Grace," as we shall observe. Wesley saw the riches of the faithful as useful not as a badge of election—which made for "Pride, Anger, and Love of the World" [81]—but as an agency of divine charity.

Traditional ways of regarding economic questions were everywhere brought into question by the advocates of the new commercial order. Certainly, it was to be expected that Wesley, a clergyman of the Established Church, would have a stake in the traditional outlook. In his sermons, for example, we find him approving of "the just price." "Do you demand, do you receive, no more than the real value of what you sell?" he inquired. "Do you demand no more than the usual price of goods of any who is in pressing want,—who must have, and that without delay, the things which you only can furnish him with?" To do otherwise was, for Wesley, "flat extortion." Wesley's Aquinian definition of extortion was that it was "a kind of legal injustice, not punishable by any human law, the making gain of another's ignorance or necessity." Wesley could not fail to observe that this kind of extortion had "filled every corner of the land." [82]

On other occasions, Wesley denounced luxury in the approved traditional manner, blaming the high price of oats, for example, on the growing numbers of horses kept for gentlemen's coaches, and the high price of beef and mutton on the fact that sheep and cattle raisers thought it more profitable to breed horses for these coaches and for export to France. He regarded such luxurious excesses as the boiling-down of "three dozen of neat's tongues to make two or three quarts of soup" as responsible for distress, and found that pork, poultry, and eggs were dear—and here the traditional critique is more distinctly heard—because of enclosures, "the monopolizing of farms," a "mischievous" monopoly which absorbed the little farms which had formerly produced such products for market, while the monopolist "gentlemen farmers" were "above attending to these little things." Wesley recommended "reducing the number of horses" by taxation, limiting sizes of farms, and restraining luxury, "the grand source of poverty," by "example, by laws, or both." Wesley regarded the use of "such immense quantities" of corn by distilling as a chief cause of the scarcity of corn and of distress: "Have we not reason to believe that half of the wheat produced in the kingdom is every year consumed . . . by converting it into deadly poison—poison that naturally destroys, not only the strength and life, but also the morals of our countrymen!" Wesley's call for the ending of distilling was primarily a call for better morals, though it was also a traditional criticism of the new market system.[83] (Much of this advice was repeated in September 1784 in a letter Wesley addressed to William Pitt, who had recently become prime minister.[84])

The new system was vulnerable not only on the grounds of high corn prices, which, after all, had been an intermittent problem for centuries, but also because of its susceptibility to periods of sharp growth and sharp reverses. This primitive "cycle"—anticipating the fully developed trade cycle of the following century—was already being observed, and was being denounced by advocates of the traditional economy. Wesley did not fail to note, and his journal and letters record, in the last two decades of his life, the ups and downs of trade. In 1773 to 1774, for example, conditions were bad; there was considerable unemployment and distress. In 1776, Wesley noted trade had "within these two last years, amazingly increased; in several branches in such a manner as has not been known in the memory of man." (Wesley attributed this prosperity, at this time of colonial troubles, to "the entire civil and religious liberty which all England now enjoys!") [85] In 1778, Wesley, in travelling through the country, found "scarce one in twenty" persons "out of employment," rather than the one in three "among the lower ranks" only six years earlier.[86] He saw the cries of alarm and ruin as due to misrepresentation "by ignorant and designing men." [87] Trade had been very good in 1786, Wesley observed, to cite still another example, but distress was again the rule in 1789. "Hearing the cry of want of business," wrote Wesley, "I considered what the meaning of it should be"; he found that while "business poured" into the industrial towns "two or three years ago," and "more hands" were employed, "when business returned into its usual channel," these men, now being without work, "spread the cry over the town." Whenever there was "an extraordinary trade for a time," Wesley concluded it "must subside again," and "then arises the cry of want of business." During the course of over half-a-century of itinerant preaching, he had observed the alternation of prosperity and distress, and he had accepted intermittent distress as an inescapable consequence of intermittent prosperity.[88] Such circumstances, however, did not lead Wesley, as it did other Englishmen, during this time of transition, to denounce commercial society or to urge a greater dependence upon the land.[89]

Throughout the century, rioting was widespread, and the "classic" motivation of the eighteenth-century rioter was his displeasure with the "dearness" of corn, a consequence, in part, of the medieval sins of "engrossing" and "forestalling," in part of intermittent bad harvests, and made chronic by the growing populations of the large commercial and industrial towns. At times of scarcity, when, in the hopes of securing higher prices, local millers and merchants bought and processed local grain, and shipped it out of the district where it had grown either to the towns or abroad, the local people became violently disturbed at the resulting high prices and rioted to deny the right to export local grain or to sell above the customary price.[90] What was Wesley's position on this critical issue?

Wesley carefully avoided the role of a Latimer. He did not denounce the rapacity of the enclosers, nor, while sympathizing with those who suffered from distress, did he undertake to combat the "engrossers," the millers and merchants, against whom the workingmen of the eighteenth century directed their venom. Certainly, he did not feed the flames of riot by insisting that grain be sold at the "customary price." On the other hand, he did do his best—as did all those associated with him—to end the rioting which resulted from the "dearness" of food. Wesley had originally gone to Kingswood because of such disturbances of the peace, and he had succeeded in quelling them. Charles Wesley wrote of a later Kingswood riot into the thick of which he had proceeded: recognizing a number of Methodist colliers among the trouble-makers, he "gleaned a few from every company," and "marched with them singing to the school" for a two-hour prayer meeting—at which they begged the Lord to chain the lion and were cautioned against apostasy.[91]

In his *Journal,* in 1776, Wesley noted that on his way to preach at Exeter, he had read "an ingenious tract" which had observed "that if corn sells for twice as much now as it did at the time of the Revolution, it is in effect no dearer than it was then, because we have now twice as much money," so "that if other things sell now for twice as much as they did then, corn ought to do so too." The tract's satisfying conclusion, with which Wesley was not disposed to argue, was that "though the price of all things increases as money increases, yet they are really no dearer than they were before." For Wesley, the "market price" had gone a considerable way toward becoming the "just price." [92] A scholar has identified the "ingenious tract" as Charles Smith's *Short Essay on the Corn Trade,*[93] a work of which Adam Smith was later to speak well. This essay was a highly persuasive description of the free market, in terms which might well have appealed to Wesley. "That, whatever may be the will of particular Persons," Charles Smith had observed, for example, "Providence, by the nature of the commodity [corn], the large sums necessary, and the number of hands required to carry on this trade, hath put it out of the power of the Cornfactors, and others concerned therein, in any considerable degree to oppress the people"; Smith also had particularly noted that forestalling and engrossing, as traditionally conceived, were essential if the people of the factory towns were to be fed, though, and no doubt reassuring to Wesley, Smith saw the prohibition of distilling at times of scarcity as moderately useful.

Wesley's conclusion, one also anticipated by Charles Smith's tract,[94] was very much the same as the sum of his previous political judgments. Of the greatest importance, Wesley observed, was this consideration: "that to petition Parliament to alter these things" was "to put them upon impossibilities"—a tribute to the persuasiveness of Smith's tract—and could "answer no end but that of inflaming the people against their Governors." [95] Just as Wesley had given up his Jacobitism when he saw that the Hanoverian dynasty could not be dislodged without violence, so did he swallow his nostalgia for the traditional ethic, especially when he became convinced that the ethic was no longer applicable. Another writer has observed that Wesley had at the same time come under the influence of Josiah Tucker's economic writings, which also tended to make him more sympathetic to laissez-faire.[96] Wesley, then, was not the simpleminded advocate of an impossible return to traditional, Aquinian economics, as some have suggested. In 1764, in discussing a key issue dividing a traditional from a modern outlook, he had written a newspaper to deny a statement which quoted him as calling it usurious to place money in the Public Funds: "I believe," he declared, that "a man may let money continue there without any sin at all." [97] Upon all the critical issues of the new economic order, Wesley was in agreement with Smith—both Charles and Adam.

In 1782, an almost octogenarian Wesley visited his native village of Epworth where, he reported, four factories for spinning and weaving had been established. In them, large numbers of women and children were employed, whose conversation had been "profane and loose to the last degree." But certain of these sinners, "stumbling in at the prayer meeting, were suddenly cut to the heart." These "never rested" until they had converted their fellows. Now, the "whole scene was changed." "In three of the factories no more lewdness or profaneness were found," Wesley observed, "for God had put a new song in their mouth, and blasphemies were turned to praise." [98] What happened in Epworth was happening wherever the new industry established itself. In 1787, Wesley and thirty-six lay preachers were invited to breakfast by the cotton magnate Robert, later Sir Robert, Peel. Peel liked Methodists and saw their usefulness; in later years he was reported to have said that "I have left most of my works in Lancashire under the management of Methodists, and they serve me excellently well." [99]

How could Wesley have condemned the new outlook when his mission, and his successes, were to be found among the proletarians to whom the new order had given rise? Especially was this the case if to articulate too forcefully the grievances of those who were disadvantaged by the new market conditions was to encourage the "lion in the streets," the forces making for revolution. Some of Wesley's practical remedies anticipated the middle-class political economy of the following generation: for example, he wished to lower the high taxes which were "laid on almost everything," and called for the "discharging half the national debt," which he believed would help lower corn prices. Moreover, as an addendum to his opinion that ending distilling would lower corn prices, Wesley suggested that if this

did not work, encouragement might be given to the importation of corn.[100]
In 1779, in a letter to a lay preacher, Samuel Bradburn, Wesley was, in a
similar spirit, to call upon "the real lovers of Ireland" to "love King
George for removing those vile restraints upon the Irish trade." [101] The
Wesleyans, thus, took up the cause of the poor as it was to be taken up by
the Anti-Corn Law campaigners of the 1830s and 1840s. To the Whig argument that the poor had no interest in legislation, John Fletcher declared that "the poor," unable to purchase meat, lived primarily upon
bread. When, therefore, "our wealthy legislators" raised the price of bread
by granting export bounties, by permitting the distilling of grain, or by
forbidding its importation, it was they who "reap the principal benefit,"
while the poor "bear the principal burden." The Whig view that legislation was of no consequence to the poor was, consequently, a ' monstrous
paradox," for "the capital branch of legislation, which raises or sinks the
price of corn, chiefly concerns the lowest class of mankind, by whom corn
is chiefly consumed." [102] Neither Wesley nor Fletcher were precisely Cobdenites before their time, but neither were they clerical purveyors of the
traditional economics.

FOR CHURCH, KING, AND COUNTRY

"Loyalty," Wesley had observed in the seventies, "is with me an essential
branch of religion"; "there is the closest connection, therefore, between my
religious and political conduct." [103] In the last years of his life, Wesley
continued his fulsome expressions of loyalty to the King and to his government. When he heard the King address the peers in 1786, he could not but
exclaim with naive delight that "I much doubt whether there be any other
King in Europe that is so just and natural a speaker." [104] In 1789, he
wrote a Methodist leader urging him to "advise all our brethren that have
votes" to use them in behalf of a candidate whom Wesley judged "a lover
of King George and the present Administration." [105] Similarly, Wesley
rarely wavered in his allegiance to the Church of England, and urged
Methodists never to speak "contemptuously of the church, or anything per-
taining to it," for "in some sense it is the mother of us all, who have been
brought up therein." [106] "I see clearer and clearer," he had observed in
1766, that "none will keep to us unless they keep to the Church";
"whoever separate from the Church will separate from the Methodists." [107]
The Church, moreover, was as much a fortress against Antinomianism as
was the King. An act of separation would be tantamount, Wesley asserted,
to "throwing balls of wild-fire among them that are now quiet in the land."

In a moving passage, Wesley declared that "we look upon England as
that part of the world, and the Church as that part of England to which all

we who are born and have been brought up therein, owe our first and chief regard. We feel in ourselves . . . a kind of natural affection for our country, which we apprehend Christianity was never designed to root out or to impair." [108] A study would probably reveal that Methodism and Evangelicalism supplied an effective nourishing ground for English nationalism.[109] Not that Wesley failed to excoriate his countrymen for their faults, particularly for their "ungodliness," which he blamed on the Puritan revolutionaries who, though "absolute strangers" to a proper fear of the Lord, had made "so large a profession" of religion that "the nation in general was surfeited, and, at the Restoration, ran headlong from one extreme to the other." [110] In calling Englishmen back to the old piety, Wesley was emulating the prophets of Israel who had chastized a chosen people, for despite its sins, Wesley had no doubts about England's continuing to enjoy the favor of the Almighty.[111]

Wesley had accomplished the unlikely feat of uniting what were apparent opposites—the bourgeois ethic sometimes associated with a republican and potentially revolutionary Calvinism (though Wesley had softened this by a more traditional cry against "extortion," and, more important, a call for charity, which smacked of the High Church's penchant for good works), and a political ethic, though similarly modified, derived from the royalist and nonjuring writers of the late seventeenth and early eighteenth centuries. During this time, Wesley was also combining the apparent theological opposites of a Calvinistic "true Protestantism" of the Dissenting sects and the Arminianism of the Anglican Church and of the Dutch Remonstrancers. This was Evangelical Arminianism, a theological synthesis elaborated by Wesley and extended by his successors. Evangelical Arminianism proved the means of uniting the emotional force of the quasi-mystical primitive Christianity of the Reformation—with its powerful capacity to create "new men"—with the "modernity" of Arminian doctrine, thus providing the spiritual instrument by the help of which large numbers of the tradition-bound lower classes might become better integrated into the industrial state. Moreover, by minimizing speculative Antinomian doctrine, it was hoped that Evangelical Arminianism would reduce the risks of a return to the practical Antinomianism of the seventeenth century. Evangelical Arminianism was the "ideology" of the Methodist Revolution.

IV

The Formation of Evangelical Arminianism

Behold the Lamb of God, who takes
The sins of all the world away!
His pity no exception makes;
But all that will receive Him, may.

Wesley, Hymns on God's Everlasting Love, 1741

We gratefully own that our creed is Arminian and not Calvinistic. Yet it is not the Arminianism of the Jesuits; of Archbishop Laud, and the high church party of his day; no, nor of some of the Dutch Remonstrants, who too soon abandoned the more tenable and scriptural ground of their master, Arminius, and made rapid strides toward the frigid region of Socinianism. To Mr. Wesley it was given, by Christ the Head of the Church, to remove the theological odium under which Arminianism had long groaned. . . . He did not, in his zeal against the peculiarities of Calvin, cast off or feebly retain those great and essential principles of Christianity, which were nobly maintained by that illustrious man. Rather, he seized them with a firmer grasp, and so interwove them with his whole theological system, as to render them essential to its existence *and so presented his children with an evangelical Arminianism which, in our humble judgment, bears the nearest approach to the faith of the first and purest churches of the Lord Jesus.*

John Anderson, The Spirit of a Great People, 1839

THE ARMINIAN COUNTER-REFORMATION

Castellio and Coornhaert, under the influence of Erasmus, had led a Protestant opposition to the rigidities of Calvinism as early as the sixteenth century. Their successor, Arminius, a professor of theology at the University of Leyden, preached a doctrine which left a wide field for free will when he declared that divine grace might be resisted, that the "saints" might not persevere, and that there still was an important niche in the scheme of salvation to be filled by good works. Crowning this theological structure, of course, was Arminius' view that Christ's offer of salvation had been made to all who would avail themselves of it, that *all* who believed might be saved. After his death in 1609, his disciple Episcopius led other Dutch Protestant clergymen in the signing of the Remonstrance of 1610, a document supporting these propositions and placing them in the setting of a rational humanism which enjoined tolerance for all religious opinions. Grotius, a supporter of the Remonstrance, was later to associate these theological doctrines with the political theory of natural rights and of a liberal, free-contract society. The stronghold of Dutch Arminianism was among the burghers of Holland and Utrecht. In 1619, the still semi-feudal rural districts of the Netherlands, whose spokesman was Maurice of Nassau, gathered at Dort a synod of the leading Protestant ministers in Europe, including Anglican theologians representing James I, to declare the doctrines of Arminius heretical.[1] This reassertion at Dort of Calvinist doctrine in its Reformation purity, imparted an invidious quality to the very name "Arminian."

Arminianism made its way to England where it influenced such groups as the Cambridge Moderates, the Cambridge Platonists, and the Latitudinarians whose rational interpretation of scripture, humanistic outlook, and broad tolerance owed much to the Dutch Remonstrancers. In England, however, the name "Arminian" was primarily identified with the Anglo-Catholic churchmen who had gathered about Archbishop Laud in the years preceding the Civil Wars, whose return to good works was dramatically marked by the restoration of many of the rituals and sacraments of the pre-Reformation Church.[2] This Laudian Arminianism, moreover, was preached not in the setting of a politics of free contract, that of Grotius and the Dutch Remonstrancers, but of one of the divine right of kings. The Calvinist Puritans did their best to extirpate Arminianism during the Interregnum, but the doctrine and liturgy of Laudian Arminianism returned with the Restoration.

John Wesley was the heir to this High Church Arminianism, but for a considerable time he avoided the name "Arminian" with its invidious association, for "true Protestants," of Laudianism or Anglo-Catholicism. It was in the seventies, at the height of his campaign against the Calvinist followers of Whitefield, that, finally and enthusiastically, he took this label for himself and his followers. Wesley, it might be argued, had felt compelled, if he were to maintain the leadership of his Connection, to maintain its growth, and to prevent its capture by Dissent (a consequence abhorrent to a loyal Churchman), to turn with increasing emphasis to those theological views which distinguished his doctrinal position from that of the Dissenters, as well as from that of his fellow Protestant evangelists.[3] His High Church Arminianism was already becoming, from his sermon on Free Grace onward, an evangelical Arminianism, stressing, along with his appeal to justification by faith, Christ's offer of salvation to all. Indeed, Wesley found himself embracing—at least on one level of his consciousness—the full system of the Remonstrants. So taken up was Wesley with the need to vanquish Calvinism, he even took St. Augustine's fifth-century opponent, the British arch-heretic Pelagius (who had preached free will and denied the existence of original sin), to his bosom, as we shall see.

Arminius himself was accepted as a brother spirit, and Wesley elaborated the articles of Arminian belief not only so as to make them appear less "Pelagian" but also to display them as identical to those of the traditional *via media* of the Church of England. Laud had introduced Arminianism into the Church, Wesley noted, "whose clergy, generally speaking, since the time of Archbishop Laud, have embraced the Arminian doctrine," a doctrine which was essentially "the same which the chief of the English Reformers"—Ridley, Hooper, Latimer, Cranmer—"held from the beginning." Later difficulties came from those who "fled to Geneva, in the Marian persecutions," and "sucked up Calvinism there." Wesley praised the Latitudinarians within the Church—the names of whose chief leaders, Hales and Chillingworth, were "still pronounced in England with veneration"—for having taken "the system of Episcopius for their model," and for having lived by Arminian concepts of religious tolerance. Wesley, at the beginning of the last decade of his long life, rejected those "among both bishops and clergy" who "breathe the narrow spirit of Laud, and who, in the language of faction, are called *High-Churchmen*," [4] and, perhaps surprisingly, virtually saw himself as a Latitudinarian Arminian, an English Remonstrancer. But, as we shall see, this was far from a definitive portrait of his views or of the views of his Connection.

During the battle between Calvinism and Arminianism in the sixties and seventies, both Wesley and his opponents saw no means of compromise, "no medium" between their divergent opinions. "For my own part," Augustus Toplady had declared, "I can discern no medium between absolute predestination, and blank atheism." "Arminianism, therefore, is atheism." [5] "Arminianism," Toplady further observed, was "the grand religious evil of this age and country" which had already "more or less, infected every protestant denomination amongst us." The "principles of the reformation" had been "generally forsaken"; "in vain do we lament the progress of popery . . . while our presses teem, and our pulpits ring, with the Romish doctrines of merit and free will." [6] Arminianism, "by despoiling the divine Being" of his "unlimited supremacy," his "infinite knowledge," his "infallible wisdom," his "absolute independency," and his "eternal immutability," by its "exempting of some things and events from the providence of God, by referring them to free will, to contingency, and to chance," was "another of those back lanes which lead, in a direct line from Arminianism to Atheism." [7]

A decade after Toplady had made his "no medium" remarks, John Wesley found himself driven to a similar conclusion. When he had begun his evangelical activities, Wesley recalled, he had been "assaulted and abused," literally "stoned in the streets" because he had been accused of preaching salvation by faith alone; now certain of his "familiar friends" had accused him of preaching salvation by works. Those who held that everyone was predestinated either to salvation or damnation could see "no medium" between salvation by works and salvation by absolute decrees, and therefore "whosoever denies salvation by absolute decrees, in so doing . . . asserts salvation by works." Now, Wesley reasoned, if salvation came by decree, it came "neither by faith nor by works"; if decrees are denied —except the "conditional one" that "he that believeth shall be saved"— then, "seeing no faith avails, but that 'which worketh by love,' which produces both inward and outward good works," Wesley felt compelled to "affirm, No man is finally saved without works." Consequently, although previously "averse" to this conclusion, Wesley granted that "there is, there can be, no medium." Either salvation was "by absolute decree," or it was "(in a scriptural sense) by works." [8] Since Wesley, in well-known hymns, had already staked his own soul that men were not saved by Calvinist decree,[9] and since, moreover, he had argued that the Calvinist doctrine of decrees would make God the author of sin, he had clearly come to the conclusion that absolute predestination, if not atheism, had at very least posited a God whom he wished to disown.[10] "Yea," Wesley declared, "this I will proclaim on the house-top,—there is no medium between these"; "you must either assert unconditional decrees, or (in a sound sense) salvation by works." [11] Had an exasperated Wesley reverted to a High Church Arminianism?

"When the first reformers shook off the yoke of Papistical trumperies," John Fletcher observed in 1775, though he acknowledged a reluctance to find fault with the reformers which a "grateful protestant" must have, they did not restore the ancient "balance of the doctrines of grace and justice," of faith and works. Luther, an Augustinian monk full of the errors of the African Saint, had denied that there was such a thing as free will, thus giving "a most destructive blow" to the doctrine of justice, "a rash deed, for which Erasmus, the Dutch reformer, openly reproved him, but with too much of the Pelagian spirit." Calvin had followed Luther in this error. To counter the direction taken by the Protestants, the Catholics, who had earlier demonstrated similar necessitarian leanings, had moved toward Pelagianism. In England, however, Fletcher continued, Cranmer had found the "exact balance"—that balance "which Augustine and Pelagius had broken, and which Luther and Calvin had ground to dust in some of their overdoing moments," for "mankind are prone to run to extremes," to "overdo or underdo," and "few people ever find the line of moderation." On the continent, Arminius had attempted to rescue the doctrine of works, "openly trampled under foot by most Protestants," while Jansenius made a similar effort to rescue the doctrine of faith or grace among the Catholics. In England, Archbishop Laud, following Arminius, had endeavored to turn "the Gospel scales" toward works, but Laud had leaned too much toward Pelagianism. At present, indeed, Fletcher declared, an overly Pelagian free will predominated in the Church of England, though there were Calvinists enough there, as well.

There were, Fletcher declared, "two modern gospels"—"Pelagianism or rigid Arminianism" on the one hand, and "rigid Calvinism" on the other. In the terms of my argument, of course, the former was "modern" and the latter "traditional." Arminianism led either to Socinianism (i.e., a proto-Unitarianism) and Deism, or to Pharisaism (i.e., a stress on the mere outward observance of the law); Calvinism led to Antinomianism, to "bigotry," and to "self-electing presumption." The true gospel way ran between "Pelagian self sufficiency"—or autonomy—and Calvinist "lawless grace," or utter dependence. Cranmer had walked the way of the true gospel. Of the divines abroad who had walked a similar path, "none came nearer the truth than Arminius." But while properly attacking "free wrath," or "lawless grace," Arminius had not set "free grace in its full Gospel light": he had not granted "the election of grace which St. Paul contends for," that is, he had not fully understood how indispensable grace was for justification. For this the Calvinists had assailed him, and thus "implacable free wrath escaped by means of Antinomian free grace"; "election proved a rock on which his doctrinal bark stuck fast." Several English divines had improved on Arminius' "discoveries," Fletcher noted, particularly Overal, Stillingfleet, Bull, Chillingworth, Richard Baxter, and Whitby. But even these "all stuck where Arminius did, or on the opposite rock." It remained for Wesley to clear "the Calvinian rock," and to present the true gospel upon which both Calvinists and Arminians might agree.[12]

While Fletcher attempted to depict Wesley's position as one of compromise between Pelagianism and Calvinism, the "medium" position whose very existence both Wesley and Toplady doubted possible—the good English compromise anticipated by Cranmer—Wesley, completely absorbed by the controversy, seemed at this time so little interested in compromise that he sought to rehabilitate Pelagius himself. "Who was Pelagius? By all I can pick up from ancient authors, I guess he was both a wise and an holy man," Wesley declared.[13] Basing himself upon recent researches of Dean Tucker, Wesley insisted that the system of decrees had been "hatched by Augustine in spite to Pelagius" who had a more proper understanding of matters. The system of decrees had been orthodox Catholic doctrine until the Council of Trent, "in furious opposition to Luther and Calvin," had disclaimed "their ancient tenets."[14] Wesley observed of Pelagius, in 1781, that "I doubt whether he was more an Heretic than Castellio, or Arminius."[15] Indeed, when Calvinist opponents levelled the charge of Pelagianism at the Wesleyans, Wesley himself, in a letter to Fletcher, was ready to acknowledge that Pelagius "very probably held no other heresy than you and I do now." [16] Wesley even seemed to suggest that from the days of the primitive church until very modern times, only Pelagius had possessed the truth, and even Fletcher, while denouncing the "rigid Pelagianism" toward which the English Church inclined, wrote of the Calvinists' "immoderate fear of Pelagius' doctrine." [17] While, of course, neither Wesley nor Fletcher—any more than Erasmus, Laud, or the Church of the eighteenth century, who all stood accused of "rigid" Pelagianism by Fletcher [18]—upheld the cardinal error of that earliest British theologian, a denial of original sin, yet they were clearly attracted by the benignity of that heretic's views, despite Fletcher's caveat that Pelagianism had robbed Christians of the "peculiar comforts arising from the election of grace." [19]

Toplady and his Calvinist supporters were justified, it might be argued, in denouncing Wesley and Fletcher as Pelagians, or, more charitably, semi-Pelagians. "The semi-Pelagians refined upon the Pelagians," wrote the *Gospel Magazine,* edited by Toplady, and "we have Arminians among us who have refined upon them," and "who may be called semi-demi-Pelagians." [20] In 1774, Toplady's journal had described Satan and Cain as Arminians "by nature," [21] and Arius and Pelagius as the fathers of the "two branches of Arminianism." [22] Sir Richard Hill, one of the more virulent Calvinist pamphleteers, denounced John Wesley as guilty of "the rankest degree of Pelagianism," [23] and declared that "Popery is about the midway between Protestantism and Mr. Wesley." [24] (Hill, in denouncing the "Romish" doctrines of Wesley, set up against him "that glorious champion of the Reformation," the "blessed Martin Luther," adding that he was "not ashamed to mention him" though the followers of Wesley probably regarded him an Antinomian; [25] in another tract, Hill declared that "next to the sacred writings, I admire and esteem above all others, that very book of that highly honoured Reformer, Martin Luther," which Wesley and his followers had "so grossly abused," the Comment on the Epistle to the Galatians, and denounced any opponent of Luther's as either a Papist or a Socinian.[26]) Wesley had gone so far beyond Arminianism, Hill declared, that "if Arminius were now living," he "would not own Mr. Wesley for a disciple." [27] Wesley's doctrines, indeed, were "a mixture of Pelagianism, semi-Pelagianism, Arminianism, Popery, Mysticism, and Quakerism," [28] and were at many points, Hill charged, at one with those Pelagian Latitudinarian free willers, "the unawakened clergy of this day." [29] Richard's brother Rowland appeared to blame Taylor's *Holy Living and Dying*—"that poor piece of Pelagian divinity"—for Wesley's distorted views, and denounced Wesley for having renounced "the grand Protestant doctrine of *justification by faith alone*" in favor of *"the Popish heresy* of *Salvation by the* MERIT *of works."* [30] (In yet another tract, the prolific Richard Hill constructed a letter in which a worldly father instructed his pious son to lay aside "those old-fashioned trumpery books you are continually poring over," "the works of the Reformers," and to study instead and to imitate the Anglican Latitudinarians, "a Clarke, an Hoadley, a Sykes, or a Tillotson," being "well assured that the doctrines maintained by these writers have gained them numberless admirers in the high and polite world" and adherence to them would lead to advancement.[31])

Hill's charges were unfair, but it cannot be denied that much of what Wesley wrote during this time appeared to justify them. Wesley seemed determined, perhaps even more than Fletcher, to identify himself unequivocally with the Arminian tradition—may one even speak of a Pelagian tradition?—which, particularly in Holland and England, anticipated certain of the most characteristic ideas of the Enlightenment.

WESLEY AND THE ENLIGHTENMENT

In attempting to understand Wesley as a man of the Enlightenment, I am not suggesting that Wesley felt any strong affinity for the ideas of the leading *philosophes*. Indeed, he regarded them as enemies to God and disturbers of the peace. Of the great philosophers of the Enlightenment, only Locke won Wesley's admiration, in part, no doubt, because he was English, but, more importantly, because "a deep fear of God, and reverence for his word" were "discernible throughout the whole" of the *Essay on Human Understanding*.[32] For French and Scottish atheists, he had nothing but disdain. Wesley claimed not to understand the fashion of admiring Montesquieu and his *Esprit des Lois;* he found the work "dry, dull, unaffecting and unentertaining: at least to all but *Frenchmen*." Montesquieu could not be forgiven for having treated Moses with no more respect than he had treated Lycurgus or Romulus. What Montesquieu lacked were "Religion and Logic"; in these he was a mere "child to Monsieur Pascal, Father Malebranche, or Mr. Locke."[33] Voltaire was a "consummate coxcomb."[34] Rousseau was a "prodigy of self-conceit," a "shallow but supercilious infidel, two degrees below Voltaire!"[35] Wesley regarded Buffon's *Natural History* as "Atheism barefaced." "I cannot, therefore," he concluded, "but place the Count de Buffon as far beneath Voltaire, Rousseau, and Hume, (all of whom acknowledge the being of a God), in religion as in understanding."[36] Yet in many ways, Wesley's ties with the liberal Enlightenment were substantial.

A number of historians, over the past two centuries, have seen an intimate connection between the Anglican *via media* and Arminianism and the eighteenth-century Enlightenment. Edward Gibbon observed that "since the days of Luther and Calvin, a secret reformation has been silently working in the bosom of the reformed churches; many weeds of prejudice were eradicated; and the disciples of Erasmus diffused a spirit of freedom and moderation," of "liberty of conscience" and "toleration."

Erasmus, Gibbon continued, "may be considered as the father of rational theology," which "after a slumber of an hundred years," was "revived by the Arminians of Holland, Grotius, Limborch, and Leclerc; in England by Chillingworth, the latitudinarians of Cambridge . . . Tillotson, Clarke, Hoadley." [37] Georges de Lagarde, to cite another example, in his magisterial work on the political thought of the Reformation, saw Arminianism, in its granting a role to free will in the work of Salvation, a view which was closely associated with a growing acceptance of natural law, as a "deliberate break" with the Reformation: Lagarde saw a line of theorists issuing from the Arminian Grotius who would lead *"insensiblement le monde protestant au Rationalisme du XVIIIe siècle";* for Lagarde, it was an error to think of the Reformation as a triumph of individualism.[38] Over forty years ago, the economic historian Sir William Ashley, in a little-known Oxford address, spoke similarly of the Arminian theology, with its basis in "a noble and necessary type of individualism," as having "marked one of the great advances in the liberation of the human spirit"; [39] and Trevor-Roper's recent study of the religious sources of the Enlightenment has charted an Erasmian tradition whose membership is roughly consistent with Fletcher's Arminian genealogy.[40]

Both Wesley and Fletcher saw themselves as belonging to this tradition,[41] and they were to some extent correct. In the end, however, it was a substantially different position which Methodism would occupy. Before we attempt to understand this latter position, we must note the very considerable links between Wesleyan Arminianism and Enlightenment liberalism.

Wesley found himself most fully in the Enlightenment tradition in his concern for the principle of religious tolerance. The importance of this principle in the making of liberalism is only beginning to receive full recognition. The view that English liberalism owed a substantial debt to Arminian Protestantism—a view most recently advanced in the essays of Professor Trevor-Roper—was maintained over a century ago by a Leeds bookseller turned London printer, James Nichols, in an 1824 volume comparing Calvinism and Arminianism. Nichols, a prominent Methodist and a friend of both Jabez Bunting and Richard Watson (two of the most important leaders of Methodism at the time Nichols wrote),[42] saw the doctrines of Calvin and his associates in Geneva, and those of Beza, Paraeus, Buchanan, and Knox, as having been responsible for the manifestations of a "restless and revolutionary spirit." He viewed the English Civil Wars as part of "a general Calvinistic crusade against Arminianism and Episcopacy," stemming from the Council at Dort. The Calvinists had been spurred on by the prophesies of "hosts of Calvinistic prophets," and by Puritan ministers, "those intolerant and infatuated zealots," who had excited a "fanatical spirit" among the common people. The chief purpose of Nichols' comparison was to demonstrate that contrary to the prevailing view, the leading Puritans were not proponents of toleration. Indeed, "their toleration of varieties in DOCTRINE extended only to those who held the opinions of Calvin, in common with themselves"; in matters of church discipline, they denied toleration even to their Presbyterian "Predestinarian brethren." (It may be argued against Nichols that a number of Presbyterians had, indeed, supported toleration, though possibly only because of an indifference to the salvation of the reprobate majority; and Calvinists such as Evans and Toplady were steady supporters of civil and religious liberty in the 1770s and afterwards.) It was John Goodwin, Ralph Cudworth, and Laurence Womack—all three converted to "the doctrinal system of the Remonstrants during the Civil Wars"—as well as both Milton and Selden, who were familiar with and influenced by "some of the most admired productions of the Dutch Arminians," Nichols insisted, who made the most critical contributions to English liberty. As firm Protestants, they understood the necessary "absence of an infallible interpreter" of the Bible, and, consequently, "they naturally learned and gave expression to the most liberal sentiments." Indeed, Nichols concluded, "in what quarter so ever Dutch Arminianism in those days achieved her conquests,—whether among Episcopalians, Presbyterians, or Independents, —she almost invariably rendered them favorable to the civil and religious liberties of mankind." [43]

Wesley, as a consequence of his early High Church Arminian loyalties, as well as, no doubt, because of the vulnerability of Methodism, became a champion of both civil and religious liberty, particularly the latter. Wesley took issue both with the persecuting spirit of Constance, and with that of a Calvinism which had secured the execution of Servetus.[44] In 1755, Wesley condemned the bigotry and presumption of the Scottish Presbyterians and the Calvinists of New England who "applauded themselves" in "showing the same spirit against all who differed from them as the Papists did against our forefathers." They united in themselves "pride, bitterness, and bigotry." [45] In 1766, Wesley observed that at the time of the Reformation, God had employed "sour, overbearing, passionate men," not, however, because they possessed such qualities, but despite these qualities; God would have used them "much more had they been of a humbler and milder spirit." "The work of God," Wesley concluded, "does not, cannot need the work of the devil to forward it." [46] Wesley observed that "papists alone are excluded" from the necessity of having toleration extended to them, because "they esteem it lawful to persecute those who will not submit to the yoke of the Roman pontiff." [47] It was this view, which most of Wesley's successors were to maintain, which has led many to regard the Methodists as narrow bigots, forgetful that Locke, probably taking his cue from continental Arminians, notably Leclerc, had made a similar exception.

Only the Methodists "do not insist on your holding this or that opinion"; "they think and let think," Wesley declared. Neither did the Methodists "impose any particular mode of worship," but "you may continue to worship in your former manner." This was true "liberty of conscience," which no other religious society, "ancient or modern" had enjoyed "since the age of the apostles." All Methodism required was that a man desire to save his soul.[48] In 1745, in his "Hymns for Protestants," Wesley had written:

> Lord, I abhor, renounce, abjure
> The fiery spirit unclean,
> The persecuting zeal impure,
> The sin-opposing sin.[49]

"Passion and prejudice govern the world," he wrote Benson in 1770; "by religion and reason joined," Methodists must "counteract them all we can."[50] Wesley proclaimed that his first objective was to attack "all the wickedness," his second "all the bigotry, in the world." What he was attempting was a "reformation, not of opinions (feathers, trifles not worth the naming), but of men's tempers and lives."[51] Wesley cautioned a lay preacher against thinking "all contrary opinions were damnable errors"; "in a few years you will find out" that mere views were not "half so *necessary* to salvation, nor half so destructive as you now imagine."[52] Bigotry, Wesley noted elsewhere, was "too strong an attachment to, or fondness for, our own party, opinion, Church, and religion."[53] A Methodist, he wrote, is one who loves God: "God is the joy of his heart, and the desire of his soul"; "he keeps his commandments" and "does good unto all men."[54] In line with such a view, it is not surprising that Wesley maintained, as had the Moravians, an ecumenical interest in Protestant unity.[55] "Is thy heart right, as my heart is with thine," he inquired; "if it be, give me thy hand"—"for opinions, or terms, let us not destroy the work of God."[56] Of course, in saying all this, Wesley might be accused of a pragmatic, pietist anti-intellectualism, subordinating all ideas to conduct.

In the contemporary philosophical debate between liberty and necessity, it is curious to observe that David Hume, Lord Kames, David Hartley, and Joseph Priestley, all undeniably men of the Enlightenment, were to join Calvin, Jonathan Edwards, and A. M. Toplady in a pessimistic fatalism, while John Wesley became a champion, under God, of that optimistic liberty which in the long-accepted simplistic stereotype typified the Enlightenment. Outright atheists or advanced Deists thus found themselves casting their lot as allies of a necessitarian Calvinism, grounded in divine omniscience and omnipotence, while the freedom of the individual to work out his own salvation and destiny, a view with a clear connection with humanistic or Deistic conceptions, was championed by a hellfire pietist, who, though he might have found "natural free will" unacceptable, yet insisted that "every man has a measure of free-will restored to him by grace."[57]

Moreover, Wesley closely united his ideas of free will with an egalitarian belief in universal salvation; the view that God had intended that *all* men be saved was certainly at one with the moral and intellectual climate of the Enlightenment.

Wesley's Arminian solution to these questions, one shared by the leading divines of the Establishment, was first propounded by him in the middle of 1740, at Bristol, where he preached his provocative sermon on "Free Grace," a superb proclamation of the doctrine of universal redemption. Wesley denounced the view that God's grace was intended only for a predestinated elect as making "all preaching vain," "needless to them that are elected" who "will infallibly be saved," and "useless to them that are not elected, for they cannot possibly be saved." This was "a plain proof that the doctrine of predestination is not a doctrine of God." It was a doctrine which tended "to destroy the comfort of religion, the happiness of Christianity," for did not those who held this doctrine often experience "a return of doubts and fears" concerning their own election and perseverance? Wesley declared that the true decree, that all those who believed in Christ as their savior, who "suffer Christ to make them alive," were "elect according to the foreknowledge of God," yielded "the strongest encouragement to abound in all good works, and in all holiness," and was "a wellspring of joy, of happiness also." It was a decree "worthy of God." Predestinarian principles, on the other hand, "directly tend to destroy your zeal for good works," for all good works, but "particularly for the greatest of all, the saving of souls from death." They undermined "several particular branches of holiness," such as "meekness and love," and "naturally" tended "to inspire, or increase, a sharpness or eagerness of temper, which is quite contrary to the meekness of Christ."

Its most pernicious consequence was that it inspired "contempt or coldness towards those whom we suppose outcasts from God!" This evil doctrine "cuts off one of the strongest motives to all acts of bodily mercy, such as feeding the hungry, clothing the naked, and the like,—*viz.,* the hope of saving their souls from death." For, a believer in predestination might ask, "what avails it to relieve their temporal wants, who are just dropping into eternal fire?" "Well," then, Wesley retorted, "but run and snatch them as brands out of the fire." A predestinarian believed this "impossible," since "they were appointed thereunto, you say, from eternity"; "you believe it is the will of God they should die," and " 'who hath resisted his will?' " Wesley dismissed the predestinarian view which destroyed "our zeal for good works," as representing "the most holy God as worse than the devil," as "more false, more cruel, more unjust." [58]

In 1774, Wesley attributed to the pagan Manicheans and Stoics the determinist doctrine which regarded God as the author of sin, and no action as "either praise- or blame-worthy." Yet, despite such absurd consequences, "this is the scheme which is now adopted by not a few of the most sensible men in our nation," and especially in its "still more plausible" variant of Hartley, the eighteenth-century philosopher-advocate of the principle of association, "adopted by almost all who doubt of the Christian system." Where "almost the whole tribe of modern philosophers" failed was that they did not "take God into their account." God "has fixed in man, in every man, his umpire, conscience": [59] this was the error not only of Kames and Hartley, but even of Jonathan Edwards.[60] Certainly it was the error of David Hume, whom Wesley depicted as "the most insolent despiser of truth and virtue that ever appeared in the world," and "an avowed enemy to God and man, and to all that is sacred and valuable upon earth." Wesley felt that Beattie's *Inquiry After Truth* had more than taken care of Hume's determinism.[61]

One of the most "dangerous consequences of Calvinism," John Fletcher observed, was its having seen man as "a mere machine in the work of salvation." [62] The philosophic counterparts of the Calvinists, Wesley charged, also made man a machine and no more. "I read Lord K [ames]'s plausible *Essays on the Principles of Morality and Natural Religion,*" Wesley noted, but he could not understand why Kames had taken "so much pains" in his essay on 'Liberty and Necessity': "what good would it do to mankind if he could convince them that they are a mere piece of clockwork; that they have no more share in directing their own actions than in directing the sea or the north wind?" Wesley observed Kames' admission that such a view would extirpate "all sense of moral obligation, of right and wrong," [63] and like Fletcher, he protested that the necessitarians were attempting to prove "the noblest creature in the visible world to be only a fine piece of clock-work." [64] Wesley could only conclude that Kames' *Sketches of the History of Man* was a "masterpiece of infidelity." [65]

Augustus Toplady amply confirmed Wesley's fears on these matters. There was "no such thing as casualty, or accident, even in things of temporal concern," Toplady observed, "much less, in matters spiritual and everlasting." To believe that God would create the universe, and then "turn us adrift, to shift for ourselves, like a huge vessel without a pilot" was "a supposition, that subverts every notion of Deity"; what was certain was that "the whole creation, from the seraph down to the indivisible atom, ministers to the supreme will, and is under the special observation, government, and direction of the omnipotent mind." If this was the case, Toplady concluded, it might be objected that "whatever is, is right"; "consequences," he granted, "cannot be helped." [66] Toplady proclaimed Jesus Christ "an absolute Necessitarian." [67] Toplady was immensely pleased by the defense of necessity by contemporary philosophers, and happily turned to the new science for confirmation of his opinions. Gravitation, he noted, the "property of attraction," was "one happy effect of physical necessity," for without "attraction" there would be chaos in the physical world; necessity was equally essential to avoid "endless confusion, wild irregularity,

and the most horrible disorder" in the moral world.[68] Toplady pursued a
warm correspondence with Priestley, who was both a Socinian clergyman
and an experimental scientist. Priestley, unlike Toplady, believed in universal salvation, but, still maintaining the insignia of his Presbyterian past,
he was also a believer in "philosophic necessity." Priestley had ingen-
uously written of the similarity of his philosophic views to Calvinism as
constituting "a strange phenomenon." Toplady, not finding it strange at all,
replied that, after all, "what is Calvinism, but a scriptural expansion of the
philosophic principle of necessity?" On the other hand, "the Arminian
scheme is no less incompatible with the religion of reason, than with the
religion of the Bible." [69] Although put off by Priestley's materialism,
which he thought "atheistical in its tendency," [70] Toplady was friendly to a
fellow determinist, even chidingly suggesting that "having set your foot in
the Lemaine lake," you may "plunge in." "Seriously," Toplady observed,
in a startling anticipation of things to come, "I think you have admitted a
Trojan horse into your gates; whose concealed force will probably at the
long run, display the banner of John Calvin on your walls, and master
your capital, though at present garrisoned by the confederate forces of Pelagius, Sozzo [Socinus] and Van Harmin [Arminius]." [71]

Could such views of universal redemption, free will, and tolerance fail
to make a decided impact upon Wesley's political ideas, leading him, even
as it had the Arminian Grotius, to the political theory of the
Enlightenment—with its liberal individualism, its view of free contract,
and of natural rights—which seemed so much a translation of Arminian theological doctrine? But Wesley was a Laudian Churchman, who feared lest
Protestant Enthusiasm be led into the paths of speculative Antinomianism,
and from thence into the fiery cauldrons of revolution. To avoid such a
calamity, he preached the doctrines of the divine right of kings and of nonresistance as essential to the Christian persuasion, although we recall that
he had on occasion described both civil and religious liberty as natural
rights. But, having set aside in his later life the "narrow spirit of Laud,"
would he move from a Laudian Toryism to a Grotian Arminian Whiggery,
from divine right more unequivocally to natural right? In one further matter, this was to prove the case, as we will see.

The interaction, each upon the other, of a "democratic" Arminian theology and a "democratic" political theory in the seventeenth and eighteenth centuries had helped, in the context of a changing social structure,
to give the death blow to Calvinism. Calvin's God was an arbitrary despot,
the master of every event who ruled through special favorites. Calvinism
had prepared men who, fortified by their conviction that they were of the
"elect" of the Lord, had possessed the confidence and courage—pride and
presumption, if you will—to resist the will of tyrants and to behead a
King. The Arminian God, not unlike the God of the Deists (which the

Calvinists, with some justice, accused Arminianism of being the source), was a benign God who countenanced considerable freedom of action, called *all* to serve him and offered his blessings to *all,* equally, who would avail themselves of them. "Should an earthly friend make me a present of £10,000," Augustus Toplady had inquired, "would it not be unreasonable, ungrateful, and presumptuous in me to refuse the gift, and revile the giver, only because it might not be his pleasure to confer the same favour on my next door neighbor?" Toplady urged men not to find themselves "embarrassed and distressed" by considering the question of the nonelect.[72] But in the century of the Lockean and Rousseauian social contract, men *were* "embarrassed and distressed." God was not a "universal debtor (as Arminianism supposes him to be)," Toplady argued, who "owes salvation to every rational being he has made." God was rather "the universal creditor, who beneficently lends every earthly, and munificently bestows every celestial happiness." There was therefore no "shadow of injustice" on his "withholding what he does not owe." The Arminian hypothesis "of man being God's creditors" rested, Toplady declared, castigating the philosophy of the eighteenth-century revolution, "on the natural claim to happiness, wherewith man is supposed to be invested, in right of involuntary creatureship," on the view that since man "derives his existence from God," "God is bound to make that existence happy." If this were admitted, Toplady concluded, "universal salvation comes in with a full tide," opening "the flood-gates of practical licentiousness," despite its "pretences to good works." [73]

But Wesley, despite his Arminianism, was no natural rights democrat, and no more, for that matter, was Toplady, a good Whig, a defender of tyranny, even though the attributes of the Calvinist God might be the same as those of the nonjuror's King. Fletcher made a small move toward harmonizing the contradictions between the Wesleyan theological and political positions, and in answer to Toplady's charge that "Arminianism robs the Father of his Sovereignty," he replied that "this is a mistake: Arminianism dares not attribute to him the grim sovereignty of a Nero," but it did "allow him *all* the sovereignty which Scripture and reason ascribe to him." [74] Wesley was to continue, to the end of his days, to appeal to divine right, so fearful was he that any other appeal might encourage Antinomianism. There were, however, critical problems which he saw as a Remonstrancer advocate of natural rights: the need to preserve religious and civil liberty, particularly the former, as we have already indicated, and the necessity of abolishing slavery. In his attitude toward slavery, indeed, where the threat of revolution did not seem at issue, Wesley fully emerged as a figure of the Enlightenment, accepting a complete translation of Remonstrance Arminianism to politics, and preaching equality and natural rights.

Wesley's views on slavery dramatized the conflict within the Wesleyan movement between the implications of its Arminian theology and its divine right politics, a conflict which was to disturb Methodism for over a century. In his tract on slavery, Wesley, whose arguments were substantially derived from the antislavery writings of the Quaker, Anthony Benezet, seemed to be taking issue with George Whitefield, the Calvinist champion. Although there had been Calvinists, like John Newton, who had campaigned against slavery, Whitefield had on occasion been a defender of the institution as supported by scripture, even though his sense of justice had obliged him to confront his American listeners with slavery's many abuses. Abraham had had slaves, Whitefield had noted, and "it is plain, that the Gideonites were doomed to perpetual slavery": "though liberty is a sweet thing to such as are born free," he reasoned, "yet to those who never knew the sweets of it, slavery perhaps may not be so irksome." [75] Wesley, who was so ready to produce scriptural arguments on all other occasions, had none to offer in his *Thoughts on Slavery* in 1774. Moved by an Arminian sensibility,[76] Wesley movingly described the seizure of the Negro by "force" or by "fraud," the horrors of the middle passage, the humiliation of the sale, the hard labor and harsh punishments meted out to him as to "brute beasts." Though usually a stalwart defender of the law, Wesley declared that "notwithstanding ten thousand laws, right is right, and wrong is wrong still." Slaveholding was "inconsistent" with "natural justice." If whites could not work in the tropics, as Whitefield had argued, "it were better that all those islands should remain uncultivated for ever." Wesley held the African "in no respect inferior to the European," and declared that if the slave seemed stupid or wicked, it was "the natural effect of their condition." "You kept them stupid and wicked, by cutting them off from all opportunities of improving either in knowledge or virtue: And now you assign their want of wisdom and goodness as the reason for using them worse than brute beasts!" Wesley appealed to all involved in the cursed business—the sea captain, the merchant, the planter—to deliver themselves from "blood-guiltiness." To those who inherited slaves, he declared that no "child of man" can "be born a slave." "Liberty is the right of every human creature, as soon as he breathes the vital air; and no human law can deprive him of that right which he derives from the law of nature." [77] On the matter of slavery, Wesley had become a complete advocate of natural rights.

When a society to abolish the slave trade arose among the Evangelicals of the Church of England, Wesley rushed to its support. He denounced the "men-butchers" [78] of Liverpool who engaged in the "execrable trade." [79] Wesley wrote to Granville Sharp in 1787 to commend "the glorious design of your Society" and to warn him of the powerful and wealthy opponents he would encounter.[80] Later that same year, Wesley reprinted a large edition of his *Thoughts on Slavery* and disseminated it throughout the country in order to assist the work of Sharp's society.[81] On February 24, 1791, shortly before his death, he wrote to William Wilberforce, who had become the parliamentary champion of the antislavery forces. Having read that day a tract written by "a poor African," Wesley had become aware of a "law" in Britain's colonies that "the *oath* of a black against a white goes for nothing." "What villainy is this!" he exclaimed; perhaps God had raised Wilberforce up as *Athanasius contra mundum* to oppose "that execrable villainy, which is the scandal of religion, of England, and of human nature." "Go on, in the name of God and in the power of His might," Wesley urged the Evangelical statesman, "till even American slavery (the vilest that ever saw the sun) shall vanish away before it." [82]

PERFECTION AND ASSURANCE

The two most characteristic doctrines of Methodism—in that they seemed peculiarly those of Wesley and his followers, and were the special targets of both Anglicans and Calvinists—were those of Christian Perfection and Assurance. The former may be seen as the most optimistic position which Wesley adopted: Wesley and his followers appeared at one with the Enlightenment in their view of man as a rational creature who might come to live in sinless perfection in this life on earth under the benign authority of a loving God. Though derived from an Arminian emphasis on man's inherent righteousness, brought into play by grace, and on works, it had a concurrent "true Protestant" appeal, one also made by the sixteenth-century Anabaptists, that the truly saved were perfect. (The Antinomian implications were countered by an insistence that a saint might fall from grace.) The latter, Assurance, possessing clear levelling tendencies, as we shall see, was derived from Reformation Protestant Enthusiasm; it was, indeed, a variation of Calvinist Assurance, seeking to produce a "new man" but of a different type from the Calvinist "new man." These two doctrines, closely related, give an insight into Evangelical Arminianism, that compound of Reformation Enthusiasm and the rational optimism, in theological guise, of the Enlightenment.

In a letter written in 1765, Wesley attributed his ideas on Christian Perfection to Bishop Taylor's *Rules of Holy Living and Dying,* as well as to Law's *Christian Perfection* and *Serious Call.*[83] The state of Christian Perfection, in Wesley's view, was an evangelically sinless perfection attained not through the purging of sin after death but here on earth, as a result (of course, under the general auspices of divine grace) of works, man's own strivings to eliminate sinful tempers and behavior and to become a "new man," replacing sinful conduct with love. This Wesleyan Perfection —like the perfectibility of the *philosophes*—centered on man's own efforts, though Wesley never ceased to stress the indispensability of faith, of

God's grace. "Error moves in a circle," wrote Fletcher; "extremes meet in one": a "warm Popish Pharisee," gets a "fresh absolution weekly by mass and confession," and the "zealous Protestant Antinomian" obtained "an eternal absolution" imputed through Christ's righteousness.[84] Wesley, on the other hand, declared that he preached an Arminian salvation by works "in a scriptural sense," not the "rigid Pelagianism" of the Latitudinarian divines.

The doctrine of Christian Perfection, in its simplest terms, was a belief that men who had been "justified," (that is, had been "saved" by faith, by the freely bestowed grace of God), might, with the further help of God's grace, strive for "holiness," for "sanctification," which was that state in which they had been "freed from evil thoughts and evil tempers." When a believer had achieved this Perfection, "all inward sin is taken away": he loves God with all his "heart, mind, soul, and strength"; "no wrong temper, none contrary to love, remains in the soul; and . . . all the thoughts, words, and actions, are governed by pure love." This Perfection was not absolute, for only God possessed absolute perfection, and consequently it might continually increase. Nor did Christian Perfection mean—as Wesley's opponents persisted in interpreting it—freedom from error, from "mistakes" and "trespasses." But such "transgressions" were not sins if motivated by love. Christian Perfection was as a rule arrived at slowly, usually it was not reached until shortly before death: after justification, "a believer gradually dies to sin, and grows in grace." But it was possible to achieve this state earlier, and although progress was most often gradual, it might be instantaneous. We could not know "infallibly" if a man had been thus "sanctified," but if he had a good character, which would suggest that he would not lie about his state, if his account appeared trustworthy, and "if it appeared that all his subsequent words and actions were holy and unblamable," then others might be brought to acknowledge his arrival at a state of sanctification.[85] But the state of Christian Perfection was not permanent, and, as Wesley came increasingly to believe in his later years, it might be lost.[86]

Was Wesley attempting to usher in—on an ecumenical scale, not merely in the form of the little utopian communities of the Moravians—a heavenly city? Wesley's doctrine of Christian Perfection was one which imposed a high degree of moral responsibility upon the believer. There was no agency of repression or supervision as in the medieval Church, except the voluntarily accepted one of the Methodist societies. Efforts to achieve holiness, though founded in faith, would proceed by works, not by works performed to accumulate merits, but performed as a part of a process by which the heart was perfected in love and freed from sin. Wesley asserted that through faith and right conduct, a man could drive sin from his heart —a "circumcision" of the heart he had called it in one of his sermons [87] —and man, thus free of sin, could be inherently righteous. Since such

97

freedom from sin was possible, an individual could no longer be excused sinful transgressions on account of his humanity.

In theory, this was a more remarkable instrument for self-discipline than that found in Calvin's theology. For Calvin, right conduct was only useful to secure a personal Assurance of salvation, since the question of who belonged to the predestinated elect had already been settled. In Wesley's scheme, there was no predestinated elect: all who believed in Christ, received his grace, and strove for holiness might become of the elect. Calvin's "Saints" could not fall—Cromwell, himself, as Wesley's *Arminian Magazine* was to report in an early issue, was comforted in his most sinful days with the doctrine of the "perseverance of the saints," insisting that "I was a good man once." [88] On the other hand, Wesley's saints could fall, if they were "back-sliders," into the fiery pits. Men had to strain to maintain their sainthood, their Perfection. To the objection of Wesley's opponents that under such circumstances, sin was "only suspended," even in the perfect, "not destroyed," Wesley replied that, "call it which you please," the perfect "are all love today." "They now experience what we teach." [89]

Wesley professed not to understand why, for over a score of years, the doctrine of Christian Perfection had proved so frightening—as if, by its having been put forth, "all Christianity were destroyed, and all religion torn up by the roots." He was ready to admit that the doctrine had been "much abused," but so, he declared, "has that of justification by faith": certainly that was "no reason for giving up this or any other scriptural doctrine." Nor, to counter another objection, did those who believed themselves "saved from sin say they have no need of the merits of Christ"; indeed, "just the contrary," they insisted that "they never before had so deep, so unspeakable, a conviction of the need of Christ in all his offices as they have now." Why was it, then, "that the very name of perfection has been cast out of the mouths of Christians; yea, exploded and abhorred, as if it contained the most pernicious heresy?" "Are we your enemies, because we look for a full deliverance from that 'carnal mind which is enmity against God?' " [90] In its grandly utopian goal of achieving freedom from sin, the Methodist Revolution, like its French counterpart, was striving for nothing less than "full deliverance" from past human frailties and errors. Yet Wesley could wonder why his doctrine of Christian Perfection had roused such strong opposition!

Was not a man who believed himself perfect a danger to society? Certainly this would seem an "enthusiastic" doctrine to a traditional theologian, whether Protestant or Catholic, for whom man since Adam was truly fallen. But for Wesley, man was not a mere sinful brute. In God's image, he maintained within himself a spark of the divine, which, with God's grace, might bring him to an almost Christ-like Perfection. This view was by no means an ignoble one, and posed an inspiring ideal. Wesley's continuing efforts to combat a speculative Antinomianism which vaunted God's righteousness and demeaned man, must be understood in the light of this doctrine. Speculative Antinomianism, Wesley believed, had the effect of increasing man's presumption while defeating his holiness.

In 1739, wrote Fletcher (next to Wesley himself the leading ideologue of the Methodist Revolution) in the seventies, "a little revolution then took place: practical Christianity revived," and were it not for the Devil, by now England might have been turned into "a land flowing with spiritual milk and honey." [91] Nor was the Wesleyan goal of Perfection cast by Fletcher in totally unreal terms: "we do not doubt," he declared, "but, as a reasonable, loving father never requires of his child, who is only ten years old, the work of one who is thirty years of age; so our heavenly Father never expects of us, in our debilitated state, the obedience of immortal Adam in paradise." "For Christ's sake," Fletcher was convinced, God "is pleased with an humble obedience to our present light," and a "loving exertion of our present powers." [92] Even this modest view of man's capacities was widely different from the picture of his inherent wickedness which dominated both Catholicism and Protestantism, as well as the cynicism of the Enlightenment opponents of religion, especially those who formed its libertine underside. Wesley, Fletcher, and their followers were convinced that men could become virtually perfect *in se* (though they never relinquished ultimate dependence on God's grace), not simply *in Christo*. This is what had horrified Zinzendorf, and was to horrify pure Calvinists, Lavington, and, indeed, all those steeped in the traditional ethos.

Closely related to the doctrine of Perfection was that of Assurance. Assurance, Wesley suggested, was "an outward impression of the soul, whereby the Spirit of God directly witnesses to my spirit, that I am a child of God; that Jesus Christ hath loved me and given himself for me; and that all my sins are blotted out, and I, even I, am reconciled to God." [93] The proof that such Assurance was genuine was the transformation of the life of the believer. It brought about a New Birth. The believer became a "new man," whose life was on its way to being perfected. The doctrine of Assurance was dismissed by Wesley's critics, both Anglicans and Dissenters, as bare-faced Enthusiasm, subject to abuse by sinful men and responsible for many distortions and enormities. (This, indeed, was Wesley's view of the Assurance experienced by the followers of Relly and Cudworth! [94]) It was for their complete Assurance of personal salvation that Wesley had so much admired the Moravian missionaries in Georgia, and it was this Assurance that he had painfully sought to acquire for himself.

It was this individual mystical experience—the believer's wrestling to achieve his conviction of God's love for himself—an extension of the Reformation doctrine of justification by faith, which was the core of Wesley's Evangelical Arminianism. The doctrine, derived from the mystics and from the younger Luther, was a levelling one, since this particular form of consciousness of salvation, though accessible to all men regardless of social condition, seemed more available to the more credulous and emotional, to the humble rather than to the mighty. Those utterly convinced of their salvation might, of course, prove dangerous to society: this fear had caused Luther, facing the revolutionary aspirations of sixteenth-century Enthusiasm, to depart from a similar view of Assurance, and to denounce the ancillary doctrine of free will.[95] The Methodist view of Assurance could not but arouse the resentment of those who did not—or could not—share such a confidence. Nor was this conviction of salvation, once attained, a certain sign that a believer would continue to enjoy this inner certainty: all efforts had to be continually directed toward perfection, toward the attainment, with divine help, of perfect love.[96]

At the beginning of the Revival, Wesley had maintained that if a man did not possess this feeling of Assurance, he was under the curse of God.[97] Wesley was subsequently to abandon this extreme position and to agree that a man might be justified without knowing it.[98] One critic of the doctrine, Melville Horne, had been a Methodist in his youth but had never been able to accept what he called "the damnatory clause, against all the Non-assured." Three years before his death, Horne wrote, Wesley had told him that "when fifty years ago, my Brother Charles and I, in the simplicity of our hearts, told the good people of England, that unless they knew their sins forgiven, they were under the wrath and curse of God, I marvel, Melville, they did not *stone us.*" "The Methodists, I hope," Horne recalled Wesley as having said, "know better now: we preach assurance as we always did, as a common privilege of the children of God; but we do not enforce it under the *pain of damnation.*" Though Wesley may have given it up, as had Fletcher, Horne further argued, yet Coke, an ordained Anglican clergyman and Wesley's leading disciple after Fletcher's death, and the other Methodists continued to adhere to "what was called, good old Methodism." (Indeed, Methodist leaders, Horne alleged, had persuaded Whitehead to eliminate evidence of Wesley's change-of-mind on this issue from his biography of Wesley.)

The Methodist doctrine of Assurance based on experience, Horne concluded, was akin to its Calvinist counterpart based on the belief in election and reprobation, and was as wicked in its consequences.[99] In 1812, Josiah Pratt, an Evangelical clergyman of Calvinist leanings, in disputing the Wesleyan doctrine, presented a stereotypically Calvinistic view of Assurance: "this doctrine should enter into our ministry in the way of exciting us to watchfulness and diligence," he urged, for, all other things being equal, "confidence will be proportioned to diligence"; "we are to *give diligence* in order to make *our calling and election sure* to ourselves," Pratt declared; "we must not preach the duty of assurance as a duty *per se,* but the duty of living in that state with which assurance is connected." (While it was true that Christ had undertaken all our sins, Pratt further observed, such a view was "liable to abuse": "doubts keep many close to Christ who would live carelessly if they had none," noting that he meant "doubts of personal interest, not of the truth of God.") [100] Whereas the Calvinists had clearly aimed at the men of the more disciplined "middling" classes, an elite, the Methodists turned their attention to those who might aspire only to that sense of conviction of salvation to be obtained through intense mystical experience, which seemed accessible to more men. Less evident, though it was noted by Horne, was that the Methodist view that there were two acts in justifying faith—first the belief in Christ for pardon, and the second the knowledge of being pardoned—was a translation of "the old puritanical one, of the *direct* and *reflex* acts of faith: the faith of reliance and adherence, and the faith of assurance." [101] An Arminian Horne defended the doctrine of Assurance held by the Church of England, as "a *knowledge* of salvation," relatively easily won through an acceptance of Christ as Redeemer.[102] This was the most readily accessible kind of Assurance, as was only appropriate for a national church.

The passive Arminianism of the Church of England, though it gave easy access of the Lord to all men, was unable to create a *new* man. This was the province of a hell-fire Calvinism and of an Evangelical Arminianism which converted the mechanism of Calvinism to its special needs. The former sought to create an elite of middling-men who would receive the personal Assurance of their election by the relative "diligence" of their lives. The latter endeavored to convert men, by means of a personal, mystical experience—more accessible, as I have suggested, to the unsophisticated, the imaginative, the disturbed—to the willingness to lead the "diligent" lives of perfect love which the Lord required for sanctification. While salvation might not be dependent on this kind of Assurance, as Wesley appears to have come to understand, it *was* necessary for the creation of the *new* men from the alienated urban proletariat, as the "good, *old*" Methodists knew. To Horne's attack, with its parting jibe that the Methodists, "as *avowed Arminians*," had "better err on the side of *free* grace, than on that of *free wrath*," [103] Coke made a strong rejoinder.[104]

"TRUE PROTESTANISM" AS A COMPONENT
OF EVANGELICAL ARMINIANISM

Despite Wesley's desire in the last decades of his life to identify himself fully with the Arminian tradition, his successors were to insist that Arminianism had dangerous tendencies toward rationalism and Socinian Unitarianism. In the middle of the eighteenth century, Calvinists frequently accused Arminians of Socinianism, and, by the later decades, it was not unusual for Methodist theologians gravely to warn each other of tendencies toward Socinianism. In 1779, for example, Thomas Coke made this accusation against Benson and Benson was forced to defend himself.[105] The most embarrassing occasion for such a charge came upon the publication of Adam Clarke's Commentary on the New Testament in 1817, in which the Londonderry-born Scotsman, a former President of the Conference in whose scholarship the entire Connection took particular pride, expressed views on the relationship of Father and Son which seemed dangerous.[106] Richard Watson, who was to become the authoritative theological spokesman of the Connection after the publication of his *Institutes* in the 1820s, rushed to counter Clarke's view [107] which, moreover, Watson suggested in a private letter, was unfortunately, in his view, not uncommon among the younger preachers of the Connection.[108] Jabez Bunting, the predominant figure in Methodism during the nineteenth century, in his last address to the Conference, in 1857, worried about an undiluted Arminianism which, he declared, led "to legality in experience, and something like Socinianism in doctrine." [109]

There was a struggle between a liberal Arminianism and a "true Protestantism"—a struggle between the modern and the entrenched forces of the traditional—which had been proceeding within the soul of Methodism throughout Wesley's lifetime. We have observed that despite all his apparent Arminian optimism, Wesley frequently found himself dwelling on the utter depravity of the natural man. Despite his paeans in behalf of free will, Wesley never ceased to wonder at the miraculous workings of providence: his history of England is replete with explanations derived from providential decrees,[110] and, on a lower level, to the end of his days, Wesley resorted to the casting of lots as a clue to the divine will. The symbolic high-water mark of liberal Arminianism upon Wesley was the founding in 1778 of the *Arminian Magazine*. With the death of first Fletcher and then Wesley, the traditional, "true Protestant" elements within Methodism, endemic to a popular, revivalistic Protestantism, reasserted themselves. The new direction of Methodism might be said to have been confirmed when, in 1797, the name of the *Arminian Magazine* was changed to the *Methodist Magazine*.

The message of Methodism, almost inevitably, was understood by great numbers who listened to it to be like that of Calvinistic Dissent. Samuel Bradburn, one of the chief leaders of the Connection, a thoroughgoing Arminian who took Fletcher for his model—his advanced Arminianism had even resulted in an accusation of Socinianism in 1775—was even offered a well-paid pulpit by Calvinistic Independents. The offer was made, Bradburn later observed, because "though I firmly believe the leading doctrines of the Methodists, and preach them clearly," yet as "I dwell mostly on the dreadful state of man by the fall of Adam, and the recovery by Jesus Christ, and on this foundation endeavour to build inward and outward holiness, saying little or nothing about the calvinian controversy," his theological leanings had been misconstrued.[111] Coke later suggested that Wesley had called all preachers of hell-fire "Croakers" and not genuine men of God,[112] and Methodists were always insisting upon the very different character of the message they preached. But Bradburn, even while he denounced, in a sermon in 1796, the Methodists who "put *hell fire* in the place of the blood of Christ," found his own sermons, with good reason, condemned by theological opponents as belonging to this category.[113]

There were many such Croakers among the Methodists, and it was evident that croaking produced converts. The traditional ethos was not lightly set aside. Whether for these "practical" reasons, or, as some were to suggest, out of ignorance, we have testimony from a number of sources that there ceased to be, especially after Wesley's death and particularly at the lower levels, significant doctrinal distinctions between the different species of evangelicalism—Wesleyan, the Calvinists of Lady Huntingdon's Connection, and the Calvinistic Evangelicals of the Establishment. In chapel meetings, more than one Anglican clergyman was to observe, Wesleyans dispensed a potpourri which, as one such clergyman insisted, although "a teacher of the sect" might deny that the doctrines he preached were Calvinistic, "I can only say, I have stated them precisely as his disciples *understand him";* and, the Anglican cleric added, "the consequences are the same." [114] Another critic of the Methodists, this time an Anglican layman, declared that "in the ordinary Methodist societies, the calamities of Calvinistic doctrines are generally prevalent" and "are dealt out in seductive or terrific language, generally proportional to the ignorance and illiteracy of the preacher." [115]

Methodist ministers of a more Arminian cast were seriously disturbed. In 1829, the Rev. James Jones, a Methodist preacher, addressed a lengthy pamphlet to Jabez Bunting, the President of the Conference at that time, in which he complained of the conquest of Arminian rationalism by Calvinist superstition. Methodists continued "tamely" to permit the "corrupt theology" of the Anglican Evangelicals, almost all of whom had some allegiance to Calvinism, to circulate among them, and as a result "our popular theology has been extensively corrupted, and awfully perverted by the constant importation of words and phrases, of notions and conceits, from our predestinarian neighbours." Jones denounced the emphasis given by Methodist preachers to the view that men were "born in sin, the children of wrath," rather than stressing that man was "a child of God, and a partaker of the blessings of human redemption," and pointed to the un-Wesleyan meaning given by Methodist preachers to the phrase, "the glory of God," making it seem that God was glorified by the everlasting misery of the wicked; he likewise protested the use of the phrase "total depravity," as one which "outrages all reason and all experience," and was "inconsistent" with Scripture. Similarly, he objected that the use of the phrase "an interest in Jesus Christ" implied in both the Calvinist and in the popular meaning unconditional election, "a moral sinecure" secured by the "arbitrary will of the Deity," and indeed, he suggested, the phrase "merits of Christ" continued to be used among Methodists in the sense in which it had been employed over half a century earlier by Hervey and the brothers Hill. "The Deity was benevolent to all," Jones declared, and not, as the Calvinists saw Him, a "partial and capricious" God; nor was the Deity the author of evil, which was the implication of the popular Methodist view of God as "an invincible agency in the moral government of the world." Jones' main grievance concerned the popular Wesleyan view of "Divine Prescience," a view which, he suggested, Wesley had not specifically condemned because it would have been impolitic "thus to have stormed the stronghold of popular ignorance, popular prejudice, and popular superstition." The Calvinist idea of "eternal prescience," Jones insisted, could never be reconciled with the Wesleyan Arminian view of "moral freedom." [116]

By the time Jones wrote this tract, the "true Protestants" had clearly won important battles. Especially on the local level, the message of Methodist preachers was reputed to be almost indistinguishable from that of Calvinistic Dissent, and the main body of Methodist members had already apparently assumed somewhat of the appearance with which they were endowed by their mid-Victorian enemies. A perceptive, if somewhat fierce, critic of Methodism, in a tract published in 1813, depicted the dour quality, the aura of melancholic gloom which hovered over Methodist pietism: he pointed to "the peculiar physiognomy of its followers," observing that "the very character of the English face is altered" by their preaching, "coarse, hard, and dismal visages, as if some spirit of darkness had got into them, and was looking out of them"; he noted the vulgar anti-aestheticism, the "bigotry, fanaticism, and uncharitableness," the "cant and hypocrisy," and the "Pharisaical expression and demeanour" of the Methodists. He was revolted at their narrow "sectarian spirit," their view of themselves as a "separate and chosen people" forbidding intermarriage with non-Methodists, and regarding the drinking of alcohol or the taking of snuff as participation in Satanic rites, and noted their insistence not only upon their own chapels, but their own schools, madhouses, magazines, and books ("their own Bible, their family Shakespear, their newspaper," etc.) He attacked their belief in the "perpetual" intervention of Providence "in all the little actions of our lives," and was horrified by their political opinions which were "made up from the Apocalypse," and by their incredible superstition, which, for example, saw Napoleon as "the beast who has risen up out of the sea, having seven heads and seven horns." [117]

Methodism never did fully become the caricature of its enemies, and many among the Methodist leadership were ready to respond to Jones' call to Wesley's "theological descendants" that they "carry out the theological principles of our system" in "perfect accordance" with Wesley's "great theological principles, the infinite benevolence of God, and the moral freedom of the human mind." [118] Jones had turned to Richard Watson's *Institutes* for support of his position,[119] and he might have secured comfort from Jabez Bunting as well. Yet the leadership had undeniably turned against a "rigid" Arminianism, not only because it had proved difficult to extirpate the "Calvinistic" doctrines of the popular Protestantism, but because to insist too strongly upon the liberal implications and consequences of Arminianism might, in the eyes of the leaders of the Connection, lead the faithful onto dangerous ground, both spiritual and political. What the leadership advocated was what they called the "middle" position of Evangelical Arminianism.

In the 1820s, under the scholarly instruction of James Nichols, Methodism was to identify "true" Evangelical Arminianism as that of Arminius himself, of Grotius, and of Wesley, distinguishing this from the looser Arminianism of some of the Remonstrancers. Though Wesley and Fletcher had seen Richard Baxter as an advocate of "practical Christianity," and as the formulator of a "medium" between Calvinism and Arminianism, Baxter was now dismissed as crypto-Calvinist, and many of the Remonstrancers and Latitudinarians—including Jeremy Taylor, a favorite of Wesley's—were denounced for having gone too far in the direction of Pelagianism. Evangelical Arminianism was depicted by Nichols as the genuine "golden mean" between Calvinism on the one hand, and Pelagianism and semi-Pelagianism on the other.[120] Nichols' friend, Jabez Bunting, in his funeral oration on behalf of Richard Watson, explicitly followed Nichols' categories when he proclaimed Watson to have been "an *evangelical* Arminian," an Arminian "of the School of Arminius himself, and of Mr. Wesley, rather than of the very different one" of "the later followers of the eloquent and learned leader of the Dutch Remonstrants." [121] (Bunting, on this occasion, specifically praised Nichols' work.[122] Richard Watson also displayed clear debts to Nichols,[123] as did Thomas Jackson, who became Connectional Editor in 1824, and was to be a leading man in the movement.[124]) In his final address to the Methodist Conference, in 1857, Jabez Bunting proclaimed Evangelical Arminianism to be "the true Gospel." [125]

Evangelical Arminianism, with its "true Protestant" component, though not by any means the pure doctrine of Arminius and Episcopius, may be understood as a partial solution to the problem with which Wesley had originally had confronted: how to reconcile the explosive Enthusiasm engendered by the appeal to salvation by faith with an Arminian concern for works. The result was, on the more elevated levels of Arminianism, free will and universal salvation modified by the necessity of grace, and of the perfection of the saved, even as among the sixteenth-century Anabaptists, but also the perfection of diligence for good works. The "true Protestant" underside of Evangelical Arminianism—the pulpit themes of man's degeneracy and the workings of providence, a medley of popular Calvinism and primitive superstition—made an appeal to a fairly widespread popular Protestantism, and was certainly, as Bradburn testified, an effective means of making masses of simple men susceptible to the desire for salvation. It also provided a counterweight, drawn from the strength of the traditional ethos, for the more heady implications of Arminianism. The emotional links of this doctrine to Reformation Protestantism, particularly to Calvinism, even made possible an alliance of the Calvinistic Evangelicals of the Church of England, whose inspiration had been Whitefield and who were still loyal to the traditional slogans, and the Arminian Methodists. While the Church Evangelicals largely devoted themselves to the conversion of the upper classes, the Methodists continued to preach to the lower. But, increasingly, they preached *a common gospel* of "practical Christianity," for just as Methodism had not yielded its "true Protestantism" even where it came into conflict with Arminian doctrine, a Calvinistic Evangelicalism was more and more preaching good works and universal salvation. The doctrinal differences between the two were easily subordinated to their common purpose of conversion, of the making of "new men."

EVANGELICALS AND PRACTICAL CHRISTIANITY

The drawing together of Evangelical and Wesleyan was anticipated in 1787 when Wesley, while preaching in Hertfordshire, encountered Charles Simeon, a leader of the Anglican Evangelicals. Simeon, after having cross-questioned Wesley, declared himself satisfied with Wesley's declaration of reliance upon God's grace to rescue him from the depravity of original sin, and for sanctification and ultimate salvation. "This is all my Calvinism," Simeon declared; "this is my election, my justification, my final perseverance"; what Wesley had stated, he continued, was "all that I hold, and as I hold it." "Therefore, if you please," he concluded, "instead of searching out terms and phrases to be a ground of contention between us, we will cordially unite in those things wherein we agree." [126]

Of course, most Anglican Evangelicals had never really advocated the extreme Calvinism of Lady Huntingdon's Connection, nor, indeed, was eighteenth-century Calvinism as unyielding a system as it had been a century earlier. Calvinism had undergone a softening even in the mid-seventeenth century. (It has been observed, for example, that the Calvinist Fast Sermons during the Interregnum had called for the diligent performance of public duties, upon which the hope of salvation was said to materially depend, almost as if their preachers had been Arminian advocates of works.[127]) By the late eighteenth century, perhaps because of the mediating doctrines of Baxter, both Dissenters and Anglican Evangelicals had also altered their view of election, though not so decisively as to make possible a genuine detente with Methodism. There is considerable evidence that many leading clergymen of the Evangelical party were still fundamentally Calvinist, although not of the sixteenth- or seventeenth-century purity to which Toplady, or the "hyper-Calvinists," had aspired. Even on the issue of redemption, upon which large numbers of Dissenters had compromised, many Evangelicals held, if not to pure Calvinism, at least to a more moderate approximation.[128] Many, however, like the Anglican Evangelical Josiah Pratt, nonetheless stressed that it was "our bounden duty to make offers of salvation to all." [129] It was this duty to evangelize, of course, which was critical, and was to undermine Calvinistic doctrine; still, these Evangelicals insisted that there be no compromise with Arminianism, which another Evangelical, the Rev. W. Goode, denounced as a doctrine that "undeifies the Deity, and deifies the creature," which, denying "the total depravity of human nature," had made "salvation depend on the will of a creature, whom the Scriptures represent as totally depraved." Yet it was clear that if the Evangelicals could not accept an Arminianism which, as Basil Woodd declared, "exalts free-will almost above God," they could nonetheless feel that "Calvinism associates too closely with necessity." Most Evangelicals were ready to go along with Pratt's view that they "be content to preach in such manner as to be accounted at one time Arminian and at another Calvinistic." [130]

This compromise acceptance of a more moderate Calvinism by the Evangelical clergy was confirmed by the program of "practical Christianity" set forth by the most prominent Evangelical layman, William Wilberforce, a program which moved even more decisively toward an understanding with an Arminian Methodism. When Wilberforce published his *A Practical View* in 1797, the "corruption of Human Nature," the "slight and superficial conceptions of our state of natural degradation, and of our insufficiency to recover from it of ourselves," was his constant theme. "Having no due sense of the malignity of our disease, and of its dreadful issue," he observed, "we do not set ourselves to work in earnest to obtain the remedy." "Set ourselves to work": was this the method to be pursued rather than the awaiting of grace? "For it must ever be carefully remembered," Wilberforce continued, "that this deliverance is not *forced on us,* but *offered to us.*" This, certainly, was not Calvinistic irresistible grace. "We are furnished indeed with every help, and are always to bear in mind, that we are unable of ourselves to will or to do rightly; but we are plainly admonished to 'work out our own salvation with fear and trembling.' . . . May we be enabled to shake off that lethargy which is so apt to creep upon us." There was nothing here to which John Wesley, or any Arminian, might take exception. More specifically Wesleyan was Wilberforce's opposition to those who pleaded Christ's "merits as their only ground of pardon and acceptance with God," and were, consequently, "sometimes apt to conduct themselves as if they considered their work as now done." Wesleyans could rejoice in Wilberforce's view, one shared by almost all Calvinist Evangelicals, that, there being "no *short compendious method of holiness";* "it must be the business of their whole lives to grow in grace, and continually adding one virtue to another, as far as may be, 'to go on toward perfection.' " Nor would Wesleyan Methodists deny—as we have suggested, they came increasingly to affirm—Wilberforce's argument that the best means "to shake off that lethargy" was "a deep practical conviction of our natural depravity and weakness."

Wilberforce praised a non-doctrinal practical, "vital" Christianity—"he only that doeth righteousness is righteous"—as having useful social and political consequences. He cited Wesley as an exemplar of this practical Christianity. Like Wesley, he also praised both Calvinist and Arminian divines who had stressed the practical, particularly eulogizing Richard Baxter, whom he found "among the brightest ornaments of the Church of England," for "his practical writings," which Wilberforce described as "a treasury of Christian wisdom." [131]

Wilberforce was widely regarded as a Calvinist, but his tract made critics wonder. He had managed to avoid taking a clear position upon the well-known issues of controversy.[132] One theological pamphleteer defended Wilberforce against the implication of a critic who doubted his Calvinist credentials, by noting Wilberforce's acceptance of the specifically "Calvinistic doctrines of human depravity." This writer further suggested that since the noted Evangelical layman was "writing a *practical* discourse, and mentioning points of doctrine only incidentally, Mr. W. (*sic*) might not think it necessary to state his principles systematically." [133] Wilberforce was certainly not the stereotypical Calvinist of the kind Wesley had combatted in the 1770s. Shortly before his death, Wilberforce pointedly declared himself "not Calvinist." [134] Writing to his son Samuel in 1829, he had remembered that "a certain strange head of a college" had observed thirty years earlier that he had been silent on the issue of imputed righteousness; "the honest truth is," Wilberforce confessed, "I never considered it." Although he had "always been disposed to believe it to be in some sort true," he thought it of no real importance compared to "the doctrine of free grace and justification by faith." [135] Although, in the context, Wilberforce seemed to mean free grace in the Calvinist sense of God's freedom to choose, yet, in 1823, he had asserted that "every year that I live I become more impressed with the unscriptural character of the Calvinistic system." [136]

The Methodists were pleased by the practical Christianity now preached by so many Evangelicals. A Methodist writer, drawing together the question of works and election, observed that it was "well known that most of the pious clergy are Calvinists," and that "unconditional election is essential to Calvinism," yet "notwithstanding the *peculiarities* of their system imply antinomianism, they are so happily inconsistent as to insist upon the necessity of obedience to the precepts of the gospel in order to find salvation." "The truth is," he continued, "that though they believe that Christ died for no more than a certain portion of mankind, they live and preach as if they believed that God 'would, without exception, have all men to be saved.' " In this way, he concluded, "are they *practically* [my italics] right notwithstanding their retaining, what I conceive to be, some speculative errors." This writer, indeed, saw "no reason why the Methodists might not hear them with pleasure and profit." [137]

Practically speaking, then, Arminian Wesleyanism and Calvinistic Evangelicalism spoke, and were understood to speak, essentially the same language. Doctrinal differences of importance there had been and might continue to be, but in the generations following Wesley's death a practical Christianity developed which made it possible for a writer inquiring into the moral tendency of both Methodism and Evangelicalism to say that "Calvinist, Methodist, and Evangelical, are to be considered synonymous," while adding that "although there is a difference between them in some respects, yet the great lines of their character are the same." [138] Methodism, withdrawing from certain of the more "enlightened" implications of Arminianism, was ready to join the Evangelicals of the Establishment in constructing a doctrine which would possess the greatest utility, as Wilberforce suggested, in producing social stability at home. Certainly it would be useful for men of God to join in preaching the gospel to all men, and thus to combat secularism and revolution. The Evangelicals, on their side, were equally ready, as we have seen in Wilberforce, to follow the Wesleyans in encouraging all men to seek after Perfection, though they were convinced it was attainable only at the time of death, and salvation. Such a practical Arminianism not only possessed domestic uses, but would be eminently suitable for the evangelization of heathen nations.

V

Fear of Revolution and Repression, 1791-1832

To you, is the civilization, the industry and sobriety of great numbers of the labouring part of the community owing.

Joseph Priestley, Address to Methodists, *1791*

Whilst, in some critical periods of our country's history, many in the middle and lower orders of societies, with whom our people were in immediate connexion, moving in the same circles, pursuing the same callings, and having a common public interest, have joined the ranks of disaffection, in attempts essentially to change, or actually to overthrow, our admirable constitution; the members of our community have retired far from these scenes of strife and disorder. . . . We tremble at the thought of what might, before this time, have been the fate of our country. . . . The infidelity and democracy which have overthrown many ancient dynasties on the continent of Europe, were fast undermining the civil and religious institutions of Great Britain; prosperous commerce was introducing unrestrained luxury and extravagance of living, when God raised up, through the instrumentality of the Wesleys, a ministry, which has proved a strong barrier against the spread of scepticism in the middle classes of society, and has exerted an influence over the dense population in our manufacturing districts, which has operated as the chief cause of the preservation of public peace in seasons of great excitement and alarm. It is not exceeding the bounds of truth to presume, that, but for the counteracting agency of that revival of religion which began with our fathers, the peasantry of England would have been as much prepared for anarchy and revolution as those of any of the continental nations, in which the most revolting scenes of insurrection and bloodshed have transpired. Who, I ask, have been the chief instruments of defeating the designs of infidel demagogues and political revolutions, among the middle and lower orders of society in this country, for the last fifty years? When itinerant orators have been running to and fro in the land, inciting the poor to deeds of faction and rebellion, and, by the dissemination of cheap literature, spreading far and wide their libertine and revolutionary principles; what class of public men have, by their open and undaunted resistance, been more than any other the objects of their ire?

Edmund Grindrod, Wesleyan Methodism Viewed in Retrospect, *1839*

In 1789, the cry of liberty, equality, and fraternity across the Channel appeared to herald the arrival of ideas which had been long awaited by many, though dreaded by others who saw them only as the dark forces of anarchy and greed disguised. For well over a half-century after the September massacres in 1792, the respectable in England feared the imminence of revolution. Certainly, the nineties—following a period of calm in the eighties which must have seemed ominous in retrospect to contemporaries—saw the spread of distress and the renewal of rioting, climaxed by the widespread difficulties of 1795. There took place a profound change of sentiment even among reformers in England. William Pitt, who in the 1780s had been a young man anxious to widen the electorate, became, in the nineties, the symbol and the direct instrument of repression. Such continued to be England's mood in the decade and a half after Pitt's death in 1806. The Luddite machine-breakers in 1811 and 1812 terrified Pitt's former associates, now entrusted with the security of the state. Sidmouth, the Home Secretary, made himself the particular spokesman of those in Church and State who dreaded upheaval, and used every means and opportunity to extirpate radicalism. The "massacre" at St. Peter's Fields in Manchester in 1819 was the climax of a year of agitation and demonstrations, a year which seemed to many one that might become a companion to 1789, and was followed by the uncovering of an undeniable revolutionary conspiracy in 1820, and by great demonstrations against the monarch in 1821. Better times brought relative social peace, but, once again, in 1829 and 1830, there was rick-burning in the agricultural districts of the South, followed by agitation by city workingmen between 1830 and 1832, an agitation spurred and led by middle-class Radicals such as Francis Place and James Mill in an effort to compel parliament to extend the franchise. The working-class leadership, disappointed by what they saw as their betrayal in 1832, organized (imitating the structural pattern of Methodism) the strictly working-class apparatus of Chartism to continue the struggle. These were the perilous circumstances which presided over the phenomenal growth of evangelical religion—the quickened pace of the Methodist Revolution—during the generation after Wesley's death, and which so powerfully affected its development.

The chief *practical* effects of the diffusion of the "vital Christianity," Wilberforce asserted, were political. "The prevalence of Evangelical Christianity" would, in every way, help "the cause of order and good government." A man motivated by "vital Christianity" would not desire "worldly gain" or "human estimation," but would wish rather to "diligently" discharge "the duties of his own station without breaking in upon the rights of others." In a society in which "vital Christianity" prevailed, "there would be no jarrings, no discord"; "the whole machine of civil life would work without obstruction or disorder, and the course of its movements would be like the harmony of the spheres." Practical Christianity, by "softening the glare of wealth, and moderating the insolence of power," would render "the inequalities of the social state less galling to the lower orders, whom also she instructs, in their turn, to be diligent, humble, patient," "reminding them that their more lowly path has been allotted to them by the hand of God." Nor need politicians be concerned lest the "religious warmth" which Wilberforce wished to encourage "might break out into mischievous irregularities," for so long as this "warmth" was confined within the Established Church, the "fervour and animation" might be restrained "within due bounds." By instructing "the rising generation" in this practical, vital Christianity, Wilberforce concluded, "an antidote may be provided for the malignity of that venom, which is storing up" in France.[1]

An Evangelical clergyman of a more decidedly Calvinist bent than Wilberforce, Josiah Pratt, could yet see the special advantages of the Arminian system in achieving Wilberforce's object: the "awful appeals to conscience on account of man's accountableness." Pratt stood ready to borrow such a useful doctrine. Pratt understood the inadequacies of the Calvinist system for such a purpose: "Say what you will of Arminian difficulties," he declared, "no difficulty can be greater than that of reconciling the sovereignty of God with the responsibility of man."[2] This problem had long troubled Calvinists: it was the new conditions in which Europe found herself which made its lack of solution glaring. The traditional discipline was breaking down, and natural depravity, no longer subdued, was rampant: this, at least, was a view widely held in Evangelical circles. "Self-will is a prominent feature in children," observed another Evangelical clergyman, the Rev. T. Scott, in 1798, declaring that "the present disorders of Europe may be assigned to the want of the old plan of discipline." "We should teach children that they must obey a *master*," he asserted. Still another Evangelical, the Rev. John Venn, agreed, noting that "Rousseau gave the tone; and many followed and repented too late."[3]

Enthusiasm—whether Rousseauian or evangelical—was, however, dangerous. What made Methodism seem particularly revolutionary, as I have suggested, was that Wesley had converted the passive Arminianism of a Church which had turned skeptical and was neglectful of its spiritual charges into an active Arminianism, preaching spiritual equality and launching a campaign against clerical indifference by the undoubted levelling methods of lay preaching. While the Church's Arminianism in the eighteenth century, not unlike that of the post-Tridentine Catholic Church, ran little risk of a meaningful political translation, Wesley's Evangelical Arminianism, tapping strong emotions, had genuinely incendiary possibilities. Yet Methodist doctrine joined elements of a repressive "true Protestantism" to a levelling, liberal Arminianism, as its theology revived the obsolete Augustinian doctrines of sin and atonement for an enlightened age. It stressed man's utter depravity before his conversion and New Birth. *All* men were, before conversion, *equally* depraved, and *all* had to experience a New Birth before they were made acceptable to their Savior.

"Their doctrines are most repulsive and strongly tinctured with impertinence and disrespect towards their superiors," the Duchess of Buckingham had observed in the mid-eighteenth century, "in perpetually endeavoring to level all ranks and do away with all distinctions." "It is monstrous," she continued, "to be told that you have a heart as sinful as the common wretches that crawl the earth." [4]

From the standpoint of doctrine, Evangelical Arminianism stirred men up only so that they might be diligent to do good works. Moreover, it accomplished this while never ceasing to assure them that meddling in politics was unbecoming a Christian and failing to honor the King was a sin against God. While a "rigid" Calvinist election might make presumptuous rebels and a "rigid" Arminianism might incite a revolutionary effort to produce a heavenly city (further spurred, perhaps, by the Wesleyan doctrine of Perfection), Evangelical Arminianism was so happily formed that it might give a spiritual satisfaction to the egalitarian and libertarian aspirations, however inarticulate, of the lower classes, without jarring their deeply ingrained unfavorable view of themselves and their fellows—so much a part of the traditional outlook—as still requiring, for a considerable time, the supervising authority of their betters.

RADICAL CHALLENGE TO
METHODIST POLITY

When the revolution came in France, it could not have surprised Wesley that the rebels marched under the banners of Rousseau and Voltaire. In February of 1790, it would appear that he viewed the Revolution itself as a foretokening that the day of judgment was at hand.[5] In quite extraordinary fashion, however, Wesley, who had feared the imminence of revolution throughout his long lifetime, appeared at this time to have had no such anxieties: "I do not know that England was ever before in so quiet a state as it is now," he observed.[6] But Wesley's uncharacteristic complacence did not extend to his successors. Indeed, Methodism itself was soon to come under attack from Radical levellers within the Connection.

During the early 1790s, accompanying the revolution in France, Tom Paine's *Rights of Man* provided an intellectual basis for challenging all authority in both state and Church. Within Methodism, the new democratic forces were represented by men like Samuel Bradburn and Henry Moore who spoke for the "people" against the rich trustees who were the predominant force in the local societies and whose spokesman was Benson. After the food crisis of 1795, popular, socially disruptive tendencies received a new force, and the government became concerned. Although previously reluctant to take action, the government now gave clear indications of a new repressive spirit. Methodism became alarmed, and the Conference at Manchester in 1795, with mobs shouting at the doors, undertook a Plan of Pacification designed to satisfy many of the principal popular demands— those at least of the more moderate leaders like Bradburn and Moore; at the same time, the Conference turned against the more uncompromising egalitarianism of men like Alexander Kilham, as a sign to the government that Methodism intended to keep its own house in order.

Nor was it surprising that there was a radical wing within Methodism, for, as we have seen, Methodism, despite the Tory sympathies of its founder, was the disseminator of a popular religion with a strongly egalitarian tendency. Its principal characteristics—in the eyes of its enemies— were those which the genteel associated with the lower orders. At a time when the upper classes had become skeptics or deists, Methodism had sought to enlist the fanatical religious zeal of the lower classes; while the genteel had turned to the new science, the Methodists tapped credulity and superstition. Wesleyan Arminianism was a levelling doctrine which made an appeal to the longings for liberty and equality which erupted so frightfully on the continent in the 1790s, even while it helped to fulfill the demands of the poor for spiritual solace, and for the establishment of new fraternal bonds to replace the weakening hierarchical authority structure. Methodism had for many decades been regarded as a threat to both Church and state, and despite all Wesley's efforts to prove his loyalty to the Church, a loyalty only rarely acknowledged by Anglicans,[7] the clergy continued to consider him an enemy, and there continued to be accusations linking him with revolutionary designs, as for example at the time of the Gordon Riots.[8] The long-held Methodist fears that the government, in response to the intermittent agitation of clergymen and prelates anxious about the role that a fanatical, mass movement might play in times of distress, might wish to restrain or to suppress the Connection became even more pressing when Methodist radicalism made its appearance after Wesley's death.

The structure of Methodism seemed, from one standpoint, a guarantee of order. Indeed, it appeared cunningly devised to keep the energies of the newly converted from spilling over into practical Antinomianism. The Methodist societies were the means by which the call to liberty and equality made by Arminian doctrine might be disciplined, thus giving the Methodist Revolution a form which, eschewing practical politics for spiritual absorption, offered pietistic (and national) fraternity, not that of rank or class.

These societies were first composed, in the Moravian manner, of Bands or Select Bands of between five and ten members (of the same sex and marital status), all joined in a common search for Christian Perfection. A Methodist was expected to lay bare all his thoughts and deeds to the members of his band, who would listen, admonish, and reprove, fulfilling the role of a surrogate family for the "alienated" poor. Subsequently, local societies were divided into classes of a dozen or more, each with a leader who exercised a sub-ministerial function. The leader was expected to visit each member of his class, to collect a penny every week from each and to "make a particular inquiry" into their behavior in order to detect "disorderly walkers." Not only the spiritual but the business activities of Methodists were under scrutiny. Members of classes who passed such a scrutiny received a ticket, which had to be renewed quarterly, as a testimony of good standing. Those who failed to pass were expelled. It was through the class leaders that the preachers kept in touch with the spiritual condition of the members. The chief figures in the Wesleyan scheme were the preachers, who, following Wesley's example, became itinerants, moving from place to place within the circuits into which the country had been divided, and being transferred periodically from one circuit to another. Wesley believed that a preacher ought not to stay in one place for more than six to eight weeks, and that no preacher ought to remain in a circuit for more than three years. In time, preachers and officers of each circuit came to hold quarterly meetings to discuss problems; and superintendents came to be appointed to govern the circuit by Wesley each quarter or half-year.

The Methodist polity was a remarkable structure, about which we need to know a great deal more than we do. The morals of all Methodists were under such steady supervision that practical Antinomianism could rarely go undetected. Methodist workingmen who had developed a superior sense of responsibility and autonomy served as band leaders, or class leaders, stewards (to keep necessary chapel accounts), or superintendents, though each was subject to the intimate guidance of superiors in the hierarchy. The system of itinerancy, it was hoped, might insure that the doctrine offered to Methodists would be relatively free of the eccentricities of a particular preacher, and that control of the Methodist polity would repose at the center. (Brief itinerancies, and an insufficient number of full-time preachers, also had the opposite effect, of course, of enhancing the authority of local preachers, at a lower level than the itinerants, and of the stewards and trustees.) John Wesley, aided by the Conference (a select group of itinerants invited by Wesley to meet with him each year) presided over a bureaucratic organization which has frequently been said to have had no counterpart other than, perhaps, the Society of Jesus.[9]

Wesley himself had ruled, apparently, by divine right, without benefit of the constitutional limitations which he regarded as useful restraints upon King George. At the 1766 annual Conference, when Wesley was asked "what power is this, which you exercise over all the Methodists in Great Britain and Ireland?" he had replied that "it is a power of admitting into and excluding from the Societies under my care," of "choosing and removing" stewards and Helpers, of "appointing them when, where, and how to help me." He had denied wielding *"arbitrary* power," that is *"unjust, unreasonable, or tyrannical"* authority. The power which Wesley had assumed had been "merely in obedience to the Providence of God, and for the good of the people," and he bore it as "the burden which God lays upon me." Wesley knew that some Methodists regarded such an authority as "shackling free-born Englishmen," and had demanded "a free Conference" of "all the Preachers, where in all things shall be determined by most votes." While ready to grant the possibility that "after my death, something of this kind may take place," Wesley was determined that it would not occur "while I live." [10] It was not long after Wesley's death that serious dissatisfaction with the Methodist polity made its appearance.

It was the generation which followed Wesley which witnessed the partial resolution of a number of the contradictions in Methodist organization and doctrine, with results which could only be disquieting to champions of the traditional ethos. Two great questions were first, how the Connection was to be governed, and secondly, whether Methodism was to remain within the Church. As early as the nineties, despite the persistence of a rearguard action by "Church" Methodists, it became increasingly clear that the Connection must be separate from the Established Church, and that the claims to a wider participation in its government would have to be met or the Methodist movement would disintegrate. In the nineties, moreover, there was a split within Wesleyanism and the most egalitarian minority seceded to form a New Connection. All this could hardly be reassuring to the forces of order when the threat of French armies shouting "Liberty, Equality, and Fraternity" seemed close at hand, and the strength of Methodism and its powerful expansive energies were in sharp contrast to the relative weakness and apathy of the Establishment.

While Wesley lived, despite occasional murmurings, as we have seen, his authority was unchallenged. At his death in 1791, the absolute authority which he had wielded was passed on by his will to a Committee of One Hundred of his ministers. At a time when democratic political theory was a powerful tide, it would have been difficult to restrain egalitarian sentiment in a mass movement. Certainly, it would have been difficult to maintain a polity which offered Methodist laymen a lesser voice than was offered to the electorate under the unreformed British constitution. In 1815, a layman belonging to the New Connection, which had seceded from the main body in the late 1790s, described the government of Methodism by the so-called Legal Hundred after Wesley's death as "unscriptural, arbitrary, and dangerous," and "so foreign to British Custom": "the grand cause of separation was that of CHURCH GOVERNMENT," he observed; "the people demanded a participation in this power," for "according to every maxim of good government, *power* emanates from the people." [11]

Within the Legal Hundred, which possessed absolute authority in the movement, there was a small group who exercised a predominating influence. The obvious successor to Wesley was Thomas Coke, who had devoted himself in the eighties to missionary work in America. For the first five years after Wesley's death, Coke served as the Secretary of the Conference, the Presidents of which, chosen annually, were not permitted to succeed to another term until eight years had elapsed, so anxious were Wesley's heirs to avoid domination by another peerless leader. Among the other leaders of the Conference were Joseph Benson, Thomas Rankin, and Thomas Olivers—all of whom had been at the right hand of Wesley—as well as John Pawson, Alexander Mather, Samuel Bradburn, Henry Moore, Thomas Taylor, Joseph Bradford, Thomas Hanby, William Thompson, and Adam Clarke, all itinerant preachers of long service, and all of whom were to serve in future years as Presidents of the Conference, a number of them more than once. After Wesley's death, the government of the Connection was in disarray.[12] Adam Clarke, in a letter written early in 1795, spoke of "our total want of government," and, observing that the Connection was "like a rope of sand from Conference to Conference," found that "the times were never more threatening." [13] John Pawson—a Yorkshire-born builder, an itinerant since 1762 who achieved a certain notoriety by burning an edition of Shakespeare's plays annotated in Wesley's own hand so as to preserve Wesley's reputation from association with such a frivolous undertaking—had for some years been a critic of Wesley's leadership,[14] as well as an early advocate of separation from the Church.[15] Seriously disturbed at the internecine warfare, Pawson was one of those who had pressed for a peaceful reconciling of differences,[16] even going so far as to write Benson, one of the leaders of the Church party, that since the Trustees, while "generally the richest, yet are not the most pious, lively, zealous men in our Connexion," it might be best for the majority of the people to have the powers of decision.[17] Pawson saw the Legal Hundred as having antagonized the great body of the people, and warned a friend, in 1795, that if many preachers attend the Manchester Conference, scheduled in that year, "the people will Mob us," most particularly since provisions were in short supply." [18]

It was the Conference which controlled the itinerant system, and which had the final word concerning the most substantial issue which beset the Connection during these years—the conditions under which a local chapel might administer the sacrament. Each year, under the direction of the Committee of One Hundred, itinerants were assigned to new districts: the Conference regarded the itinerant system, as had Wesley, as the heart of Methodism's perpetual evangelism, preventing preachers from slipping into settled, comfortable ways, and keeping the missionizing fervor keen. A chapel was constrained to accept a preacher assigned by the Conference no matter how undesirable the members of the chapel might feel him to be. But there was considerable unhappiness within the laity concerning all these arrangements. At the Conference of 1795, a Committee on General Pacification composed by Bradford, Pawson, Mather, Coke, William Thompson, Bradburn, Benson, Moore, and Clarke (representing both the firm "Church" Methodists and a more moderate, Whiggish view whose chief spokesman was Samuel Bradburn), sought to stem the rising irritation with the conservatism of the dominant "Church" Methodists—a group whom Clarke denounced as "the vilest Persecutors." The Committee, while affirming the exclusive right of the Conference to appoint preachers (insisting, moreover, that "the hundred Preachers mentioned in the enrolled Deed, and their successors, are the only *legal* persons who constitute the Conference: and we think the junior brethren have no reason to object to this proposition, as they are regularly elected according to seniority"), introduced a method whereby unwelcome preachers might be removed from the circuit as a concession to the laity. Despite the anxiety of the leaders of the Conference to follow Wesley in attempting to avoid separation from the Church of England, the Committee was obliged to yield to the most intense pressure from local stewards and class leaders to relax restrictions against the administration of the Sacrament. The Sacrament was to be offered when the majority of the trustees of a chapel, as well as the majority of the stewards and class leaders, were ready to allow it (though only if the Conference endorsed such a move), and only on Sunday evenings, except where the majority of the stewards and leaders wished it during church hours, and even then only to Methodists but "never . . . on those Sundays on which it is administered in the parochial church." [19]

These were the lines along which further concessions were to be made in the years to come, and while they were, for a time, sufficient to prevent a major split in the Connection, it became clear that the price of maintaining the Connection and the leadership of the One Hundred relatively unimpaired was to permit the drift of Methodism from the Church to Dissent. As early as 1793, the Conference, in explaining why it felt compelled to yield to the wish of local societies to administer communion, declared "that it is the *people* . . . who have forced us into this further deviation from our union to the Church of England." If the Conference had not yielded, it was feared that many members would withdraw from the Connection: "We cannot, however, we will not, part with any of our dear flock, who loves God and man, on account of unessential points." The need of the leadership to maintain control of the movement had, as in the past, determined policy—in ritual as well as doctrine: "for we love you *all*," the Conference of the Legal Hundred concluded, "and are servants of you all for Jesus' sake." [20]

There were a few members of the Conference, whose spokesman was Alexander Kilham, an itinerant preacher since 1785, who were not content with the extent of the concessions granted by the Legal Hundred, and who campaigned to speed the course of Methodism along the road upon which it had reluctantly entered. The fears of the Connection on almost all matters of controversy—uncertainty concerning Connectional government, separation from the Church, concern over popular radicalism and government repression—had come to center on Kilham. The leaders of the Hundred saw in their own midst men who were biding their time, since they "expect a Revolution to take place in a while."

"I understand," Pawson observed in 1796, "that the people in and about Newcastle are almost mad with rage against the Preachers and are determined to support Kilham." [21] The chief men of Methodism saw Kilham as a grave threat to the Connection. Under these circumstances, the leadership of the Connection was disturbed by rumors that their enemies had informed the ministry that the Connection was subversive.[22] Bradburn, at one time Kilham's friend and sympathetic to his views, fearing Pittite repression, now denounced Kilham totally: in 1796, he described Kilham's "dream of Equality" as "worthy only of such inexperienced novices," and to the Kilhamite "cries about the *poor*," Bradburn declared "the distress of nine in ten of the poor *is entirely their own fault*." [23] The Methodist leaders were convinced, in Pawson's words, that "the spirit of leveling is become so prevalent in our Connection, as well as in the nation at large, that it is to be fear'd, it will bring total ruin in the end." [24] Pawson wanted Kilham and his followers to be exposed as "mere Tom Paineites," in order to deprive them of their "influence among our people." [25]

The Conference moved to clamp down on the rebels, and in 1795 determined to expel those who continued to object to the decisions of the Legal Hundred.[26] In 1796, the Conference, while acknowledging that "the liberty of the press being considered as our undoubted privilege," was nonetheless anxious that nothing should be done by any individual which would be prejudicial to the whole," and determined that *"no Preacher shall publish anything* but what is given to the Conference and printed in our own Press," with the Book Committee determining "what is proper to be printed." [27] The 1796 Conference further insisted that "no man, nor number of men, in our Connexion, on any account or occasion . . do or attempt to do anything new." [28] Despite this remarkable injunction, new rules were adopted in 1797 by which the Conference yielded to Quarterly Meetings, with a broader representation, a great part of its financial supervision of the Connection, and much of its power over admissions and expulsions: "in short, brethren," the Conference reported, "out of our great love for peace and union, and . . . to satisfy your minds, we have given up to you far the greatest part of the Superintendent's authority." [29]

ARMINIAN WHIGGERY: BRADBURN
AND KILHAM

The political ideas of both Alexander Kilham and Samuel Bradburn may be understood, in part, as translations of an egalitarian Arminian theology. The two Arminian Whigs were to have very different fates in the Connection.

Samuel Bradburn, an itinerant preacher since 1774 and an admirer of the Whig leader Charles James Fox, the Secretary of the Conference in 1796, 1797, and 1798, and again in 1800, and the President in 1799, was one of the inner circle of the Conference leadership. During its early years, Bradburn was very sympathetic to the French Revolution. As late as 1792, probably before the massacres of September of that year, Bradburn had vaunted the "spirit of Philanthropy" which had accompanied the "spirit of Liberty" in a Revolution which had "in some measure affected all Europe." In a tract denouncing the slave trade, Bradburn took issue with those who suggested that Methodist efforts to end slavery were "pushing things to extremes." A radical Bradburn declared that "if *moderate* men, as they affect to be called, had been attended to in France, that infernal mansion, the Bastille, had still remained; and millions of intelligent human beings had continued in the galling chains of servile oppression, who are now rising to the privileges of a free people." [30] Was it a wonder that Pawson might suspect that the enemies of the Methodists had supplied the ministry with Bradburn's writings in order "to give them an unfavorable opinion of the Body at large"? [31]

At Bristol, in February 1794, Bradburn preached a sermon on *Equality,* a dangerous title at a time when, as Bradburn understood, if a man "say anything in defence of the privileges of the people, especially if he name the 'Rights of Man,' he is immediately termed a REVOLUTIONIST," and "an enemy to all subordination." But its mood was very different from that of his 1792 tract. While opposing, in the best Whig fashion, those "who would exalt the royal prerogative above all law," as well as those "who would level all orders of men, and overturn the state," Bradburn presented a careful Arminian case for equality as the immediate *spiritual* condition of man, even if its practical, mundane realization, so far as politics or property were concerned, might have to be postponed until the millennium. The word "Equality" was at root "scriptural," Bradburn insisted, and all men were equal in that they were "all equally *creatures,*" "all equal with respect to their total depravity," all equally "under the same necessity of being saved by the free grace of God." But temporal Equality, "in the present state of things," was "impossible," since "a natural consequence of a variety in men's powers and employments, was an inequality in their

PROPERTY." Nor was it "an evil in itself" that "mankind were rendered *unequal*" by "being divided into GOVERNORS and THE GOVERNED," and Bradburn called on the governors to exercise paternal care on behalf of their children. Like Wesley, Bradburn observed that a Christian's "political sentiments" were "determined by the New Testament."

But there were two causes for which Bradburn would brandish the sword of resistance: to protect religious liberty and to defeat slavery. In discussing these matters, Bradburn's sermon was replete with threatening Whiggish phrases which could only disturb the government. The assertion that "Man has no rights!" was "downright TREASON," Bradburn proclaimed, since it struck "at the root of all order and government," "opening the way for rebellion, anarchy, and all the miseries that man can bring on man." "When men of rank treat their inferiors with supercilious insolence, as if they were beings of another species," the "consequence" was likely to be "the insurrections, rebellions, and revolutions, recorded in the histories of various countries"; but of course, he granted, insolent behavior was no excuse for rebellion on the part of Methodists, who, for conscience sake, subjected themselves to the higher powers. Man's prime right was "the unalienable birthright of every human being to choose his own religion, and to worship God as he pleases." Methodists did "not look upon ourselves as called to reform Civil governments, or spend much of our time in disputing about state affairs," he declared; "who ever knew any of our Ministers, or even private members of our society, concerned in mobs or riots, or any way disturbing the peace?" "But by subjection," Bradburn observed, "we must not understand an absolute or implicit resignation of their persons, legal privileges, or consciences to the arbitrary decisions of any man or body of men upon earth." It was "criminal" to resist magistrates "in the lawful execution of their office," but "when men require any thing contrary to the commandments of God, submission to them is treason against the Most High." In the same category as the freedom of religious conscience, "which our very existence as a people compels us to defend," Bradburn put the Methodist interest in the abolition of the slave trade.[32]

In taking up the theme of liberty of conscience, Samuel Bradburn, in Arminian fashion, argued that "the human mind" be left "free to exercise, as it deemed best, the right of private judgment in matters of faith and worship." Bradburn observed further that "all who object to this are persecutors in principle, whatever may be their conduct."[33] Within the ranks of Methodism, Bradburn revealed himself in an ambiguous position in conduct, if not in principle, in the case of Kilham.

Alexander Kilham, an itinerant preacher since 1785, was very proud of his birth at Epworth, the native town of the Wesleys, and we may gain a further insight into his view of himself when we recall his use, on one occasion, of the pseudonym *Martin Luther*.[34] Kilham made himself the champion, within the Conference, of the principles of "liberty and equality," and of the program of separation from the Church of England, of the equal participation of all in the government of the Connection, and of the necessity of scrutinizing Methodist doctrine by the light of scripture, reason, and conscience. While praising, in 1795, "our father in the gospel, Mr. Wesley" for his clear insight into many questions of doctrine, Kilham was disgusted when the Conference, following Wesley's method, cast lots in 1792 to determine whether the Lord's supper ought to be administered by Methodists in the following year. This was *"contrary to God,* and an eternal reproach to scripture, reason, and common sense." [35] Kilham pointed out doctrinal contradictions within the body of Wesley's sermons and his notes on the New Testament which the Conference had made the canonical guide for preachers. Were there not passages in those writings which spoke of the imputation of Christ's personal righteousness and hence "border upon Antinomianism," and had not Wesley's "Calvinist opponents availed themselves of these passages and fought our venerable father, with his own words?" "Were the people requested to examine everything," Kilham urged, and "point out in leaders', quarterly, and district meetings, any thing that militates against the scriptures, or the avowed doctrines of Methodism, would there be any harm in laying them aside?" [36]

Kilham, translating by his own lights the implications of Arminianism into political theory, emerged with a defense of democracy—for the government of the Connection, at any event. Decisions within societies ought to be taken by direct vote, Kilham insisted, and the majority ought to rule on such questions as the hours of services, the sacrament, baptism, burial, etc. It was a "sin in the sight of God, to hinder" such a majority decision: "we all have an equal right to vote in these matters, as we all are redeemed by Christ, and have each a soul to save, *equally precious in the sight of God,* with the souls of our trustee brethren." Kilham had no doubt that "if the Conference, a body of trustees, or any person or number of persons, prevent a society from having the privilege of determining these matters, it is *tyranny on their part, and oppression to the people."* Kilham hoped that minorities would "submit, saying 'The will of the Lord be done,' " but declared that their liberty of conscience would be protected in any case. Was it not intolerable, Kilham inquired, that Methodists were "at a vast distance from that portion of religious liberty among ourselves, which the nation enjoys of civil liberty"? Was "it not amazingly strange, that any sect or party should refuse to give to their brethren what the laws of our country so cheerfully allow"? At bottom, the issue was the failure of the leaders of the Conference to "collect the sense of the people": reception into or exclusion from the society ought to be "by the consent of the people"; the creation of itinerant preachers ought to be approved by the people, through their representatives; class leaders ought to be chosen by the people. No Methodists—whether preachers, trustees, class leaders, or stewards—"have a right to lord it over the consciences of their brethren." [37]

Views of this sort were disconcerting to the leaders of the Conference not only because their authority was being challenged, but because they were evidence of revolutionary, republican, and even Jacobinical sentiments which the enemies of Methodism had always insisted were to be found within Wesleyan ranks.[38] Those opposed to Kilham, we have observed, linked his name to that of Tom Paine, and spoke of his "levelling principles." [39] Writing in 1796, Kilham endeavored to counter such charges. "Whatever new plans we have proposed for our connexion," he declared, "no person can charge us with agitating new plans for the state." "We have never introduced anything into the pulpit on the subject," he continued, and "we pray for our King and country, and seek the salvation of both." Less reassuringly, Kilham associated himself "with the principle (*sic*) gentlemen of this country . . . in seeking for peace," these "gentlemen" being the Foxite opponents of the government.[40]

Motivated, consequently, by fears for Methodist survival, and by the need to defend its own authority, the Conference disregarded the opposition's numerous appeals in behalf of liberty of conscience, and mounted a trial of Alexander Kilham before the General Conference in London, in July 1796. The leadership demanded that Kilham bind himself, in the future, to agree with the views of the Conference. Kilham was ready to do so only "as far as they are consistent with scriptures." When Joseph Benson, the friend and associate of Wesley, urged Kilham to give such a pledge, Kilham replied by quoting Benson's own words that in matters of doctrine "as every man must give an account of himself to God, so must everyone judge for himself." In his account of his trial before the Conference, Kilham reported that "Mr Benson seemed a good deal confused" by this rejoinder, "yet he attempted to prove, that every Methodist Preacher ought to engage to submit to the [Conference] minutes without any condition being expressed." During this encounter, Kilham reported, Samuel Bradburn "smiled and sat down"; "perhaps he thought I should be quoting a few passages from his excellent Sermon on Equality." The subject was quickly changed. An overwhelming vote for expulsion, under far from unimpeachable circumstances, was obtained. All the preachers present were asked to sign a paper testifying to "the *justness* and *uprightness*" of the proceedings; and Samuel Bradburn, at this time the Secretary of the Conference—"I cannot relate the tragical story without weeping," Kilham wrote—"who had formerly professed himself," Kilham continued, "a friend to liberty and the rights of the people; Mr. Bradburn, I say, stood by the rails of the Lord's table, like the governor of an inquisition, to see that all his brethren signed." [41]

Bradburn had clearly determined that the best means of defending Methodist liberty of conscience, and perhaps even of securing the abolition of the slave trade and slavery, was to display a Methodism free of radical taint. Equality was to be exclusively a spiritual condition—having no meaning even in the government of the Connection. Methodist preachers were the heirs of the authority of Wesley, and were determined, like good stewards, not to squander their inheritance. Another preacher who earlier had been sympathetic to Kilham's ideas, Jonathan Crowther, was to declare that "it would be a miserable degrading sight to see a minister of Christ, and an ambassador of the KING OF KINGS, reduced to the humiliating situation of being the mere *executioner* of the wills and plans of a few individuals, who called themselves THE PEOPLE." Crowther further suggested that Kilham was engaged in "a mere struggle for power." [42]

In 1797, Kilham and his few followers in the Conference, formed a New Connection. In 1800, they possessed but twenty preachers; by 1814, they claimed some 273 preachers, 101 chapels, and 8,292 members. [43]

MEETING THE THREAT OF SUPPRESSION

In these revolutionary decades when the governing classes suffered from a growing paranoia, they saw the Methodists under the tight discipline of a committee of One Hundred which dispatched scores of itinerant preachers throughout the kingdom to guide hundreds of chapels, having many thousands of members. These Methodists, in their view, were moved by fanatical fervor, and were, or so it seemed, determined to undermine one of the pillars of the state—the Established Church. With revolution rampant on the continent, the government could not but dread it at home. It might be noted, furthermore, that the Methodists were the only body of the "People" who were so organized as to be capable of making a revolution. Might not the Methodist Revolution in the nineties follow the lead of Whitefield's American followers in the seventies?

The nineties and the first two decades of the nineteenth century were a time when political radicalism and widespread economic distress were causing the government to be apprehensive, and with good cause. It was the time of Paineite Radicalism, Luddism, and Peterloo. This was also the time when Methodism, 100,000 strong in 1791, had reached the point of organizational take-off. In the following quarter of a century, the Methodist preachers seemed to be keeping pace with the successes of the French armies, extending the sway of their own revolution. Methodist claims, possibly inflated, indicated a growth of members—not merely hearers who were thought to be more than twice the number of members—to some 200,000 by 1802, 270,000 by 1806, and 367,000 by 1812. [44] A more moderate claim saw about 167,000 members in England alone in 1815, with 631 preachers and 1,355 chapels, and over a half-million members and hearers combined.[45] (Of course, other, non-Wesleyan evangelists were by no means idle during this time, as we shall see.) Methodist evangelism, long confined to the savage mining areas or the new-grown industrial districts which the Established Church had, practically speaking, declined to serve, had reached the point where its evangelistic energies required new fields of activity. The Connection was boldly moving into the more settled towns and villages of the older, rural England, and directly challenging the Church. The evidence suggests that there were many within the Established Church who were enormously fearful of the consequences of Methodist missionizing.

The breakdown in social discipline which accompanied the progress of the French Revolution saw a popular reaction against the Established Church and its clergy, as well as against the upper classes. Yet, this reaction was accompanied by an outburst of popular religious feeling: interdenominational and undenominational adult and children's Sunday Schools, many under Methodist inspiration and control, were set up; societies were established, sometimes under denominational auspices, to forward largely undenominational missionary enterprises across the seas; most interestingly, the Dissenters were joining in setting up united itinerant ministries over large parts of the country, particularly in the rural areas, to take advantage of the widespread hostility toward both the upper classes and the Established Church. In all these activities, though most obviously in the itinerancies, the example of the Methodists was consciously imitated. This outpouring of religious sentiment, with its antiestablishment, even revolutionary, implications, made many in both state and Church tremble. The great enemy to stability seemed to be Methodism, whose evangelism had now spread to other religious groups, scoring remarkable successes even in the rural preserves of Anglicanism.[46] Yet, one might argue, it was this popular religious revolution which helped to put a society falling apart politically and economically, growingly hostile to the national church, under a religious discipline.

The Anglican clergy was especially disconcerted by the "levelling principle" in Methodism which spurred the creation of a body of lay preachers, a principle which, in the words of one clergyman, "if it do not entirely destroy, certainly weakens all the claims of abilities, learning, and diligence." Methodists, moreover, were "called on unequivocally to surrender their reason, and to place an implicit confidence in their illuminated instructors." Fanaticism was an enemy to stability.[47] A Cornish clergyman who, in the late nineties, witnessed some riots near Cornborne, saw this as evidence of Methodist designs to seek "the destruction of subordination, and a share in the plunder of all property." [48] Almost a decade later, in 1805, an anonymous clergyman, denouncing this *"levelling* tendency," declared the Methodist teachers to be "perfectly orthodox in explaining the doctrines of *Thomas Paine"* concerning *"natural* and *equal rights."* He further warned that the Connection constituted a full blown revolutionary conspiracy with "the preacher of the most obscure village" constituting a "link in the chain, and intended for a further use perhaps than either himself or his followers are at present aware of." It was clear, he declared, that "the principal leaders of this sect, are looking forward to a *Revolution* and of course of the *democratic* kind"; the Methodist leaders, like the Puritans of the seventeenth century, "have only to point their fingers to the place of attack," and "their forces will immediately follow with all the violence of false enthusiasm." [49] An Anglican pamphleteer warned, in 1806, that unless the Toleration Act were amended to restrain the Methodists, "unless some method be adopted to check, if not to annihilate, the extensive and extending *imperium in imperio* of Methodist government, and their autocratic priesthood," a "formidable mischief threatens us." Did not the Methodist abhorrence of episcopacy resemble the "fanaticism" of "the dark days of our republican hypocrisy"? [50] The same mood was apparent in a series of letters from a curate to his rector, entitled *Puritanism Revived,* which displayed the parallels between Methodism and Puritanism—even itinerancy had been a Puritan device.[51] Nor were the enemies of Methodism only obscure, and obscurantist clergymen. The Bishop of Rochester, in 1801, observed that "the Jacobins of this country" were "making a tool of Methodism," while "the real Methodist" was "kept in utter ignorance of the wicked enterprize," [52] and the Bishop of Gloucester depicted the Methodists as "malignant and subtle adversaries," who through "their private conferences, their local classes, their extensive connections, their general assemblies . . . cooperate from one part of the kingdom to another . . . for the purpose of concerting measures to undermine our civil and religious Constitution." [53]

The growing conversions obtained by Methodist preaching during this period frightened the clergy. A writer, who described himself as no Methodist, "but a friend to universal toleration and religious liberty," was much troubled that "in the conduct that has lately been exhibited" by the Methodists "in *recruiting* . . . for converts throughout every town and village in the country, there may be more zeal than judgement." [54] The clergy complained to their Bishops of the increase of itinerant preachers, whose sermons were proving so seductive. One writer, in a pamphlet in 1806 arguing for the correction of Church abuses, addressed to the Archbishop of Canterbury, wrote of "a regular *propaganda societas* under Methodist protection": a likely town is chosen, and a congregation "clandestinely secured"; no minister is appointed, but an itinerant missionary is "sent down for the Sunday, and perhaps for one evening in the week"; this congregation, "first procured by strategem" was then turned against "the established clergyman," "undervaluing his labours, and misinterpreting his motives." The clergy of the Establishment demanded protection.[55]

Dissenters, many with attachments to political radicalism, could not but fear that if the government felt sufficiently threatened, the protection afforded them by the Toleration Act might be rescinded, now especially because of their new participation in interdenominational itinerancies. The Methodists, given their entire dependence upon a system of itinerancy, had special grounds for concern, since, as foes of the Connection observed, it was the clear implication of the Toleration Act that the preacher of a dissenting congregation had to be permanently settled.[56] Furthermore, there was some question as to whether the Toleration Act properly applied to Methodists at all, since they regarded themselves not as Dissenters but as members of the Church. Of course, the most important grounds for Methodist concern was that many in both Church and state felt threatened by their expansion.

There were two responses from the Connection: the Methodists continued, following Wesley, to insist that their religious scruples made loyalty to the king and his government a spiritual imperative; moreover, to counter the argument that Methodism, like seventeenth-century Puritanism, was interested in promoting revolution, the preachers of the Connection proclaimed that Methodism served rather to dampen the discontent of the lower orders. Not only had the spread of Methodism, they argued, made for a more stable society, but the fact that there had been no revolution in England, despite considerable revolutionary pressures, might be directly attributed to its beneficent influence. These arguments were adopted as the party-cry of the Connection almost immediately after Wesley's death, and continued to be proclaimed by Methodists as a badge of respectability until at least the middle of the following century.

In the last decade of the eighteenth and the first three decades of the nineteenth century, Methodist sermons, conference resolutions, and tracts were a veritable pasacaglia upon these two themes. The first of the themes—eulogies of the Toleration Act, and endless protestations of loyalty, for conscience sake, to the government and to the King—was, of course, a continuation of long-standing tradition. In 1792, the year after Wesley's death, the Conference warned members of the Connection that "none of us shall, either in writing or conversation speak lightly or irreverently of the Government under which he lives," and further observed that "the oracles of God command us to be subject to higher powers" and "that honour to the king is there connected with the fear of God." [57] In that same year, Samuel Bradburn proclaimed that there were no "better subjects in the British Empire than the Methodists," since "our principles, respecting Civil Government" were founded "not upon political manoeuvres, but upon the holy scriptures," that "whatever government we live under, we are 'subject, not only for wrath, but also for conscience sake.' " [58] In 1793, Joseph Benson noted that the Methodists "uniformly and constantly inculcate" the command of "Fear God and honour the King"; indeed, Benson continued, the Methodists were "most notorious" for the practice of this principle.[59] The same theme was pressed by itinerants Henry Moore, in 1794,[60] and Jeremiah Brittell, in 1796,[31] in sermons which both bore the title of *Fear God and Honour the King*. We have examples of dozens of conference resolutions and sermons during these years in which this hymn of loyalty was sung.[62]

At times, these proclamations of loyalty were accompanied by denunciations of Radicalism—whether the Radicalism of Tom Paine, as in Thomas Taylor's answer to the *Age of Reason*,[63] or, more generally, the doctrines of "French philosophy." [64] When the Irish rose in rebellion in 1798, the Conference passed a resolution condemning France, that "infatuated nation," for its responsibility in "spreading carnage and desolation" in order to establish "a lawless freedom and a chimerical equality," and called upon Methodists "to do all in our power to suppress whatever tends to molest the quiet of the best of kings, or derange, in any degree, the happiest of all civil Constitutions." [65] An itinerant, John Stephens, described a Jacobin as "a political madman" who "hates his native land," "raves at the dearness of provisions and the enormity of taxes," and turns "his attention from the proper duties of his station," all traits stemming from Jacobinical infidelity. It was therefore impossible, Stephens insisted, as some had erroneously suggested, that "Methodists and Dissenters, and even the pious part of our Brethren in the Establishment," were Jacobins.[66]

The second theme was initially stated in a funeral sermon for Wesley by his friend Whitehead, who, conscious of the forebodings inspired by the French Revolution, had observed that Methodist influence was uniformly exerted to bring about "peace and good order." "If all the people were Methodists," Whitehead had declared, "no times of difficulty could come"; "but if such times should arrive, the more numerous this body of people is, the better it will be for the country." [67] The theme was further developed in response to clerical accusations. The leaders of the Connection recognized, as, in 1798, had Thomas Taylor, an itinerant for nearly forty years by that time, that "the poor, in general, are very profligate, murmuring and discontented, often combining against their masters or employers," yet, he added, quite different in every respect were the Methodists, "a remnant, who are squaring their useful lives by reason and by grace." "I hope their numbers will increase," Taylor concluded.[68] John Pawson observed in a sermon in the following year, 1799, that "in a time of general danger and distress, the wicked have been very ready to lay the blame upon the people of God, as if they were the cause of it," and have been ready to regard the Methodists as "enemies both to the Church and state." Methodists, Pawson replied, had always been "among the peaceable and quiet of the land," having "nothing to do with strife or contention, with mobs and tumults," and he urged his co-religionists, "in these dangerous days," to "study to be quiet." [69] The argument appeared full blown in

1805, in a tract by Joseph Sutcliffe, a Methodist itinerant since 1788, who not only attributed the "perfection" and "extent" of British commerce and industry to the spread of evangelical religion, but suggested that the fact that "vast groups of loose and disorderly men, subject as they have been to sudden stoppages in trade, to exorbitant advances of provisions, have been governed almost without mobbing and confusion" was also the fruit of Methodism and of evangelical religion generally. In the past, "there frequently happened very serious riots among the colliers and manufactures (*sic*)," but these formerly disorderly classes were "now more mixed with men of honest principle, with men of industry and property, who awe the wicked by their love of order, and reverence for the magistrate." The overall grounds for such a satisfactory situation, Sutcliffe concluded, were that "the sermons and writings of the Methodist preachers abound with effusions of loyalty and patriotic affection." "Let any gentleman, however prejudiced he may be against us," Sutcliffe declared, "make a tour through the manufacturing parts of the nation, and he will find almost as many chapels as villages, and crowded with attentive hearers." Such a gentleman would discover "that the proprietors of factories are either religious characters themselves, or actuated by interest, they choose sober and pious men for their foremen and overlookers," and that "the commerce of the country" was "principally conducted by persons who are attached, in one form or other, to evangelical truth." [70]

These Methodist arguments, conforming so well with Wilberforce's views as to the practical, political effects of "vital Christianity," were becoming more widely accepted outside the Connection. In 1804 an anonymous writer, probably an Anglican, while granting that some Methodists could not but have "imbibed, in some measure, the disorganizing spirit of the times," nonetheless acknowledged that since "their religious economy prevented them from entering into the turbulent and dangerous field of politics" and "taking a part in civil reforms," Methodists of a radical bent, such as Kilham and his associates, had turned to reforming Methodism itself. The more the doctrines of Methodism "are received in any civil community," the writer concluded, the less that community had "to fear from either popular rage or foreign invasion." [71] Another anonymous writer, perhaps an Evangelical businessman, writing in 1806, agreed with Sutcliffe that "great assemblies of men," "being particularly susceptible of religious impressions, may, on this account be more effectually controuled (*sic*) by the Scripture doctrine of submission to authority." [72] Still another writer, more a man of the Enlightenment, writing in 1810, praised the political "utility" of religion as a means of maintaining stability in society, adding that it was "to John Wesley and George Whitefield," that "we owe all the religion which now exists among the lower orders of society." [73]

This last writer was moved to write in praise of Methodism because of his objections to legislation then being proposed to make preaching licenses more difficult to obtain. Because of the political utility of Methodism, he wrote, he did not wish to see Methodism ridiculed or persecuted, and he favored "absolute unrestricted toleration." [74] This proposed legislation, part of a larger effort on the part of members of the clergy and of the Tory government, particularly the Home Secretary, Lord Sidmouth, to counter the growth of Methodist societies, was, in the view of most Methodists, the beginning of the repression they had long feared.

During those years, many would have agreed with an Anglican friend of the Connection that Methodists had never accepted "the *right of resistance*" as "residing in the governed," the position of Locke which, he declared, "if even *theoretically true,* would if reduced to practice, deprive all governments of stability." [75] Yet perhaps surprisingly, in view of Methodist political views, the Methodists *had,* indeed, promised resistance, and again and again, in sermon after sermon, should they be denied toleration. On this matter, clearly, Protestant determination that every individual had to be granted his own way to seek God triumphed over the New Testament injunction to obedience to constituted authority. Henry Moore, for example, in 1794, after urging the fear of the Lord and the honoring of the monarch, nevertheless enjoined that "should the heavens again grow black with the clouds of persecution . . . call to mind the former days"— the Revolution of 1688–and "suffer not as evil-doers." [76] As Benjamin Rhodes suggested in 1796, a King "has no divine right to govern ill," so if liberty of conscience were interfered with, obedience to God meant the necessity of resistance.[77] Another itinerant, Thomas Roberts, in a sermon preached in 1802 exulted that Britain had a "constitutional King," under whose reign, "Religious Liberty, the corner stone of the Reformation, the basis of Protestantism has been inviolate." In the latter part of his sermon, in which he described the Revolutionary settlement of 1688 as "providential," Roberts asserted that while "every Christian man must deprecate, from principles of conscience, 'all sedition, privy conspiracy and rebellion,' " such an injunction did not apply when matters of conscience were at issue: "no human power is to be obeyed where obedience to magistrates is rebellion against the laws of God"; in such circumstances, Roberts urged, "resist unto blood." [78]

Nor did this seem an idle threat. Methodists, a non-Methodist observed, "compose among themselves the most powerful affiliated society in existence"; their number is prodigious," and their "discipline" formidable; "it is not to be conceived that a people who are in the constant exercise of that animation and ardour which so peculiarly distinguishes Methodism from every other religious sect whatever, will tacitly suffer a preparation for war without striking the first blow themselves." "In the most perilous times," he continued, clearly persuaded by the Connection's party-cry, Methodists had "been of essential service in maintaining subordination and loyalty." "Is it now a due reward for their patriotism," the writer inquired, that "such an opposition should be uselessly excited against them?" [79]

The Home Secretary, Lord Sidmouth, who as Henry Addington had served as prime minister between 1801 and 1803, began an effort in 1811 to secure the passage of legislation which would have placed restraints on the system of preaching central to the Methodist scheme. For some three years, Sidmouth had been collecting information through the agency of the episcopate of the Establishment concerning the number of licensed teachers and places of worship in the kingdom and concerning the condition of the Church of England. The results of his survey revealed that the considerable growth of Methodism contrasted sharply with what seemed an increasing weakness of the Established Church. Sidmouth and the Anglican bishops could only see the rapid spread of Methodism by such irregular means as lay preaching and itinerancy—methods which the Dissenters were now also adopting—as subversive to the Church and the state, a foretokening of what had already come to pass on the other side of the channel. Worried, Sidmouth framed a bill which he introduced on May 9, 1811 "to explain and render more effectual" the Toleration Acts, which specified that licenses were to be required of dissenting preachers, and which required that such licenses be granted only to those preachers whose respectability could be vouched for,[80] a provision which would place a considerable discretion in the hands of local justices. The Home Secretary described himself as a friend to "these Acts of Toleration," but they had given rise to "abuses"; there were persons claiming preaching certificates, "who were coblers (*sic*), tailors, pig-drovers, and chimney-sweepers," "situations" which "disqualified them from being teachers and instructors of their fellow subjects." England's "security depended upon the firmness" of the foundation of the Establishment, Sidmouth declared, and unless action were taken to defend the Church, "we should be in danger of having a nominal Established Church, and a sectarian people." Lord Holland rose "irregularly" to oppose the bill at its first reading, defending absolute freedom of religious conscience, and warning that "meddling with the Toleration act" would "only tend to excite Dissenters." Earl Stanhope agreed and further warned the Home Secretary against trying "his hands with the Dissenters." [81]

A great agitation was set in motion. During May, enemies of the Methodists supported Sidmouth's bill, while denouncing the Methodists as "the pious champions" of Jacobinism who had "decreed the subversion of all the established religions in the world," and whose "real object" was "REVOLUTION" and the revival of the Commonwealth.[82] On the other side, Methodism continued to boast that the Connection had successfully worked to counteract the pressures making for revolution. At a Methodist meeting on May 14, 1811, a resolution was passed which described "the manifest effect which the diffusion of religion has had for the last fifty years, in raising the standard of public morals, and in promoting loyalty in middle ranks, as well as subordination and industry in the lower orders of Society"; the adoption of the Sidmouth measure, the framers of the resolution were convinced, would "weaken these great sinews of the nation," as "the ardent affection of many a conscientious and loyal subject would be involuntarily diminished." [83] A similar resolution passed by the Methodist ministers of the Manchester district, over a week later, attributed "the preservation of this happy country from the horrors of that revolutionary frenzy which has so awfully desolated the nations of the Continent" to "this high degree of Religious Liberty" which England enjoyed.[84] In parliament, on May 17, Earl Grey regretted the introduction of the bill, "particularly at a period like the present, when so many circumstances required that religious dissensions should, if possible, be prevented." [85] A joint committee of Methodists and of the Three Denominations—Baptist, Congregational, and Unitarian—was organized to fight the bill, using methods which had already been successfully employed, a few years earlier, to bring pressure upon parliament to end the slave trade. Hundreds of petitions were assembled in a relatively short space of time, all demanding the defeat of Sidmouth's bill.

On May 21, 1811, before the bill could be submitted for its second reading, some five hundred petitions in opposition had been placed before the House of Lords by Stanhope, Holland, Grey, Lord Erskine, the Earl of Lauderdale, the Earl of Moira, and the Earl of Rosslyn. The Earl of Liverpool, the spokesman for the government in the upper house, rose to urge Sidmouth to drop his bill because of "the inconvenience arising from the agitation and alarm" which had "prevailed" since its introduction, declaring it "impolitic" to "interfere without a real and absolute necessity" into religion. The Archbishop of Canterbury, though agreeing with the principles of the bill, thought it "unwise and impolitic to press it," and the Lord Chancellor agreed. The Home Secretary, determined to pursue his effort, observed that he had anticipated opposition from the Establishment, which might regard the bill as "inefficient for what was requisite," but not from Dissenters. Lord Holland, in his reply to Sidmouth, denounced the bill as an "infringement" of the "natural rights" to religious liberty, adding that "the evil complained of" was "visionary," while "the remedy" was "violent." "If this Bill were to pass," he declared, with considerable exaggeration, "they would find 50,000 methodist teachers applying immediately for licenses, for fear of persecution." Earl Stanhope expressed delight that "the immense heap of petitions" had contradicted "a kind of silly talk" which had been "going abroad, that there was no public." This was proof that "there was a public, and a public opinion, and a public spirit." Lord Erskine, the noted Whig barrister, asked whether it had not been the "intention of the Saviour of the World" that his doctrines be "propagated, not by the high and learned but by the humble and lowly," concluding by bestowing encomiums upon "the late lady Huntingdon, and to Mr Westley (*sic!*), as well as to his followers, for the rectitude of their lives, and abstinence from political affairs." [86] The bill was withdrawn.

Although there had appeared to be no legal difficulties for itinerant preachers under the provisions of the Toleration Act for many decades, quite suddenly, after the failure of the Sidmouth bill, there was a rash of cases in which itinerants were brought before the magistrates and asked to prove themselves the teacher or preacher of some particular congregation, and when they were unable to do so they were refused permission to preach. The enemies of the Connection were determined to destroy the itinerant system.[87] Throughout the country, the minutes of the 1812 Methodist conference reported, there was "a new spirit of hostility." The Methodists began to see that the local itinerant preachers, so "absolutely necessary to our economy" had, in the past, "been *tolerated* by the general *consent* of the country, rather than *protected* by the *law.*" The press, the minutes continued, was "teeming with the grossest slander and falsehood," and they were "represented as '*vermin fit only to be destroyed.*'" Such statements, moreover, were not "casual" but were "reiterated in certain popular publications month after month." This was especially worrisome at a time when parliament was "loudly and repeatedly called upon to adopt measures of coercion against them, under the pretence that evangelical religion was inimical to public security and morals." [88]

It was in such a climate that the Methodists petitioned for and received protection. On June 2, 1812, Stanhope gave notice of his intention to relieve the "very great anxiety" which "prevailed in the minds of a numerous body of his Majesty's subjects," the nonconformists,[89] and on July 3, in rising to move the second reading of a Dissenters Relief Bill so as "to prevent religious opinions from being made the stalking horse for exciting disorder," Stanhope reminded the House that a recent survey had revealed that the Establishment had 2,533 places of worship in England, while the Dissenters had 3,454, "thus proving," was Stanhope's debatable conclusion, "that the majority of the people were non-conformists." The Bill was defeated so that Lord Liverpool, the new prime minister, might present a Government bill [90] on July 23, 1812, by whose terms both the Conventicle Act and the Five Mile Act (legislation of the 1660s directed against Dissenters) were repealed. Liverpool received the full support of Stanhope and Holland, while Sidmouth offered only a reluctant, grudging approval.[91] In the Commons' debate on the bill, the Chancellor of the Exchequer Nicholas Vansittart vaunted the abolition of these "relics of religious animosity and civil faction," sprung from "the embers of a civil war," that were "both in their spirit and their provisions wholly unsuited to times of settled tranquillity, and mutual liberality of sentiment." (Vansittart was relieved, however, that the bill continued certain "precautions," such as that of insisting upon public and open meetings of Dissenters, a provision necessary "to prevent the possible danger of clandestine meetings for dangerous purposes.") [92]

The Methodist Conference of 1812 showered its thanks upon Lord Liverpool, the Archbishop of Canterbury, Lords Holland and Erskine, as well as upon Messrs. Wilberforce, Stephens, and Babington, all Church of England Evangelicals, for their help; they also thanked the Quakers and the Dissenters who had constituted the Protestant Society for the Protection of Religious Liberty. The Act, the Conference observed, was "of peculiar excellency," more "especially in times like the present," for "the effect it will have upon the happiness of *the religious poor"*: it was religion which "soothes them under poverty and distress, and, by the grace of God, makes them content under the apparently adverse dispensations of Divine Providence, and teaches them to wait with patience for the 'inheritance which is incorruptible.' " [93] The preachers assembled at the 1812 Conference framed an address in which they expressed confidence that they owed this great boon to their "well-known loyalty," "their dutiful attachment to their King and Country, and the simplicity and purity of their object in promoting their own salvation, and that of others." The confidence in them displayed by the government, the address observed, "strengthens our motives for obedience" and "our alacrity in the path of Duty." Turning from "the contemplation of the benefits with which we are favoured" to the consideration of the "State of Society" which prevailed in "some of the Northern Counties," where Luddism was rampant, the address of the preachers observed that

we look at the principles which have given birth to this state of things, with the utmost horror; principles which are alike destructive to the happiness of the Poor, and of the Rich. And although we are well assured that our Societies are uncontaminated with that spirit of insubordination, violence, and cruelty, which has caused so much distress and misery, yet we cannot but dread the operation of its insidious and infectious nature, and the speciousness with which it aims to seduce the credulous and simple. We, therefore, as faithful Ministers, cannot refrain from sounding a solemn alarm, lest any of our dear people should be drawn away by the dissimulation of evil-disposed men. We proclaim loudly and earnestly, 'Fear the Lord and the King: and meddle not with them that are given to change. Avoid them. Come not near them. Say of them, O my Soul, come not thou into their Secret: unto their assembly, mine honour, be not thou united.' Destruction and Misery are in their Ways: and The Way of Peace have they not known. . . . We know well, and feel for, the situation of the poor, their want of employment, and the dearness of provisions; but murmuring and discontent will not alleviate their sufferings: they will rather aggravate them. Be ye therefore patient. Let the richer Brethren assist those who are poor, and let all hope and trust in Him, who hath said, I will never leave thee nor forsake thee; and in due time you shall reap if you faint not.

The preachers entreated the members of the Societies to remember that if "after having in the face of the World vouched for your loyal, your peaceable and honest deportment, we should be deceived in any of you," they would be overwhelmed by "grief and distress." "Justify our expectations," they enjoined, "and ye shall be the Crown of our rejoicing when those times of delusion shall have passed away." [94]

The houses of parliament, during the sessions of 1811 and 1812, it was later argued by the Methodists, had debated the issue which has been the subject of recent historiographical controversy, and had, patently, concluded that Methodism was a force for stability rather than for upheaval. Methodist sermons rang with a new confidence. In 1813, a Methodist answering an accusation of disloyalty, asked whether the critic of the Connection did "not know that the LOYALTY OF THE METHODISTS has stood the test of more than half a Century, against attacks as much more formidable than his, as the roaring of a Lion is to the yelping of a cur." [95] Another Methodist, the itinerant preacher John Hughes, denying the analogy drawn by a High Church opponent that displayed Methodism as a revival of a rebellious Puritanism, countered that the Methodists, by their religious instruction, had contributed to the "industry, sobriety, good order and moral decorum" of the lower classes; "the arguments offered on this head in the house of Lords, by those illustrious Peers who opposed Lord Sidmouth's Bill, were incapable of being contraverted." [96]

In a sermon on *The Divine Mission of the People Called Methodists* in 1814, Joseph Sutcliffe repeated his arguments of some nine years previously that Britain's "commercial grandeur" was due to the triumph of Methodism, and that, given the "groups of profligates" attracted by "the vast extent of our mining and manufacturing concerns," without Methodism, "atheism, impurity, and revolt" would have triumphed. The charge that Methodism aimed at "anarchy and revolt" which ran "through most of the books and reviews, written against us" was patently false. Methodism had revealed its unrevolutionary character "in its greatest fort, the commercial districts, during the severest pressures from the loss of trade with America, and the Baltic, connected with the dearness of bread, of which circumstances, the Luddites availed themselves to excite revolt." Methodist preachers, on the other hand, had, during this time, "circulated books and sermons on loyalty, and social order," and "warned the unwary." [97]

The charges against the Methodists did not cease. In 1813, after parliament had supposedly "settled" the question, it was still possible to accuse the Methodists of spreading "confusion and anarchy," and of warning, in the words of one pamphlet, that "our lives, our property, and all that we hold dear in life will be at the mercy of these wild and ungovernable enthusiasts." The writer urged Englishmen to look at France if they wished to see "the effects of freedom of conscience in religious matters." [98] Other

Anglicans, with more charity, merely continued to urge Methodists to return to the Church, reminding them of Wesley's loyalty.[99] In defense, then,
against these charges of disloyalty and of fomenting revolution, the
Connection and its friends in parliament not only continued to insist upon
the absolute loyalty of Methodists, but, anticipating the views of later historians like Guizot, Taine, Lecky, and Halévy, asserted that the spread of
Methodism had actually served to prevent a revolutionary outbreak during
a time of social and economic distress, and political turmoil.

Valentine Ward, writing in 1815, while insisting upon the loyalty and
patriotism of the Methodists, was ready to admit that there had been dis-
loyal Methodists, but in 1797 "nearly, if not quite, all of that description
left the Society" with Alexander Kilham. At this time, Ward could observe that "the Loyalty and Patriotism of the Methodists is now well
known, both to the government itself and to the nation in general." Ward
concluded, most sensibly, that the "usefulness" of the Methodists "in preventing the spread of French principles, both political and religious, is
only fully known to God." [100] This last is a judgment a responsible historian would find difficult to fault. What I am suggesting, however, is that
the Methodists may have been able to help prevent the violent forms which
egalitarian principles were taking on the continent by propagating these
principles in altered, spiritual forms to the restless and rootless eager to
receive them. Sidmouth and the Anglican bishops had a sense of the Methodist Revolution, and dimly saw its spread as an English counterpart to
what was happening on the continent. Others, more keen-sighted, understood that to attempt to repress it was to invite violence, while to permit it
to flourish would mean that Methodist itinerants could continue to be, for
practical purposes, agitators for order.

A NEW COURSE

Yet this is only one part of a more complex story. Wesleyan itinerants
were in close competition with radical agitators, and the latter had an undeniable advantage because the Methodists labored under the accusation of
supporting a repressive government. Methodist preaching no doubt helped
to undo apathy, but its message of spiritual liberty and equality, at a time
when, because of rapid growth, the Connection did not possess sufficient
resources to imbue discipline, probably served to swell the radical ranks as
well as the Methodist membership. It was at this time, also, as we have
seen, that the government attempted to block Methodist evangelism. Methodism required a new course of action, and a number of men in the
Connection, particularly Jabez Bunting and his leading collaborator Richard Watson, understood this. First of all, it was necessary—in the interests

of relieving the anxieties of both state and Church and, indeed, preventing Methodism from inadvertently stirring dissension and possibly revolt—to concentrate Methodist energies on disciplining the converted rather than extending even farther the nominal sway of the Connection.[101] Of course, it would be impossible to dam up evangelistic impulses completely, and especially at the peripheries of the movement the work of propagation continued despite the efforts of the leadership to induce restraint. Methodism was inherently an evangelistic system which required an outlet for its energies.

In the early years of the new century, groups of Methodist-inspired "revivalists" came upon the scene, men who aroused the fears of the Legal Hundred even as Wesley had once stirred those of the Bishop of London. The most prominent of these were the Primitive Methodists under the leadership of Hugh Bourne and William Clowes, who were to be the largest of the groups to secede from the Wesleyan main body. Starting at Mow Cop, in Staffordshire, in 1800, Bourne's Methodists spread through the countryside, stressing the immediate attainability of Christian Perfection, and under the influence of Lorenzo Dow, an American—much as Wesley and Whitefield had come under the influence of the preachings of the Welsh evangelists—Bourne adapted the "camp-meeting" techniques of the American frontier. The hostility of the leaders of the Connection closed many Methodist chapels to Dow and his followers, and separation became unavoidable. Primitive Methodism spread into Derbyshire, Lancashire, Cheshire, and South Staffordshire, and in 1817 through 1819 great camp meetings were held throughout the midlands. Just as in the first period of Wesley's awakening, when preachers sought to convert the most distressed and rebellious, the efforts of the revivalists were made in the same districts in which Luddism was most evident. In 1819, the Primitive Methodists had a membership of 7,842; by 1824, their membership had more than quadrupled, standing at 33,507. Primitive Methodism was even to be successful among the peasantry of East Anglia and Wessex in the second quarter of the century, and its efforts and successes were especially notable in the time of the rick-burnings in the late twenties and early thirties. It was in these rural areas that there was later considerable persecution of Primitive Methodists, many of whom also engaged in radical and trade-union activity, as may be seen in the case of the Tolpuddle martyrs, most of them Methodists, in 1835.[102]

By the second decade of the nineteenth century, there was already substantial reason to fear that Wesleyan Methodism had overextended itself. Those in the working and laboring classes who were hungry for the message of liberty, equality, and fraternity were increasing at a rate greater than the ability of Methodism to bring them under the restraints of its bands, classes, and societies. The years after the war also brought, once again, hard times. Eighteen-nineteen was a particularly bad year, marked by severe economic depression. The difficulties faced by Methodist preachers in the industrial North during the last months of 1819 were depicted by Thomas Jackson. Jackson, the preacher son of a Yorkshire farm laborer, at that time stationed in Manchester, wrote of the misery of the people, and of having witnessed "scenes of immorality and wretchedness which I can never forget": "Political agitators went about inflaming the passions of the suffering multitudes"; "thousands of people desired the overthrow of all government, and a general scramble for the property which the rich possessed"; the town was looked upon as in "a state of incipient rebellion," and the soldiery was prepared for "immediate action." In one of the popular Manchester papers, Methodist preachers were denounced as "enemies of the people" because of their support of the government; indeed, "the poor members of the Society were taught to hate us as their oppressors," and "to guard them against this delusion, in every instance, was impossible." "Not a few of our people," Jackson reported, "in this 'day of rebuke and blasphemy,' lost their piety by the indulgence of a worldly and malignant spirit." [103]

The Annual Address of the 1819 Conference, written by Richard Watson, already a man of some influence in the Connection, warned Methodists of "wicked men" who used "the privations of the poor" as "instruments of their own designs," and urged them not to be "led astray from your civil and religious duties by their dangerous artifices." The Address reminded Methodists of their traditional submission to magistrates, and enjoined them "to follow your occupations and duties in life in peaceful seclusion from all strife and tumults." [104] The Address was written in August, but the uproar in the country continued, particularly after the Peterloo Massacre, and in November the Committee on Religious Privileges, still worried about repression by the government, felt obliged to send another message to the faithful, stressing the irreligion of the preachers of sedition, and calling for the "discountenancing and repressing" of all "infidel and blasphemous publications" and of "tumultuous assemblies." The Committee urged Methodists to abstain from such meetings, and warned that those who did not obey would be expelled from the Connection. Methodists were further reminded that by joining with the forces making for "tumult and anarchy," they ran the risks of losing their religious liberties: in the past, "the soundness of your principles, and the order of your public conduct, have at once been our boast, the strength of our defence, the ground of our success." While sympathizing with the distress of the poor, the Committee urged those in distress "to bear their privations with patience, and to seek relief, not in schemes of agitation and crime, but in a reliance on Divine Providence." "The poor we shall always have, while men vary in their moral, mental and personal faculties," the message continued; "to the state of mankind, which admits of such a variety of conditions, with its concomitant trials and discipline, our holy religion is admirably adapted." We cannot "alter the temporal state of man" but must "seek for glory, honour, and immortality, in that better world, to which this short and transient life is but a pilgrimage." [105]

The same message was to be found in a tract by the Methodist itinerant, John Stephens—whose son, the future Chartist, Joseph Rayner Stephens, was to be expelled from Methodism in the thirties—on "the rich and the poor" (the first edition was sold out in five days), written in order "to counteract that daring spirit of insubordination, which threatens at once to subvert the Religion and Government of the country." Stephens bemoaned that "the ribaldries of Paine are openly set in opposition to the word of God" in what he called a "contest" between "anarchy and social order," and declared that "levelling schemes" were opposed to "all history, all facts, all reason," to "all the best interests of mankind" as well as to both God and the Bible. The poor had to be restrained from reading "infidel, seditious, and blasphemous" tracts, and taught "to be contented . . . in doing their duty in that state of life in which providence has placed them." They must be encouraged to turn to religious works—and the rich must set a "good example" in this matter—so that "the thoughts of another world shall be excited and kept alive in their minds." The poor had many advantages: their condition taught them industry, temperance, humility, gratitude and contentment; most important, poverty "predisposes" the poor "to feel their need of, to receive and value, the glorious Gospel," which "prepares for the true, the eternal riches!" The rich, Stephens continued, "derive many advantages from the continuance of the poor in the world": they gain "full scope for the exercise of *Condescension* and *Humility.*" If only "the poor be taken out of the hands of the disturbers of the public peace," then "respectable gentlemen" might again consider "the state of the *poor weavers.*" Stephens did remind middle-class Methodists that the "widest extremes of poverty and riches" though "permitted" were not "sanctioned by God." But he did not fail to note that it was commercial fluctuations and glut which caused "unprincipled and desperate manufacturers" to "beat down the workmen's wages"; of course, he observed, a lack of industry and of temperance on the part of the workmen produced similar consequences.[106]

John Stephens was relieved to report, in a letter to Jabez Bunting in 1821, that radicalism was no longer rampant in Manchester. The "poor people are getting better wages" and "provisions are cheap," Stephens wrote; "their leaders have deceived them in their promises of revolution," and "they are growing tired of radicalism." As radicalism "dies religion will revive," he reported. "Our congregations are good," and "Methodism stands high with respectable people." Stephens was especially delighted with the new chapel, which he regarded as "a reward for all I have suffered in Manchester." There was still trouble from the radicals in the Manchester societies, for, Stephens wrote, "we wish to be careful in rooting up the tares lest we should root up the wheat also." Nonetheless, he concluded, "they are down and I intend to keep them down." [107]

Clearly, in the troubled times of 1819, the Connection continued its effort to lead Methodists away from radicalism, indeed, away from all concern with political questions. But, this was not an easy task. John Stephens' and Thomas Jackson's account of Manchester in 1819–1821 have an authentic ring. They were relatively free of the party-cry boasting of how Methodism had dampened the flames of revolution, and presented, between the lines, not only a picture of the probable usefulness of Methodism to the cause of stability, but of the preachers' feelings of helplessness when the popular mood, possessing strength even within the Methodist societies, was that of "incipient rebellion." A similar insight into the efforts of Methodism to counter tumult may be seen in the 1824 Annual Address, written by Richard Watson, which observed that because of their itinerancy, Methodist preachers were "never so connected with any individual society as to become the organs of those changes and innovations which, in particular places, might be often advocated." [108] This, too, was a recognition of real difficulties—the danger that Methodist itinerants might be "radicalized" by their flocks—and far from the usual Methodist self-praise. Methodism, in the decades after Waterloo, still anxious about charges associating the Connection with revolution, was undeniably strongest in those districts where the possibility of revolution seemed most real. A distrustful Sidmouth remained one of the chief spirits behind the government's efforts to repress political dissent, and the Methodist fear of repression hovered just beneath the surface. [109]

Methodists continued to take great care to avoid suspicion. A Methodist pamphlet of 1821 denounced perverters of the poor such as Cobbett, Paine, and Carlisle, vaunted patriotism in opposition to liberal cosmopolitanism, and declared the phrase "the liberties and rights of the people," to be "the cant word, or rather the watch-word of treason and rebellion." While "thousands are poor through their own idleness, profligacy, and drunkenness," the pious poor had "every reason to submit, with the most entire resignation, to that lot which their heavenly Father and benefactor has appointed them." [110] At times Methodist efforts to ward off suspicion seem ludicrous, as when Richard Watson, in reviewing a political tract by the Methodist minister David McNicoll, published in 1820, the tenor of which he found "moderate and safe," expressed concern at McNicoll's even discussing "the delicate subject of resistance to Governments in extreme cases," since in such a free country as England, the idea of revolution was "at the farthest possible remove." [111] When, in 1822, Thomas Jackson's biography of the seventeenth-century Puritan advocate of universal salvation and liberty of conscience John Goodwin appeared, Jackson reported that the *Methodist Magazine* was wary of praising a book by a Methodist minister which eulogized a defender of regicide, though Jackson did manage to clear Goodwin of the charge that he had been a Fifth Monarchy man.[112]

In 1822, Adam Clarke, one of the great men of the Connection, published a volume which once again set forth the traditional Wesleyan view of politics. Clarke, a scholar who performed useful service for the Public Records Commission, was a Whig: an advocate of peace during the wars with France and sympathetic to the idea of parliamentary reform, he had come into repeated conflicts with such Tories as Jabez Bunting, and he had even supported the Whigs and Queen Caroline in 1820 while Bunting, Richard Watson, and other Tories stood by the King.[113] Yet no less than Wesley did Clarke insist that "God is the very Fountain of *magistracy* or *dominion,*" while the King, especially the British King to whom God gave special support, was "the viceroy, lieutenant, or deputy, of God." The British constitution was "the object of God's most peculiar care" because "it is most like his own administration"; "God alone can overthrow it," but "He will not destroy the work of His own hands." "Democracy *aims well,*" an Arminian Clarke might concede, but it was "*violent, indecisive, and fickle.*" As a good Wesleyan, Clarke could only proclaim that if the king ruled "according to the Constitution, nothing can justify rebellion against his authority." While as a Whig, Clarke might have no doubt that "*rebellion and tyranny* are equal abominations," as a Wesleyan, he insisted that "he who does anything to alienate the people's minds from their loyalty to their King, and attachment to the constitution, is worse than a public incendiary." "*Rebellion* is no cure for public evils," and "a *revolution* in a *free state* will in all probability make it *worse.*" Clarke concluded by citing Prov. xxiv.21, which enjoined "My son, fear thou the Lord, and the king; and meddle not with them that are given to change." [114]

This continued to be the mood of the Methodist leadership in the decades ahead. In 1820, the Connection had experienced a decline in its membership, a fact the Annual Address attributed to the fact that "commercial embarrassment, and consequent distress, have largely prevailed, and especially in those districts where usually we have had the greatest success in 'turning many to righteousness,' " and that, as a result, "political agitations have spread through the land." [115] But by 1822, the Annual Address could give thanks that "the days of tumult are passed away," and that "our people so generally evinced, in times of disorder, loyalty to our Sovereign, and attachment to his Government." [116] The thirties brought new troubles, and we find the Annual Address in 1831 again urging members not to let "worldly politics engross too much of your time and attention." [117] Indeed, the Connection's obsession against meddling in politics, led it, in 1832, the year of the Great Reform Act, to ask those Methodists who now possessed the vote whether they could "with perfect security to your religious character, and your peace of heart, become the ardent agents" of any political party.[118] The Address of 1833 once more warned Methodists not to listen "with too warm an interest" to political debate. "In those times of conflict among certain classes of the community," it continued, "keep at the utmost distance from all associations which are subversive of the principles of true and proper liberty, employing unlawful oaths, and threats, and force . . . to accomplish purposes which would tend to destroy the very frame-work of civil society." [119] The Conferences of 1834 urged Methodists to "aim at possessing and manifesting the ornament of a meek and quiet spirit" [120]—and that of 1836 [121] repeated this advice.

The years after Waterloo heard echoes of old controversies, but there was a new mood. Of course, extreme Calvinist writers still attacked Arminianism, and Methodists denounced the Genevan demons; [122] the tracts belonging to the fierce Calvinist controversies of the 1770s were even at times reprinted and circulated,[123] and, inevitably, Methodists and Calvinists continued to accuse each other of Antinomianism.[124] Yet, as we have already observed, a "vital," practical Christianity had triumphed. Church of England clergymen and laymen, no doubt, still saw Methodists and Evangelicals as subversive to both Church and state,[125] and Methodists continued to defend themselves with protestations of loyalty,[126] for conscience sake and by citing the passage of the legislation of 1812 as virtually unanswerable proof; [127] but now only cranks among the Anglicans continued to make such charges, and the Methodist defenses were a routinized, almost mechanical reaction, touched with more confidence and less concern. One rabidly anti-Methodist Cornish clergyman who as late as 1820 had urged that Methodism as the "importer of sedition" from the North, and "the vender of treason," be actively combatted—observing that "we owe the preservation of 'liberty and law' to the vigilance and spirit of anti-jacobinism" [128]—was to find himself in 1833 suggesting the possibility of "a coalition" of Arminian Methodists and Anglicans.[129]

Methodism was becoming respectable. Older Methodists looked back with some regret to the time when Methodists had constituted a persecuted sect of the rootless poor, when, in the words of one veteran, "under the pretended dread of an 'imperium in imperio,' they were viewed with a suspicious eye." [130] Another also recollected the time when Methodists "generally, were considered outlaws," "vile and contemptible," and were denounced by government as "stirrers up of sedition." Now, Methodists stood "acquitted from every charge of that nature," and "as a body, they seldom meddle with politics, except to show their disapprobation of radicalism, and their attachment to the king and Constitution." Indeed, he concluded, "now, in 1823, it [Methodism] has become so fashionable." [131] Of course, this new respectability had transformed the character of the denomination. Our first veteran observed that Methodists no longer wore plain dress, and that the poor who were accustomed in past years "presumptuously to mingle with the rich, are now placed in two rows of benches at a respectful distance, in some *airy* situation, where they may hear distinctly the flapping of the doors, and the noise of lobby loungers, and see their superiors ushered from their chariots to their elegant pews by the courtly stewards and chamberlains." [132] Class divisions—already apparent in the 1790s—were sharpening. Many in the Connection, especially among the leadership, accepted the new respectability as a fitting culmination to their lives' work. Others yearned for the days of the traditional Enthusiasm, even as they sought to free themselves from the control of the Legal Hundred, less rigid perhaps than in the nineties, but still providing firm lines of authority. The same resentment of autocratic rule, we have seen, which had led to the founding of the New Connection in 1797, and was to propel the rise of the Primitive Methodists and of William O'Bryan's Bible Christian Methodists in 1811 and 1815, provoked similar breakaways in the following decades.

By the mid-1820s, Methodism felt that its own house was once again in order and resumed boasting of its services to national stability in what had become a tedious party-cry. In a rebuttal to critical remarks about the Connection made in a book by Lord John Russell, for example, Humphrey Sandwith, writing in 1830, reminded Russell of the time when the Conference had secured "the *loyalty* of our members in the manufacturing districts, when Radicalism was at its height, only eleven years ago." [133] Another Methodist, William Vevers, writing in 1831, noted that the rick-burning in the South of England of the previous year had left the North "reposing in domestic security" despite the laboring classes of the North being "in a state of greater destitution," and suggested that "the prevalence of Methodism in Yorkshire, and the want of Methodism in Sussex" was "quite sufficient to account for the immense difference in the intelligence, morality, and religious principles, of the operative classes in the two counties." [134] The same arguments were repeated in the late thirties, at a time of Chartist agitation. Simeon Woodhouse, for example, also attributed the incendiarism in Sussex, Kent, and Hampshire to the circumstance that they were "counties where Methodism is the least prevalent." "During periods of political agitation, commercial distress, and 'privy conspiracy,'" Woodhouse concluded, "Methodism has been of essential service to the nation." [135] In 1839, during the Chartist troubles, Edmund Grindrod, one of the leaders of the Connection, also observed that at those times when there had been "many in the middle and lower orders" with whom Methodists were associated, "moving in the same circles, pursuing the same callings, and having a common public interest," who had "joined the ranks of disaffection," Methodists had loyally "retired far from these scenes of strife and disorder," and had kept England from revolution.[136] When Revolution again came to Europe in 1848, the Rev. William Arthur, a Methodist missionary stationed in Paris who had witnessed the events there, similarly had no doubt but that England's social peace was due to the "remarkable spread of Christian light and principle during the last century." [137] By that time, having been repeated so often, the view appeared wearisomely indisputable.

In the generation following Wesley's death, Methodist leaders were, as we have seen, determined that the call to order (the effort to prevent the political translation of spiritual egalitarianism) would triumph over the revolutionary stimulus of evangelizing itinerants as well as the radical implications of Arminian doctrine. This determination had, more or less, as noted, silenced most critics of the Connection in both state and Church who had so long decried—with good reason—the radical potentialities of Methodism. Yet the leaders of the Connection could not be fully confident that Methodist radicalism was entirely defeated. Indeed, the revolutionary pressures on working-class Methodists, on the one hand, and the rise to middle-class status of a good portion of Methodists, on the other, made for an increasing uncertainty of vocation on the part of the Connection. Certainly, as suggested earlier, there were great dangers in continuing to press for the evangelization and conversion of the nation. But there was enough Arminian Enthusiasm in Methodist ranks to present another kind of problem for the leadership. Though Methodists had preached the need for the believer to be absorbed not by this but by another world, it was a sect whose vocation was very much in this world, and which had mobilized enormous energies for the dissemination of Evangelical Arminianism. An absorption with heaven might not long prove practicable. In the years after 1812 the Connection leadership seized the opportunity of a new means of fulfilling the evangelical vocation of Arminianism, with the minimum possibility of stirring dissension.

The answer to all these problems seemed to lie in turning Methodism to the cause of the missions. The Methodist Revolution would be directed at objectives over the seas, just as Napoleon had directed the forces of the French Revolution beyond the frontiers of that nation. In a letter in 1795, in which he denounced Kilham and Radicalism, John Pawson, one of the leaders of the Legal Hundred, had noted the founding of the London Missionary Society by the Dissenters—observing that "all those have lighted their [cand]le at the Methodist lamp"—and warned that the Dissenters might yet "rob us our glory," and "out do us in zeal and activity." Would it not be better for Methodism to take up this lamp and cease their intestine squabbling? Certainly, "ever since the death of our venerable Father," Pawson concluded, "our great adversary has found us one thing or other to contend about!" [138] The leaders of Methodism after Wesley's death, floundering and confused in purpose, seeing the Connection divided between the rich and the poor, and hoping to separate the Methodist poor from the forces threatening social revolution, sought to turn Methodism to the grand purpose, in John Stephens' words, of "sounding forth to distant climes" the "Gospel of our salvation." [139] In this way the doctrines of Evangelical Arminianism, and the evangelistic Enthusiasm of the converted might continue to be fulfilled with safety, even while Methodism, in pursuit of respectability, contributed to the national mission.

VI

"Practical Arminianism" and England's World-Mission

What think you of our new set of Fanatics called the Methodists? I have seen White-field's Journal, and he appears to me to be as mad as ever George Fox the Quaker was. These are very fit Missionaries, you will say, to propagate the Christian Faith among Infidels. There is another of them, one Wesley who came over from the same [Georgia] Mission. He told a friend of mine . . . that he will return thither, and then cast off his English dress, and wear a dried skin like the savages, the better to ingratiate himself with them. It would be well for Virtue and Religion, if this humor would lay hold generally of our overheated bigots, and send them to cool themselves in the Indian marshes.

Bishop Warburton

Let the rich and the poor come forward in this great and important work; the pence of the multitude of the pious poor, will produce funds to carry on the greatest designs. God will sanctify what you give, and put his especial blessing on what remains, and you will have the consolation to reflect that you have contributed your part, through these your proxies, to publish the Gospel of Christ to Nations whom you can never see; and to tribes, of whose names you have never heard. Your support of the Gospel has been hitherto, in a great measure, confined to yourselves:—by coming heartily forward in this glorious missionary work, you will now especially benefit others; and thus give proof of your obedience to the command of Christ, ye shall love your neighbour as yourselves.

Adam Clarke, 1815

In *Adam Bede,* George Eliot described the coming of the revival in 1799 to the rural village of Hayslope. By the nineties, in the midst of the wars with a revolutionary France, we have observed that Methodism had commenced a serious invasion of villages like Hayslope, and that this had brought a renewal of the hostility of the Established Church. But these efforts were not to prove very successful. Methodism, I have suggested, had expanded beyond its powers to absorb and discipline those attracted to its message. Wesley had blamed Whitefield for having stirred up the Americans by his preaching and then having failed to make certain there would be no backsliding. Now, Wesleyanism saw the danger that large sections of the people who had been stirred up by the rash of itinerant evangelists in the

1790s and 1800s to desert the Church might "backslide" into radicalism and revolution. Anxious to establish its respectability, fearful of repression by a state determined to prevent revolution, what was Methodism to do? Methodism, if it was to survive, had to maintain an evangelizing fervor, yet without descending to the camp meetings of a far-from-respectable Primitive Methodism, or seeming to threaten either state or Church either by excessive Enthusiasm or by a political translation of its Evangelical Arminianism.

The great conflict within Methodism was, in Hume's terms, that between Enthusiasm and Superstition, between sect and Church. Wesley had endeavored to counter the revolutionary implications of enthusiastic sectarianism by continuing to insist upon his adherence to the Church of England, its liturgy and its doctrine. But if the exigencies of the movement made separation almost inescapable, when it came, Methodism had virtually become, in Halévy's phrase, the "High Church of Non-conformity." Yet the popular character of the Methodist movement, the need to insure its growth and to maintain his leadership over it, had brought Wesley to identify the Connection more and more fully with what I have called Remonstrance Arminianism, with its emphasis upon spiritual egalitarianism. Wesley even stood ready to borrow—on the issues of slavery, and civil and religious liberties, we recall—the idea of natural rights espoused by Arminius' disciple Hugo Grotius and his many English successors. Given Wesley's obsessive concern with revolution, would this not prove a dangerous proceeding? How could Wesley's successors find the means of restraining the egalitarian Enthusiasm of this sectarian Arminianism, so much at the heart of the Methodist Revolution, at a time of social malaise, before it flowed beyond the bounds of order and invited repression?

Half a century later, the difficulties had apparently been resolved. When it seemed as if Arminian Enthusiasm might become a threat to order, its force was diverted to foreign missions, and the character of Methodism was transformed. As George Eliot was to observe, Methodism would come to mean to many Englishmen "sleek grocers, sponging preachers, and hypocritical jargon"; while the "old fashioned" Methodist "believed in present miracles, in instantaneous conversions, in revelations by dreams and visions," the "modern type" Methodist "reads quarterly reviews and attends in chapels with pillared porticoes." [1] Other commentators—Charles Dickens and Thomas Carlyle, for example—depicted the Methodism of the mid-nineteenth century less charitably, and, indeed, denounced all the evangelical Protestants who had joined in philanthropic enterprises collectively known as "Exeter Hall," the edifice off the Strand, in London, where many of these enterprises were housed. According to its critics, Exeter Hall was the cant of religious hypocrisy made flesh: while neglecting the plight of England's poor, evangelical philanthropy stirred up the country concerning the wretchedness, spiritual and temporal, of England's colored wards across the seas. In an article written in 1848, Dickens, denouncing such false priorities, proclaimed that "it might be laid down as a very good general rule of social and political guidance that whatever Exeter Hall champions, is the thing by no means to be done." [2] What had happened was that the leaders of the Connection had turned Arminian idealism from the succoring of the poor to the furthering of the world-mission of the English middle classes.

PRACTICAL ARMINIANISM

The first English Protestant missions of any consequence had been those of the English Moravians, in imitation of their German parent branch. The Moravians, like their offspring the Wesleyans, were opponents of election, and as James Hutton, an early associate of John Wesley and one of the founders of English Moravianism, wrote in 1769, the Moravian "zeal for the conversion of the Heathen" had its origin in the Moravian belief "that our Saviour had died for the whole world, and would have all men to be saved by the knowledge of the truth, which he had ordered to be preached to all nations." In appealing for funds for missionary endeavors, the Moravians urged that conversion changed the "hearts and whole life" of the pagan, and that "true faith cannot but produce good works and a proper behaviour." Christianity, Hutton noted in 1769, made "the Negroes in particular very faithful to their masters." [3] But while the Moravian belief in the equality of souls made them opponents of slavery, the Moravians had sought to avoid political disputation, and urged the Brethren to be subject to the higher powers. Consequently, Moravian missionaries were instructed to teach "those heathen who are under the yoke of slavery, as the negroes in the West Indies," to be "obedient to their masters, for it is not a matter of chance, but of God, that they are come into that state." [4] Nor must the missionary permit the slave "to imagine, that after his conversion, he should no more be treated severely by his master." [5] Porteus, the Evangelical Bishop of London, whose diocesan duties included "the Ecclesiastical superintendence" of the British West Indies, found himself likewise urging, in this approved style of what may be called a "practical Arminianism" and the cautious political program of the Moravians, the conversion of the Negro slaves.[6] The early Methodist missions, of necessity, followed the same program.

The first Church of England missionary to go to Africa, in 1792, at least in part under Methodist auspices since he had been recommended for the post by Thomas Coke, who supervised the Connection's missions, was Melville Horne. Horne, who we recall had been close to Methodism and to both Coke and Fletcher, was born in 1761, the son of a West Indian planter. He felt a strong missionary vocation, and wished nothing more than to spend the rest of his life converting the heathen in Sierra Leone. To his enormous disappointment, he proved unable to bear the climate and returned to England in 1793, determined to preach the missions.[7] He had endeavored "to do in India, China, or the Southern Islands, what the late venerable John Wesley and others connected with him have done in this country," he wrote in 1794, in his reflections on missions, and, by so doing, permit "our pigmy generation" to "grow up to the stature of primitive Christians." Horne urged that "liberal Churchmen and conscientious Dissenters, pious Calvinists and pious Arminians, embrace with fraternal arms," let previous doctrinal controversies be forgotten, "build our religion on facts and not on arguments," and as missionaries, teach neither Calvinism nor Arminianism, but Christianity. Methodism had a decisive role to play in Horne's plan. Moravian zeal was "calm, steady, persevering"; the Moravian "would reform the world, but is careful how he quarrels with it." In contrast, "the zeal of the Methodist blazes"; "he is open, active, bold, and ardent"; "he sees himself in a pushing world, and pushes with the foremost"; the Methodist "lives in action," and "is dejected and uncomfortable, if he wants active employment." "A Methodist preacher would think his life thrown away," Horne concluded, "in spending twenty or thirty years upon a few converts," and "the Methodists are too well acquainted with themselves, to engage in such undertakings, while so many large and populous Kingdoms are accessible to their labours." If the Methodists "do not split themselves," Horne was ready to predict that "there is hardly anything in the missionary line, which they may not attempt and succeed in."

To the objection that there were heathens enough in England, Horne observed that "foreign missions will have the same influence on religion, as foreign commerce has upon agriculture and manufactures," and "as Christianity prevails abroad, so it will flourish at home." It was necessary to "obtain for Christianity a firm footing, and extensive spread" in the heathen world; "a few scattered missionaries, and paltry funds" would prove "inadequate," for "such conquests." "Men and money are the nerves of war," and to obtain these and the protection of government, the missionaries must demonstrate that they and their converts were "the most peaceable, loyal, and affectionate of subjects, and this not from policy, but for conscience sake." [8] Methodism, clearly, was particularly well suited for this role.[9] Horne's terms—e.g., "to obtain for Christianity a firm footing, and extensive spread"—repeated, almost precisely, those used by contemporary British manufacturers who wished to secure foreign markets for their product. Nor were Horne's explicit comparisons of missionary activities to foreign commerce ever entirely absent from the minds of the advocates of Methodist overseas evangelization. Horne saw practical Arminianism, a religion built "on facts, and not on arguments," as attractive for a mass mission market. Just as foreign commerce had stimulated the prosperity of the manufacturer or agriculturist at home, Horne argued, so would foreign missions stimulate the piety of Christians at home. This was a time, moreover, when British Methodists, like British manufacturers, not infrequently Methodists themselves, found the home market risky. The evangelistic energies of Methodism, "active, bold, and ardent," were invading markets where a competing firm, the Church, had long enjoyed a monopolistic position, and the Church, deeply disturbed, had petitioned the national legislature for protection. Yet, "a Methodist preacher would think his life thrown away," as Horne had observed, "in spending twenty or thirty years upon a few converts"; a Methodist "is dejected and uncomfortable, if he wants active employment." Just as manufacturers were turning to foreign markets, seemingly infinite in extent, might not Methodism do the same, joining the Church with which it was forced to compete at home but with whom it might cooperate in marketing Christianity abroad? Evangelistic energies had to be properly directed if difficulties were to be averted.

Both Bradburn and Kilham were Arminian Whigs with an egalitarian bias, yet, as we have seen, they represented different policies. Kilham had been expelled because he had translated Arminian spiritual equality too rigorously into political terms, in his demand that the Connection be transformed into a working democracy with the unexpressed threat of the extension of such democratic demands to society as a whole. Bradburn's Arminianism, on the other hand, concerned itself with spiritual equality and the dim possibility of a temporal equality far in a millennial future. There were but two political causes which Bradburn regarded as essential to Methodists, if they were not to invoke divine displeasure: first, freedom of religious conscience, and secondly, a cause which "our very existence as a people compels us to defend," was the extirpation of the slave trade. Bradburn, following Wesley, urged Remonstrance political idealism toward an objective where it might satisfy the egalitarian promise of Methodism without threatening the stability of the state, the Church, or the Connection, toward harnessing the egalitarian and libertarian ideals of Arminianism to the goals not only of defending religious toleration, but also of ending the slave trade and slavery, and at the same time of bringing the good news of salvation to the slaves and to all the heathen world. There was a close connection between the abolition of the slave trade and the success of missionary activity, for, as Bradburn observed, "the *slave trade* is the *chief,* perhaps the *sole obstacle* to our ministers' spreading it [the gospel] in Africa."

The overflow of Arminian Enthusiasm, contained at home by the desire to avoid social disturbance, poured out in a root-and-branch opposition to the slave trade, and, not too far beneath the surface, to slavery as an institution, and this, more and more, as a necessary preliminary to the conversion of the heathen. The need to abolish the slave trade and slavery was not "an *opinion,* or *a point of private judgement,*" but "*a case* of conscience," Bradburn maintained in fervent tones. (Unlike Wesley, who, in his essay on slavery, had declined to discuss the implicit scriptural justification for the institution, Bradburn argued that the "Jewish dispensation" could not be claimed except by Jews, and that in any event "the gospel has entirely abolished all national distinctions, and annulled for ever any right in one man to enslave another.") Following Wesley's example, all Methodist ministers supported the abolition of the slave trade, despite the view that Methodists ought not to meddle in politics. A Whiggish Bradburn might even remonstrate that the Negroes in the British dominions were "our *fellow subjects,*" and asked whether Methodists had "ceased to be a part of the people of England, because you wish to secure the salvation of your souls in a coming world?" There was a "moral obligation," he observed, proceeding onto dangerous waters, to obey only laws "designed upon the whole, to promote the *good of the governed.*" Bradburn insisted even more strongly than had Wesley that the slave trade was "a complete System of Robbery and Murder," that slavery was "unconstitutional," and "an utter disgrace to any nation of people, *said to be free.*" Arminian Methodists had special reasons to "believe that 'God hath made of *one blood all* nations of men,' " Bradburn declared. "Our society and constant hearers" were numbered at some 400,000 in England alone by Bradburn; would it not be possible for so substantial a number of Methodists, he asked, to work, by petition and by foregoing the use of sugar and rum, to end the slave trade, and thus to prepare the way for the evangelization of the entire world? [10]

Arminianism in its Wesleyan form thus turned its evangelistic energies to the conversion of the hundreds of millions in the West Indies, in Africa, and in Asia, an enterprise in which the Connection might join the Church as a colleague rather than a rival, and advance the interest of the nation as a whole. The way had already been prepared for by the special character of Wesley's Evangelical Arminianism. Wesleyanism, we have seen, in accepting what appeared to be "Calvinistic" doctrines of human depravity in a "practical" Christianity which enveloped both Methodism and Church Evangelicalism, rejoiced to see Calvinist Evangelicals similarly yielding to a "practical" Arminianism, with an increasing emphasis upon good works and a new stress upon the view that salvation was offered to all who would strive to attain it. The ideological battle between Calvinist and Arminian had ground to a halt. When there was a brief encounter, as in 1814–1815, it was clear that there was nothing essential left in the controversy.

This latter skirmish, between Thomas Jackson, whom we have already met, and John Cockin, a Calvinist Dissenter, concerned the usefulness of their respective creeds to the new interest in the missions. The Arminian

Jackson urged that without Wesleyan Arminianism there would have been no Revival in England, and no missionizing among the heathen: [11] "It is well known," he declared, that a "Methodist Missionary believes in his heart that 'such a salvation as it becomes God to give, and man to receive, is within the grasp of every human soul' "; "the advantage of this conviction to a 'Missionary,' " Jackson continued, "must be obvious." [12] The following year, Cockin denied that Calvinism was any less useful in the Mission field: "We [Calvinists] make the decree of election as extensive as actual salvation," he declared, and "therefore in our plan the multitude of the redeemed is as great as in yours, but our peculiarity is to ascribe their final happiness to discriminatory mercy and special grace," which Cockin described as eminently "Calvinistic doctrine." [13] W. Hutton, one of the Connection's spokesmen on overseas evangelization, accused Cockin of attempting "to revive old disputes," but was ready to conclude that "the *heart is better than the head"* and many who "verbally maintain your doctrines" nonetheless "preach and write as though Christ died for all": "I am happy in giving it as my opinion, that there are but few Calvinist ministers who are not nearer Arminius than Calvin in their general discourses," Hutton declared; "when a man, even of your persuasion is inspired with a *true* Missionary spirit, that moment his *particulars* became *generals,* and he at once flies, with open arms, to evangelize the world." [14] Jackson rushed to agree with Hutton. [15]

THE ANNI MIRABILES OF THE MISSIONS
(1813—1815)

During the last two decades of the eighteenth and the early years of the nineteenth centuries, Methodists, in imitation of the Moravians, did what they could to set up missions abroad. Thomas Coke, who had been Wesley's right hand after Fletcher's death, had set off in the eighties on missions to the New World, particularly to the West Indies. Upon his death, in 1813, he was described by one Methodist missionary as the "Apostle to the Africans," and "the most indefatigable Missionary that this or any former age has produced." [16] Certainly the mission field was the primary focus of Coke's interest, and the minutes of the Methodist conferences are filled with his pleas to congregations to collect money for missionary work wherever "practicable," and to preachers to volunteer to be missionaries. [17] At times it seemed advisable to make "private collections" for the missions with the help of local preachers, especially in cases where, because of the poverty of the congregation, a public collection might prove offensive.[18] Not unimpressive amounts were collected in this haphazard fashion for missions, mostly in the British West Indies.[19]

Resentment concerning the collection of money from poor Methodists for use in the mission field was inevitable but apparently not widespread. A member of one Methodist society who called himself "Thomas Attentive" wrote abusively, in 1788, of Coke—though without actually naming him—as one who "schemed for the superintendency of the western world," and aimed at being "a second Count Z_____ to reign over you." Thomas Attentive grandiloquently described Coke's imperial design:

> And what shall we say of the law which he got passed this year [1788] to make extra collections every quarter to raise supplies for his *Don Quixote* schemes, where the poor people are not able to supply their own ministers with food and raiment? Is this not grinding the face of the poor, with a witness: yea, sucking the very blood out of their veins? But missionaries must be sent from hence, at any rate, or at any expense to the West Indies, to secure the government thereof to himself. . . . the brain indeed of this political genius is fertile in producing new plans. . . . seeing that nothing else will satisfy it, but to become Hierarch from sea to sea.[20]

Coke's private collections for the missions continued to grow, and more missions were established in the West Indies and even in Africa.

In 1813–1815, the Methodist Connection was to determine to devote a very substantial portion of its energies and its monies to foreign missions. Since the plan for financing the missionary effort which was adopted at that time seemed deliberately designed, or so it might be argued, in Thomas Attentive's phrase of twenty-five years earlier, "to grind the faces of the poor," one may well ask why it was that at this time of distress because of wartime conditions, a time, further, when the Connection was hard pressed by its enemies, such a crusade was undertaken. Of course, we have suggested that these seeming obstacles were among the principal reasons that the turn to the missions was undertaken, and such a reading of Methodist history is confirmed by the words and events surrounding the reorganization of mission activities in 1813, 1814, and 1815. In this, we must take count of the spur of Arminian idealism, and the impetus given by the final repeal of the slave trade (to a substantial extent accomplished through the good work of the Methodists and Evangelicals in 1807). Nor can we fail to stress, as Joseph Sutcliffe observed in 1798, that "in England, for some years past, the minds of Christians have been unusually enlarged with a desire for the conversion of the heathen," an event regarded as "a happy token, that our blessed Lord is about to accomplish a glorious work in the earth." [21]

In 1813, a good part of England seemed obsessed by a frenzy for foreign missions. The Methodist mission fever which was to strike at Leeds in the latter part of 1813 can of course be explained as the culmination of the tendency of long-existing forces within the Connection, but such a great departure on the part of so large and influential a denomination cannot be fully understood in terms of Connectional politics alone. Not only Methodism but the Dissenters and the Evangelicals of the Church of England as well were all to mount successful campaigns to raise funds for overseas evangelization during the years 1813, 1814, and 1815. The times certainly gave rise to millenarianism, and the permission granted in 1813, in the new charter of the East India Company, for Christians to evangelize in the Company's domains (a victory for the Evangelicals against the better judgment of the Company) gave an opportunity to speed the blessed event.

The London Missionary Society was founded in 1794 as part of a non-denominational effort—though its auspices were those of the older Dissent —to unite the missionary efforts of all evangelical groups. In 1799, in part inspired by the activities of the L.M.S. and spurred by Venn, Simeon, and Grant, the Eclectic Society, founded by Evangelical clergymen in 1783, launched the Church Missionary Society to bring the Gospel to the heathen world.[22] The prelates and clergy of the Church, even those generally friendly to the Evangelical cause, however, were not stirred by the call of the C.M.S., not quite accepting the view of its first secretary, the Rev. Thomas Scott, who, in 1801, urging that England "declare offensive war against the kingdom of the devil," declared that "a soul in China, or Africa is of as much value, as one in our own families or congregations," and "its salvation as important"; nor did they credit his opinion that "well conducted and successful plans for evangelizing the heathen, would prove the most powerful means of more fully evangelizing Britain." [23] The interests of Anglicanism were more parochial. The Church was not moved when, in 1805, the Rev. John Venn urged a missionary offensive on the grounds that Christianity "tends more speedily and effectually to civilize a country, than any other means of civilization," [24] nor when the Rev. Basil Woodd, in 1807, told them that when they sent missionaries to preach to the heathen, "you imitate God." [25] In 1811, the Rev. Melville Horne, a pioneer of the missionary cause, hoping that Anglicanism would respond more generously to his pleas than had Methodism, was, in a sermon to an Anniversary Meeting of the C.M.S., to anticipate the call to the missions which was to become widespread in 1813. "At this hour, religion, PROTESTANT RELIGION," Horne declared, "is the bulwark, shield, sword, and glory of Britain; and if Providence has placed under her dominion the provinces of the distant East it is . . . that we may impart to them the blessed religion of Jesus." "The trumpet of the Millennial Jubilee is, at last, heard," Horne concluded, and "serious Christians of all denominations are espousing the cause of Missions, and anxious to *prepare the way of the Lord*." [26]

In 1813, an *annus mirabilis* for the missionary movement, the imagination of large numbers of Englishmen was seized by the missionary impulse. Prelates who had previously been shy of the C.M.S. quite suddenly embraced it; leading evangelical clergymen were sent by the C.M.S. to visit cities and market towns all over the kingdom to preach missionary sermons and to address missionary meetings, and they were enthusiastically received.[27] While Evangelical laymen had played an important role in the nation's politics, witness the abolition of the slave trade in 1807, they had made comparatively little headway among the bulk of the clergy. In 1813, clergymen known to be hostile to the Evangelicals as no less subversive than Methodists, made their pulpits available to Evangelical clerics for the preaching of missionary sermons. These sermons, we are told, filled those who heard them with an evangelical fervor,[28] and during 1813 and 1814, the C.M.S. formed dozens of local societies, even penny societies, to raise money for the missions, in imitation of the methods of the London Missionary Society. (After the founding of the C.M.S., the L.M.S. became more clearly nonconformist and Calvinist in orientation; it was probably the most successful of the missionary societies before 1813.) Methodists at Leeds who were to form the first Methodist Missionary Society in the fall of 1813, could not help but be stimulated by the vigorous efforts of the Evangelicals, and were immediately spurred by a "West Riding Missionary Society" begun in Leeds in the summer of 1813 under the auspices of the Congregationalists, as a local branch of the L.M.S. This local society, from its initiation, had even succeeded in winning impressive contributions from well-to-do Leeds Methodists.[29]

How can we account for this new missionary temper of the nation? In the early months of 1812, England seemed caught in a mood of profound dejection: Napoleon, widely regarded as the Anti-Christ, had extended his empire into Russia, and had the continent at his feet; Luddite rioters, provoked by keen economic distress, were terrifying the North. The *Gentleman's Magazine* in July 1812 bemoaned the triumphs of "that Individual, who, by the mysterious dispensations of Providence, has, for so long a period, been permitted to erect his conquering throne upon the misery and anguish of the Nations of the Earth." [30] By the end of 1812, however, it had become clear that Napoleon had been dealt a fatal blow in Russia. "A Star has at length appeared from the North," that journal now observed; "surely now, the elasticity of the human heart will be restored to its due confidence in the gracious dispensations of Providence".[31] In June 1813, the monthly lyrically proclaimed that "the British Eagle once more towers aloft above its foes," [32] and in December it congratulated Englishmen upon "a succession of Victories the most important, the most splendid, the most glorious that are found in the pages of History." "Once more the auspicious wings of favouring winds waft our deeply-laden Barks to every quarter of the Universe." [33] Of the year 1813, a more sober observer, the *Annual Register,* proclaimed "the commencement of a new era in the political system of Europe"; at home, moreover, there was "a remarkable state of tranquility" owing to the "spirited measures taken for suppressing the disturbances," and improved trade and harvest prospects. "That the wheel of fortune should revolve with so much rapidity, who could hope or foresee?" [34] The *Gentleman's Magazine,* in the succeeding months, dramatically mounted paeans to British glory, and to the apocalyptic defeat of the Anti-Christ: "We candidly acknowledge ourselves to be so dazzled with the glorious splendour, which at the present moment envelopes the atmosphere of Britain, that it is not without difficulty we obtain the self-command, temperately to express our emotions of rapture and gratitude." [35] Six months later, with Napoleon at Elba, the magazine cherished "the exultation arising from the idea, that Babylon, the mighty Babylon is fallen." [36] In June 1815, it observed concerning the returned and the again defeated Napoleon that he was veritably "the Arch-daemon." [37] "How are thou fallen, Lucifer," [38] it proclaimed in December 1815, and in June 1816, it pictured "the Oppressor, fallen, fallen, fallen from his high estate, by the exertions, and of Peace restored under the auspices of Britain." [39]

The vision which moved the *Gentleman's Magazine,* a journal which spoke the sentiments of much of the public, was, undeniably, in its rhetoric at least, millennial. Surely the apocalyptic events of the preceding quarter of a century which had miraculously led to Waterloo had a supernatural significance. The magazine, in giving voice to the thoughts and feelings of many hundreds of thousands of Englishmen after the long travail, was relatively restrained. What it attempted to convey by implication was proclaimed explicitly by the Evangelicals—whose extravagances the *Gentleman's Magazine* had been accustomed to regard with suspicion. In an address before the Church Missionary Society, in 1813, for example, the Dean of Wells, who was about to become the Bishop of Gloucester, observed that "at the coming of the Saviour," a "peace of extraordinary unanimity and duration prevailed," and "seemed to usher, as it were, the Prince of Peace into his own World"; "and may not this period of extraordinary harmony and tranquility, now to all appearances approaching, prove the herald and preparation for another coming of the Messiah"—at least, the Dean added in a concession to a skeptical age, "in a figurative sense?" Did these events not herald "the awakening of the Gentile World"? "We acknowledge our national duties." "Native Britons" have at long last "accepted the call," to venture forth "from this island of ease" to conquer "the strongholds of sin and Satan." [40]

In the years ahead, there were many repetitions of these themes. In 1817, for example, the Reverend Daniel Wilson, a prominent member of the C.M.S., inquired why it was "that our whole Empire, at this moment, perhaps exceeds, both in extent and population, any one of the Four great Empires of the Antient World," and "that our national wealth and constitutional liberty, our wealth, our power, and our commerce, far surpass those of other people, antient or modern?" "Do not these circumstances," he demanded, "like the union of so many nations under the Roman Emperors at the first promulgation of Christianity, obviously point out the design of Providence?" [41] Five years later, in a sermon before the C.M.S., the Rev. J. W. Cunningham rejoiced that England, "a country possessing the Gospel in its purest form," preaching "a genuine Protestantism" and not "a spurious Christianity," would effect "the complete overthrow of the Kingdom of Satan," would vanquish "the Empire of Satan upon Earth." [42]

With the defeat of Napoleon, many of the pious of Great Britain saw one remaining imperial Adversary—the Devil himself—and sensing the approach of the last days, enlisted the power, the pounds, and the prayers of England to hasten the second coming. This was the mood clearly apparent in the *Gentleman's Magazine*, secularized and subdued in the *Annual Register*'s "new aera," and made into a battle sermon for Christ's soldiers by Evangelical clergymen. This was the mood which saw, in 1813, 1814, and 1815, the expansion of the work of the London Missionary Society and the Church Missionary Society, and which confirmed the dramatic shift in the energies of the Methodist Connection which was to characterize its principal role in the nineteenth century. In a letter to Hannah More in 1818, the Evangelical layman Zachary Macaulay rejoiced that "the duty of evangelising the heathen" had been "solemnly recognised by the highest authorities in the State," and that the work of the missions had "become national." [43] Indeed, it may be argued that the initial force of Wesley's Revival, begun in 1739, had diminished by 1813, and that Methodism, and the evangelicalism of the Church and the Dissenters so powerfully affected by Wesley's example, had turned to the new imperial mood which struck Britain in the last years of the wars with Napoleon, as the impetus for a new Revival, as the best means of making Englishmen think again of their own salvation, by linking evangelical religion to the national mission.

The decision to turn the expansive energies of Methodism to the foreign mission field must also be viewed in terms of the inner politics of the Connection, an intricate story which has not been systematically set forth. [44] Although the decision was the seemingly inevitable solution to the difficulties facing the Connection, the Connection had to be persuaded, and the men who were chiefly instrumental in this process—Jabez Bunting and Richard Watson—found themselves, as a result of their successful efforts to turn the Connection's evangelical gaze overseas, catapulted into leading positions. Bunting was to be the dominant figure in Methodism for four decades; Watson was to be acknowledged its leading doctrinal spokesman until his death in 1833. If these were circumstances surrounding a decision taken by a purely political party, we would be obliged, and quite properly, to describe what occurred as a *coup*.

The decision to turn to the missions might have been taken at any time after Wesley's death. What had helped to delay it was the jealous superintendence of the mission field by Thomas Coke. Coke, made a Bishop of American Methodism, no doubt thought of himself as Wesley's natural successor, and this made him suspect to many in the Connection. Coke was at his core an evangelist and an expansionist, and in the early years of the new century, when Methodism was finding itself the object of growing fears, Coke became the spokesman of those forces in Methodism which sought vigorous expansion, despite the warnings of those who advised caution. In 1810, Coke wrote optimistically: "Let us go on, and not regard any croakers, and God will be with us in spite of the Sidmouths and all our enemies, and we shall, I believe, have a leaven in every Village in England in twenty years." [45] Similarly, Coke earnestly believed in the foreign missions he supervised on behalf of the Connection: he had been active in America, in Wales, and in Ireland; in 1791, having improved his French, he undertook a French mission, taking advantage of the postrevolutionary religious freedom; again and again, he had urged the Methodists to match the Calvinists of the L.M.S. mission for mission in the West Indies. But such an expansionary policy met with great obstacles, primarily financial, for Methodists tended to think that charity ought to begin at home. In 1803, when Coke was out of the country, a missions committee of which Jabez Bunting was a member had been appointed to put Coke's accounts in order, for he was a poor administrator; on his return, Coke vented his quasi-episcopal irritation at this usurpation, and in the years ahead he resisted other efforts by the Connectional leadership to deal with the missions.

It is not unlikely, given the political pressures which bore down upon Methodism, that the solution of subordinating home evangelization to the missions which was seized upon in 1813–1815, had occurred to Bunting, and probably to others as well, some years earlier. But the jealous control of the Methodist mission field by Coke, with his great prestige, combined with Coke's simultaneous fervor in behalf of the home missions, made action difficult. In late 1812 and early 1813, an opportunity arose when Coke, no doubt weary of jealousies at home, still nourishing unfulfilled ambitions, and stimulated by the current mission fever, determined to head a mission to India. An ordained clergyman, he even made efforts to become the Anglican Bishop of India! Unsuccessful in this, he moved from circuit to circuit urging the leaders of Methodism to overcome their deep prejudices against overseas activities—he had had difficulties in obtaining Conference approval for foreign missions—and to lend their support to his imperial venture.[46] When Coke spoke to Jabez Bunting at Halifax in 1812, where Bunting was Superintendent, the latter had enthusiastically offered to join him, despite his obligations to his wife and three young children, but Coke, probably not much to Bunting's surprise given Coke's previous proprietary behavior, urged him rather to work at home in support of the missions.[47] At the Conference in August 1813, there was a vigorous debate as to whether the Connection ought to give financial support to Coke's mission. Many opposed Coke's plan, and Benson even declared such a mission "would be the ruin of Methodism." [48] Not only Benson but Henry Moore, who had also travelled with Wesley and enjoyed considerable prestige in the Connection, opposed the expense of the Asian journey. Even Bunting agreed that a plan for securing needed financial support had first to be discovered. Coke made a passionate, tearful plea in favor of his mission, and offered to provide much of the funds from his own money. The Conference could not, under the circumstances, deny its approval.

In 1813, Jabez Bunting, then only 34 years old, was stationed as an itinerant at Leeds, serving under the superintendency of George Morley; stationed nearby was Richard Watson. The three preachers addressed themselves to the problem of the missions and their support, in the spirit of the suggestion made by the London District meeting to the 1813 Conference that Circuit Committees be formed to raise money for the missions, a suggestion which the Conference had ignored. Bunting, although a young man, was already much respected within the Connection, and was clearly destined to take a leading part in its future. Watson, on the other hand, had had a chequered past and an ambiguous future. Born in 1781, the son of a Lincolnshire saddler, Watson had been received as a Wesleyan itinerant in 1800. Almost immediately afterwards, he had left the ministry to go into business, having decided to marry, but soon regretting his decision to leave the old Connection, he applied for reinstatement. This request having been denied, Watson joined the New Connection, which he served as an itinerant from 1804 until 1812. It was at Stockport in 1811, during the height of the agitation against Sidmouth's bill, that, by chance, Watson met Bunting, at that time helping to organize the opposition to the bill. Bunting found in the consumptive Watson, a man of considerable intellectual powers, a talented journalist, a kindred spirit, and a potential ally. They formed a close friendship, and Bunting urged Watson to apply again for readmission to the Old Connection. Watson's early sympathy for the system of government of the New Connection had by this time vanished—his biographer quoted him as having declared that while it was "a great evil to be Priest-ridden," it was "a still greater to be ridden by the people" [49]—and six months later, in early 1812, he applied for readmission, and because of the considerable efforts exerted by Bunting, he was, not without difficulty, once more accepted as an itinerant. In Leeds in 1813, Watson was able to offer his voice and pen to Bunting, with whose views he had clearly found himself in agreement at the time of their original meeting. The three—Bunting, Morley, the senior man, though he seemed to be guided by Bunting, and Watson—planned the organization of the Leeds Missionary Society as a model for the Connection.

Bunting's son and biographer thought only the special "urgency" of the situation might have justified these three, aided by half-a-dozen others, in attempting to organize such a movement without the specific authorization of the Conference. While granting that "there was a sense" in which all the leading organizers were first in conceiving the plan, T. P. Bunting knew that "my father organized the whole movement." "Each detail" of the Leeds meeting, Bunting's son was to report, "was carefully pre-arranged —as carefully as if the whole result had depended exclusively upon it." [50] Jabez Bunting's hand, indeed, was everywhere. He began to write friends about his plans before the Leeds meeting took place. On September 28, 1813, for example, in a letter to the Rev. Robert Smith, who had friends on the Missionary Committee in London, he urged upon Methodism the necessity of *"eclat* & publicity," and warned that "if we refuse the weekly help of the lower classes," then "the Dissenters will gladly accept it" and were "sure to profit by our scruples." He also asked Smith for information concerning the reaction of the men in London to his plans.[51] Two weeks later, on October 11, Bunting wrote Smith that "I hope & believe the hand of God is in the business." [52]

The founding meeting of the first Methodist Missionary Society, that of the Leeds District, was held in that city on October 13, 1813, with Thomas Thompson, M.P., a prominent Methodist layman, in the chair. William Dawson, of Barwick-in-Elmet, an early speaker, professed to see the origin of the overseas missionary movement in the great Revival undertaken by Wesley and Whitefield nearly three-quarters of a century earlier. The doctrines of Methodism, Dawson declared, "bind this duty upon us in an especial manner" since "we believe that in the Gospel is provided a *full, free,* and *present salvation* from all the moral evils consequent on the fall of Adam" and "that wherever the Gospel is faithfully preached, this salvation is within the reach of all." Since, Dawson further noted, the *"duties"* of the Gospel "are imposed upon *all,* its *benefits* are offered to *all,"* and "if we act consistently with our principles, we shall not be the least nor the hindmost in Missionary efforts"; and since, furthermore, we ourselves had been saved by Methodist Gospel Ministers, we could not "see our poor fellow creatures going blindfolded to ruin." This was to be the philanthropic spirit of the Conference, but the imperial note was not lacking. W. G. Scarth, of Leeds, with full pride in Britain's new position as a commercial emporium, saw "our happy isle, which, from the peculiarity of its situation, the extensive nature of its connexions, and the strength of its resources," as "well calculated to become the grand Missionary depot of the world." The Reverend John Braithwaite, of neighboring Huddersfield, asked whether Methodists "ought not" then "feel a holy emulation, stimulating us to the greatest exertions in the noble cause," since "many of our enterprising countrymen are encountering the greatest dificulties, and exploring distant climes, for the extension of a lucrative commerce"; "shall we feel less anxious to encourage and support these 'servants of the most high God,' who are willing to go to the ends of the earth, with a view 'to teach the way of salvation'?" John Wood, of Wakefield, declared that in Africa, in contrast to England, missionaries of other denominations were not "our rivals or opponents, they are our contemporaries and coadjutors," and concluded that "missionary exertions may be regarded as a system of warfare, in which Christianity is opposed to Paganism," and "like our countrymen" who were "engaged in a momentous conflict" with "the Tyrant of the Continent," so were Christians with "the Tyrant of the World."

What was being proposed at Leeds was a plan of weekly contributions, to be raised, even in pennies, among the societies, which, Scarth suggested, "affords to persons in the lower ranks of society an opportunity of uniting in this good work." The Reverend Thomas Vesey of Halifax declared that "many of the comparatively poor, by giving a small sum, weekly or monthly, are gratified with the opportunity of assisting in this benevolent design." "They believe," Vesey added, "and not on slender grounds, that God will more abundantly bless them in the labour of their hands." "Only let a man contribute though in small degree, to the Missionary cause," Scarth had argued, "and it will excite an interest in his mind which he would never have felt without such a contribution"; "only let him *regularly* contribute, and it will keep that interest alive in his mind." The Rev. Jabez Bunting made an appeal to "British and Christian Females" particularly to further the work of seeking contributions.

George Morley, as the Leeds Superintendent, took a leading role at the meeting. Morley noted that the Connection had been "absolutely terrified" at the thought of expanding the missions "on account of the exhausted state of the funds"; but, he added, revealing much, the 1813 Conference had "at last agreed to diminish the number of preachers at home, in order that we might be enabled, by our frugal savings, to maintain a greater number of missionaries in foreign countries." By such a shift, Morley continued, once more confirming the argument we have pursued, Methodists might continue to gather financial support from nonmembers who were ready to give money for their foreign missions but not for their home missions; moreover, it would better enable the Connection to garner the monies which the Dissenters had been collecting for foreign missions in Methodist chapels. The chairman, Thomas Thompson, concluded the meeting by a ringing proclamation of loyalty to the King, and a paean of rejoicing for the "repeal of the Conventicle Act" during the previous year, by which "the Methodists have been delivered" from "harassing perplexity." Jabez Bunting called for "the evangelization of the world," and described "the Methodist Missionary Ship" as "one, among others, of the Grand Fleet, by which it is intended to carry to the ends of the earth the blessings of the Gospel." Bunting then made a final motion that to the Rev. Richard Watson of Wakefield be entrusted the task of preparing an address which would incorporate the views of the Conference upon missions, observing that "no man is better qualified for the task." [53] Watson, who was to become one of the Secretaries to the Committee for the Management of the Wesleyan Methodist Missions, thus became, virtually from the start, the official spokesman on missions for the Connection.

In his address, Richard Watson observed that the influence of the Revival, already "felt through almost every part of the British empire," was perhaps only "now" acquiring its "full play." "England, the greatest Protestant state, was roused from its slumber," and "with the revived spirit of religion, compassion for the heathen, long neglected by Protestants, revived also." "Religious feeling gives rapid birth to action," he observed, and the conversion "of the distant colonies of the empire, was early attempted" by the Methodists, with "unparalleled" success. Watson noted that a recent parliamentary decision "has opened a more effectual door for the introduction of the Gospel among sixty millions of British subjects" in India, now "darkened and corrupted by the grossest Idolatry," and possessing "a double claim upon our regards, both as benighted Pagans and as British subjects." If it had pleased God "to moralize so great a portion of the community at home" through the instrument of Methodism, and if "this great work" of evangelization had "been effected without any counter-balance of evil, civil or religious," Watson was "emboldened" to offer the Methodist Missionary Society "as the proper and effectual medium," through which the "bounty" of "the pious" might be "distributed to the heathen." [54]

The following month, in November 1813, Watson, speaking at Halifax, on the occasion of the formation of a Methodist Missionary Society in that city, saw Christianity in England as having assumed "an *offensive* attitude," in preparation "for her grand assault upon the Heathen World." An excellent and "evident indication" that Providence favored Missions was that "the missionary spirit which now pervades these islands" had not been "excited" in a continental nation "without a navy or maritime connexions"; if such had been the case, "it is difficult to conceive how any efficient plans for the instruction of the Heathen could have been devised." "But this spirit has been excited in Great Britain, the country to which God has given the ocean, whose colonies extend to every quarter of the globe, whose vessels crowd every port of every shore, and whose sons speak almost all the languages of the bubbling earth." Such "a co-incidence, between our duties and our opportunities, our wishes and our means, cannot be overlooked"; it was "more than accidental," "it is the finger of God pointing out our way." Britain's "vessels" were carried by "His winds to every clime" so that they might carry "not only our *merchandise,* but our *Missionaries;* not only our *bales* but our *blessings;* . . . . 'that where Britain's *power* / Is felt, mankind may feel her *mercy* too.' " By joining the gospel to her merchandise, it might prove possible to "consecrate our commerce": while, in the past, commerce had proved "volatile and inconstant," when "seen in connexion with religion," when made the "handmaid" of both wealth and charity, it would be fixed "to our shores forever."

Watson could anticipate but one objection to Methodism's renewed and vigorous dedication to the missions—"that charity begins at home." While denouncing such an objection as "a neat pocket-edition of selfishness," he nevertheless declared "our purposes and plans are not inconsistent with this principle." Indeed,

Charity to the Heathen is charity begun at home. This is not difficult to prove. We cannot take a step towards evangelizing the Heathen, without entering into many inquiries as to the extent of our moral wretchedness; and such inquiries are eminently useful to ourselves. In our present state, we are seldom brought to value our own blessings but by their loss, or by comparing our condition with that of others. By the loss of our religious privileges, I hope we shall never learn the value. But if, by comparing our light with the darkness of the Heathen, our riches with their poverty, we learn to prize those blessings more, and to use them better; then, Sir, Missionary efforts will prove a blessing to us, to our Societies, and to our country, and *charity to the Heathen* will be charity begun at home.

Moreover, Watson concluded, "the pleasure we have in attempting to do good, the joy we feel in anticipating success, the good effects produced upon our minds by the prayers we are excited, by meetings like this, to offer for others, are all home-blessings." [55]

In a sermon preached at Wakefield in July 1814, Watson summed up the new Methodist view of missions. He urged his fellow countrymen to unite to secure the universal abolition of the slave trade in favor of "enslaved Africa," and to work "to evangelize the world." Declaring himself "no admirer of that universal civism" which "would extinguish our partialities for our own country," Watson confessed to a special regard for England and its mission: "the distribution of the word of God, and the support of missions to the heathen, may almost be denominated national acts, because the institutions which have been formed for these great objects number a great part of the nation among their active supporters." England had a "particular reason" for pleasure, since its missions to the heathen would be a means of establishing "our national prosperity by continuing to us the blessing of God." "The enterprize of the merchant will open the way for the enterprize of the missionary"; "our bales and our bibles will be conveyed across the ocean at an easier freight, and the diminished burthens and increased opulence of the country will enable the lovers of Christ and of the souls of men to make more liberal sacrifices for the promotion of truth." Foreign commerce would civilize and Christianize the globe, and by making themselves the agents of this process, England would prosper since "that portion of our wealth which is offered in acts of benevolence" would "consecrate the rest." [56]

.   .   .

Coke, who was kept carefully informed about the proceedings at Leeds, was extravagant in his approval of Bunting's plan, as were most of the members of the missionary committee. "It is the Lord who has put into your hearts thus to step forth," Coke wrote to Bunting.[57] In the light of Coke's prestige, his approval was important, for there were dissenting voices. Moore and Gaulter, for example, thought the time was not ripe, and suggested that the money might be better employed in support of the Connection's educational enterprises. But the Leeds meeting, given the temper of the times, spurred similar meetings in other districts. After Leeds, Bunting urged his friends among the itinerants to imitate his example, and helped in the detailed planning of their meetings. After telling the itinerant preacher at Halifax how to arrange his program, and suggesting speakers—among them Nichols, Watson, and Thomas Jackson—he explained that "I mean not to dictate, but I am anxious that your Meeting should go off with some degree of eclat." [58] In the months ahead, Bunting continued to do what he could to encourage the formation of local missionary societies and to overcome the "tardiness and timidity" of the Connection. He observed to a correspondent that while in 1813, only about £300 had been collected for the missions at Halifax, in 1814, as a result of "the new system of public meetings and Auxiliary Societies," nearly £1300 had been raised. "This *fact* is worth more than a score of theories," he declared. At Leeds, moreover, not only had more money been collected for all purposes—"the Mission business is no hindrance, but a great help"—but "our monthly prayer-meetings grow in interest and in *attendance.*" Bunting concluded from all this that "there is nothing like public meetings!" The new system had taught "the poorer classes . . . by experience the privilege of giving." The poor now knew "the consequence and efficiency conferred on them by their number," and were "resolved to maintain, by actively assisting every good work, the dignity to which they have been raised." [59]

Methodist societies, urged by the Conference of 1814 to follow the Leeds model,[60] took up the cause of the missions with enthusiasm. Halifax, Hull, Sheffield, York, Newcastle, and many other districts of the Connection formed societies. The first report of the Missionary Society for the Leeds District exulted at the "spectacle" of these many acts of "piety and benevolence" inspired by "the great idea of Christianizing the whole earth," proclaiming that the Methodists were "especially called" to this task.[61] By undertaking this calling, Methodists, moreover, confirmed the respectability assigned to them by parliament in 1811 and 1812. How could a Methodist hesitate to answer the call of the Missions, Humphrey Sandwith declared in January 1814, at a meeting which established an Auxiliary Missionary Society at Beverley, "when in so doing we are associated with . . . the most distinguished societies, churches, and governments." [62] In November 1814, on the occasion of the founding of a Missionary Society at Plymouth-Dock, the Rev. W. Burgess, Jr. of Liskeard, noted that "missionary efforts confer honor upon the country in which we live and contribute to its safety." What had saved Britain during "her late dreadful conflicts," and had "elevated her to her present rank among the nations," was "not so much the power of fleets and armies" as "the prayers of the pious," the "bible societies, missionary societies, &c." [63] At the meeting which saw the foundation of the London District's Missionary Society, in December 1814, the Rev. Joseph Entwistle proclaimed that "London, the metropolis of the Empire," ought to "stand foremost in the cause." Adam Clarke, who held the chair at this London meeting, told his fellow Methodists that those they send overseas "will, under God, be your missionaries" and Methodists would have an "interest in their prosperity," and the result must be "a revival, increase, and deepening of true religion among ourselves." [64] "We are called to the honour of joining issue with God himself in converting the world," declared David McNicoll, at the establishment of a Missionary Auxiliary Society at Bolton, in May 1815, thereby "resembling him not only in conduct, but also in the grand governing qualities of our nature." "Missionary benevolence," he continued, was "a noble course of godlike action in which we may all successfully contend for the prize"; "in our attempts to convert" the heathen, "we resemble him [Christ] as a Saviour." [65]

John Stuart, at the formation of the Methodist Missionary Society of the Dublin District, in May 1814, had rejoiced that "the people who, under God, have kept this vast machine in motion, are in general poor." [66] The first report of the Leeds District described with pride the sacrifices which the poor were ready to make for the missions and the spiritual comfort they received as a consequence. A needy woman in Wakefield had pledged 1d. per week to aid the Methodist missions: "it was immediately said to her, 'Surely you are too poor to afford it' "; she replied, " 'I spin so many hanks of yarn every week for a maintenance' "; " 'I will spin *one more, that will be a penny for the Society.' "* [67] The first report of the Society of the Sheffield District spoke of the "poor and labouring youth" of the Methodist Juvenile Association having "cheerfully paid their voluntary tax in this Holy War," and reminded its readers that Methodism, "as a peculiar form of Christian profession, is literally a Missionary system." [68] The missionary movement, indeed, the first report of the Society at Hull declared in 1815, had the happy effect of reducing religious tensions at home: "compared with the vast worlds of unreclaimed territory on which the weeds and poisons of pagan superstition luxuriate, the enclosures, which at home distinguish the sects of Christians, shrink into insignificance." [69]

"All this money," moreover, as Bunting observed, "is raised without the personal exertions of the preachers," for "the people themselves beg it and collect it." [70] Under the Leeds scheme, laymen would have a large role in collecting funds. Joseph Entwistle wrote to Bunting, on October 25, 1813, that although "we must guard against lay influence," yet there was "great propriety in making Circuit stewards members of the [mission] committee, and we ought to avail ourselves of their talent and influence." [71] It was to this moderate view that Bunting subscribed at this time when the laity, though not as noisily as during the nineties, was demanding a greater share in the government of the Connection. (Joseph Butterworth, a Methodist M.P., and a brother-in-law of Adam Clarke, for example, felt deeply on this matter.) On the other hand, Samuel Bradburn, long past his radical days, was reported in a letter by Grindrod to Bunting as having "condemned the proceedings of the Leeds meeting in strong terms, declaring that some of its measures were little less than Kilhamism." Even Grindrod expressed fears lest the lay committees "by degrees take the Missions out of our hands, and even control of all our affairs." [72] But Bunting, insisting that the Dissenters must not be allowed to steal a march on Methodism, went from circuit to circuit urging the adoption of the Leeds plan. Entwistle was one of those stirred by the example Bunting had offered at Leeds. In December 1813, he, too, spoke of the need for "publicity" or "our Calvinistic B [rethr]en will *shove* our *Missions* out of sight, and *in part at least* drain our resources." [73]

From shipboard, on his way to India, Coke sent a last message to Bunting by the pilot, asking that "the Lord reward you a thousand-fold for this." [74] The Annual Conference not only accepted, as had Coke, the usefulness of Bunting's and Watson's initiative, which had already demonstrated its appeal to the interests and imaginations of the rank-and-file, it urged, as we have noted, that the Leeds example be followed in the circuits which had not yet done so. The appeals for the democratization of the Connection, to which the Leeds plan was in part a response, were answered in still another way by the 1814 Conference. Although ministers representing district meetings had been welcome to participate in the Conference, their decisions could be vetoed by the vote of the Legal Hundred, and ministers were received into that body by a system of strict seniority; moreover, only members of the Legal Hundred could elect or serve as President or Secretary. In 1814, a new rule was adopted: although three out of every four vacancies in the Hundred would be filled by seniority, the fourth would be the nominee of all the preachers at the Conference, providing the nominee had had at least fourteen years of travelling and was confirmed by the Legal Hundred. The first member of the Conference to benefit from the new system was Jabez Bunting. The extent of the success of his initiative may be further seen in his election as Secretary of the Conference as well.

PARADOX RESOLVED

Methodism had been at a point of crisis. From the standpoint of the tensions within Wesleyan ideology, as we have observed, and from that of the increasing political pressures (climaxed by Sidmouth's bill), a turn to the missions was a resolution of critical problems. There was concern that the impetus of 1739 was weakening—this despite the steady growth in numbers of nominal adherents—and the Connection, having lost much of its confidence in the role which it had pursued for three-quarters of a century, required a new role consistent with its traditional doctrine, conduct, and purposes. Writing to Bunting in 1814, Watson declared that "your missionary news does me good," adding that "if we can but turn the energies of Methodism into that channel, the work must go on; for 'God is with us.' " [75] One of the early opponents of Missions, Henry Moore, was ready to concur in June 1815 that "the Lord was with us in our Missionary business." [76] In December 1816, Moore, apparently seeing it as the consequence of the Lord's favor of Methodist missionary activity, declared that "I never knew the Society in a better state with respect to every appearance of earnestness"; "our congregations and prayer meetings are crowded." [77] What was, in effect, a mission party was formed in the Connection,[78] and with the growing acceptance of the plan, even those formerly hostile were converted. Thomas Jackson observed that "when Missionary Meetings became general among the Methodists, the great body of the Preachers were expected to take a part in them"; "it was interesting in many places to hear aged and venerable men publicly retract their former opinions": [79] the missions were the platform and the program which were to dominate the Connection for the greater part of the nineteenth century, and the work of the missions enabled Bunting to join the efforts, at home and abroad, of an increasingly respectable Methodism to those of the better-placed Evangelicals of the Church of England.[80]

Methodism, in the nineteenth century, preserved much of its Arminian idealism, seemingly paradoxically, by maintaining the national, indeed, the imperial standard. This was a period when Evangelicals were determined to convert Hindostan, even as they worked to end West Indian slavery. Methodism was caught up in the national mood. Joseph Entwistle, in Bristol in May 1813, had found the petition campaign of the Evangelicals to permit Christian missionaries to go to India so powerful that he joined in it, not only seeing "no impropriety" in doing so, but thinking "it would be *almost criminal* in us to be silent in Bristol when the whole city was moved." [81] On the occasion of the first General Meeting of the Wesleyan Methodist Missionary Society, in 1818, Jabez Bunting, advocating the extension of the missions in India, spoke of the "singular dispensation of

Providence which has placed sixty millions in Asia under the political direction of fourteen millions in Britain." At a time when Englishmen— under both utilitarian and Evangelical influence—were still speaking of preparing India for independence, Bunting saw as "the moral design of this dispensation" a "way to keep it *British*"! Dismissing the view that support for the missions would injure "domestic exertions," he declared that "opposition to that spirit which originates Foreign enterprise will infallibly damp and quench the spirit of domestic exertion." [82]

In the years ahead, the ties between Evangelicals and Methodists became closer as both continued to pursue the same objectives, the abolition of slavery and the conversion of the heathen. Those two causes, indeed, seemed united by still another tie—that of evangelical guilt. At the general meeting of the Wesleyan Methodist Missionary Society, in 1818, the Rev. J. Gaulter of Rochester proposed a resolution "that the Commercial Christian Nations of Europe, owe it in reparation for the wrongs inflicted upon Africa, to endeavour the civilization and Christianizing of the natives of that continent." The resolution was unanimously approved. [83] "Was it right," the Rev. Thomas Kelp asked a meeting of the Auxiliary Society for the London District in 1819, "was it just and equitable, that we should receive so many comforts, so many luxuries; from the labours of the poor African, degraded by us to toil, to sweat, to languish beneath a tropical sun, and not endeavour to make some reparations for the injuries they have received?" [84] This was the tone of many of the addresses made to the succession of Anniversary Meetings of the W.M.M.S. by both the Methodist leaders, and the leaders of Evangelicalism who spoke to them over the years. William Wilberforce addressed the 1819 Anniversary Meeting, for example, and the younger James Stephen joined Wilberforce in speaking in 1822; Wilberforce was a speaker, again, in 1823, and in 1829, T. F. Buxton spoke in 1833 and in 1834, and there were others. [85] In 1823, William Wilberforce described his particular pleasure in being associated with the Methodists in the great task of dissipating "the darkness of paganism." [86]

There was a debate within the Connection, in 1818 and 1819, between the "mission party" and its opponents. Adam Clarke spoke for the "mission party" when he observed that "at present we have comparatively little more to do, especially in this nation, than to maintain the conquest we have gained, conduct the rising generation into the fold of Christ, and continue to sow and water a seed which, through the mercy of God, is, almost every place, falling into good ground." The immediate call for the Connection, Clarke suggested, lay in the foreign mission field. [87] Valentine Ward, very doubtful of such a conclusion, wrote of those Methodists who "are in great danger of being so dazzled by the splendour of Foreign objects, as to neglect those of equal, if not superior importance, because they happen to be near at hand." There was only a limited fund upon which to draw,

Ward warned. What Ward had in mind were such areas as the Scottish Highlands, although even in England there were "numerous villages and market towns, where the voice of a Methodist Preacher is never heard" and where "the Gospel is not preached." Even in the large manufacturing towns, there were "thousands of people who still attend no place of worship." Ward quoted "an able friend of the Connexion" as having said that " 'Should Methodism cease to exist as a Missionary System, its existence will cease.' " This was true, but Ward added that "should Methodism cease to exist as a Missionary System at home," its foreign activities would also cease. "And will not the blood of souls be found in the skirts of some, who throw every obstacle" in the way of facilitating the preaching of the gospel to "these outcasts of society, and the rising generation?" [88] Ward, in a spirit far from the dominant one of reconciliation between all evangelicals, even suggested that the *"Truth as it is in Jesus"* was to be found only among Methodists, a view which one member of the mission party was to denounce as bigotry. The latter also was to take issue with Ward's criticism of Clarke: "I trust," he was to observe, "that every Methodist preacher ardently longs, and prays and labours for the entire evangelization of Britain"; but "how little is this, compared with the vastness of his desires, compared with the evangelization of the whole world!" [89]

In making this decision to redirect the evangelistic energies of Methodism to the mission field, the leaders of the Connection had at last in good part resolved the paradox with which Wesley had been faced at the beginning of his mission: how to reconcile the Enthusiasm inherent in Methodist evangelism, with its revolutionary, Antinomian tendencies, with an obsession with order in both Church and state. As Methodism separated from the Church, the tension had become sharper, but by redirecting Methodist Enthusiasm, the threat it posed to domestic stability might be overcome. (It was certainly easier for the leaders of the Connection to make such a decision when there existed a body of Evangelicals who were carrying out Wesley's mission within the Establishment.) Such a redirection also put into harmony the conflict between what we have called Laudian politics and those of a Remonstrance Arminianism. Both the need for order and loyalty, of nonresistance and divine right, and the dedication to spiritual equality and natural rights, might, in such perilous times, be satisfied by the new direction taken in 1813. The alternative to this course of action was to accept the revolutionary risks inherent in releasing the evangelistic energies of a Methodism, seemingly near the zenith of its powers, upon the ancient preserves of the Establishment. The result of such a choice might be repression and the necessity of a loyal Methodism invoking the right of resistance.

VII

The Methodist Synthesis:
Liberalism, Order, and
National Mission

Socinianism, moonlight; methodism, a stove. O for some sun to unite heat and light!

Coleridge, Anima Poetae

There is no way of knowing how realistic were the apparently widespread fears—shared, as we have seen, by Methodist leaders, Churchmen, and government ministers—that Methodists might become a force for violent revolution. Of immediate concern was the existence of a body of people who were enrolled in a movement whose ideology was revolutionary, both modernizing and liberal, and seemed to uphold, in religious doctrine and organization at any rate, the threefold goals of the Parisian mobs—liberty, equality, and fraternity. Moreover, it was an ideology that was energetically propagated, in an extra-legal manner, by methods associated with the enthusiasts who had helped to make a revolution a century earlier. It was the "levelling" aspect of Methodism, we recall, that gave special concern, the itinerant preaching by ill-educated mechanics. We have traced the particular conditions growing out of Wesley's personal circumstances and the requirements of his movement which led Wesley and his associates to develop this modern and liberal doctrine. Among people who took their faith seriously, such a doctrine might well have been translated to the political sphere—as it was, to a considerable extent, to the social sphere—and with unsettling repercussions. We have seen that Wesley, still devoted to the scriptural injunction of passive obedience, and his equally conservative-minded associates well understood this. The history of Methodism in its first three-quarters of a century of existence may be seen, in good part, first as an effort to provide the Evangelical Revival with a theology free of the potentially subversive Antinomian doctrine—whether actually tending to disorder or not these "Reformation" doctrines were certainly illiberal and out of line with a growingly modern society—which they attributed to their Calvinist rivals; secondly, it was to labor to prevent the revolutionary (liberal and modern) implications of Methodist doctrine or the revolutionary manner of its propagation from being translated to the political scene.

In so doing, the Wesleyans made themselves leading opponents of revolution and the defenders of divine right and passive obedience in the sixties and seventies, and again during the wars with a revolutionary France. Moreover, insofar as the possibility of Methodist Enthusiasm might spread beyond control—during the days of the French wars and the rapid growth of the Connection—the leadership endeavored to divert these energies of Arminian evangelization to the mission field. There had been radical efforts, as we know—it is difficult to judge their real strength but the Wesleyan leaders thought them serious—to translate Arminian liberalism into the political life of the Connection. These were roundly defeated. In order to persuade the government not to repress the Methodist movement which it regarded as revolutionary, in the nineties and afterward, the Wesleyan leadership insisted that it had succeeded in helping to block revolution— even while it threatened resistance should government fail to heed its plea, an illuminating display of Methodist ambivalence. That Methodism prevented revolution became, as we saw, the party-cry of a Connection whose badly frightened leadership was at least relieved to have prevented radicalism and revolution, in the form of the Kilhamites, from taking over the Methodist movement!

The "revolutionary" implications of Methodist doctrine thus led to the contradictory effort of the Connection leadership to counter the political translation of this doctrine: the consequence of this clash was what I call the Methodist synthesis. The Methodist synthesis, with its combination of the modern and the traditional and its peculiar resolution of the forces making for liberty and order, for revolution and counter-revolution, may be said to be at the heart of the success of Wesley and his Connection as the mediator between the traditional England of the *ancien régime* and that of the modern, industrial nation-state. For nearly three-quarters of a century, Wesley and, though less successfully, his immediate successors managed to control the tensions produced by these contradictions and yet maintain, virtually unimpaired, much of the Enthusiasm of the early days of the Revival. When the traditional disciplines of the hierarchical society were breaking down, neither the Church nor the Protestant sects seemed able to build an alternative means of discipline which might make an appeal to masses. The Methodists may have succeeded in doing this. Moreover, Evangelical Arminianism, by its widespread preaching (supplemented by the efforts of its evangelical allies and competitors) made *real* the egalitarian and libertarian message of the main body of the Anglican Church in a way perhaps best calculated to serve liberal purposes. The new sense of community instilled by the initial experience of the revival meeting and by personal conversion was reinforced by the submission of the "new" men, the new proletarians, uncertain and fearful about the exercise of the autonomy thrust upon them, to the moral guidance of their brethren in Christ. Other denominations followed a modified system of supervising the morals of their members, spurred by the example of the Methodists, making increasingly possible the relatively orderly social transformation to a modern, individualistic society during the eighteenth and nineteenth centuries.

In the first third of the nineteenth century, the various doctrinal parts of this synthesis were presented in scores of sermons, tracts, and public addresses. The most systematic effort—though even here the elements must be pieced together—was made in the writings of Richard Watson, the principal ideological spokesman of the Wesleyan Connection from the early 1820s until his death in 1832. Watson's views, indeed, were regarded as authoritative in the Connection until the later decades of the nineteenth century.

WATSON, THE METHODIST SYNTHESIS, AND LIBERALISM

Richard Watson, after Wesley and Fletcher, came closest to being the official theologian of Methodism. Though Watson was not trained in a University as both his predecessors had been, his *Theological Institutes,* published in the early 1820s and dedicated to Jabez Bunting, became the authoritative statement of Wesleyan doctrine during the period when Bunting's influence was predominant. Watson—a translator of the Dutch Remonstrancer Episcopius [1]—invoked Arminius on the title page and John Locke on the first page of his *Institutes,* setting the tone of both its religious and political philosophy. Yet Methodist liberalism was hardly that of John Stuart Mill, and, indeed, Watson even prided himself on being an opponent of "liberalism," as it was understood by the Radicals and Unitarians.

"As a mutual dependence has been established among men, so also are there mutual *rights,* in the rendering of which to each other, justice, when considered as a social virtue, consists," Watson declared in his *Institutes.* "Ethical Justice" concerned "men's *natural* rights, which are briefly summed up in three,—*life, property,* and *liberty.*" "To the natural rights of life, property," Watson continued, "may be added the right of CONSCIENCE," that is, the right to pursue one's own religious views and opinions. (Watson, like Rousseau, pointedly excluded atheists from freedom from "civil penalties" which might be imposed upon them, since, denying God, they could not be protected by the natural—i.e., God-given —right to liberty of conscience.) Watson was convinced that the government had the duty to see to it that no sect was allowed to interfere with the rights of others. The government, however, had no right to restrain men or sects for the simple possession of opinions, "however erroneous," or "involving a corrupt conscience," or "fatal to the salvation of those who hold them," so long as the holding or propagation of these views did "not interfere with the peace, the morals, and good order of society."

Because of the Wesleyan inheritance, no doubt confirmed by a wish to counter fears to which Methodism had given rise, there were more explicit references to the need to restrain revolution and anarchy than secular liberalism usually permitted itself. This greater consciousness of original sin —Satan's domain—decidedly altered the liberal mood of the *Institutes*. Mindful of the dangers of Antinomianism, Watson insisted that no sect or individual ought to be permitted "ignorantly, fanatically, or corruptly" to "so interpret the Scriptures as to suppose themselves free of moral obligation, and then proceed to practise their tenets by any such acts as violate the laws of well-ordered society." Similarly, the government had the right to restrain men "where political opinions are connected with religious notions," as in the case of "the Fifth Monarchy Fanatics," though if only a few held such deluded views, Watson advised, the government would be wise to leave them alone. However, "should a fanaticism of this kind seize upon a multitude" and "render them restless and seditious," the State might justifiably use force to restrain it.

While expounding in Arminian fashion the equality of all men, Watson, like Bradburn earlier, saw equality in the next and not in this world. Religion reminded men that they were all equal "in the sight of God," that they all had an "equal share in the benefits of redemption," and a "title to the common inheritance of heaven, where all these temporary distractions on which human vanity is so apt to fasten, shall be done away with." Without religion, masters would treat servants "with contempt, contumely, harshness," and servants would, without religion, "from their natural corruption," be "inclined to resent authority, to indulge selfishness, and to commit fraud, either by withholding the just quantum of labour, or by direct theft." In this world, however, "equality of condition" was "alike contrary to the nature of things, and to the appointment of God." [2]

A seeming—though, as we have earlier suggested, not necessary— variance with this liberalism was Watson's adherence to the old slogans of Wesley's Laudian inheritance. The origin of power was not from man, by the "pure fiction" of a social compact, but from God, he noted in his *Institutes*. Government "in the first ages of the world" was "paternal," and it was clear that Scripture favored monarchical government. Yet, with all this, for Watson, as for Wesley and, indeed, Burke, the principles of 1688 prevailed. "The rights and duties of sovereign and subject are reciprocal," and Watson, like Wesley, was ready to accept the reality of a constitutional compact by which the sovereign was obliged "to bind himself to observe those fundamental principles and laws of the State by solemn oath, which has been the practice among many nations, and especially those of the Gothic Stock." Unless good government was in jeopardy by misrule, only when there were "real encroachments upon the fundamental laws of a State," or a "serious maladministration of its affairs," could resistance be justified, and then only when approved of by "the fairly collected public sentiment."

The talk of revolution, of recourse to arms, was so constant during Watson's lifetime and the vision of Satanic revolution was so ingrained a part of Methodist thinking that Watson felt obliged to devote a considerable discussion to a question which later English political theorists largely ignored. Watson continued to recommend *"subjection* and *obedience"* not only for wrath but for conscience sake—and this had become one of the most essential parts of Wesleyanism. There were three cases to be examined. In the first, and Watson clearly had contemporary England in mind, where a nation enjoyed and valued good institutions, "a prompt resistance of public opinion" to any effort to abridge the laws and customs would probably carry the day; the "danger in that state of society" lay in "persons, who from vanity, faction, or interest, are ready to excite the passions and to corrupt the feelings of the populace." Under those circumstances, the true patriot must "support a just authority" because "licentiousness in the people has often, by a re-action, destroyed liberty, overthrowing the powers by which alone it is supported." In the second case, "public liberty and other civil blessings are in gradual progress," and are maintained by only a minority, "whilst a great body of ignorant, prejudiced, and corrupt persons are on the side of the supreme power, and are ready to lend themselves as instruments of its mis-rule and despotism." France was in such a condition at the time of the Revolution, and England during the time of the Civil Wars: an appeal to arms under such circumstances would be "hopeless" and "impolitic," since no good can come of an appeal to "an ignorant and bad populace"; "the result would be a violence which, it is true, overthrows one form of tyranny, but sets up another under which the best men perish." In the third case, a majority of the public opposed "infringements on the constitution," but the sovereign, "in attempting to change the fundamental principles of his compact," uses mercenaries against the people, or was aided by a foreign power. Here alone, wrote Watson in detailing the conditions which existed in England in 1688, "the renunciation of allegiance is clearly justifiable," and constituted "a deliberate national act," an act "of the people under their natural guides and leaders,—the nobility and gentry of the land."

Revolution, then, was justifiable in England in 1688, but apparently at no other time or place. Indeed, Watson's antipathy to revolution was so intense that he even denied Methodists the right to resist when suffering religious persecution, a right to which, as we have noted, so many Methodist preachers had appealed between 1795 and 1812. In sum, Watson vaunted, as had Wesley and Fletcher, Christian allegiance and proclaimed that a religious man must not "become a factious man," and must "avoid all association with low and violent men, the rabble of a State and their designing leaders." [3]

A Christian received the privileges of heavenly citizenship: "the first is freedom," freedom from sin and from Satan's dominion.[4] Christians gladly accepted "the reign of God," Watson declared in another sermon in 1814: notwithstanding the "sovereignty and certainty" of God's government, it "interferes not with human liberty," for "we have the freedom of moral agents." "We may not be able to reconcile the sovereign control of God with the freedom of his creatures," Watson argued, but this was a result of "our own ignorance" since "the Scriptures assert both propositions."

In a review of the writings of Thomas Chalmers, Watson, while displeased by Chalmers' Presbyterian belief in predestination, approved of the grand conclusion of the Scottish clergyman-economist that the "great reason" for social evils was "the non-application of Christianity, on a scale sufficiently extensive to our national ignorance and vices." Noting the "spread of misery and murmuring" throughout the working classes, a condition which "disposed them to riot and rebellion," Watson dismissed the views of many Tories that this discontent was due either to "religious fanaticism," or "the diffusion of education." It was those ignorant of religion who were rebels. What was "generally meant by fanaticism" by those who denounced it was "that very theological system which they themselves profess to reverence in their own religious formularies, fully drawn out and earnestly impressed by others." The way to deal with the poor, Watson concluded, was not merely, as the economists urged, to abolish poor laws which injuriously encouraged "the spirit of dependence," but to remove "the spirit of pauperism," i.e., "dishonesty, idleness, improvidence, disregard of character, want of affection for children"—"moral evils, which can not submit to a scientific or political cure . . . but must have a moral one." This is what Methodism had set out to do. Watson agreed with Chalmers that "true Christianity, when applied by a faithful Christian labourer," served "to bring out the results contemplated by the economist." It turned darkness "into light, confusion to order, shamelessness to character, squalidness to decency, prodigality to frugality, improvidence to foresight, and sloth to industry." [5]

Nations, too, had to be regarded as free moral agents, Watson declared. God judged nations as well as individuals, estimating their character "by majorities, and by public national acts." If a nation "welcome his religion, and pay him the homage which he claims," that nation would receive "special political favours," a fact confirmed for Watson by the special political and commercial position in the world held by Christian nations, and especially by Protestant nations. God had peculiarly favored England, countering its sins by the spread of religion rather than by severe punishment. Purified by religion and by its victories over Napoleon, England—whose commercial pursuits had brought her into contact with pagan nations— seemed on the threshold "of that great end, the Christianizing of the world." [6]

At the Anniversary Meeting of the Wesleyan Methodist Missionary Society in 1830, Richard Watson delivered a paean for a liberal, evangelical and imperial Protestantism. Watson knew that it was "in the order of God and his providence" to "extend civilization, and to carry it through to the whole earth." But men could not be civilized without Christianity, and indeed, if by civilization we meant that "mankind live under equal laws and enjoy all that liberty which is requisite to the general order and prosperity," then "none of the most celebrated states of antiquity were civilized." Medieval Christianity had been exceedingly slow in civilizing Europe because it was "a mixed and adulterated Christianity," bearing "the fatal principle"—Watson continued, almost in the mode of a present-day sociologist discussing Protestant "autonomy" and "self-orientation"—which compelled it to "treat the body of the people like children, not men"; instead of Christianity, they gave the people superstition, thus "hiding from them the manly and elevating truths" with which true Christianity "arouses the dormant spirit." These "manly and elevating truths," Watson asserted, had been "put into operation on as large a scale, only by two of the leading nations of the earth"—Great Britain and the United States. These nations had, by "the circulation of the Scriptures, and by preaching the word of God," made the "verities of Christianity" to "bear on the moral and civil condition of the whole body of the people." Though not entirely successful in accomplishing this, it came as no surprise to Watson that these were the two countries which "lead in the great march of nations, and are in fact the lights of the world": "their liberty, and public virtue, and religion, are set on high, and are hailed as an example by the wise and good in distant lands who wish to conform their institutions to ours." [7]

In the missionary sermons of Richard Watson, we may see an early statement of the distinctive "liberalism" which Methodism, as well as the other Protestant denominations, under similar pressures, maintained through much of the nineteenth century.[8] This was the position of Exeter Hall, the complex of Protestant missionary societies, and of humanitarian groups such as the Aborigines Protection Society and the Anti-Slavery Society. Exeter Hall was not to be anticolonialist, as were, say, the Cobdenites. Rather, in the manner anticipated by Watson, it sought to assure that the process which saw the spread of British commerce, and thereby the colonization and control of a great part of the globe, would not work undue hardship and injustice upon the native races. Exeter Hall was derided by Carlyle as the Universal Abolition of Pain Association for its fervent support for the abolition of slavery and the improvement of the lot of the freed man, and for its protection of, successively, the Dyaks, the Indians, the Maori, and the Jamaican rebels of 1865 against the seemingly unavoidable callousness of imperial policy. Of course, through these efforts the evangelical Protestants of Exeter Hall expected, also, to save their own souls, and to invoke the blessings and help of God to "preserve" and "consecrate" their markets, a position already clear in the addresses at Leeds in 1813.[9]

The policy of Exeter Hall was the peculiar product of the nonconformist liberalism of nineteenth-century England. Its philanthropic concern for the welfare of "natives" was accompanied by a more callous attitude toward the condition of the working men at home, the quasi-reprobate victims of the natural laws of political economy. Charles Dickens satirized Exeter Hall in the character of Mrs. Jellyby, a woman who neglected her own children while she employed her energies in the work of the missions, thus fulfilling the role which Jabez Bunting had assigned to "British and Christian Females." Others, most prominently John Ruskin and Thomas Carlyle, were similarly to regard themselves as enemies to Exeter Hall because its devotees, while compulsively watchful over the interests of its black, brown, and yellow men overseas, largely disregarded the hardships faced by ignorant, overworked, and underfed Englishmen.[10] This was the argument that "Charity begins at home," that "neat pocket-edition of selfishness," which Watson had attempted to answer. Watson's reply that the missions were "charity begun at home" because "by comparing our light with the darkness of the Heathen" and "our riches with their poverty," Englishmen might "learn to prize these blessings more," though hardly persuasive, does provide a useful insight into the role which the missions played in the economy and polity of Methodism through much of the nineteenth century. As Watson and others at the Leeds Conference had suggested, the missions were employed as a means of enlisting the imagination and sympathies, as well as the meager resources, of the poor in such a fashion as not only to overcome an otherwise inevitable absorption with their own wretchedness, but to give them a stake in the spiritual and material welfare of others, overseas, depicted as more wretched still.

Is it possible to trace this callousness of Exeter Hall in good part to the compulsive absorption with the fear of revolution—and the overwhelming passion to avert such a calamity—of Wesley, his associates, and those who led the Connection after his death, as I have suggested? And might the forces making for revolutionary disorder be diverted to "constructive" purposes by thus transferring the demands growing out of the political implications of spiritual egalitarianism to such "otherworldly," in the sense of the overseas world, pursuits as ending slavery, converting the Negro, and serving as his protector? In this great effort, in any event, a "respectable," increasingly middle-class Methodism was able to join the other "respectable," middle-class nonconformist denominations, substantially revitalized by the influence of the evangelical Revival, which also were to give their first priority to the heathen. Having long abandoned their seventeenth-century revolutionary inheritance, the sects, implicitly following the logic and in part the rhetoric of Cromwellian policy, could see a liberal, Protestant Britain as an elect nation with a divine mission. This was a view which an Arminian Methodism, as we have seen, had come to share. In this fashion, as the nineteenth century advanced, while continuing to maintain a distinctive position, Methodism became largely, though not entirely, absorbed in an evangelical alliance, which increasingly subordinated the concern for the saving of the lower orders—which had inspired Wesley's Methodism—to the new goals of the more affluent middle classes.

EVANGELICAL ALLIANCE AND METHODISM

What the Methodists had been doing among the lower classes, the church Evangelicals were attempting, with considerable success, among the higher. When Wilberforce had met Wesley in 1789, he regarded him with admiration mingled with patronization: Wesley was "a fine old fellow." [11] But, as Wilberforce's sons and biographers observed, Wesley's "mission was chiefly to the poor": "there was need of some reformer of the nation's morals, who should raise his voice in the high places,"—which Wesley at times seemed to regard almost as the sites of Baal's temples—"and do within the church, and near the throne, what Wesley had accomplished in the meeting, and amongst the multitude." [12] It was only in this that there lay the possibility of Wilberforce effecting his purpose—"the reformation of manners." [13] In this effort, if we are to believe the testimony of Tocqueville and Taine and other foreign observers of Victorian England, the Methodists and Evangelicals, aided by the older nonconformist sects, were successful.

Moreover, for the nineteenth-century evangelical of whatever denomination, there was no contradiction between advancing the nation's morals and commercial gain. Indeed, the two objectives were intimately intertwined. It was, perhaps, the Evangelicals who led Methodism increasingly to accept the middle-class outlook. Certainly the Church Evangelicals did not neglect the trading advantages of the humanitarian and mission movements. For example, the annual report of the Evangelical-founded African Institution in 1819 proclaimed that the slave trade was "the only impediment" to the civilizing of Africa, since it "at once turned aside the attention of the natives from the more slow and laborious means of barter, which industry presented, to that of seizing upon and selling each other";[14] the Institution urged Great Britain to obtain for its navy arrangements "for enforcing by visitation and search in time of peace, the abolition laws of the different states." [15] When the West India interest took note of the link between philanthropic and private interest, citing primarily the case of Zachary Macaulay, who made his living in trading with Sierra Leone,[16] James Stephen, a humanitarian and a prominent Evangelical layman, observing that the enemies of the Evangelicals continued to throw at them "the old watch-words of methodists, enthusiasts, fanatics, and jacobins," defended Macaulay's motives. Nothing was so "likely to promote so much the purposes" of Great Britain and of the African Institution "in that unfortunate continent," Stephen declared, "as the success of individuals who engage in its innocent commerce." Indeed, Stephen concluded, "the man who gains a thousand pounds in that trade, will be a more effectual benefactor to the African people, than if he had charitably subscribed a hundred thousand, for their instruction in the arts and sciences or any other direct means of their improvement." (On this occasion, Stephen was also obliged to defend himself against the charge that he had procured a job for his son in the colonial office.) [17]

Even before the turn of the century, the Evangelicals had come to think of themselves as the protectors of the Methodists, and the Methodist leadership was flattered by this attention. In the early twenties Bunting was invited by Zachary Macaulay to join "the London Society for Mitigating and Gradually Abolishing the State of Slavery throughout the British Dominions." True to his Arminian and Wesleyan principles, and flattered by the invitation, Bunting insisted on joining and on remaining a member of that society despite the fact that Methodist missionary instructions framed by a discomfited Watson, had taken a neutral line on abolition. By 1824, Bunting had succeeded in winning the Methodists over to full abolition, and the Connection took up the cause with enthusiasm.[18] The Methodist Conference in 1830, addressing itself to Methodists who would soon vote for the first time, urged them to choose candidates primarily with a view to electing friends of emancipation.[19] (Bunting faced a dilemma. Although described as "a Whig of the Old School," and "a firm Royalist"—he has often been quoted on the virtual identity of democracy and sin—in practical politics, he, like Wilberforce, was a Tory.[20] At Liverpool in 1832, Bunting let it be known that he gave his support to Earl Sandon, the Tory candidate who had made no public commitment on emancipation, over a Liberal and Radical, Thomas Thornley, a well-known friend of the abolition of slavery. When attacked for this stand, Bunting allowed it to be understood that he could not conscientiously give his vote to a candidate, however favorable to abolition, whose other political views he regarded as destructive to society, and whom he did not regard as a Christian. Thornley was a Unitarian.[21] The Conference in 1833 supported Bunting in this position.) [22] In Leeds, a stronghold of Methodism, the Tory candidate, Michael Sadler, had for many years been a Methodist, indeed even a local preacher, though no longer active, and had, anticipating the work of Shaftesbury, been energetic in the defense of both the factory worker and the agricultural laborer. The Whig candidate was T. B. Macaulay, the son of the Evangelical leader. In a letter to a Methodist minister at Leeds, Richard Watson declared that he could not "for a moment hesitate to whom to give the influence we may have": ignoring Sadler's humanitarian efforts, Watson noted that Sadler, while claiming to hate slavery, had not been one of the leaders of the abolition campaign, while Macaulay had been "trained up to abhor" slavery by his "venerable Father" to whom "that sacred cause of Negro liberation owes more perhaps than to any man in the empire." (Watson, like Bunting, also declared he "would not vote for a radical candidate even for the sake of his vote against slavery," for God would not choose to free the slaves "by such means.") [23]

Nor did the Evangelicals fail to display their appreciation for Methodist support, and for the role the Connection was playing in the pagan world. If Watson's vaunting of the missionizing role of evangelical Christianity, discussed earlier, appeared to include Calvinists and Anglican Evangelicals, a prominent Evangelical and the son of a founder of the African Institution, James Stephen, who would in 1836 become the permanent undersecretary for colonies, saw Methodism as the most important Christian agency in the expansion of the British Empire. At the Anniversary Meeting of the W.M.M.S. in 1834, with T. F. Buxton in the chair, Stephen spoke as a lifelong member of the Church of England. "I love that Church," he declared. Nevertheless the Church had disappointed him, especially in his hope that it would take an important role in the evangelization of the West Indian Negro. But "the Established Church is essentially parochial: it was formed, chiefly for England and Wales: it was not adapted for ready expansion to the colonies and dependencies of Great Britain." It was because of this essentially parochial character of the Establishment that "the great Apostle of modern times, John Wesley, born in the Church of England, and living in its communion, holding its faith, and feeling a common interest in all connected with it," had found it necessary to venture "into paths in which spiritual rulers were unable to obstruct him, and into which few cared to follow him." Methodists still continued in the divinely mandated work of evangelization. "It is enough for me to know," the future colonial undersecretary concluded, "that wherever I find a colony the most peaceful, the most orderly, and in which the views of the British Parliament are most fully carried into effect, there I find a colony where Wesleyan Missionaries have been most laborious and successful." [24]

The mission party, led by Bunting and Watson, had triumphed, and the intensity and scope of Methodist missionary activity increased considerably during the century, even while the rate of growth, though not the absolute growth, of the Connection at home sharply declined. In 1813 there had been forty-two Methodist missionaries, and about two-thirds of these had been stationed in the West Indies, with the remainder in British North America and Gibraltar. In that year, there were some 15,000 Methodist adherents in the West Indies, and 1500 in Nova Scotia and Newfoundland (compared to probably over 200,000 in England, and 400,000 in the United States). By 1863, the golden jubilee year of the Leeds Methodist Missionary Society, there were eighty missionaries in the West Indies; thirteen on the mainland of Central and South America, and thirty in British North America (without Canada); twenty-five in West Africa, and seventy in South Africa; eleven in Ceylon, and twenty-eight in South India; and seven in China (the first had come in 1852). There had been over 200,000 mission converts since 1813, equal to almost one-half the total membership of British Methodism.[25] The evidence seems to suggest that British Wesleyan Methodism had, of course, also grown during these years, but far from dramatically, although one historian has argued that Bunting's opposition to the growth of the Connection reduced Methodist numbers by over 100,000.[26] Jabez Bunting, in 1854, commenting on complaints of declining growth, was to observe that Methodists had been "guilty of the sin of David in numbering the people, and had made too much boast of numbers as such." [27]

Even without the missions, an increasingly respectable Wesleyan Methodism—eschewing revivals and fearing Enthusiasm—would probably have had difficulties in maintaining its earlier rate of growth. What appears with some certainty, however, is that Methodism, a missionary system, had a stock of energy which it decided would best be expended abroad. At the 1838 Conference, for example, although the pressing need for home missions was explicitly acknowledged, the limited funds of the Connection were again devoted to the foreign missions—once more confirming the determination made over two decades earlier.[28] On the other hand, the New Connection as early as 1817 founded, by an accidental symbolism at Leeds, a "Leeds Home Mission Society." While not condemning foreign missions—which the New Connection described as raising "us, as a nation, to the highest pinnacle of honour and dignity"—the Kilhamites of the New Connection were convinced that "a *Home Mission* is not inconsistent with the existence and exercise of *love to all* mankind." The New Connection beheld "with painful concern the vast number of their countrymen yet involved in the darkest ignorance, and polluted by the most shocking impiety," and saw them in "a situation equally deplorable, but much more *awful* than the most untutored Indian." [29] The New Connection and the Bible Christian Methodists,[30] as well as the Primitive Methodists who followed a similar policy, were to exhibit a very considerable growth during the nineteenth century.[31]

By mid-century, there was questioning of these priorities. For example, at Cambridge, on Degree Day in 1859, there was an interchange between two of the speakers, W. E. Gladstone, and Sir George Grey, the just-returned Governor of the Cape Colony: Gladstone criticized the spending of large amounts on foreign missions and urged a concentration of those resources against the "practical Heathenism" of the great cities, while Grey defended the position of the mission parties of the denominations. The mission party was virtually unchallenged in Wesleyan Methodism until the 1880s, when the great depression, the revival of socialism, and the renewal of trade union agitation compelled a re-examination and helped to turn the attention of Methodism to the plight of the heathen at home and to building popular halls in urban centers, designated as "missions." The mission-hall movement of progressive Methodism, the Forward Movement, was led by Charles Garrett and Hugh Price Hughes, the editor of the *Methodist Times,* who was to become the dominant figure of Methodism even as Bunting had been earlier. In 1889, the year of the Dock Strike, the *Methodist Times* attacked the Methodist mission in India in a blow against the established Connectional leadership which was very much oriented to the foreign mission field. These charges, however, were not sustained, and after his predominant position in the Connection was acknowledged, Hughes himself became reconciled to foreign missions.[32]

One historian has described Wesleyanism as having fulfilled its inner purposes by becoming, increasingly, a part of the nonconformist block which backed the Liberal Party,[33] and a recent investigation of pollbooks would suggest that even Methodist ministers, contrary to the usual view, were overwhelmingly Liberal by mid-century.[34] Another recent historian, John Kent, has continued to see important differences between Methodism and the rest of nonconformity. Kent has maintained that Bunting's Toryism was essentially loyal to Wesley and his system, and that there were no real differences on political questions between Wesleyan Methodists and their non-Wesleyan Methodist brethren; later in the century, he continued, the Wesleyan Methodists supported Rosebery, the Liberal Imperialists, and the Boer War. Kent has taken note of "the rather vulgar Liberal imperialism" of Sir Robert Perks, Sir Henry Fowler, Sir William McArthur, and Hughes,[35] and of the xenophobic, even racist, "social Imperialism" of Hughes as well as of other leading Wesleyan Methodists who saw Rosebery's social imperialism as a block to socialism.[36] (Methodism, it might be noted, had waged war against socialism which it saw as "the old scheme of INFIDEL ATHEISTICAL NECESSITY," as early as the second quarter of the century.) [37] Hughes, not unlike Richard Watson earlier in the century, lauded the Pax Britannica, which he saw as maintained not only by England but by an Anglo-Saxon America (as had Watson) and other "Teutonic" nations true to Reformation principles as the only means of ending bloodshed and anarchy. Like Sir James Stephen, he saw an "Imperial Methodism" as especially suited to the British Empire.[38]

THE SECTS, THE "DEMOCRATIC REVOLUTION," AND LIBERALISM

It might certainly be argued that if we wish to explore the religious origins of English liberalism, we would do better to turn to Unitarianism or Quakerism. Were not Priestley, Price, or the Quaker-Deist Paine better exponents of liberal, democratic doctrine than John Wesley and Richard Watson? Undoubtedly. But could one of these sects or the Anglicanism of the *via media* have made "new men" of the lower classes and presided over their nonviolent rites of passage into modern society? It was Methodism, the facts show, not Unitarianism or Quakerism, which attracted hundreds of thousands of the lower classes to its standards during this critical time of transition.

The divisions among the faithful in England were not dissimilar to those that had existed among the Jews at the time of Christ. Many of the clergy of the Establishment, like many of the priestly Sadducees, had turned to a worldly model. The Methodists, following the example of Jesus, adhered to the vision of the Pharisees who desired only to pursue a godly life and urged that Caesar be given his due. But the Pharisees, in pietistic, sectarian fashion, had sought to separate themselves from the godless, the *Am-ha-eretz,* the common throng, a decision which permitted the Zealots and the dagger-wielding Sicarii to lead the people to destructive revolution in 66 A.D. Wesley, who feared the worst from Antinomian zealots, was determined to take the commonalty of England to his bosom and make it God-fearing, for Wesley, unlike the Pharisees and the older nonconformists, took up an evangelistic vocation: he did not think of himself as the leader of a sect, but as the reformer of the nation. Not only in politics and philosophy, but in matters of social ethics, Wesley found himself—it is difficult to say how consciously—in the moderate Pharisaic tradition rather than in that of the more rigid, deterministic sects; certainly both the Methodists and the Pharisees saw providence ruling all while men had free will, a compromise between High Church and Sadducean free will and the determinism of the Calvinists and Essenes. There is some evidence that Wesley thought of Methodists as akin to the Pharisees; certainly, Wesley described the latter in much more sympathetic terms than had the Gospels.[39]

Wesley, as early as 1741, had observed that the Calvinist doctrine of predestination was an immobilizing doctrine, making any effort at spiritual or social amelioration appear futile. While Wesley, with his belief in free will, had urged charity to the poor, Joseph Priestley, a Unitarian minister and a philosophical determinist though occupying an "advanced" political position, anticipated the later economic outlook—with its illiberal and traditional determinist underside—of the liberal middle classes, and believed charity worse than useless. In having "defeated the purposes of Providence," Priestley observed, parish relief "reduced him [the pauper] to a condition below that of any of the brutes." The Unitarian determinist, as early as the 1780s, raised the laissez-faire banner in just this quasi-Calvinist spirit, declaring that "nothing . . . seems so likely to answer the purpose as undoing, as fast as we can, all that we have hitherto done, and getting back into the plain path of nature and of Providence," that of making every man look after himself and his family.[40] What if Wesley's fight against Calvinist predestinarianism had not been as successful as it was in banishing determinism not only from the denomination which was to contain the most numerous body of Dissent, but also, and more important, in helping thoroughly to undermine its credibility in parts of the Established Church and in the ranks of much of the older Dissent? In that case, might not organized Christianity have confirmed, rather than counteracted, the secular predestinarianism of the main branch of orthodox political economy? Without Evangelical social reforms, might not an industrial England have succumbed to the "fatal inevitability" of class conflict prophesied by Ricardian political economy?

Yet Quakerism and Unitarianism have been more clearly associated with nineteenth-century liberalism than has a pietistic Methodism. Indeed it has become a commonplace to suggest that the sects, with their Puritan descent, were the means by which seventeenth-century ideas of liberty were transmitted to the nineteenth century. Like Methodism, both Quakerism and Unitarianism were universalist, seemed optimistic concerning man, and were relatively nonsystematic in theology, as well as committed to the ideal of tolerance, and concerned with the importance of works. There were, of course, doctrinal differences between them and Methodism —as, for example, in the strand of Unitarian determinism—which deserve consideration, and it may be argued that it was in their organization and in their methods of propagation that the chief differences lay. Certainly, neither of the "liberal" sects managed, as did the Methodists, to tap Protestant fervor and thus to enlist great numbers, to make "new men" on a mass scale. These sects might, it may be further argued, have served as a spur for a "democratic revolution," but one more like that which took place in France: their doctrines might have served as a way station to a secular religion of liberalism and democracy and thus, in all probability, as a force for promoting violent revolution by masses in search of a faith. Methodism, on the other hand, served as an effective agent in the dissemination of the liberal ethos while still keeping its adherents devoted to order.

First of all, what of the Quakers and liberalism? In George Fox and the Society of Friends in the seventeenth century we may see clear anticipations of certain of the more important organizational and doctrinal features of the later Methodism. The Friends, like many of the seventeenth-century Puritans and the later Methodists, regarded themselves as belonging to a religious fellowship whose members exercised a strict moral supervision over each other; they possessed, again like the Methodists, a lay and itinerant ministry, ready to preach indoors and outdoors, to which women were admitted, which sought conversion by inducing a personal mystical experience of an intense emotional order. They stressed the importance of repentance and personal striving after divine truth, and preached tolerance, universal salvation, and the possibility of achieving perfection in this life. (This last was a complete victory over sin, though Robert Barclay, the foremost theologian of the Friends, was ready to grant the existence of degrees of perfection and the possibility of a fall from perfection.) Fox and Dewsbury established a system of discipline and a form of church government which would supervise the orderly dispatch of itinerant preachers and the payment of their expenses, although there was considerable opposition from Quaker advocates of the inner light. Like the Methodists, subsequently, Quakers displayed a great interest in missions, in philanthropy generally, and in education, and they became the great opponents of slavery.

What kept the Friends from producing a Quaker version of the democratic revolution? They were not successful evangelists, certainly not on the scale of the Methodist Revival. In the eighteenth century Quaker zeal declined, and no longer did Quakers claim to embody the future form of the entire church. More and more they saw themselves as a "peculiar people," and occupied themselves with maintaining their purity rather than in seeking converts. Moreover, they so stressed the inner light during the century after Fox's death that there seemed little interest in the written word of Scripture or of outward works as a means of attaining holiness. (Similar ideas of perfection were, of course, present in the Revival in the doctrines of men like Relly or Cudworth, whom Wesley denounced as Antinomians.) By the middle of the eighteenth century, it might be said that their time had come, and they were not equal to the opportunity.

Clearly, despite similarities to Quakerism, Wesleyanism moved in a very different direction. Unlike the mystical, sectarian Quakers, Wesley, a good Churchman, could not neglect the importance of the word, of reason, and of the attainment of outward holiness; he would not do without the sacraments, liturgy, or formal creed, as did the Quakers. Nor did he separate himself from the Established Church and from the nation as a whole, although at one time, in his later life, he was to regret that his followers were not, as were the Quakers, distinguishable from others by their dress. Wesley, rather than challenge the state by the exercise of a conscientious pacifism, or by a refusal to take oaths in Quaker fashion, urged a positive loyalty to the King and his ministers, and a readiness to defend them in time of war for conscience sake. An Anglican writer spoke in 1804, of "the passive obedience of the Quakers in principle and practice," and of how, in contrast, "the Methodists as a body join" to this passive obedience an "active obedience, without the smallest scruple or reluctance." [41] There was, moreover, a strain in Methodism, barely present in eighteenth-century Quakerism, one congenial to popular and traditional Protestantism as well as to *practical* Christianity, which laid great emphasis upon man's natural depravity as well as on the joys of paradise and the dreads of hellfire, which gained converts and helped to discipline Enthusiasm. [42]

What, then, of the Unitarians? The differences between the Methodists and the Unitarians are sharp. Despite Priestley's praise of their social utility, [43] the Unitarians, through the decades of our study, regarded the Methodists as illiberal and therefore dangerous. In the 1780s, for example, the Unitarian minister Richard Price, Wesley's political foe, denounced the "absurdities" of the established faith lest religion "go on to lose its credit" until "little of it will be left except among the lower order of people," many of whom, Price continued, "are sinking into a barbarism in religion lately revived by Methodism." [44] A half-century later, an anonymous pamphlet on Methodism published by the British and Foreign Unitarian Association and written by R. B. Aspland, a prominent Unitarian preacher, attacked the Wesleyan "priestly oligarchy" as well as Methodist doctrine. "About two millions" of persons were in one way or another, by attending Methodist meetings or Methodist Sunday Schools, Aspland argued, "terrified into obedience" by this "church militant," whose *"esprit de corps"* dominated absolutely on all "moral and political questions," and, indeed, in all "the ordinary pursuits of life." Methodism had made priests of fanatics, "men who but yesterday exchanged the apron for the black coat," and was "an enemy to the principles of dissent." These men, "tyrants themselves," inevitably "incline to the side of tyranny." Indeed, Aspland observed, as Methodism, "in the stormy times of 1792, . . . has gone into the strong-holds of dissent—it has gone among the people, and bound those who, in the natural course of things, would have been on our side, with a seven-fold cord." Although Aspland was ready to concede that Methodism had "done good service in the field against the monstrous doctrines of Calvin," thus liberating "the minds of thousands" from "the strong agony which these tenets occasion in all who, earnest in their religious convictions, sit at the feet of the Gamaliel of Geneva," and that the Methodist leadership had "so far" been "friends to religious emancipation," he still concluded that Methodism "has done more than any other thing to check the progress of liberal sentiments within the last century." [45]

The Methodists, on the other hand, insisted that authority and discipline were a necessary means of making the lower classes virtuous and self-reliant. In 1789, for example, a defender of the Methodists, John Holloway, in a reply to Price's attack, suggested that Price's "sublime ideas are more calculated for theory than for practice," since there was "as yet too much barbarism in the world to allow any prospect of such refined ideas of liberty being realised in society." Holloway urged Price first to "begin to labour among the lower classes of society, reform their manners, and make them sufficiently virtuous." The aim of Methodism was "to civilize and disciple (*sic*) the nations of the world." Why did the Unitarians not go abroad to "convert the heathen-nations," or turn with charity to the "dissolute and profane" poor at home? [46] In 1830, Aspland, like Priestley, could acknowledge the past usefulness of Methodist discipline to which Holloway alluded. Methodism had undertaken "to rule those who could not rule themselves." But "however Methodism may have suited the last century," he nonetheless insisted, "it will not suit the present, except the tone of its domination be lowered, and its spirit assimilated to the liberal spirit of the age." [47] This, indeed, was already happening at the time Aspland wrote.

What would have happened if Methodism had chosen the way of these sects, in the process refining, as had the Quakers and Unitarians, the purity of the liberalism inherent in the most characteristic parts of Arminian theology? By chance, we have an experimental sample of such a sectarian Methodism. The "Arminian Methodists," about seven hundred people and thirteen local preachers, led by Henry Breeden, in the vicinity of Derby, seceded from the Wesleyan Methodist Connection in 1832, [48] one of the very few secessions on grounds of doctrine in Methodist history. The so-called Derby folk moved Arminianism to its liberal and Pelagian conclusion. Although man was undeniably sinful, they maintained, nonetheless "the grace of God operates upon every heart," and the Holy Spirit "powerfully inclines (but not irresistibly forces) people to be saved." Faith was available as soon as sought, and fervent prayer for the bestowal of God's grace was not necessary. [49] Of course, the Latitudinarians of the Establishment had almost reached such a view of man, one much like that being reached by liberal political theorists, but Wesleyan Methodism was horrified by what seemed a flight not to the passive Pelagianism of the Anglican Church, but an evangelical Pelagianism. A critic of the "Derby folk," correctly saw these doctrines as antiscriptural: the Scriptures had been insistent upon "man's total degeneracy, his own utter inability to employ remedial measures, and consequently the indispensable necessity of an immediate agency from above." The Derby Arminian Methodist—"rash enthusiast" that he was, "would fain limit Jehovah's prerogative—trespass upon his peculiar province—and place the proud meritoriousness of a human agent in the high seat of the Divine Majesty." [50]

The Arminian Methodists, indeed, declared their independence even of divine grace in a way which left very little specifically Christian about their doctrine. Their appeal was very limited. They did not prosper, and their creed became rather a way station to the English middle-class Liberalism of the latter part of the century,[51] almost a secularized faith like liberalism, positivism, or socialism. It is interesting to observe that the families of both George Eliot and Herbert Spencer had been among the Arminian Methodists of Derby.[52]

Methodism has been described as a denomination, bearing the marks of both sect and church. John Wesley was an archetype of the charismatic leader of a sect. Even when still a High Church Anglican priest in Georgia, he banished the woman he had earlier sought in marriage from the communion table. While insisting, in churchly fashion, that he parted from no man on account of his opinion, he denounced and separated himself from the Moravians, expelled Cennick and his allies, and waged doctrinal war against Calvinism, all for opinions which might easily have found expression in the Church of England. He insisted that salvation by faith and the New Birth were at the heart of his doctrines, and stressed the doctrine of Assurance—all appeals undeniably in the mold of enthusiastic Protestant sectarianism. Like the sects, Methodism accepted lay preaching by the spiritually gifted regardless of education or social status; even women were welcomed as preachers. Like the sects, the Methodists sought to include only the morally and spiritually qualified in their societies, imposing upon them a strict supervision, employing a ticket system adopted from earlier sectarians, and never hesitating to expel backsliders. As a sect, of course, Methodism was more akin to the highly disciplined Puritan associations, even to imitating their ascetic ideals, than to less orderly sects like the Anabaptists.

Yet despite such sectarian tendencies, Wesley, as a good Churchman, was ready to rely on the Church of England for the sacraments, for Baptism, and for Communion, and, during his lifetime, even insisted that meetings of his societies not take place during hours of Church worship. Wesley regarded himself as making real and vital the true message of the Anglican *via media,* the doctrine of Hooker and Tillotson, rather than the false Calvinistic one of the dissenting sects. He strove to balance unsettling, sectarian salvation by faith by making churchly works necessary for sanctification. If lay preaching by the spiritually gifted was encouraged, the Connection always endeavored to keep the doctrine of the preacher free of personal eccentricities; first Wesley and then the Legal Hundred meeting in Conference were responsible for assigning itinerant preachers, taking care that none remained sufficiently long in a circuit either to establish independence of the Connection or to become subject to the will or opinions of members of local societies. Moreover, in the best churchly, as well as denominational, fashion, Wesleyanism invited *all* Christians to attend prayer meetings, and, later, Methodist Sunday Schools, and these "hearers" far outnumbered the actual "members" of Methodist societies.

After Wesley's death, the Methodists emerged as a fully independent "church." In 1793, Methodism ended the distinction retained by Wesley because of his Anglican prejudices between ordained and nonordained ministers, while retaining a similar one between itinerant and local preachers. Only the itinerants could administer sacraments; the local preachers, frequently part-time, continued as the instrument of Methodism's sect-like thrust. (Indeed, by the 1820s Bunting was to see them as a source of democratic meddling with the government of the Connection.) In the nineties, the forces within Methodism which had sought complete separation from the Church moved to have the Connection offer communion independently. The Connection regularly denied the requests of local congregations that they be permitted to reject ministers whom they thought unworthy, while dissenting congregations were freely choosing theirs. The ministers, not the laity as among the Dissenters, governed Methodism. With separation from the Anglican Church, the Connection inherited all the functions which it had formerly permitted the Church to perform in its behalf, while continuing to stress the church-like features of both its theology and organization. By the second decade of the nineteenth century, Adam Clarke was to see Methodist evangelism at home as completed, the only domestic function of the Connection being the continuing disciplining and superintendence of the faithful and their children. At this point Methodism saw itself as fully a church.

Abroad, in the interests of the national mission, it was to remain, not officially but in fact, a most effective proselytizing arm of the national Church, which had for so long been its role at home. Though at first still distrustful of the dissenting sects, seeing them as the republican heirs of Puritan revolutionaries and therefore as dangerous to both Church and state, the Connection gradually grew to understand that the latter were being transformed into the Methodist image, and by mid-century was ready to join with Dissenters, as we have seen, in a host of humanitarian and missionary undertakings.

There have been a wide variety of opinions concerning Wesley's "system." Some have seen him and Methodism as fundamentally Lutheran;[53] others have regarded Wesley as at bottom a Puritan or a Calvinist.[54] He has been set down as a Moravian, a Pelagian and even a quasi-Catholic.[55] But although Wesleyans—at different times—appeared ready to assume these frequently conflicting labels,[56] none of them really fits. Methodism owed much to the Anglican *via media,* and, one might say, could hardly have performed the function here assigned to it had it not been for the confirming influence of the national Church. Certainly, in distinguishing pragmatic, individualistic English liberalism from certain absolutist continental counterparts, this *via media* played a most useful role. Wesley opposed the Calvinist *system,* with what one writer has called the "liberal method," a method in theology based upon reason and scriptural tradition which Hooker set forth and which the Cambridge Platonists and the Latitudinarians had developed.[57]

Methodism, like Anglicanism, had an ingrained antipathy to the idea of "system," which it saw as inevitably Calvinistic in its tendencies. So strong was Wesley's antagonism to a theological *system* that he found himself discouraging the reading of any books except the Bible and the Homilies because "I find they who read many books usually neglect the Bible, and soon become eager disputants, and in the end turn out Predestinarians." [58] Theological soundness was less important than good conduct, and Wesley was first of all the advocate of a practical Christianity. Although declaring that it was "our bounden duty to labour after a right judgement in all things," since "a wrong judgement naturally leads to wrong practice," Wesley insisted that "right opinion is at best but a very slender part of religion," which "properly and directly consists in right tempers, words, and actions." Wesley even suggested that right opinion might exist "where there is no religion at all; in men of the most abandoned lives; yea, in the devil himself." [59] In its obituary of Wesley in 1791, the *Gentleman's Magazine* understood Wesley's attraction to the views of Arminius as not only "more benevolent in their nature," but as more "practical in their tendency, than Calvin's" doctrines. [60]

It may have been because of its lack of a theological system, as I suggested earlier, that liberal, secular-minded historians tend to think of Wesleyan Methodism as the narrowest pietism and to compare it, to its disadvantage, to seventeenth-century Calvinism. This certainly seemed the view of Sir Leslie Stephen, a good radical and consequently an admirer of the "system," of the rigor of Puritan theology and political thought,[61] as well as of E. P. Thompson, with a similar predilection for the liberating role of the Puritan revolution.[62] One recent scholar, Michael Walzer, has adopted a more persuasive view when he concludes that Calvinism, however systematic, was "not a liberal ideology."

Though Calvinist associations were voluntary, Walzer has argued, they gave rise to "a new political discipline—impersonal and ideological," one not based on patriarchal kingship, nor upon loyalty, nor upon the desire of men for salvation. Adapting Weber's economic categories to politics, Walzer viewed the Calvinist saint as preeminently a revolutionary, disciplined by an ideology with a "military and political work-ethic" directed not toward capitalist acquisition but toward struggle, toward challenging the old order. Seeing his work as "an endless struggle with the devil," the saint, in a mood of an apocalyptic millenarianism, saw "violence and systematic warfare as the necessary price of reformation." Calvin saw men as entirely wicked, unredeemed by a survival of Adam's original innocence, as a kind of powerless rationality. Calvin's political theory, neither patriarchal nor contractual, saw the state as a necessary order of repression, anticipating the authoritarianism of Hobbes as well as that of Rousseau. Calvinism, although it looked forward to an internally accepted discipline and therefore helped prepare for liberalism, Walzer concluded, was not liberalism but radical Enthusiasm, and he suggested that "the spread of the capitalist and liberal spirits parallels the decline of radical enthusiasm." [63] I have suggested that the spread of these spirits accompanied the rise of Evangelical Arminianism.

THE METHODIST REVOLUTION AND ENGLISH LIBERALISM

The eighteenth century was a time in England when, in Smollett's words in 1771, "no body reads sermons but Methodists and Dissenters." Between the nominal Churchman and the Dissenter there was an enormous chasm, social and theological, as well as the burden of the Interregnum of the preceding century. Smollett's Methodist servant, Humphrey Clinker, did not represent a challenge to his master, as might a middle-class Dissenter; indeed he was by the very character of his calling a client—in the novel, his master's long-unrevealed natural son—and maintained religious principles which bade him know his place, and which seemed little different from those his master pretended to espouse. Much the same could be said of the proletarian Methodists of the Northern villages, who also made the claim of being well-behaved subordinates seeking sympathetic patronage. John Wesley and George Whitefield called upon all Englishmen to listen to the inner voices which bid them to turn to God, and the message was taken up by regiments of lay preachers who wished to reawaken the dormant sensibilities of a generation wary of yielding to Enthusiasm. Though the governing classes feared the possible consequences, in the years ahead they were compelled to grant that Methodist Enthusiasm appeared to bring sobriety rather than disorder.

Nor could they deny the wide appeal of Methodism. When Humphrey Clinker, the footman-preacher, addressed a Methodist meeting, "we were altogether confounded at finding all the females of our family among the audience." "What right has such a fellow as you to set up for a reformer," asked Clinker's master? "May not the new light of God's grace shine upon the poor and the ignorant in their humility, as well as upon the wealthy?" Clinker replied. "In a word, Mr Clinker," came the employer's retort, "I will have no light in my family . . . unless it be the light of reason, which you don't pretend to follow." Clinker's victory came when the events of 1789–1792 persuaded the gentlemen to join the ladies. By that time, they would have recourse to a more "proper ghostly director" than a servant.[64] But it was the servant's Enthusiasm, not the master's reason, which triumphed.

As early as 1759, Oliver Goldsmith had seized the issue, though without fully perceiving the Methodist role. Goldsmith described the sermons of Tillotson, the great Arminian divine, as having become the model for Anglican ministers. Such sermons, "long, dry, tedious discussions," served "to amuse only divines and are utterly neglected by the generality of mankind." Goldsmith urged the ministers of the Church of England to discard their "lazy manner of reading sermons," and to forget the road of preferment in favor of the "pleasures of improving society." If he endeavored "to be great, instead of being prudent," thus risking being called "an enthusiast," the Anglican minister might perhaps counter the illegal activities of the Methodists, who though seldom "endowed with common sense," yet manage to "affect their hearers." Why did not the bishops, "testify the same fervour, and *entreat* their hearers, as well as *argue*"? "The enthusiasms of the poor" were at present "opposed to law." If the established Church were, legally, to "conspire with their enthusiasms," England would be "the happiest nation upon earth." For, Goldsmith declared, "enthusiasm in religion, which prevails only among the vulgar, should be the chief object of politics": "a society of enthusiasts governed by reason among the great, is the most indissoluble, the most virtuous, and the most efficient of its own decrees that can be imagined." All strong nations "have had their enthusiasms, which ever serve as laws among the people." Goldsmith noted the ancient Greek *Kalokagathia,* and the Roman *Amor Patriae;* England had "the truer and firmer bond of the *Protestant Religion."* Goldsmith, in calling upon "those whom the law has appointed teachers of this religion" to "raise those enthusiasms among people, by which alone political society can subsist," [65] could not see that the Methodists, however illegally they might preach, were doing precisely this.

If as we have been persuaded by contemporary historians, all of Western society was prepared, in the last quarter of the eighteenth and the first quarter of the nineteenth centuries for a revolution whose message was to be *liberté, egalité,* and *fraternité,* certainly, it matters very much whether the vehicle for this revolution was to be an anticolonial rebellion as in America, a political and social revolution as in France, an imposition of a conquering army as on much of the European continent, or a religious revival. Such a revolution, espousing in a variety of forms the new social and political faith which the modern, industrial state required, could not be produced routinely or accepted perfunctorily. It required a pervasive, all-embracing Enthusiasm to make "new men," and it required a well-organized system of fraternal discipline to keep them on the road to Christian Perfection. In England alone, this explosion of the energies of the masses was accompanied by a minimum of physical violence and bloodshed. Certainly among the more important reasons for this happy transition to the modern world, I have argued, was the Methodist Revival which incorporated an attenuated, spiritual version of the new, democratic faith in its Arminian Christianity, mobilizing popular energies in pursuit of personal salvation, while strengthening the motives for obedience and subordination.

We must see this Methodist Revolution as Tocqueville saw the French Revolution: both were, in good part, revolts by masses of the humble, ignorant, and superstitious, yearning, at times of social transition and of spiritual crisis, to be made whole again by faith. They were spectacular displays of religious Enthusiasm. For decades, there had been "a civil war in every soul," between reason and fanaticism, between skepticism and faith. In France, the religious skepticism of the intellectual elite and the governing classes had so fully triumphed over revealed religion that faith had to seek its realization elsewhere: the religion of the Goddess of Liberty, with its climax in the fanaticism of the Terror, and in the religion of imperial grandeur under Napoleon. In England the Revival had enlisted, ever since 1739, the Enthusiasm of the most susceptible and most critically placed. When the hour of revolution arrived in France, not only were the numbers of enthusiasts in England enrolled at an increasing rate but a considerable part of the governing classes were also, with understandable haste, converted to the evangelical standard.

That standard, indeed, was also to enlarge the sense of communion of the uprooted and those formerly alienated from God, from the Methodist fellowship to the nation as a whole, and to its world mission. If Methodism muted the calls to liberty and equality in order to restrain enthusiastic, revolutionary propensities, the same motive made it stress fraternity. In the century of Voltaire's *sauve qui peut* and Smith's *laissez-faire,* when the paternalism of the traditional hierarchical society was breaking down, Methodism sought to endow the lower classes with a sense of their own worth, and to revive traditional religion as a source of warmth and solace, of comfort and joy. In a cosmopolitan century in which wars and ties of allegiance seemed more dynastic than national, Methodism expounded a new loyalty to the King and State, and to the Church and the Nation.

Seventeenth-century Arminianism—both Dutch Remonstrance and Laudian—had proved incapable of inspiring the masses, unable to tap the profound emotions. Laudian Arminianism—that is, Anglo-Catholic ritualism—had obviously been limited in its appeal, and while the Arminianism of the Remonstrancers might influence thinkers like Grotius and the Cambridge Platonists, it could not convert the miners of Kingswood. It was Wesley's Evangelical Arminianism—supported by a functionally Arminian (in that they called on all to be saved) though still (in sentiment and slogan) Calvinistic Evangelicalism—which had aroused masses of believers, and *was* capable of effecting the Protestant Counter-Reformation which the seventeenth-century Arminians had sought, as well as helping to effect the objectives of the "democratic revolution." Wesley went through Great Britain and Ireland to announce that *all* men—not merely a predestined elect—could avail themselves of Christ's offer that those who believed in

Him should be saved. Those justified in this fashion would obtain sanctification by voluntarily submitting themselves to the discipline of their fellows in their joint pursuit of freedom from sin, and the joy of Christian Perfection. A man might be saved, in an "instant," through the free gift of God, but his perseverance was not preordained, and he must earnestly strive, through love and works, to achieve and to maintain Perfection and a state of sanctification.

Wesley intermittently disavowed the Pelagianism immanent in his view of Perfection, insisting that, unlike Pelagius, he had no doubt of the reality of original sin and of the certainty that God's grace was necessary to put man in a condition wherein he might seek after holiness. But the essentially Pelagian *tendency* of Wesley's views was nonetheless clear to Wesley's Calvinist opponents. And may not Pelagius be set down as the first British liberal? With the necessary Christian qualification, Wesley saw man as inherently good.

If Wesley called the poor from riot to the New Testament politics of divine right and passive obedience, he also insisted upon spiritual liberty and equality, which helped to provide a positive alternative to tumult. Evangelical Arminianism, fulfilling the optimistic implications of Arminian theology, saw the possibility of Christian Perfection on earth, an incentive to good works and self improvement, with its offer of full participation in the heavenly Kingdom, and by easy extension, in the earthly one as well. Wesleyanism made the extension even easier, despite its authoritarian structure, by welcoming the perfected, and even the partially perfected poor into the service of the Connection as lay preachers, class leaders, and stewards.

Such an Arminianism seems more useful, in the shaping of a capitalist ethic than a Calvinism which saw man as irremediably under the aegis of sin, and his salvation or damnation as irrevocably preordained. Methodism proved to be—not unlike the earlier Calvinism—the means by which many men of the lower orders joined the ranks of the middling-orders. The older Protestantism, directed toward a few, had equipped its adherents with the self-discipline and self-assurance for participation in revolution or in the political life of the oligarchic republics of the seventeenth century. In casting its net much wider, Methodism was better suited to the era which England was then entering, both in the evangelizing of great numbers, and in its quasi-democratic principles of organization—lay preachers, the mutual supervision of the bands, societies, and so on. Wesley foresaw the probability that Christian habits would make for an improvement in social station; the Wesleyan denial of irresistible grace, the recognition that steady effort was necessary to attain and to retain Perfection, seemed a theological mirror of the liberal theory of a relatively mobile society. Would not a growingly liberal and commercial England require the disciplined energies of previously untapped sections of its population to manage its commerce and industry and the increasing complexities of its local and national politics?

For a number of these reasons, despite his Toryism, Wesley has been described as a democrat and as a social-reformer by his admirers, and Methodism has even been accounted an important force in the development of the British labor and socialist movements.[66] Certainly, in the Arminian religion of universal redemption, as we have seen, there can also be found a source of antislavery sentiments and missionary activity, and of the Wesleyan interest in the education of the working classes. And, very much at the core of this doctrine of the burghers of Amsterdam and Utrecht, with its contractual view of man's relationship with God, was a plea for tolerance and against bigotry, a cornerstone of modern liberalism. In carrying the banner of free will, Wesley was making himself the spokesman of the creed which underlay both the humanism of the Enlightenment and the liberalism of the nineteenth century, even as other men were preparing to carry forward the Augustinian and Calvinian proclamations of man's helplessness against the great forces of history. It was, consequently, a dedicated Tory, convinced that revolution was sin, who proved an instrument of a liberal revolution.

Very much linked to the role of Methodism as a vehicle for its spiritual version of a democratic revolution, as I have suggested, was its simultaneous determination to battle against both "speculative" and "practical" Antinomianism, which it associated with Calvinist Dissent. Wesley's desire to avoid revolutionary violence may be regarded as pervading and unifying virtually all of his leading ideas; it had become, like his loyalty to the King, a fundamental part of his religion, and was rooted not only in the New Testament and in the views of the High Church, but also in the circumstances of his personal history. Wesley was understandably fearful of the consequences of his own enthusiastic methods, and disturbed that his preaching might be thought provocative, most particularly since his first arenas of activity were amid the violence of the new industrial towns. His attacks on "speculative" Antinomianism must often have seemed far-fetched to his far-from-revolutionary theological opponents, and certainly there seemed a great gap between "speculative" and "practical" Antinomianism; yet in earlier centuries that gap had proved frighteningly narrow.

What, one might ask, would have happened in the seventies, or during the wars with revolutionary France, if the Wesleyans had not been so committed to obedience and subordination? If the rabble assembled by Lord George Gordon caused such a fright,[67] what if Methodism had provided an organized popular movement, grounded in the pristine Protestantism, the sectarian Enthusiasm, of the Reformation, dedicated to producing "saints" on the American model, rather than seekers after Christian Perfection? [68] The eighteenth century was a time of turmoil, and the Methodists took the opportunity of panics, riots—even those of Church-and-King mobs directed against themselves—and other disturbances to spread their message. Wesley, for example, described the "general expectation" of "calamities" in 1756, after the Lisbon earthquake and the renewal of hostilities with France, as "a means of abundant spiritual blessings": "we endeavoured," he declared, "in every part of the kingdom, to avail ourselves of the apprehensions which we frequently found it was impossible to remove, in order to make them conducive to a nobler end; to that 'fear of the Lord' which 'is the beginning of wisdom.' " [69] What if Wesley, and his successors, had been moved by a more mundane end?

If Mary Wollstonecraft saw in Burke a man who might have been "a violent revolutionist," had he not suppressed such inclinations,[70] does not our portrait of Wesley and his ideas suggest something quite similar? Burke, a good Whig and a defender of the Revolution of 1688 and of the cause of the American colonists in the 1770s,[71] found himself advocating Lockean principles until the coming of the French Revolution. It has been suggested recently by C. C. O'Brien that beneath the English Whiggery of Burke there was a covert Irish Jacobite who was repelled by Dissenters such as Dr. Price (to whom Burke was replying in his *Reflections*) whom he regarded as potential rebels, and whose modes of thinking he believed conducive to revolution.[72] Wesley, while respectful of Locke, could not fail to denounce such disciples of his as Price (who, we recall, had also been Wesley's opponent in the seventies) when they extracted Locke's political principles from their theological setting, and, in so doing, seemed to direct them toward the goal of unsettling society. For Wesley as for Burke, the Protestantism of the dissenting sects was potentially revolutionary, and the "superstition" of the Churches—both Catholic and Anglican—was a block to Jacobinism and a citadel of order. For both, there was an inner struggle between the politics of the Jacobites and that of the Whigs, and for both of them the struggle derived a special psychological urgency because of family circumstances: Burke's father had shed his Catholicism, just as Wesley's parents had shrugged off Dissent, to conform, each for his own motives, to the Establishment. Their sons can be seen as having struggled to bring this ambiguous ideological inheritance into some harmony.

The French and the Methodist Revolutions were calls both to a democratic revolution, though on different levels, and to order. In France, the call to liberty and equality, a call to democracy, was an unsettling thrust; the call to fraternity was an appeal to social cohesion, and at bottom to national unity against a cosmopolitan aristocracy as well as the foreigner. But even the call to order had revolutionary implications and was readily converted into a call for imperial grandeur under Napoleon, to spread the message of the revolution. The call to order in Methodism was articulated at every point with the call for a spiritual revolution by a leader who was at once a revolutionary and the most rabid opponent of disorder. Wesley's heirs, faced like the French Directory with the instability of these conflicting calls, with the threat of a continuing revolution still present and with the enemies of that revolution ready to move against it, were ready to

yield to the millenarian urge to conquer the world for Arminian Christianity, spurred in good part by the failure of Napoleon to conquer it for the
principles of the revolution. Given this conflict, clearly apparent in Wesley, and passed on by him to his successors, it cannot be surprising that
contemporaries were puzzled, even as some historians are today, as to
whether Methodism constituted a force for radicalism or for stability.

J. L. Talmon has discovered the antecedents of the secular religion of
"totalitarian democracy" in the chiliastic religious movements of the middle
ages and the Reformation, and in the Puritan Revolution of the seventeenth century. But it was in France, Talmon continues, that egalitarianism, in opposition to liberty, took a decisive direction toward a centralist,
"totalitarian" democracy, the roots of which were to be found in the left
wing of the Enlightenment—in Rousseau, Morelly, Mably, Helvétius, and
Holbach. These absolutist theories came to flower in the Revolution under
the Jacobins and were carried into the nineteenth century in the "political
Messianism" of the Saint-Simonians and the disciples of Marx. Support for
an empirical, individualist, liberal democracy was to be found among the
Girdondists, and among men like Condorcet, and, later, Benjamin Constant,
Guizot, and Lamartine. In nineteenth-century England, John Stuart Mill
was the embodiment of liberal democracy, calling for the maximum scope
for individual freedom, eschewing the strand of coercion which lurked beneath abstract, absolute political dogma, that faith in a "system" which has
revealed "the truth" in the form of a blueprint of the future ideal society,
not unlike the millenarian blueprints of Puritanism, held to be imminently
realizable, frequently enough by violent revolution.[73] It is interesting to observe that among the historians in the nineteenth and early twentieth centuries who understood, each in his own way, the tension between liberty
and equality of which Tocqueville wrote, four of them—Guizot, Taine,
Lecky, and Halévy[74]—also observed, though without making any specific
connection between the two, the peculiar usefulness of Methodism in preventing an English counterpart of the French Revolution.

Wesley's Evangelical Arminianism, I have argued, may have played a
more positive role, in the course of pursuing its efforts to counter violent revolution, with its almost inevitable, history would suggest, aftermath of terror and repression? The Protestant Reformation was a revolution which
helped to usher in modern times, and Protestant ideas, as they were displayed by the leading denominations and in Catholic Jansenism, were
rooted in the conception of the essential corruption of human nature, for
which there was no earthly remedy, and in a divine despotism. As Georges
de Lagarde observed, such a conception made Reformation Protestantism
antagonistic to individualism and to rationalism, and caused it to envision
the need for organs of state repression akin to those which were to be described in Rousseau's "Religion Civile." Would the spirit which inspired

modern democracy be that of Luther and Calvin, Lagarde inquired. "La question est ouverte," was his cautious conclusion. [75]

Wesley, I suggest, may have contributed both directly and indirectly to making England a liberal and not a "totalitarian" democracy. Of course, Methodism preached reason, tolerance, and both civil and religious liberty, all essential to liberalism. Moreover, Methodism saw men as good, indeed, envisioned the possibility of Christian Perfection in this life. Its Enthusiasm transformed men, summoning them to assert rational control over their own lives, while providing in its system of mutual discipline the psychological security necessary for autonomous conscience and liberal ideals to become internalized, an integrated part of the "new men" awakened and regenerated by Wesleyan preaching. In all this, Methodism may also have helped to soften the brutalities of a rapidly growing industrial society. Of course, it is as difficult to estimate the importance of the contribution that Methodism may have made toward such ends as it has been to gauge the role of the Protestant ethic in the birth of capitalism. Evangelical religion, moreover, may also have had less happy effects on English life in the nineteenth and twentieth centuries, as we have indicated. But in its Arminian —and in its "practical" Christian—variant, it proved a strong support to a society which, almost uniquely, sought to extend liberty, and was able to enjoy that liberty because it had mastered, again almost uniquely, a large measure of self-discipline.

"Despotism may be able to do without faith," Tocqueville wrote in his study of American democracy, "but freedom cannot." "How could society escape destruction if, when political ties are relaxed, moral ties are not tightened . . . and what can be done with a people master of itself if it is not subject to God?" This was Tocqueville's final judgment concerning the relative stability of England and America, more particularly in comparison to France. Tocqueville did not fully understand how this had come about in England, even as France was moving in an altogether different direction. This may have been the function, I have argued, of the Methodist Revolution. "Almost every revolution which has changed the shape of nations," Tocqueville declared, "has been made to consolidate or destroy inequality." At its core, the Methodist Revolution, which was such a movement, aimed at countering the destructive spiritual consequences of certain of the illiberal, traditional doctrines preached by the Reformation. It may have been this spiritual Revolution which made possible the essential peculiarity of what Tocqueville called "Anglo-American civilization"—the "product" of "two perfectly distinct elements which elsewhere have often been at war with one another." "I mean," he concluded, "the *spirit of religion* and the *spirit of freedom*." [76]

Notes

I / THE METHODIST REVOLUTION

1. For a fuller discussion of the historiography of what has become virtually a "classic" problem, see B. Semmel, "Elie Halévy, Methodism, and Revolution," introductory chapter to Elie Halévy, *The Birth of Methodism in England* (Chicago: University of Chicago Press, 1971), pp. 1–29. See also Gertrude Himmelfarb, *Victorian Minds* (New York: Knopf, 1968), pp. 292–99.

2. See for example, J. L. and B. Hammond, *The Town Labourer, 1760–1832* (London: Longmans, Green, 1918), Chapters X, XI, XII. V. Kiernan, "Evangelicalism and the French Revolution," *Past and Present*, I (1952), 44–56; E. P. Thompson, *The Making of the English Working Class* (New York: Pantheon Books, 1964), pp. 41–46, 53–54, 350–51, 355–58, 362–63, 367–70, 375–82, 385–94. Thompson has denounced Methodism for having helped to subject the factory worker to the grinding discipline of the factory. Thompson's doubts concerning the Halévy thesis are set forth on p. 45. His exhilarating chapter "The Transforming Power of the Cross," however, may be regarded as confirming the thesis; see also p. 42. A further discussion of some of the complexities of Thompson's position on the Halévy thesis may be found in his postscript to the paperback edition (London: Penguin Books, 1968), pp. 917–23.

3. Thompson, *Making of the English Working Class*, p. 362.

4. Leslie Stephen, *History of English Thought in the Eighteenth Century* (New York: Harcourt Brace, 1962), II, 368, 362. (Originally published in 1876.)

5. Thompson, *Making of the English Working Class*, pp. 362–64.

6. See the Hammonds, *Town Labourer*, p. 287, and, indeed, the entire chapter on "The Defences of the Poor." Also see the works of the historian and Methodist minister, R. F. Wearmouth, especially *Methodism and the Working-Class Movements of England, 1800–1850* (London: Epworth Press, 1937); and the discussion in Harold Perkin, *The Origins of Modern English Society 1780–1880* (London: Routledge & Kegan Paul, 1969), pp. 353–57, and *passim*. See also E. J. Hobsbawm's protest against the view that much of "British socialism is descended from Wesley rather than from Marx," in his *Labouring Men: Studies in the History of Labour* (New York: Basic Books, 1964), p. 232; in same volume, see also pp. 23, 378, and *passim*.

7. Hammond, *Town Labourer*, p. 287.

8. Hobsbawm, "Methodism and the Threat of Revolution in Britain," in *Labouring Men*, pp. 31–32; much the same view is taken in E. J. Hobsbawm, *Primitive Rebels* (New York: W. W. Norton, 1965), pp. 128–32, 145 and *passim*.

9. "Let us take a pair of extreme examples. In 1855 the state-quarrymen of Trelazé, discontented with their economic conditions, decided to take action: they marched on Angers and proclaimed an insurrectionary Commune, presumably with the memory of the Commune of 1792 in their minds. Nine years later the coal-miners of Ebbw Vale were equally agitated. The lodges from the valley villages marched on to the mountains, headed by bands. Speeches were made, tea provided by the Ebbw Vale lodge at 6d. a head and the meeting ended with the singing of the Doxology. Both Welsh miners and Breton quarry-men were engaged on rather similar economic agitations. Clearly they differed, because the histories of their respective countries had differed. The stock of past experience, upon which they drew when learning how to organize, what to organize for, where to pick their cadre of leaders, and the ideology of those leaders embodied, in part at least, specific French and British elements: broadly speaking we may say, in the former case, the revolutionary, in the latter the radical-nonconformist traditions." E. J. Hobsbawm, "Labour Traditions," in *Labouring Men*, pp. 371–72.

10. Halévy, *The Birth of Methodism*, p. 62.

11. Quoted in C. B. A. Behrens, *The Ancien Regime* (New York: Harcourt, Brace & World, 1967), p. 10.

12. Alexis de Tocqueville, *The Old Regime and the French Revolution* (Garden City, N.Y.: Anchor Books, 1955), pp. x, 4–13, 19–21, 148–57.

13. This point of view is identified with R. R. Palmer, *The Age of the Democratic Revolution* (Princeton: Princeton University Press, 1959), 2 vols. Various writings of Jacques Godechot have also supported this view. Certainly, the critics of this view who stress the differences between the movements in the various countries are right when they warn against the search for rigid parallels: one such is to be found, for example, in R. C. Cobb, "The English Jacobins and the French Revolution," reprinted in P. Amann, ed., *The Eighteenth Century Revolution: French or Western* (Boston: D. C. Heath, 1963), pp. 23–25; for criticism of such parallelism, see Alfred Cobban, "The Age of the Democratic Revolution," *History*, XLV (1960), 234–39.

14. See F. Fanon, *The Wretched of the Earth* (New York: Grove Press, 1966), pp. 27–83, and *passim*. For a discussion of the difficulties which beset masters and men when the traditional relationship of dependency has become outmoded, and a new relationship of the modern sort is being formed, see O. Mannoni, *Prospero and Caliban; The Psychology of Colonization* (New York: Frederick A. Praeger, 1956). Mannoni was writing specifically about a colonial situation; for an application of his analysis to European conditions in the eighteenth and nineteenth centuries, see the discussion in B. Semmel, "The Issue of 'Race' in the British Reaction to the Morant Bay Uprising of 1865," *Caribbean Studies*, II (October 1962), 3–15. See the very able discussion of the late-eighteenth-century fight for autonomy in Fred Weinstein and G. M. Platt, *The Wish to be Free: Society, Psyche, and Value Change* (Berkeley: University of California Press, 1969).

15. It may be argued, as a French demographic historian did, that since eighteenth-century France was not industrialized, her additional population could not be absorbed, as could England's, in new economic activities; in both the countryside and in the growing towns, they remained idle, "ready and waiting for adventures"—a matter of "considerable significance for political history." L. Henry, "The Population of France in the Eighteenth Century," in D. V. Glass and D. E. C. Eversley, eds., *Population in History; Essays in Historical Demography* (Chicago: Aldine Publishing Company, 1965), p. 435.

16. David Hume, "Of Superstition and Enthusiasm," *The Philosophical*

Works of David Hume (T. H. Green and T. H. Grose, eds.) (Dormstadt: Scientia Verlag, 1964), III, 144–50. See R. A. Knox, *Enthusiasm; A Chapter in the History of Religion* (New York: Oxford University Press, 1950), which is indispensable.

17. For a comprehensive list, see R. Green, *Anti-Methodist Publications Issued During the Eighteenth Century* (London: C. H. Kelly, 1902).

18. The Methodists were kin of the Puritans of the previous century. Lavington argued, but it was Wesley's misfortune that the tolerance of the times was "very unpropitious to the fortunes of a new Sect": Lavington urged the clergy to continue to support both the letter and the spirit of the Toleration laws in order to frustrate the Methodist need for persecution, even though Methodists, he observed, as members of the State Church, were not legally entitled to this protection. [Bishop Lavington], *The Enthusiasm of Methodists and Papists Compared* (London: Knapton, 1749 and 1751), Preface, Part I, pp. 10, 22–26, 45; Part II, pp. 2–19, 27, 36, 43–45, 53–56, 113 f., 145–54, 160 f., 164, 167 ff., 184; Part III (1751), pp. xxvii, 141, 144, 241, 279 ff., 306 ff., 311–41, 381–90.

19. William [Warburton] Lord Bishop of Gloucester, *The Doctrine of Grace; Or, the Office and Operations of the Holy Spirit Vindicated from the Insults of Infidelity, and the Abuses of Fanaticism: With Some Thoughts (humbly Offered to the Consideration of the Established Clergy regarding the right method of defending Religion against the attacks of either Party)* (London: A. Millar, 1763, 2nd ed.), Book II, 86, 91–95, 105 ff., 115 ff., 122, 124, 130 f., 134, 139, 142–45, 175 f., 190, 198 f., 204, 222 f., 237, 243.

20. T. Parsons and E. A. Shils, *Toward a General Theory of Action* (Cambridge, Mass.: Harvard University Press, 1962), pp. 77–91, and *passim*.

21. T. Smollett, *The History of England from the Revolution to the Death of George the Second* (London: Cadell, 1791), V, 375.

22. A. Friedman, ed., *Collected Works of Oliver Goldsmith* (Oxford: Clarendon Press, 1966), II, 431.

23. G. B. Hill, ed., *Boswell's Life of Johnson* (Oxford: Clarendon Press, 1934), I, 458–59; see also II, 123.

24. P. P. Howe, ed., *The Complete Works of William Hazlitt* (London: J. M. Dent, 1930), IV, 60.

25. See the discussion in J. H. Chamberlayne, "From *Sect* to *Church* in British Methodism," *British Journal of Sociology*, XV (1964), 139–49; also D. A. Martin, "The Denomination," *British Journal of Sociology*, XIII (1962), 1–14.

II / THE BATTLE AGAINST "SPECULATIVE" ANTINOMIANISM

1. See R. W. Evans, "Relations of George Whitefield and Howell Harris, Fathers of Calvinistic Methodism," *Church History*, XXX (June 1961), 179–90.

2. There are a number of accounts of the life of Wesley; unless it is otherwise stated, I have drawn from Rev. L. Tyerman, *The Life and Times of the Rev. John Wesley* (London, 1890), 3 vols.

3. Despite his earlier loyalty to the Stuarts and to the doctrine of divine right, he did not fail to write in defense of the Revolution of 1688, dedicating his work to Queen Mary, and receiving as a reward the living of Epworth, in Lincolnshire. See Samuel Wesley, *Elegies on the Queen and Archbishop* (London: B. Motte, 1695). Wesley described Queen Mary, when she arrives in

heaven, welcomed by the "Martyr'd Charles," as "Thou best! thou dearest *Name* of all my Race!" (p. 16) In a similar manner, Queen Anne was to be eulogized as "sacred Anna," in Samuel Wesley, *Marlborough; or, the Fate of Europe: A Poem Dedicated to the Right Honourable Master Godolphin* (London: C. Harper, 1705), p. 11.

4. Some months before the death of William III, as John Wesley later told the story, in the course of his customary prayers for the King, Samuel Wesley observed that his wife had failed to say "Amen." Upon questioning her, he discovered his wife's continued loyalty to the Stuarts. Horrified, he swore that he would refuse to cohabit with her unless she joined in a loyal "Amen," and when she declined, he left the family to secure a chaplaincy on a man-of-war. With the accession of Queen Anne, who was of the blood royal, the Wesleys regained a united household. John was the first child born after this separation. See Robert Southey, *The Life of Wesley; and the Rise and Progress of Methodism* (London: Longmans, 1820), I, 10–11; Maximin Piette, *John Wesley in the Evolution of Protestantism* (New York: Sheed and Ward, 1937), p. 219. Further details of the quarrel, possibly unknown to Wesley himself, were uncovered by the recent discovery of letters written by Susanna seeking the advice of Jacobite friends and clergymen in the solution of her difficulties. Contrary to the story believed by Wesley, it appears to have been a fire in late July 1701–1702 which Samuel saw as the hand of God condemning him for his rash oath, not the death of King William, which had occurred the preceding March, which brought Samuel home. See Robert Walmsley, "John Wesley's Parents: Quarrel and Reconciliation," in *Proceedings of the Wesley Historical Society* [hereafter referred to as *PWHS*], XXIX (1953), 50–57.

5. See Southey, *Wesley*, I, 12–14, 19; and Piette, *Wesley*, pp. 226–28.

6. The portrait is identified and discussed in *PWHS*, III (1902); also XI (1918), 158–59.

7. See the perceptive essay by John Walsh, "Methodism and the Mob in the Eighteenth Century," in G. J. Cuming and D. Baker, eds., *Popular Belief and Practice* (Cambridge: Cambridge University Press, 1972), pp. 213–27.

8. See Tyerman, *Wesley*, I, 99.

9. J. Telford (ed)., *The Letters of John Wesley* (London: Epworth Press, 1931), I (July 29, 1775), 22–23. [Hereafter referred to as Wesley, *Letters*.]

10. John Wesley, "Minutes of Several Conversations between the Rev. Mr. Wesley and others; From the Year 1744 to the Year 1789," in John Wesley, *The Works of the Rev. John Wesley, A.M.* (London: John Mason, 1860), Fifth Edition, Vol. VIII, 300. [Hereafter cited as Wesley, *Works*.]

11. See "The Life of the Rev. John Wesley," in Wesley, *Works*, V, 5.

12. Quoted in *ibid.*, p. 6. Halévy's *Birth of Methodism* is especially good on Wesley's conversion.

13. C. Wesley, *The Journal of the Rev. Charles Wesley, M.A.* (London: Culley, 1909), p. 143; see also p. 166.

14. Wesley, "Salvation by Faith," in *Works*, V, 7–16.

15. A schism was later to bring many of these Inghamites into the ranks of "Daleites," a Scottish sect formed by the Glasgow industrialist whose daughter Robert Owen was to marry, establishing a link between Herrnhut and New Lanark, and New Harmony. See Halévy, *Birth of Methodism*, p. 74. In America, the community of Harmony, Indiana, had been a Rappite utopia, not dissimilar in its organization to Owen's secular successor of New Harmony, thus providing another display of the ties between seventeenth- and eighteenth-century German pietism and nineteenth-century "utopian" socialism. See J. F. C.

Harrison, *Quest for a New Moral World* (New York: Scribner's, 1969), pp. 54, 100.

16. See A. W. Harrison, "Why the 18th Century Dreaded Methodist Enthusiasm," in *PWHS*, XVIII (1931), 40–42; also Umphrey Lee, *The Historical Backgrounds of Early Methodist Enthusiasm* (New York: Columbia University Press, 1931). One clergyman, Joseph Trapp, was to declare in later years that "Methodism was nothing but a revival of the old fanaticism of the last century; when all manner of madness was practised, and all manner of villainy committed in the name of Christ." (Quoted in Tyerman, *Wesley*, I, 242.) The mood of the time can be gauged by the story, told by Wesley in a letter to James Hutton, that on visiting Bath, in 1739, Wesley's sermon was interrupted by Beau Nash who warned Wesley that there was "an Act of Parliament against conventicles"; Wesley replied that "the conventicles there mentioned were seditious meetings," but that "there was no such here." See Wesley, *Letters*, I (June 7, 1739), 320.

17. C. Wesley, *Journal*, pp. 208–9.

18. *Ibid.*, p. 223.

19. See Halévy, *Birth of Methodism*, pp. 60–72. See also N. Curnock (ed.), *The Journal of John Wesley, A.M.* (London: Epworth Press, 1909–16), II (Nov. 27, 1739), 322. [Hereafter referred to as Wesley, *Journal*.]

20. Halévy, *Birth of Methodism*, p. 69.

21. Wesley, *Journal*, II (March 31 and April 1, 1739), 167–68.

22. Wesley, *Journal*, II (Nov. 27, 1739), 322–23.

23. Wesley, *Journal*, II (Aug. 27, 1739). 262; see also II, 275–76, 326; III, 28.

24. Wesley, *Journal*, II (April 26, 1739), 184.

25. For Law, see J. H. Overton, *William Law, Nonjuror and Mystic* (London: Longmans, 1881); S. Hobhouse, *William Law and Eighteenth Century Quakerism* (London: Allen, 1927); H. Talon, *William Law* (London: Rockliff, 1948); and E. W. Baker, *A Herald of the Evangelical Revival, a Critical Inquiry into the Relation of William Law to John Wesley and the Beginnings of Methodism* (London: Epworth Press, 1948).

26. Josiah Tucker, *A Brief History of the Principles of Methodism, Wherein the Rise and Progress, together with the causes of the several Variations, Divisions, and Present inconsistencies of this sect are attempted to be traced out, and accounted for* (Oxford: James Fletcher, 1742), pp. 8–15, 18, 20, 31–35, 37–43, 46–48.

27. Quoted in Southey, *Wesley*, II, 185. G. C. Cell, *The Reaiscovery of John Wesley* (New York: Holt, 1935), found the Wesleyan ethic "thoroughly Calvinistic."

28. See Wesley, *Journal*, II (April 21, 1741), 447–49; see also III (November 27, 1750), 502 ff. See C. W. Towlson, *Moravian and Methodist Relationships and Influences in the Eighteenth Century* (London: Epworth Press, 1957).

29. Wesley, *Journal*, II (1738; 1741), 496.

30. Wesley, *Journal*, III (June 7, 1746), 243.

31. See discussion in Southey, *Wesley*, I, 350.

32. In 1740, for example, he charged the Moravians with being too ready "to conform to the world . . . by joining in worldly diversions in order to do good." Wesley, *Journal*, II (August 8, 1740), 490–91.

33. It was vain of Zinzendorf to affect, in manifestoes to his English followers, the de-Germanization of his name to "Count Louis." "But why is he ashamed of his name?" Wesley inquired some years after the break. "The

Count's name is Ludwig, not Louis; no more than mine is Jean or Giovanni."
Wesley, *Journal*, III (September 28, 1749), 435; see also Wesley's warning to
"beware of the German wolves (falsely called Moravians)," III (October 20,
1750), 499.

34. "And in many of you I have more than once found (what you called
'being wise as serpents')," Wesley declared, "much subtlety, much evasion and
disguise, much guile and dissimulation." See Wesley, *Journal*, II (August 8,
1740), 492; see also II (April 21, 1741), 447–49; III (November 27, 1750),
502–6.

35. After reading, in 1742, a biography of Ignatius Loyola, Wesley described the Spanish Jesuit as "setting out (like Count Z.) with a full persuasion that he might use guile to promote the glory of God or (which he thought
the same thing) the interest of his Church." See Wesley, *Journal*, III (August
16, 1742), 40.

36. Wesley, *Journal*, II (August 8, 1740), 490–95.

37. Wesley, *Journal*, II (December 14, 1739), 327; see also II, 328–31.

38. Wesley, *Journal*, II (August 8, 1740), 490–95.

39. Wesley, *Journal*, II (September 3, 1741), 488–90. The account of the interview in Wesley's *Journal* appeared in Latin, the language in which it took
place, "to spare the dead," Wesley declared.

40. See "James Hutton's Second Account of the Moravian Work in England, Down to the Year 1747," in *PWHS*, XV (1926), 208–9, 212, 214.
For the influence of Taylor and Law upon Wesley, see *Journal*, V (May 14,
1765), 117–18.

41. Wesley, *Journal*, II (June 15, 1741), 467.

42. Wesley, *Journal*, II (June 16, 1741), 468.

43. Letter appears in Tyerman, *Wesley*, I, 312–13.

44. Letter in *ibid.*, pp. 313–14.

45. Letter in *ibid.*, p. 314.

46. Letter in *ibid.*, p. 316.

47. Letter in *ibid.*, pp. 316–17.

48. Letter in *ibid.*, p. 324.

49. Wesley, *Journal*, II (March 28, 1741), 439.

50. Letter in Tyerman, *Wesley*, I, 315–16

51. Wesley, *Journal*, II (April 4, 1741), 441.

52. Wesley, *Journal*, II (June 19, 1740), 353.

53. Wesley, *Journal*, II (June 20, 1740), 353.

54. Wesley, *Journal*, II (December 20, 1740), 408–9.

55. Wesley, *Journal*, II (December 26, 1740), 410.

56. Wesley, *Journal*, II (February 22, 1741), 427–28.

57. Wesley, *Journal*, II (February 28, 1741), 430; see also II (March 7,
1741), 432–33.

58. See John Cennick, "An Account of the Most Remarkable Occurrence in
the Awakenings at Bristol and Kingswood etc.," in *PWHS*, VI (1908), 110;
also *PWHS*, VI (1908), 133, 135, 138. Cennick reported Charles Wesley as
having at this time described Calvin as "the first-born son of the Devil." (p.
138) See also William Leary, "John Cennick, 1718–55: A Bicentenary Appreciation," *PWHS*, XXX (1955), 30–37.

59. Wesley, *Journal*, III (December 8, 1745), 228. Five years later, Cennick's mother came to tell Wesley that the Moravians had imposed a wife on
her son and had expelled her from her son's house. Wesley felt duty-bound to
make public these evil results of authoritarian communitarianism. Wesley,
Journal, III (October 24, 1750), 500.

60. Wesley, *Journal,* III (August 24, 1743), 84–86.

61. In 1750, for example, Wesley patronizingly observed that "even the little improprieties both of his [Whitefield's] language and manner were a means of profiting many who would not have been touched by a more correct discourse, or a more calm and regular manner of speaking"; "how wise is God," declared Wesley, "in giving different talents to different preachers!" Wesley, *Journal,* III (January 28, 1750), 452. There were a number of occasions when Wesley was invited to occupy the pulpit in a place occupied by Whitefield's followers. In 1753, for instance, he described how he "willingly accepted" such an offer adding "thus it behoveth us to trample on bigotry and party zeal." Wesley, *Journal,* IV (August 14, 1753), 79. As the years passed, Wesley's suspicions vanished. In January of 1766, Wesley reported a visit by Whitefield, who "breathes nothing but peace and love"; "bigotry cannot stand before him," Wesley wrote, "but hides its head wherever he comes." Wesley, *Journal,* V (January 31, 1766), 154. See also Wesley, *Journal,* V (February 27, 1769), 303.

62. Wesley, "On the Death of the Rev. Mr. George Whitefield," (1770), in *Works,* VI, 167–182.

63. Wesley, *Journal,* V (May 14, 1765), 116.

64. Wesley, *Letters,* VI (August 18, 1775), 175.

65. Wesley, *Letters,* IV (May 14, 1765), 297–98.

66. "We break with no man for his opinion," Wesley wrote; "we think, and let think." *Journal,* III (May 29, 1745), 178. See also Wesley, *Letters,* II (November 1747), 110; II (1748), 293; and IV (November 26, 1762), 347.

67. See, for example, John Wesley, "Some Remarks on 'A Defence of the Preface to the Edinburgh Edition of Aspasio Vindicated'" (1766), *Works,* X, 346–57.

68. Wesley, *Journal,* V (May 14, 1765), 116–17.

69. John Wesley, *Serious Thoughts Upon the Perseverance of the Saints* (London, 1751), pp. 23–24, 4.

70. Wesley, "Predestination Calmly Considered" (1752), *Works,* X, 207, 231–32, 242 f., 256–57, and *passim.*

71. Wesley, *Journal,* III (April 1, 1751), 519.

72. Wesley, *Journal,* IV (April 25, 1753), 64–65.

73. Wesley, *Letters,* VI (September 16, 1774), 113. See G. Huehns, *Antinomianism in English History* (London: Cresset Press, 1951).

74. Wesley, "Minutes of Some Late Conversations" (1744), *Works,* X, 278.

75. Cudworth declared "that the giving of scandalous names, such as Antinomian, or the like, has no warrant from scripture, and appears to men of sense but a mean way of making good the cause one is engaged in." See William Cudworth, *A Dialogue between a Preacher of Inherent Righteousness and a Preacher of God's Righteousness . . . ; Being an Answer to a Late Dialogue between an Antinomian and His Friend* (London, 1745), p. 2; Luther is cited against Wesley on p. 6. Recourse to Luther against Wesley is also sought in William Cudworth, *A Second Dialogue Between a Preacher of Inherent Righteousness and a Preacher of God's Righteousness* (London, 1746), pp. 39–40, and in William Cudworth, *The Discovery of the most Dangerous Dead Faith* (London, 1747), pp. 56–60. In the fifties, turning the tables, Cudworth accused Wesley of the "most dangerous doctrinal Antinomianism, which leavens all you write in the eyes of judicious readers." See William Cudworth, *To Mr John Wesley, occasion'd by the revival of his Dialogues, in a late treatise, called A Preservative against Unsettled Notions* (London, 1806), for a defense of Cudworth against Wesley. Relly answered the charge of Antinomianism made by another Methodist writer, W. Mason, in James Relly, *Antichrist resisted; in a*

reply to a pamphlet, written by W. Mason, intitled: Antinomian Heresy ex-ploded (London, 1761), pp. 4, 10, *passim.*

76. Wesley, "A Short History of Methodism" (1764?), *Works,* VIII, 349–51; see also Wesley, *Journal,* IV (July 25, 1756), 178; and Southey, *Life,* I, 314–16.

77. See Wesley, "A Dialogue Between an Antinomian and His Friend," (1745), *Works,* X, 267, 268, 270–72, 275–76.

78. John Wesley, *Thoughts on the Imputed Righteousness of Christ* (London: W. Strahan, 1762), pp. 9–11.

79. Wesley, "A Second Dialogue Between an Antinomian and His Friend" (1745), *Works,* X, 277, 280–81, 283–84.

80. Wesley, *Journal,* III (January 16, 1751), 510–11.

81. Wesley, *Journal,* IV (April 2, 1755), 108.

82. Wesley, *Journal,* III (March 23, 1746), 237–38.

83. Wesley, *Journal,* III (April 10, 1750), 463.

84. Wesley, *Journal,* III (March 23, 1746), 238.

85. See Wesley's letter to the Bishop of London, in *Letters,* II (June 11, 1747), 279.

86. John Wesley, "A Blow at the Root; or, Christ Stabbed in the House of His Friends" (1762), in *Works,* X, 366, 368.

87. Wesley, *Letters,* III (October 15, 1756), 372, 379, 381, 387–88.

88. Wesley, *Letters,* III (October 14, 1757), 229–30.

89. Wesley, *Letters,* IV (November 29, 1758), 47.

90. Sellon, one of Wesley's principal lieutenants, even suggested that Cudworth had really written *Aspasio Vindicated* in Hervey's name, and that Hervey, whose pen was "dipt in *Antinomian venom,*" was entirely managed by Cudworth. See Walter Sellon, *An Answer to 'Aspasio Vindicated' in Eleven Letters* (London, 1767), p. 166, and *passim;* see also John Wesley, "Some Remarks on 'A Defence of the Preface to the Edinburgh Edition of Aspasio Vindicated' " (1766), *Works,* X, 347 and *passim.* A denial of this appeared in Anon., *Mr Wesley's principles detected; or, a defence of the Preface to the Edinburgh edition of Aspasio vindicated* (Edinburgh, 1765).

91. Quoted in A. C. H. Seymour, *The Life and Times of Selina Countess of Huntingdon* (London: W. E. Pointer, 1844), I, 187–91.

92. See Seymour, *Countess of Huntingdon,* II, 233–34.

93. In 1780, after Toplady's death, Wesley could not resist publishing, in the *Arminian Magazine,* III (January 1780), 54–55, a letter which Toplady had written him in 1758. "I have long been convinced," Toplady had observed at that time, "that Self-righteousness and Antinomianism are equally pernicious; and that to insist on the imputation of Christ's Righteousness as alone requisite to Salvation, is only strewing the way to Hell with flowers." Such a doctrine, he then noted, was "very agreeable to corrupt nature."

94. In a sermon delivered in 1774, Toplady declared that "it pleased God to deliver me from the Arminian snare, before I was quite eighteen." See A. M. Toplady, "Free Will and Merit Fairly Examined; Or, Men Not Their Own Saviours" (1774), in *The Works of Augustus M. Toplady* (London: Baynes & Son, 1825), III, 170. [Hereafter, Toplady, *Works.*]

95. A. M. Toplady, "The Doctrine of Absolute Predestination Stated and Asserted" (1769), *Works,* V.

96. A. M. Toplady, *Historic Proof of the Doctrinal Calvinism of the Church of England* (London, 1774), 2 vols.

97. Wesley, "The Doctrine of Absolute Predestination Stated and Asserted by the Reverend Mr. A————— T—————" (1770), *Works,* XIV, 198.

98. Wesley, *Letters*, V (June 24, 1770), 192.

99. A. M. Toplady, "A Letter to the Rev. Mr. John Wesley Relative to His Abridgment of Zanchius on Predestination" (1770), *Works*, V, 333–34.

100. The full text appears in Tyerman, *Wesley*, III, 72–73; see W. R. Cannon, *The Theology of John Wesley with Special Reference to the Doctrine of Justification* (New York: Abingdon Press, 1946); H. Lindström, *Wesley and Sanctification* (Stockholm, 1946).

101. The text of Shirley's letter appears in John Fletcher, "First Check to Antinomianism; Or, A Vindication of the Rev. Mr. Wesley's Minutes" (1771), in *Checks to Antinomianism in a Series of Letters* (New York: Carlton & Porter, n.d.), I, 7; see also I, 26, 63; also Tyerman, *Wesley*, III, 94.

102. See *ibid.*, III, 71–75, 92; see also Wesley, "A Short Account of the Life and Death of the Reverend John Fletcher," *Works*, XI, 298.

103. Wesley, *Letters*, V (June 19, 1771), 258–59.

104. Wesley, *Letters*, V (July 10, 1771), 263–65.

105. See Wesley, *Letters*, V (August 14, 1771), 274–75.

106. A. M. Toplady, "A Letter to the Rev. Mr. John Wesley Relative to His Abridgment of Zanchius on Predestination" (1770), *Works*, V, 340.

107. Wesley, *Letters*, VI (December 23, 1773), 60.

108. Wesley, *Letters*, VI (January 14, 1777), 250.

109. Wesley, *Letters*, VI (December 9, 1778), 331.

110. Wesley, *Letters*, VIII (September 30, 1778), 95; see also VIII (January 19, 1791), 256.

111. Wesley, *Letters*, VI (October 18, 1778), 326.

112. Wesley, *Letters*, VI (October 22, 1773), 51.

113. Wesley, *Letters*, V (July 13, 1771), 266–67.

114. Wesley, *Letters*, VI (December 23, 1773), 60.

115. Wesley, *Letters*, VIII (July 15, 1789), 154. See also *Letters*, V (May 23, 1768), 90–91; V (November 30, 1770), 211–12; V (June 11, 1771), 256–57; V (November 20, 1771), 290. On February 26, 1783, Wesley wrote of Calvinism, Mysticism, and Antinomianism as "the bane of true religion, and one or other of them has been the grand hindrance of the work of God wherever it has broke out." *Letters*, VII (February 26, 1783), 169.

116. In W. Sellon, *An Answer to 'Aspasio Vindicated, in Eleven Letters'* (London, 1767); see also Tyerman, *Wesley*, II, 526–32.

117. See W. Sellon, *Church of England Vindicated from the Charge of Predestination* (London, 1771). See Tyerman, *Wesley*, III, 108; also Wesley, *Letters*, V (February 21, 1770), 183, and V (June 24, 1770), 192.

118. See Thomas Olivers, *A Letter to the Reverend Mr. Toplady* (London, 1770); especially forceful was his attack on the predestinarian view that "Whatever is, is right" (pp. 5 ff).

119. See Thomas Olivers, *A Scourge to Calumny* (London: R. Hawes, 1774); and Thomas Olivers, *A Rod for a Reviler: Or A Full Answer to Mr. Rowland Hill's Letter Entitled Imposture Detected, and the Dead Vindicated* (London: J. Fry, 1777). In the latter tract, "Calvinist" and "antinomian" are used virtually as synonyms (p. 28, and *passim*).

120. Charles Perronet, *Leviathan or the Crooked Serpent; Being an Antinomian Creed, Taken from Rich. Hill, Esq.* (n.p., 1773), pp. 2, 4.

121. Richard Hill, *Conversation between Richard Hill Esq.; the Rev. Mr. Madan, and the Superior of a Convent of English Benedictine monks at Paris,* etc. (London, 1772), pp. 8, 10, 13. See also Tyerman, *Wesley*, III, 87–108, 136–45, 158–62, 179–83, 209–10, 232–34, 255–60.

122. In Sir Richard Hill, *Three Letters written by R. Hill, Esq. to the Rev.*

J. Fletcher, . . . in the year 1773. Setting forth Mr. Hill's Reasons for declining any further controversy relative to Mr Wesley's principles (Shrewsbury, 1775?), Hill observed: "I am told that one Thomas Oliver, (alias Olivers) a journeyman Cordwainer, has attempted to write a pamphlet against me. . . . I hear also that the man has begged a *Greek motto,* being himself . . . most profoundly ignorant of the very rudiments of the language, to stick up in his title page; however if this important disciple of St. Crispin was like Pontius Pilate of old, to have prefixed an inscription in Hebrew, Greek, and Latin . . . I should not take the least notice of him, or read a line of his composition, any more than, if I was travelling on the road, I would stop to lash, or even order my footman to lash every impertinent quadruped in a village that should come out and bark at me. . . . But I ought to implore the kind reader's forgiveness for having dwelt so long upon a *subject,* as well as upon an *object,* of such absolute insignificance." (pp. 4–5) Hill seems to have backed away, to some degree, from this attitude; see Olivers *A Rod for a Reviler,* p. 32.

123. See Wesley, *Letters,* V (June 24, 1770), 192.

124. J. Wesley, "The Consequence Proved" (1771), *Works,* X, 7 and *passim.*

125. J. Wesley, "Some Remarks on Mr. Hill's 'Review of All the Doctrines Taught by Mr. John Wesley' " (1772), *Works,* X, 413–14.

126. *Ibid.,* pp. 375–76, 413.

127. J. Wesley, "Some Remarks on Mr. Hill's 'Farrago Double-Distilled' " (1773), *Works,* X, 415–46.

128. J. Wesley, "An Answer to Mr. Rowland Hill's Tract, Entitled 'Imposture Detected' " (1777), *Works,* X, 451.

129. Among them William Mason, a former Methodist class leader who in 1770, when he was a Surrey magistrate, wrote his *Axe Laid to the Root of Antinomian Licentiousness.* The reply in 1777 to Rowland Hill by the mechanic, Matthew Goodenough, must also be noted. See Tyerman, *Wesley,* III, 71–75, 255–60.

130. Wesley, *Letters,* V (September 18, 1772), 340.

131. For Fletcher's life, see J. H. Overton, "John William Fletcher," in *Dictionary of National Biography,* VI, 312–14 Wesley, *Life of Fletcher* (London, 1786).

132. Wesley, *Fletcher,* pp. 364–65.

133. Wesley, *Letters,* VI (March 22, 1775), 146.

134. Wesley, *Letters,* V (March 20, 1768), 83–84. Even after Fletcher, in his voluminous writings during the seventies, had amply proved his loyalty, Wesley could not fully accept the well-born and learned Genevan's trust in plebeian Protestantism. In early June of 1781, Wesley remarked to a correspondent that he had not had a letter from Fletcher for some time. See *Letters,* VII (June 10, 1781), 67. When, a few weeks later, he still had not heard from Fletcher, he wrote anxiously to his brother Charles wondering "why it is that we hear nothing from Madeley." Hopefully, Wesley observed, "prejudice has not stepped in, or Calvinism!" *Letters,* VII (June 27, 1781), 70. It was neither. Fletcher was absorbed in the process of courting his future wife.

135. Wesley, *Letters,* VI (January 15, 1773), 10–11.

136. Wesley was to blame "the reading of those poisonous writers the Mystics" for having "confounded the intellects of both my brother and Mr. Fletcher and made them afraid of (what ought to have been their glory) the letting of their light shine before men." Wesley, *Letters,* VIII (September 26, 1788), 93. Toplady, in a letter in January 1774, noting the rumor that Fletcher was to succeed "pope Wesley, as commander in chief of the societies," observed that it was "no wonder, therefore, that the cardinal of Madeley is such a

zealous stickler for the cause." "One would think," Toplady snidely concluded, "that the Swiss were universally fated to fight for pay." Letter of A. M. Toplady to Ambrose Serle, January 11, 1774, in Toplady, *Works*, VI, 209–10.

137. Quoted in Wesley, *Fletcher*, p. 299.

138. J. W. Fletcher, "Second Check to Antinomianism" (1771), in *Checks to Antinomianism*, I, 130.

139. J. W. Fletcher, "Logica Genevensis; Or, A Fourth Check to Antinomianism: In Which St. James' Pure Religion is Defended Against the Charges, and Established Upon the Concessions, of Mr. Richard and Mr. Rowland Hill" (1772), in *Checks to Antinomianism*, p. 259; J. W. Fletcher, "An Equal Check to Pharisaism and Antinomianism, Part I" (1774), *Checks to Antinomianism*, I, 427.

140. J. W. Fletcher, "Fourth Check to Antinomianism" (1772), in *Checks to Antinomianism*, I, 213.

141. J. W. Fletcher, "Last Check to Antinomianism" (1775), in *Checks to Antinomianism*, II, 485–86, 489, 495.

142. Although, by the time Tucker's tract was published, Wesley had already broken with Zinzendorf on the question of imputed righteousness, Wesley had earlier attended Tucker's Church in Bristol, and had approved of his sermons. He is reported, for example, to have been much comforted by Tucker's Good Friday sermon in 1740. Wesley's first work of controversy, *The Principles of a Methodist*, was written in reply to Tucker's tract. See Wesley, *Letters*, III, 272.

143. See, for example, A Lover of Free Grace [J. Wesley], *The Question, What is an Arminian? Answered* (London, 1770), pp. 5–7 and *passim*.

144. See Peter Toon, *The Emergence of Hyper-Calvinism in English Nonconformity, 1689–1765* (London: The Olive Tree, 1968).

145. Wesley, *Letters*, VI (November 29, 1775), 192.

III / CONFRONTATION WITH "PRACTICAL" ANTINOMIANISM

1. John Wesley, "How Far Is It the Duty of A Christian Minister To Preach Politics?" (1782), *Works*, XI, 154–55.

2. John Wesley, "Free Thoughts on the Present State of Public Affairs" (1768), *Works*, XI, 14–16.

3. John Wesley, *A Concise Ecclesiastical History from the Birth of Christ to the Beginning of the Present Century* (London, 1781), IV, 116.

4. Augustin Léger, *L'Angleterre religieuse et les origines du Méthodisme au XVIIIe siècle; la jeunesse de Wesley* (Paris: Hachette, 1910), pp. 30–32. In his Appendix (Pièces Justicatives), pp. *24–*26, Léger described a political pamphlet, in the Bodleian Library, published by Samuel Wesley with the title *What Has Been May Be: Or, Fair Warning to the Good People of England, Against the Commonwealth Principles Industriously Propagated by the London Journal, and Too Unwarily Received by Some Amongst Us* (London: J. Roberts, 1721). See J. T. Rutt, "The Wesleys,—An Attempt to Account for Their High Church Principles, 1808," *PWHS*, XI (1918), 155–59.

5. John Wesley, *A Concise History of England from the Earliest Times to the death of George II* (London: R. Hawes, 1776), IV, 75 n. While accepting Samuel's authorship, Southey thought the speech not consonant with his vows. See Southey, *Wesley*, I, 20.

6. Quoted in Walmsley, "John Wesley's Parents," *PWHS*, XXIX (1953), 57.

7. See Tyerman, *Wesley*, I, 438–41. In his "Advice to the People Called Methodists," issued in 1745, Wesley observed that it was the Methodists' "uniting of yourselves together" which had proved "offensive" to many: "because this union renders you more conspicuous," Wesley wrote, "placing you more in the eye of men; more suspicious,—I mean, liable to be suspected of carrying on some sinister design, (especially by those who do not, or will not, know your inviolable attachment to His present Majesty)." See *Works*, VIII, 355. Wesley, in his *Journal*, reported the gossip "that it was beyond dispute Mr Wesley had large remittances from Spain, in order to make a party among the poor; and that, as soon as the Spaniards landed, he was to join them with twenty thousand men." See Wesley, *Journal*, II (September 26, 1741), 487.

8. Wesley, "A Word in Season: Or, Advice to an Englishman" (1745), *Works*, XI, 182–84. Whitefield also pledged his loyalty to the Hanoverian dynasty: See his *Britain's Mercies and Britain's Duty . . . Occasioned by the Suppression of the late Unnatural Rebellion* (Boston, 1746), pp. 7, 9; and his *An Alarm in Zion: . . . on the alarm of Invasion written . . . in 1756* (London, 1803), pp. 13–14.

9. Letter appears in Tyerman, *Wesley*, I, 491–92; see also pp. 483–84.

10. Wesley, "A Short Address to the Inhabitants of Ireland, Occasioned by some late Occurrences" (1749), *Works*, IX, 173–78. When war broke out with France in the fifties, Wesley offered to raise a company of volunteers to defend England against invasion. See Wesley, *Letters*, III (March 1, 1756), 165.

11. Wesley, "A Word to a Freeholder" (1748), *Works*, XI, 196–97. See also Wesley, *Letters*, IV (October 1764), 271–72.

12. See Tyerman, *Wesley*, II, 235–36.

13. Wesley announced that the marriage in 1209 between King John and Isabella, the daughter of Count Angoulême was not "lawful," and that consequently the children of this marriage were illegitimate. Therefore, "their posterity, the Stuarts in particular," had no right "by birth" to the crown. John himself had no "right to the throne"; Matilda, Wesley proclaimed, "had a prior right, from whom King George is lineally descended." See Wesley, *History of England*, I, 189.

Wesley's father had taken a more pragmatic approach in an anti-Jacobite stanza of a poem in 1695:

> Shou'd some old lost *Plantagenet* arise,
> And plead his *lineal Title* to the *Throne*
> Who'd not his *Antiquated claim* despise,
> And still the *brave* and *just Possessor* own?"

See Samuel Wesley, *Elegies on the Queen and Archbishop*, p. 27.

14. Quoted in Mary Warnock, Introduction to J. S. Mill, *Utilitarianism, On Liberty, Essay on Bentham* (New York: World, 1962), pp. 14–15.

15. Henry Brooke, [*A Fool of Quality; Or,*] *The History of Henry Earl of Moreland*, revised and ed. by J. Wesley (Plymouth: J. Bennett, 1815).

16. Wesley, *Letters*, VII (December 24, 1785), 305–6; the Westminster School at which Samuel Wesley was head usher was High Church and Jacobite, as were all the members of his circle. See T. E. Brigden, "Samuel Wesley Junior and his Circle, 1690–1739," *PWHS*, XI (1917), 25–31, 74–81; (1918), 97–102, 121–29, 145–53.

17. John Wesley, "Free Thoughts on the Present State of Public Affairs" (1768), *Works*, XI, 16, 20 ff., 24, 26–28, 30.

18. Wesley, *Letters*, V (January 16, 1770), 176.

19. Wesley, *Journal,* V (May 8, 1770), 366.

20. John Wesley, "Thoughts Upon Liberty" (1772). *Works,* XI, 34–46.

21. John Wesley, "Thoughts Concerning the Origin of Power," *Works,* XI, 48–53.

22. Wesley, "Thoughts Upon Liberty" (1772), *Works,* XI, 45–46. The practical conclusion of the tract was that the "licentiousness of the press" be restrained, and that all those who told "palpable lies" which "manifestly tend to breed dissension between the King and his subjects" be punished.

23. Wesley, *Letters,* V (December 1768), 379.

24. The text of the letter to Lord North is in the Appendix to Wesley, *Journal,* VIII, 325–28.

25. The text of this letter to Lord Dartmouth is in the Appendix to Wesley's *Journal,* VIII, 334–35; for Wesley's high opinion of Dartmouth, see *Journal,* VI (February 2, 1778), 179–80. At the preceding general election at Bristol, Wesley had supported Burke's policies, and he was later quoted by Rowland Hill as having on that occasion described the Americans as "an oppressed and injured people," and to have urged them "to exert themselves, if they wished to continue a free people." All of which prompted Hill to describe Wesley, "this *crafty man,*" as a rebel. See Rowland Hill, *Imposture Detected and the Dead Vindicated* (London, 1777), pp. 33–34, 40.

26. See Wesley, *Letters,* VI (December 26, 1775), 199.

27. John Wesley, *A Calm Address to Our American Colonies* (London: R. Hawes, [1775]), pp. 3, 5–7, 9, 11–18, 23; see also *Letters,* VI (August 13, 1775), 173; VI (November 3, 1775), 187; VI (November 11, 1775), 188.

28. John Wesley, "National Sins and Miseries" (November 1775), *Works,* VII, 401–4. In a letter to Thomas Rankin, Wesley observed "the clouds are black both over England and America. It is well if this summer passes over without some showers of blood. And if the storm once begins in America, it will soon spread to Great Britain." *Letters,* VI (April 21, 1775), 148; see also *Letters,* VI (May 19, 1775), 149–50; and VI (June 2, 1775), 152.

29. A Lover of Peace [John Wesley], "A Seasonable Address to the More Serious Part of the Inhabitants of Great Britain, Respecting the Unhappy Contest Between Us and Our American Brethren: With An Occasional Word Interspersed to those of a Different Complexion" (1776), *Works,* XI, 119–20, 124. In this tract, Wesley repeated many times the metaphor to which we have referred: e.g., "the devouring flames of an unnatural civil war" were "already kindled"; it was "so terrible a conflagration," and Englishmen were "contending who set the building on fire"; but since "the flames are actually spreading, and may soon reach from them to us, let us do our utmost to extinguish them," etc. Charles Wesley was so anxious not to contribute to the flame that, during this period, he objected to Wesley's having censured Charles I, on the ground that "at such a time as this especially, when it is the fashion to 'blacken the tyrant,' you and I should not join in the popular cry, but rather go against the stream." See Wesley, *Letters,* VI, 186 f.n. That John Wesley *did* become more sympathetic to Charles I is evident in *Journal,* VI (December 28, 1781), 341.

30. John Wesley, "Some Observations on Liberty; Occasioned by a Late Tract" (1776), *Works,* XI, 93–94, 97–98, 104–6, 109, 116–17. In his *Journal,* VI (April 4, 1776), 100, Wesley wrote of Price's "dangerous tract" whose principles, "if practised, would overturn all government and bring in universal anarchy."

31. Americanus [Caleb Evans], *A Letter to the Rev. Mr. John Wesley Occasioned by His Calm Address to the American Colonies* (London: Dilly, 1775), pp. reverse of title page, i, 4, 10–11. Evans, following the arguments of

Bristol's M. P. Burke, approved of the taxation of the colonies for purposes of trade, but not for revenue. Massachusetts Bay, in its resistance, he declared, were not the dupes of English conspirators; they were the heirs of John Hampden. (pp. 18–20, 22.)

32. Hanoverian [A. M. Toplady], "An Old Fox Tarred and Feathered; Occasioned By What Is Called Mr. John Wesley's Calm Address to our American Colonies" (1775), *Works,* V, 441–43.

33. Among them was one by T. S. which suggested Wesley was seeking royal favor, and accused Wesley of attempting to inculcate "the detestable doctrines of passive-obedience and non-resistance." If there was a revolutionary conspiracy afoot, T. S. suggested, it was engineered by "tories and jacobites, friends to the Pope and Pretender, who hate his Majesty, and are, by a variety of means, endeavouring to overturn the constitution." These men, T. S. indicated, were the King's Ministers and a "corrupt" Parliament. See T. S., *A Cool Reply to a Calm Address, Lately Published by Mr. John Wesley* (London: J. Plummer, 1775), pp. 4, 6, 30; also Anon., *A Constitutional Answer to the Rev. Mr. John Wesley's Calm Address to the American Colonies* (London: Dilly & Almon, 1775), pp. 7, 20, 22.

34. In the preface to a subsequent edition of the *Calm Address;* see Wesley, *Works,* XI, 80. Wesley, in a letter published in *The Gazeteer,* in which he admitted Evans' charge that he had "once 'doubted whether the measures taken with respect to America could be defended either on the foot of law, equity, or prudence.' I did doubt of these five years, nay indeed, five months ago. You affirm that I 'declared' (last year) 'the Americans were an oppressed, injured people.' I do not remember that I did, but very possibly I might. . . . I am now of another mind." *Journal,* VI (December 9, 1775), 88–89.

35. Wesley, *Journal,* VI (November 11, 1775), 82–83.

36. Wesley, *Journal,* VI (November 27, 1775), 84–85.

37. Wesley, *Journal,* VI (February 3, 1777), 138.

38. John Wesley, *A Calm Address to the Inhabitants of England* (London: J. Fry, 1777), pp. 9, 14–23.

39. John Fletcher, *A Vindication of the Rev. Mr. Wesley's 'Calm Address to Our American Colonies': In Some Letters to Mr. Caleb Evans* (London: R. Hawes, 1776), pp. iii, vi, 17–18, 41–44, 46, 49, 52, 59, 62, 65–66, 70–71.

40. See Wesley, *Letters,* VI (December 24, 1775), 197, which also makes it clear that the Earl of Dartmouth was asked to make suggestions concerning Fletcher's manuscript before its publication, and that he did so.

41. Caleb Evans, *A Reply to the Rev. Mr. Fletcher's Vindication of Mr. Wesley's Calm Address to Our American Colonies* (Bristol: W. Pine, n.d. [1776]), pp. 3–4, 34, 37–38, 78–79, 81–84, 87–88.

42. Rowland Hill, *A Full Answer to the Rev. J. Wesley's Remarks Upon a late Pamphlet, Published in Defence of the Character of the Rev. Mr. Whitefield and Others* (Bristol, 1777), p. 31.

43. Sir Richard Hill, *The Tables Turned, A Letter to the Author of a Pamphlet, entitled Observations on the Election of Members for the Borough of Ludlow In the Year 1780* (Shrewsbury: T. Wood, 1782), p. 12.

44. Rowland Hill, *A Full Answer,* p. 31 n.

45. A Gentleman of Northumberland, *A Compleat Answer to Mr. Wesley's Observations, Upon Dr. Price's Essay on Civil Liberty* (Newcastle: Robson, 1776), p. 16.

46. W. Mason, *The Absolute and Indispensable Duty of Christians, in this Critical Juncture* (London: Pasham, 1776), pp. 9, 16.

47. Thomas Taylor, *The World Turn'd Upside-down* (Leeds: J. Bowling,

1784), p. 7. "But let the Gospel take place," Taylor declared, "and man's rebellion is at an end, he fears God, he honours the King and all that are in authority." (p. 8)

48. Thomas Olivers, *A Full Defence of the Rev. John Wesley, in Answer to . . . the Rev. Caleb Evans* (London, 1776), pp. 6, 8.

49. John Fletcher, *American Patriotism Farther Confronted with Reason, Scripture, and the Constitution: Being Observations on the Dangerous Politicks Taught by the Rev. Mr. Evans, M.A. and the Rev. Dr. Price* (Shrewsbury: Eddowes, 1776), pp. 129–30, 101, 107, 120–21, 92, 66.

50. Caleb Evans, *Political Sophistry Detected, Or Brief Remarks on the Rev. Mr. Fletcher's late Tract Entitled 'American Patriotism'* (Bristol: W. Pine, 1776), pp. 15, 17–18, 22.

51. John Wesley, *Some Account of the Late Work of God in North America in a Sermon on Ezekiel 1:16* (London: R. Hawes, 1778), pp. 7–8, 9–13.

52. Alan Heimert has no doubt but that the Arminian "Enlightenment" (a term which he employs to include not only the "official theology" of the Church of England in the colonies, but the views of all exponents of a liberal, "rational" religion) was "profoundly conservative, politically as well as socially." Calvinist "pietism," on the other hand, was in the forefront of the forces which made the revolution. (A reader may well bogle at the yoking of Wesleyan Arminianism and Deism under one head!) From its earliest days, the American revival, Heimert has demonstrated, invoked the name and spirit of Oliver Cromwell, and Calvinist ministers were Commonwealthmen of a fierce order. See Alan Heimert, *Religion and the American Mind; From the Great Awakening to the Revolution* (Cambridge, Mass.: Harvard University Press, 1966), pp. vii–viii, 4, 6, 12, 14, 18–19, 21, 34, 58, 92, 346, 351, 357–58, 375, 424.

53. A. M. Toplady, "Moral and Political Moderation Recommended" (1776), *Works*, III, 293–99.

54. Toplady, "Historic Proof," *Works*, II, 342–43.

55. Though Toplady bemoaned that "the sad ravages of civil war" would, "too probably, people the regions of the grave with additional thousands," he concluded that "providence, unerring providence, governs all events." A. M. Toplady, "Reflections for the Beginning of the Year 1776," *Works*, III, 451.

56. This is the argument of C. R. Haywood, "Was John Wesley a Political Economist," *Church History*, XXXIII (1964), 314–21.

57. See, for example, K. W. MacArthur, *The Economic Ethics of John Wesley* (New York: Abingdon Press, 1936).

58. This was, more or less, the view of W. J. Warner, *The Wesleyan Movement in the Industrial Revolution* (New York: Russell & Russell, 1967).

59. Haywood, for example, considered only Wesley's letter to *Lloyd's Evening News* in his "Was John Wesley a Political Economist." More balanced accounts can be found in R. M. Kingdon, "Laissez-faire or Government Control: A Problem for John Wesley," *Church History*, XXVI (December 1957), 342–54; and C. M. Elliott, "The Ideology of Economic Growth: A Case Study," in E. L. Jones and G. E. Mingay, eds., *Land, Labour and Population in the Industrial Revolution* (New York: Barnes & Noble, 1967), pp. 75–99.

60. Southey has suggested that Wesley liked the farmers least: "they were the least susceptible of Methodism," for Methodism "could be kept alive only by associations and frequent meetings; and it is difficult, or impossible, to arrange these among a scattered population." Southey, *Wesley*, II, 67–68.

61. Wesley, "Short Address to Inhabitants of Ireland," p. 177.

62. Quoted in Southey, *Wesley*, II, 65.

63. Wesley, *Journal*, VI (May 1, 1776), 104; see also VI (September 9, 1776), 127. Price's estimate of an English population of four or five millions was based on the assumption that an average of about four or four and a half persons were to be found in a house; Wesley's information led him to believe that there were, on the average, about seven to a house in a great number of regions in the Kingdom. Moreover, in Wesley's view, Price had "miscomputed" the number of houses, there being, perhaps twice as many as Price had calculated in the growing commercial and industrial districts, such as Bristol and its environs.

64. Wesley, *Journal*, VI (March 28, 1781), 309–10.

65. Wesley, *Journal*, IV (October 8, 1753), 232. Wesley felt more friendly to the quasi-communitarian Trevecca, which had been set up by Howell Harris, the Welsh evangelist whom he regarded as a friend. The setting, he wrote in 1763, was "a little paradise"; Trevecca, moreover, was morally useful, since "about six-score persons are now in the family," all of whom were "diligent, all constantly employed, all fearing God and working righteousness." *Journal*, V (August 19, 1763), 25. For more on Trevecca, see Morgan H. Jones, *The Trevecka Letters, or the Unpublished MSS. Correspondence of Howell Harris and His Contemporaries* (London, 1932). Trevecca was "the first attempt at applying the pietistic regulations of the Moravians to a Welsh settlement." (p. 187)

66. When Wesley visited Fulneck near Leeds, in 1780, his conclusion was: "I see not what but the mighty power of God can hinder them from acquiring millions," since they used the best materials, and had several hundred persons, "all of whom are employed from morning to night, without any intermission, in various kinds of manufactures, not for journeymen's wages, but for no wages at all, save a little very plain food and raiment." Their goods were, moreover, in good demand, and were sold for "ready money." Wesley, *Journal*, VI (April 17, 1780), 273–74.

67. Wesley, *Journal*, VI (June 28, 1783), 428.

68. Wesley, *Journal*, V (May 22, 1765), 118.

69. Wesley, *Letters*, V (April 24, 1769), 133–34.

70. Wesley, "Use of Money," *Works*, VI, 130.

71. *Ibid.*, pp. 127–28. In this sermon appears the following remarkable statement: "So I am convinced, from many experiments," he observed, that "I could not study, to any degree of perfection, either mathematics, arithmetic, or algebra, without being a Deist, if not an Atheist: And yet others may . . . without sustaining any inconvenience." (p. 128)

72. Wesley, "A Word to a Smuggler" (1767), *Works*, XI, 174–75; see also *Letters*, VII (March 21, 1784), 214–15.

73. Wesley, "Use of Money," *Works*, VI, pp. 128–30; see also *Letters*, VII (August 3, 1781), 77.

74. Wesley, "Thoughts upon Methodism," *Arminian Magazine*, X (March 1787), 156. Max Weber discussed this "apparent paradox between the rejection of the world and acquisitive virtuosity," in a number of places in his writings. See, for example, Max Weber, *The Religion of China* (Glencoe, Ill.: Free Press, 1951), p. 245. The ambivalence of the Wesleyan view toward riches is ably discussed in Elliott, "Ideology of Economic Growth," in Jones and Mingay, eds., *Land, Labour and Population*, pp. 76–86.

75. Wesley, *Journal*, IV (January 5, 1761), 428–30.

76. Wesley, "The Danger of Riches," *Works*, VII, 11.

77. Wesley, "On Riches," *Works*, VII, 217.

78. Wesley, "On the Danger of Increasing Riches" (1790), *Works*, VII, 355.

79. Wesley, "Thoughts upon Methodism," *Arminian Magazine*, X (March

1787), 156. The Moravians had attempted to solve this problem, although Wesley did not seem aware of this, by making the community rich rather than individuals. Wesley, on the other hand, saw such Moravian riches as a danger to the entire community. In describing the prosperity of Fulneck, Wesley asked: "But can they lay up treasure on earth, and at the same time lay up treasure in heaven?" *Journal,* VI (April 17, 1780), 274.

80. Wesley, "Thoughts upon Methodism," *Arminian Magazine,* X (March 1787), 156. See also Wesley, "The Use of Money," *Works,* VI, 126, 131, 134.

81. Wesley, "Thoughts upon Methodism," *Arminian Magazine* X (March 1787), 156.

82. Wesley, "Upon Our Lord's Sermon on the Mount," *Works,* V, 323, 320.

83. Wesley presented a moving picture of this distress: "I have seen it with my eyes in every corner of the land. I have known those who could only afford to eat a little coarse food every other day. I have known one picking up stinking sprats from a dunghill and carrying them home for herself and her children. I have known another gathering the bones which the dogs had left in the streets and making broth of them to prolong a wretched life. Such is the case at this day of multitudes of people in a land flowing, as it were, with milk and honey, abounding with all the necessaries, the conveniences, the superfluities of life!" Wesley, *Letters,* V (December 9, 1772), 350–54.

84. See Tyerman, *Wesley,* III, 451–52.

85. Wesley, *Journal,* VI (May 1, 1776), 104.

86. Wesley, *Journal,* VI (February 2, 1778), 180.

87. Wesley, *Journal,* VI (February 17, 1778), 180–81; also VI (May 9, 1778), 189–90.

88. Wesley, *Journal,* VII (March 20, 1789), 479.

89. See, for example, B. Semmel, "Malthus: 'Physiocracy' and the Commercial System," *Economic History Review,* XVII (1965), 522–35.

90. See E. P. Thompson, "The Moral Economy of the English Crowd in the Eighteenth Century," *Past and Present,* No. 50 (February 1971), 76–136.

91. See Tyerman, *Wesley,* I, 295; also Halévy, *The Birth of Methodism,* passim.

92. Wesley, *Journal,* VI (September 2, 1776), 125–26.

93. See *JWHS,* IV, 209.

94. See Charles Smith, *A Short Essay on the Corn Trade, and the Corn Laws. . . . First printed in 1758* (London, 1766), pp. 32, 61, 63.

95. Wesley, *Journal,* VI (September 2, 1776), 125–26.

96. Kingdon, "Laissez-faire or Government Control," *Church History,* XXVI (December 1957), 342–54.

97. Wesley, *Letters,* IV (October 29, 1764), 270–71.

98. Wesley, *Journal,* VI (May 14, 1782), 352–53.

99. Quoted in Tyerman, *Wesley,* III, 499–500.

100. Wesley, *Letters,* V (December 9, 1772), 353–54.

101. Wesley, *Letters,* VI, (December 29, 1779), p. 366.

102. See Fletcher, *Vindication,* p. 30. In opposing Whig sympathizers with colonial claims, Fletcher exposed the undemocratic character of the franchise employing later Radical arguments and examples—the contrast between Old Sarum and Birmingham—to cite one instance; Fletcher's purpose was not to extend the franchise, which he believed would have an unsettling effect, but to insist that disenfranchised American colonists deserved no greater privileges than the English poor. See *ibid.,* p. 14.

103. Quoted in Tyerman, *Wesley,* I, 441.

104. Wesley, *Journal,* VII (January 24, 1786), 136–37.

105. Wesley, *Letters,* VIII (October 1, 1789), 173. Wesley had for some time regarded George III as particularly protective of Methodism. See *Letters,* VI (February 9, 1774), 72.

106. John Wesley, "Reasons Against A Separation From the Church of England" (1758), *Works,* XIII, 229–30. For a full discussion of Wesley's relationship with the Church, see Frank Baker, *John Wesley and the Church of England* (Nashville: Abingdon Press, 1970).

107. Wesley, *Journal,* V, (August 4, 1766), 180. Wesley made the same observation in *Letters,* V (November 27, 1770), 209.

108. Wesley, "Reasons Against A Separation" (1758), *Works,* XIII, 225, 228–30. While ready to accept the presence at the meetings of the Dissenters of Methodists who had been brought up as Nonconformists, for all others, Wesley insisted, "repeated experience shows it is not wholesome food; rather, to them it has the effect of deadly poison."

109. See K. S. Pinson, *Pietism as a Factor in the Rise of German Nationalism* (New York: Columbia University Press, 1934).

110. John Wesley, "An Estimate of the Manners of the Present Times" (1782), *Works,* XI, 159, 162–63; for English "ungodliness," see also John Wesley, "A Serious Address to the People of England, With Regard to the State of the Nation" (1778), in *Works,* XI, 148–49. See also Wesley, *Letters* VI (July 10, 1779), 348.

111. "Most of those who have the fullest intercourse with God," he noted, "believe our enemies will never be permitted to land in England," citing, as proof, the "malignant fever" which had killed thousands in the enemy fleets. Wesley, *Letters,* VI (October 10, 1779), 358. More practically, he vaunted the power of the British navy, "in a better condition than it ever was since England was a nation," and rested secure in the knowledge that the government possessed troops which could put down internal revolts. John Wesley, "A Compassionate Address to the Inhabitants of Ireland" (1778), *Works,* XI, 151–52. See also Wesley, *Letters,* VII (August 3, 1782), 133; IV (July 28, 1762), 185.

IV/THE FORMATION OF EVANGELICAL ARMINIANISM

1. See Hugh Trevor-Roper, *The Crisis of the Seventeenth Century; Religion, the Reformation and Social Change* (New York: Harper & Row, 1968), Chapters 1, 4, and *passim.* "And why was it Arminian Amsterdam," Trevor-Roper inquired, "which created the amazing prosperity of the United Provinces, while Calvinist Gelderland remained the reserve of booby squires?" (p. 7)

2. See R. L. Colie, *Light and Enlightenment; A Study of the Cambridge Platonists and the Dutch Arminians* (Cambridge: Cambridge University Press, 1957), pp. x–xi, 3, 11, 17, 21, and *passim;* also Trevor-Roper, *Crisis of the Seventeenth Century,* pp. 193–236.

3. See again the argument in Tucker, *Brief History of the Principles of Methodism, passim.*

4. John Wesley, *Concise Ecclesiastical History,* III, 116–27, especially 119–20, 126–27; see also IV, 100, 103–7, 112–13. In this history, Wesley took the opportunity to rail not only at "the seditious sect of Anabaptists," but also at " a more rigid kind of Calvinists" in the seventeenth century "called by their adversaries *Antinomians.*" See III, 269, and IV, 110. The *Concise Eccle-*

siastical History, in four volumes, was based upon the continental Arminian Johann Lorenz Mosheim's well-regarded work.

5. Toplady, "Doctrine of Absolute Predestination," *Works*, V, 160–66.

6. *Ibid.*, pp. 156–58.

7. A. M. Toplady, "Historic Proof of the Doctrinal Calvinism of the Church of England," in *Works*, II, 356, 354.

8. J. Wesley, "Thoughts on Salvation by Faith" (1779), *Works*, XI, 492–96.

9. See, for example,

> My dear Redeemer, and my God
> I stake my soul on Thy free grace;
> Take back my interest in Thy blood,
> Unless it stream'd for *all* the race:
> I stake my soul on this alone,
> THY BLOOD DID ONCE FOR ALL ATONE.

The Poetical Works of John and Charles Wesley (London: Wesleyan Methodist Conference Office, 1869), Hymn XIII, III, 29.

10. See Hymn XVII, *ibid.*, p. 34.

> O HORRIBLE DECREE,
> Worthy of whence it came!
> Forgive their hellish blasphemy
> Who charge it on the Lamb. . . .

11. Wesley, "Thoughts on Salvation by Faith," pp. 492–96.

12. J. W. Fletcher, "Zelotes and Honestus Reconciled; Or, The Third Part of An Equal Check to Pharisaism and Antinomianism" (1775), *Checks to Antinomianism*, II, 273–82.

13. Wesley, *Letters*, IV (July 7, 1761), 158.

14. Wesley, *Letters*, VI (August 18, 1775), 174–75. [J. W.] "Introduction," *Arminian Magazine*, I, No. 1, vi, viii. See Josiah Tucker, *Letter to the Rev. Dr. Kippis* (Gloucester: Raikes, 1773), pp. 84, 88, 94, 96–98.

15. Wesley, *Concise Ecclesiastical History*, I, 248 n.

16. Wesley, *Letters*, VI (August 18, 1775), 175.

17. Fletcher, "Second Check to Antinomianism," in *Checks to Antinomianism*, I, 91.

18. Fletcher, "Last Check to Antinomianism," in *Checks*, II, 601, 606.

19. Fletcher, "Zelotes and Honestus," *Checks to Antinomianism*, II, 314.

20. *The Gospel Magazine*, VI (January 1779), 48; see also VI (February 1779), 86–90.

21. *Ibid.*, I (1774), 144–45.

22. *Ibid.*, I (1774), 303.

23. [Sir Richard Hill], *Five Letters to . . . Mr Fletcher relative to the Vindication of the . . . minutes . . . of John Wesley* (n.p., 1772), p. 52.

24. Hill, *Conversation between Hill, Madan, and the Superior*, p. 10; see also pp. 8, 13.

25. Sir Richard Hill, *A Review of all the Doctrines Taught by the Rev. J. Wesley; Containing a Full and Particular Answer to a Book, Entitled, "A Second Check to Antinomianism" etc.* (London, 1772), pp. 4, 13, 25.

26. Sir Richard Hill, *Daubenism Confuted, and Martin Luther Vindicated* (London, 1800), pp. 18–19.

27. Sir Richard Hill, *Logica Wesleiensis: or the Farrago double distilled* (London: Dilly, 1773), p. 52.

28. Hill, *Review of all the Doctrines*, p. 92 n.

29. *Ibid.*, pp. 31, 40, 52.

30. Rowland Hill, *Imposture detected & the dead vindicated* (London, 1777), pp. 7, 10–11.

31. Sir Richard Hill. *A Lash at Enthusiasm etc.* (n.p., 1792). p. 47.

32. John Wesley, "Remarks Upon Mr. Locke's 'Essay on Human Understanding'" (1781), *Works*, XIII, 455–64. Wesley's remarks, and monthly excerpts from Locke's *Essay*, appear in the *Arminian Magazine*, Vol. V (1782), Vol. VI (1783), and Vol. VII (1784). For a view of Wesley as a man of reason, stressing his interest in science, see Stuart Andrews, "John Wesley and the Age of Reason," *History Today*, XIX (January 1969), 25–32.

33. John Wesley, "Thoughts Upon Baron Montesquieu's Spirit of the Laws," *Arminian Magazine*, IV (1781), 206–09.

34. Wesley, *Journal*, VII (August 26, 1784), 13.

35. Wesley, *Journal*, VI (May 31, 1774), 23.

36. John Wesley, "Remarks on the Count de Buffon's 'Natural History'" (1782), *Works*, XIII, 448–55.

37. Edward Gibbon, *The History of the Decline and Fall of the Roman Empire* (London: Methuen, 1907), [Bury ed.], VI, 127–28, 128 n.

38. Georges de Lagarde, *Recherches sur l'esprit politique de la Réforme* (Paris: Auguste Picard, 1926), pp. 189–94, 424, 459, 460, 462, 464.

39. See excerpt of speech by W. J. Ashley, "An Economist on Calvinism, Arminianism, Puritanism," *PWHS*, XVI (1927), 32–34.

40. Trevor-Roper, *Crisis of the Seventeenth Century*, pp. 193–236. Calvinism was depicted as the "enemy" of the Enlightenment. (p. 214)

41. See, for example, Fletcher, "An Equal Check to Pharisaism and Antinomianism," *Checks*, I, 447, 515, 578, and *passim*.

42. Nichols was associated with Jabez Bunting in initiating the Leeds Methodist Missionary Society, and in 1820, once more working with Bunting, he became the publisher and editor of the first Methodist venture in journalism, the *Christian Reporter*. Nichols described his political principles as being those of such "Whigs of the Old School," as Lord Somers and the first Earl of Chatham; he devoted many years to a translation of the writings of Arminius, of whose principles, both religious and political, he declared himself a disciple. Letter of James Nichols to Jabez Bunting, 29 July 1820, among many others to Bunting, 1816–20, in James Nichols Papers, Methodist Church Archives; see James Nichols, *Works of Arminius* (London, 1825).

43. James Nichols, *Calvinism and Arminianism Compared* (London, 1824), pp. xli–xlviii, l–liii, lx–lxviii, lxxiv f., lxxix, ciii, xcvii f., xciii, 264, 294, cxiii–cxiv; 515 f.; also 242–308.

44. See, for example, Wesley, *Letters*, VII (March 31, 1780), 10–11. In 1749, Wesley observed that though Luther had been "a man highly favoured of God, and a blessed instrument in His hand," he ought to have been rebuked "plainly and sharply for his rough untractable spirit and bitter zeal for opinions, so greatly obstructive of the work of God!" Wesley, *Journal*, III (July 19, 1749), 409.

45. Wesley, *Journal*, IV (June 23, 1755), 123.

46. Wesley, *Journal*, V (June 23, 1766), 171–72.

47. Wesley, *Concise Ecclesiastical History*, IV, 126.

48. Wesley, *Journal*, VII (May 18, 1788), 389.

49. See Wesley, "Hymns for a Protestant" (1745), *Poetical Works*, VI, 6; see also VIII, 266.

50. Wesley, *Letters*, V (October 5, 1770), 203.

51. Wesley, *Letters,* VI (December 28, 1773), 61.
52. Wesley, *Letters,* VIII (March 20, 1762), 271.
53. J. Wesley, "A Caution Against Bigotry," *Works,* V, 490.
54. J. Wesley, "The Character of a Methodist," *Works,* VIII, 341, 344, 346.
55. Wesley, *Journal,* IV (October 26, 1754), 101.
56. Wesley, "Character of a Methodist," *Works,* VIII, 347.
57. J. Wesley, "Remarks on Hill's 'Review' " (1772), *Works,* X, 392; see also Wesley, *Letters,* V (March 22, 1771), 231.
58. John Wesley, "Free Grace" (1740), *Works,* VII, 373–86.
59. Wesley, "Thoughts Upon Necessity," (1774), *Works,* X, 457–58, 464, 469, 473.
60. J. Wesley, "A Thought on Necessity," *Works,* X, 474–76, 479.
61. Wesley, *Journal,* V (May 5, 1772), 458; for further allusions to Hume, see *Journal,* V (December 11, 1772), 491; V (August 8, 1773), 523; V (March 5, 1769), 303.
62. Fletcher, "Equal Check," *Checks,* I, 445.
63. Wesley, *Journal,* VI (May 23, 1774), 21–22.
64. J. Wesley, "Thoughts Upon Necessity" (1774), *Works,* X, 457.
65. J. Wesley, *Journal,* VI (July 6, 1781), 326.
66. Toplady, "Doctrine of Absolute Predestination." *Works,* V, 160–66.
67. A. M. Toplady, "The Scheme of Christian and Philosophical Necessity Asserted. In Opposition to Mr. John Wesley's Tract on That Subject" (1775), in *Works,* VI, 48; see also 48–66.
68. *Ibid.,* p. 67. See also Toplady, "A Dissertation Concerning the Sensible Qualities of Matter," *Works,* VI, 107, 112–13, 132; cf. Wesley's argument in "Thoughts upon Necessity," X, 470.
69. Letter of A. M. Toplady to J. Priestley, December 23, 1774, in Toplady, *Works,* VI, 240–43.
70. Letter of A. M. Toplady to J. Priestley, January 20, 1778, in Toplady, *Works,* VI, 291.
71. Letter of Toplady to Priestley, December 23, 1774, in Toplady, *Works,* VI, 240–41; for Wesley on Priestley, see *Letters,* VII (April 3, 1785), in which Priestley is described as "one of the most dangerous enemies to Christianity that is now in the world." (p. 265)
72. Toplady, "Absolute Predestination," *Works,* V, 158–59.
73. A. M. Toplady, "More Work for Mr. John Wesley: Or, A Vindication of the Decrees and Providence of God," *Works,* V, 381–82.
74. J. W. Fletcher, "An Answer to the Rev. Mr. Toplady's 'Vindication of the Decrees' " (1775), *Checks,* II, 467.
75. See W. J. Townsend, H. B. Workman, G. Eayrs, *A New History of Methodism* (London: Hodder and Stoughton, 1919), I, 225. The text of White-field's letter, written on March 22, 1751, appears in Tyerman, *Wesley,* II, 132. Speaking more practically, Whitefield had observed that "hot countries cannot be cultivated without negroes." Whitefield had himself purchased slaves on behalf of his Georgia orphans-home and, after his death, the Countess of Huntingdon, as his heir and executor, continued, without compunction, to make such purchases. See A. A. Dollimore, *George Whitefield; The Life and Times of the Great Evangelist of the Eighteenth Century Revival* (London: Banner of Truth Trust, 1970), pp. 495–501, 508–9.
76. A very different view of Wesley, one which sees him as having a strong prejudice against primitive peoples—the Georgia Indians, Hottentots, Lapland-ers, Senegalese, etc.—seeing them as unmerciful, corrupt, degenerate, and beset by original sin, is to be found in M. T. Hodgen, *Early Anthropology in*

the Sixteenth and Seventeenth Centuries (Philadelphia: U. of Penn. Press, 1964), pp. 366–67.

77. J. Wesley, "Thoughts Upon Slavery" (1774), *Works,* XI, 61–79.

78. Wesley, *Journal,* VI (April 14, 1777), 143.

79. Wesley, *Letters,* VIII (November 24, 1787), 23.

80. Wesley, *Letters,* VIII (October 11, 1787), 17.

81. Wesley, *Letters,* VIII (November 24, 1787), 23.

82. Wesley, *Letters,* VIII (February 24, 1791), 265; see also *Journal,* VII (February 24, 1789), 471.

83. Wesley, *Journal,* V (May 14, 1765), 117–18. For a discussion of Christian Perfection see W. E. Sangster, *The Path of Perfection, An Examination and Restatement of John Wesley's Doctrine of Christian Perfection* (London: Hodder and Stoughton, 1943).

84. Fletcher, "Equal Checks," *Checks,* I, 440.

85. John Wesley, "A Plain Account of Christian Perfection, As Believed and Taught by the Reverend Mr. John Wesley" (1777), in *Works,* XI, 366, 375–76, 387, 394–95, 398, 442, and *passim.*

86. John Wesley, "Brief Thoughts on Christian Perfection" (1777), *Works,* XI, 446.

87. John Wesley, "A Circumcision of the Heart" (1733), in *Works,* V, 202–12.

88. *Arminian Magazine,* V (March 1782), 149–50.

89. Wesley, "A Plain Account of Christian Perfection" (1777), *Works,* XI, 442–43.

90. *Ibid.,* pp. 441–45. Wesley's descriptions of the sinful state are, of course, suggestive of the kind of sin which was, apparently, very prominent in his mind: Wesley asked for "a full deliverance" from a "carnal mind"; his metaphor of "the circumcision of the heart" is not without significance, nor is his preoccupation with the idea that the chief allure of the "practical" Antinomians was the common possession of women.

91. Fletcher, "Equal Check," *Checks,* I, 442.

92. Fletcher, "Last Check," *Checks,* II, 494.

93. Quoted in Rupert Davies, "The People Called Methodists; 1. Our Doctrines," in R. Davies and G. Rupp, eds., *A History of the Methodist Church in Great Britain* (London: Epworth Press, 1965), I, 165. By Assurance, Wesley wrote elsewhere, quoting the words of the homily, "I mean 'a confidence which a man hath in God that, by the merits of Christ, his sins are forgiven, and he reconciled to the favour of God.'" Wesley, *Journal,* IV (December 20, 1760), 425. See A. S. Yates, *The Doctrine of Assurance with Special Reference to John Wesley* (London: Epworth Press, 1952).

94. See Wesley, *Letters,* IV (April 2, 1761), 144.

95. See Wesley, *Letters,* III (February 5, 1756), 159.

96. See, for example, an early entry in Wesley, *Journal,* II (October 6, 1738), 82–83.

97. "I never knew one soul thus saved without what you call 'the faith of assurance'; I mean a sure confidence that, by the merits of Christ, he was reconciled to the favours of God.'" See Wesley, *Journal,* II (January 25, 1740), 333–34.

98. "We believe a man may be a real Christian without being 'assured of his salvation.'" Wesley, *Letters,* IV (April 2, 1761), 144.

99. Melville Horne, *An Investigation of the Definition of Justifying Faith. . . . Held by Dr. Coke, and other Methodist Preachers* (London: Longmans et al., 1809), pp. 1–4, 7–10, 12, 14.

100. J. H. Pratt, ed., *Eclectic Notes; or Notes of Discussions on Religious Topics at the Meetings of the Eclectic Society, London. During the Years 1798–1814* (London: J. Nisbet, 1865), pp. 500–507.

101. Horne, *Investigation of Justifying Faith*, pp. 19–20.

102. *Ibid.*, p. 5, and *passim*.

103. *Ibid.*, pp. 107–8.

104. Thomas Coke, *A Series of Letters Addressed to the Methodist Connection* (London: Blanshard, 1810); see also another Methodist reply, Edward Hare, *A Letter to the Rev. Melville Horne; Occasioned by his Investigation of the Doctrines Imputed by him to Certain Methodist Preachers* (Sheffield: J. Montgomery, 1809).

105. See George Smith, *History of Wesleyan Methodism* (London: Longmans, Green, 1866), I, 442–43. Both Benson and Coke later produced "Commentaries" on the Bible which acquired a quasi-authoritative status within the Connection; Coke's, written between 1800 and 1803, was largely taken from a commentary by a Dr. Dodd, which the latter had based on what he thought was a work of Locke, but was in fact Ralph Cudworth's *True Intellectual System. Ibid.*, II, 652–54.

106. See *ibid.*, II, 654–60.

107. Richard Watson, "Remarks on the Eternal Sonship of Christ; and the Use of Reason in Matters of Revelation; Suggested by Several Passages in Dr. Adam Clarke's Commentary on the New Testament" (1818), in *The Works of the Rev. Richard Watson* (8th ed.; London: Wesleyan Conference Office, 1865), VII, 3–86.

108. Richard Watson, in London, to Rev. R. Reece, in Manchester, 7 March 1818. Watson Papers. Methodist Church Archives.

109. Quoted in T. P. Bunting, *The Life of Jabez Bunting* (London: T. Woolmer, 1887), II, 382.

110. Wesley, *History of England, passim*.

111. E. W. Bradburn, ed., *Memoirs of the Late Rev. Samuel Bradburn* (London: R. Edwards, 1816), pp. 45, 86, 91–95 n.

112. See John Vickers, *Thomas Coke; An Apostle of Methodism* (London: Epworth Press, 1969).

113. See William Vidler, *A Letter to Samuel Bradburn and all the Preachers in the Methodist Connection* (Tottenham, 1796), p. 3; and Samuel Bradburn, *Methodism Set Forth and Defended* (Bristol: Lancaster and Edwards, 1792), pp. 5–13, and *passim*.

114. [Anon.], *Letter to a Country Gentleman on the Subject of Methodism* (Ipswich, 1805) p. 44; see also pp. 4, 42–43, and *passim*.

115. Member of the Church of England, *Hints for the Security of the Established Church* (London: Hatchard, 1806), p. 36.

116. Rev. James Jones, *Moral Freedom and Divine Benevolence; A Letter Addressed to the Rev. Jabez Bunting, M.A., President of the Methodist Conference* (Margate: R. Osborne, 1829), pp. 4–13, 15, 17, 21 f., 28.

117. Anon., *Methodism Exposed: With the History and Tendency of That Sect* (London: Cradock and Joy, 1813), pp. 20–22, 12–13, 16, 14–15.

118. Jones, *Moral Freedom*, p. 28.

119. *Ibid.*, p. 22.

120. Nichols praised the Arminianism of Laud, the Latitudinarian leaders Hales and Chillingworth, the Cambridge Platonists (More, Cudworth, and Whichcote), and, of course, Archbishop Tillotson, but condemned the Pelagianism of Jeremy Taylor and of Arminius' later disciples, Curcellaeus, Poelenburgh, and Locke's friend, Limborch. The true evangelical Arminianism of the

master might have triumphed in England, Nichols observed, if Arminianism had not been altered by the doctrinal tendencies, e.g., on the matter of original sin, toward Pelagianism; as it was, English Calvinism rejected "the *free gold* of General Redemption" because of the "dross" of Pelagianism. Nichols felt bound to conclude that "though Courcelles, Poelenburgh, and Limborch are seen to have been deficient in evangelical purity of doctrine," yet they were "entitled to the gratitude of posterity as asserters of civil and religious freedom." Nichols, *Calvinism and Arminianism Compared*, pp. xlii–xlvi, lxxx–lxxxvi, cxv, 795–96, 801–6.

121. Jabez Bunting, *Memorials of the late Rev. Richard Watson: including the Funeral Sermon . . . January 18, 1833* (London: J. Mason, 1833), p. 29.

122. *Ibid.*, pp. 30–31 n.

123. See, for example, Watson, *Works,* VII, 421.

124. Thomas Jackson, *Recollections of My Own Life and Times* (London: Wesleyan Conference Office, 1878), pp. 215–16, 479–81, 473.

125. Quoted in T. P. Bunting, *Jabez Bunting,* II, 382.

126. Wesley, *Journal,* VII (November 1787), 337–38; Tyerman, *Wesley,* III, 510–11.

127. See discussion, for example, in Nichols, *Calvinism and Arminianism Compared,* pp. xcviii ff.

128. Rev. Basil Woodd, as an instance, at a meeting of the Eclectic Society in 1800, while granting that all men were "in a general sense redeemed," yet declared, using Baxter's distinction, "none but the elect are actually redeemed"; while the offer of redemption had been made to all, "the effectual application of the redemption is to the elect." "Election is the free act of God effectually applying redemption to men equally sinful in themselves with those who are not so brought to Him": "Yet all," Woodd concluded with evident wonder, "is the result of wisdom and justice." Pratt, ed., *Eclectic Notes,* April 14, 1800, pp. 167–68.

129. *Ibid.*, p. 168.

130. *Ibid.*, April 13, 1812, pp. 511–12.

131. William Wilberforce, *A Practical View of the Prevailing Religious System of Professed Christians in the Higher and Middle Classes in This Country, Contrasted with Real Christianity* (London: Cadell, 1797), pp. 50–51, 462, 464, 466 n., 379–80 n.

132. Thomas Belsham, *A Review of Mr. Wilberforce's Treatise* (London: J. Johnson, 1798), pp. 6–8, and *passim*.

133. Thomas Williams, *A Vindication of the Calvinistic Doctrines of Human Depravity etc. . . . in a Series of Letters to the Rev. T. Belsham: Occasioned by His "Review of Mr. Wilberforce's Treatise"* (London: A. Parns, 1799), pp. v, 90. The view that Wilberforce's stress on hereditary depravity as the foundation of all religion placed him unreservedly in the Calvinist camp was also to be found in A. Layman, *Letters to William Wilberforce on the Doctrine of Hereditary Depravity* (London: J. Johnson, 1806), p. 35 and *passim*. For a link with the Calvinian Controversy of the seventies, see Richard Hill, *An Apology for Brotherly Love . . . With a Vindication of Such Parts of Mr Wilberforce's Practical View As Have Been Objected to by Mr Daubeny, in his . . . Guide to the Church* (London, 1798).

134. A. M. Wilberforce, ed., *Private Papers of William Wilberforce* (London: T. Fisher Unwin, 1897), p. 260.

135. *Ibid.*, p. 248.

136. Quoted in R. I. and S. Wilberforce, *The Life of William Wilberforce* (London: John Murray, 1838), V, 162. This appears also to have been the view

of the Evangelical Bishop of London, Porteus. See Rev. Robert Hodgson, *The Life of the Right Reverend Beilby Porteus, D.D., Late Bishop of London* (London: Cadell and Davies, 1811), p. 265.

137. Careful Observer, *Strictures on Methodism* (London: R. Edwards, 1804), pp. 65–66.

138. William Burns, *An Inquiry into the Moral Tendency of Methodism and Evangelical Preaching* (London: J. Johnson, 1810), pp. 7–8. Burns, sympathetic to Evangelicalism without being himself an Evangelical, suggested that, in reality, the old Calvinist "fear" had departed. "The merciful disposition of the divine character is so well established, and the gracious purpose of our Saviour's mission so well known, that men are more apt to presume too much on the goodness of God, than to be terrified by the fear of his justice." (pp. 135–36)

V / FEAR OF REVOLUTION AND REPRESSION, 1791–1832

1. Wilberforce, *A Practical View*, pp. 393–94, 405, 419–20.

2. Pratt, ed., *Eclectic Notes*, April 13, 1812, p. 512.

3. *Ibid.*, Sept. 17, 1798, pp. 72–74.

4. Quoted in Preserved Smith, *The Enlightenment, 1687–1776* (Vol. II of *A History of Modern Culture;* New York: Collier Books, 1962), p. 401.

5. Wesley, *Letters*, VIII (February 4, 1790), 199–200.

6. Wesley, *Letters*, VIII (March 1790), 204.

7. Only the rare clergyman—noting that Methodists regarded themselves as belonging to the Church of England—might argue that "did they [the Methodists], like the Puritans of the former Age . . . seduce Believers from the established Church, we should have Reason to be alarmed; but the direct contrary is manifest." Rev. Moore Booker, *Two Letters Concerning the Methodists* (Dublin: Kilburn, 1751), p. 11.

8. See A Consistent Whig, *Considerations on the late Disturbances* (London: J. Almon, 1780), p. 13. In 1769, an anonymous writer, probably a Dissenter, in discussing a report of an impending crackdown on Methodists and Dissenters for their supposed support of Wilkes, and seeing the move as spurred by the clergy, had intoned "O, what a happy World would this be, if there was never a toryfied Clergyman in it!" Anon., *An Alarm to Dissenters and Methodists* (London: G. Keith, 1769), pp. 14, 21, 23, and Appendix.

9. For a discussion of the organization of Methodist Societies, see Townsend, Workman, Earys, eds., *New History of Methodism*, I, 279–91, and *passim*; also Robert Currie, *Methodism Divided: A Study in the Sociology of Ecumenicalism* (London: Faber, 1968).

10. *Minutes of the Methodist Conferences* (1766), I, 60–62. [Hereafter *Conference Minutes.*]

11. A Trustee and Layman, *An Apology for the Methodists of the New Connexion* etc. (Hanley: Conference Office, 1815), pp. 8, 18–20, 22, 39. Although by 1815 important steps had been taken toward a more democratic participation in the government of the Old Connection, in part to combat the appeal of the New, it was still possible, at that time, for a disgruntled Methodist of the Old Connection to contrast the "self-elected, absolute, and arbitrary Government" of his denomination with the "excellent civil constitution which

we enjoy as Englishmen," and with the "Equitable and Constitutional" government of the New Connection. See A Member of the Old Methodist Society, *An Exposition of the Proceedings of the Old Methodist Conference With Reflections on the Nature and Tendency of its System of Government* etc. (Manchester: G. Innes, 1815), 2nd ed., pp. 5–8, 15–18. "Nothing indeed can be more inconsistent with the Religion we profess, with the enlightened age and place in which we live, the principle of our admirable constitution, nor, above all, with the unerring and infallible word of God, than our present system of Church Government." (p. 12)

12. See John Pawson to Charles Atmore, 11 February 1793, 22 February 1793. Pawson Papers. Methodist Church Archives. City Road, London. Hereafter M.C.A.

13. Clarke was disturbed at the High Church Party's boast that they were supported by "a Majority among the Preachers"; "my love would mourn to think," he declared, that "I had got into a Connexion, the majority of which was so base." Clarke doubted the accuracy of this boast. Adam Clarke to George Marsden, 8 January 1795, Clarke Papers, M.C.A.

14. See John Pawson to Charles Atmore, 20 October 1787, 17 March 1788, 19 March 1789. Pawson Papers. M.C.A. The Shakespeare incident is recounted in G. J. Stephenson, *Methodist Worthies; Characteristic Sketches of Methodist Preachers of the Several Denominations* (London: T. C. Jack, 1884), I, 171.

15. See, for example, John Pawson to Charles Atmore, 30 March 1786. Pawson Papers. M.C.A.

16. John Pawson to Thomas Benson, 21 November 1794. Pawson Papers. M.C.A.

17. John Pawson to Thomas Benson, 5 March 1795; see also Pawson to Benson, 1 [9] March 1795 and 27 March 1795. Pawson Papers. M.C.A.

18. John Pawson to Charles Atmore, 15 July 1795. Pawson Papers. M.C.A.

19. *Conference Minutes (1795)*, I, 339–42.

20. *Conference Minutes (1793)*, I, 292. As the anonymous "Trustee" understood, in his *Apology for the Methodists of the New Connexion*, "though slowly, the Old Connexion will be impelled to follow our steps." (p. 46)

21. John Pawson to C. Atmore, 14 February 1796. Pawson Papers. M.C.A.

22. John Pawson to Charles Atmore, 22 February 1793. Pawson Papers. M.C.A.

23. Bradburn added that, "considering it abstractedly (*sic*)," the war "has done more good than hurt to the nation." Samuel Bradburn, at Bath, to J. Reynolds, 12 April 1796. Bradburn Papers. M.C.A.; see also Samuel Bradburn, at Frome, to Pritchard, at Halifax, 10 May 1796. Bradburn Papers. M.C.A.

24. John Pawson to Charles Atmore, 4 July 1797. Pawson Papers. M.C.A.

25. John Pawson to Thomas Benson, 14 December 1796. See also John Pawson to Rodda, 10 September 1796; and John Pawson to Thomas Benson, 25 November 1797. Pawson Papers. M.C.A. Also see a Samuel Bradburn letter in which the writer denounced Kilham's autobiography as "an endeavour *to sow discord among brethren*," and urged it be burned "by the common hangman in every town in Britain!" Samuel Bradburn, at Manchester, to Benson, at Hull, 5 February 1800. Bradburn Papers. M.C.A.

26. *Conference Minutes (1795)*, I, 342.

27. *Conference Minutes (1796)*, I, 361–62.

28. *Conference Minutes (1796)*, I, 364.

29. *Conference Minutes (1797)*, I, 377, 392, 394.

30. Samuel Bradburn, *An Address to the People Called Methodists; Concerning the Evil of Encouraging the Slave Trade* (Manchester: T. Harper, 1792), pp. 20, 21, 23.

31. John Pawson to Charles Atmore, 22 February 1793. Pawson Papers. M.C.A.

32. Samuel Bradburn, *Equality* [Sermon preached at Bristol, February 28, 1794] (Bristol: Lancaster & Edwards, 1794), pp. 1, 6–11, 13–25, 27–28, 25–26, 22–23, 27 n. The Rev. Isaac Keeling was to suggest that Bradburn's sermon on Equality was designed to procure "an indirect and dexterous clearing of himself from holding French notions of equality, to which his early admiration of the Revolution of 1789 had seemed to make him liable." Quoted in T. W. Blanshard, *The Life of Samuel Bradburn; the Methodist Demosthenes* (London: E. Stock, 1871), p. 206.

33. Bradburn, *Equality*, p. 22.

34. See Alexander Kilham, *The Progress of Liberty, Amongst the People Called Methodists* (Alnwick: J. Catnach, 1795), p. vii.

35. *Ibid.*, pp. 9, 15.

36. [Alexander Kilham], *A Defence of the Account Published by Alexander Kilham on his Trial Before the London Conference* [16 December 1796] (Leeds: Binns & Brown, 1796), pp. 37–38. In *A Short Account of the Trial of Alex. Kilham, At a Special District Meeting, Held at Newcastle, On the 18th, 19th, & 20th, of February 1796* (Alnwick: J. Catnach, 1796). Kilham observed: "The papists are required to receive the doctrines which are taught by their priests, without examining them by the word of God. Every member of the Church of England, is to receive the scriptures, as they are explained by the church, and every methodist preacher is to mould his doctrines according to the notes and sermons of Mr. Wesley." (p. 10)

37. Kilham, *Progress of Liberty*, pp. 12–13, 17, 19, 24–26, 35–36.

38. See Paul & Silas [Alexander Kilham], *An Earnest Address to the Preachers Assembled in Conference* (n.p., 1795), in which Kilham, in the name of "liberty and equality," praised a plan for church governance which would make the Connection "a pure republic." (pp. 12–13) See also Anon., *A Dialogue Between James, A Member of the Old, and Jacob, A Member of the New Connexion of Methodists* (Leeds: T. Hannam, 1797), which presented Jacob attempting to refute but in actuality confirming James' charge that the governing plan of the New Connection would "lead to republican principles": "our form of *church* government is nearly modelled upon the form of *civil* government in England," Jacob argued, and just as the king was "the head of civil government," so "our Head of Spiritual government, is Christ the Annointed." (pp. 11–12)

39. Kilham, *A Defence of the Account*, p. 50.

40. Alexander Kilham, *Appeal to the Methodist Societies of the Alnwick Circuit* (n.p., 1796), p. 10.

41. [Alexander Kilham], *An Account of the Trial of Alexander Kilham, Methodist Preacher, Before the General Conference in London: On the 26th, 27th, and 28th of July, 1796* (Leeds: Binns & Brown, 1796), pp. 3–4, 37. In an earlier appeal to the Alnwick circuit, Kilham had declared that "no government under heaven, except *absolute monarchies*, or the *papal hierarchy*, is so despotic and oppressive as our's (*sic*) is." (p. 8) In his *Account of the Trial of Alex. Kilham, at Newcastle*, Kilham complained of "the *secret* and *popish* method of my trial." (p. 24) See also Alexander Kilham, *A Candid Examination, of the London Methodistical Bull* (Alnwick: J. Catnach, 1796).

42. Jonathan Crowther, *Christian Order: Or, Liberty Without Anarchy; Government Without Tyranny; and Every Man in his proper Place* etc. (Bristol: R. Edwards, 1796), pp. 2–4, and *passim*.

43. See Trustee, *Apology for . . . New Connection*, p. 33.

44. See W. Vipond, *The Doctrines, Discipline and Mode of Worship of the Methodists* (Canterbury, 1807), p. 91; and Jacob Stanley, *The Increase, Influence, and Stability, of Unestablished Religion, No Cause of Alarm to Established Christians* (Wednesbury: J. Booth, 1813), p. 13. Stanley suggested the likelihood of a continuance of the same rate of growth! (p. 14)

45. See Valentine Ward, *A Brief Statement of Facts, Designed for the Information of Those Who from Good Motives Enquire 'What are These Methodists?'* (Leeds: James Nichols, 1815), p. 14. Samuel Bradburn estimated 120,000 members in 1804, adding that "these are not a fourth part of our congregations; so that we have never less than half a million people who have on Sundays, regularly attended our places of worship." Samuel Bradburn, *God Shining Forth, From Between the Cherubim* (Bolton: Garner, 1805), p. 64.

46. See W. R. Ward, "The Religion of the People and the Problem of Control, 1790–1830," in G. J. Cuming and Derek Baker, eds., *Popular Belief and Practice* (Cambridge: Cambridge University Press, 1972), pp. 237–57.

47. George Croft, D.D., *Thoughts Concerning the Methodists and the Established Clergy* (London: Rivington, 1795), pp. 49–50.

48. See Samuel Drew, *Observations (In behalf of the Methodists) on a Pamphlet Lately Published by the Rev. R. Polwhele* (Falmouth, 1800). Drew had checked into the facts and reported that "not one Methodist ever did join the mob from choice; but many were compelled to join through necessity." Nevertheless, he declared that Methodists were "a check upon the mob during the day." (p. 54)

49. Anon., *A Letter to a Country Gentleman*, pp. 18, 19 n., 20, 21, 23–25, 31, 33, 41 n., 41–42. The following year, the same author, in his *An Address to the Lower Class of His Parishioners, on the subject of Methodism* (Ipswich: J. Raw, 1806), made reference to "that *system of terror* the Methodist pursues." (p. 15) Compare with Lecky, *History of England*, II, 582.

50. Member of the Church of England, *Hints for the Security of the Established Church*, pp. 28–29.

51. Anon., *Puritanism Revived; Or Methodism as Old as the Great Rebellion. In a Series of Letters from a Curate to his Rector* (London: Rivington, 1808), pp. 36–37, 95, and *passim*.

52. Quoted in the *Evangelical Magazine*, IX (1801), 162. The *Evangelical Magazine*, however, defended Methodist loyalty, though without denying the specific accusation, and proclaimed that "the leading men among the Methodists are known to be as inveterate enemies to it [Jacobinism] as any prelate on the Bench." (p. 164)

53. G. I. Huntingford, Bishop of Gloucester, *A Charge Delivered to the Clergy of the Diocese of Gloucester* (London: Cadell & Davies, 1807), pp. 22–23, 26, 29–30.

54. Cursitor, *A Letter to the Lord Bishop of Lincoln, Respecting the 'Report from the Clergy of a District in the Diocese of Lincoln, In Which Report the Increase of Methodism Is Considered as a Cause of the Declension of Religion* (London, 1800), pp. 11, 22.

55. Member of the Church of England, *Hints for the Security*, pp. 21, 16–20; see also pp. 23–24, 28–29.

56. See, for example, Member of the Church of England, *Hints for the Security*, in which the writer asks for an act stating "that a minister, preacher, or

teacher, shall *be licensed to and confined to his own appropriate registered place of worship."* (p. 24)

57. *Conference Minutes (1792)*, I, 270–71.

58. Bradburn, *Methodism Set Forth and Defended,* pp. 51–52. In 1805, Bradburn was to praise the "illustrious House of Hanover" who "not from political motives, but from Christian Principles . . . have not suffered anyone to be persecuted for conscience sake." Bradburn, *God Shining Forth,* p. 62.

59. Joseph Benson, *A Defence of the Methodists in Five Letters Addressed to the Rev. Dr. Tatham* (London, 1793), pp. 42, 58.

60. Henry Moore, *Fear God: Honour the King* (London: G. Paramore, 1794).

61. Jeremiah Brittell, *Fear God and Honour the King* (n.p., 1796).

62. For example, see *Conference Minutes (1792)*, I, 270–71; *Conference Minutes (1793)*, I, 294 (at this time, the conference insisted that a charge of disloyalty was "cruelty itself," enjoining those who made it to "show us the men and the proofs of their guilt, and we will instantly cut them off from our Connexion"); *Conference Minutes (1799)*, II, 28; *Conference Minutes (1800)*, II, 59; *Conference Minutes (1803)*, II, 190; *The Address of the Members of the Sixteenth Annual Conference* (Manchester, 1803), p. 4. A pledge of loyalty is accompanied by the conviction that "there is no country, where, from age to age, personal liberty and property and the sacred rights of conscience have been so well secured," in Thomas Rutherforc, *The Voice of the Rod* (London: R. Edwards, 1803), pp. 12–13; John Stephens chanted "loyalty to the best of kings, and profound attachment to the happiest of Constitutions," and added that "we enjoy the blessings of a republican form of government, in our House of Commons, without feeling the direful effects of its restless and revolutionary spirit," in his *The Privileges, Sins, Dangers, and Duties of Britons* (Edinburgh: Chapman, 1803), pp. 2, 9; and Thomas Wood, in his *Victory and Death* (Huddersfield: T. Smart, 1804), appealed for loyalty on grounds that under the "equally extended protection" of the British Constitution, "the industrious poor rest as securely in their humble dwellings, as those of exalted ranks do in their princely palaces." (pp. 6 n., 8) Also see Thomas Wood, *Essays on Civil Government and Subjection and Obedience* (Wigan: Lyon, 1796), pp. iii, 10, 11, 18 f., 57 f., 60, 63 f.

63. Thomas Taylor, *An Answer to the First Part of the Age of Reason. Printed in 1794* (Manchester, 1796).

64. T. Thompson, *French Philosophy: Or, A Short Account of the Principles and Conduct of the French Infidels* (London, 1803), 3rd ed. "If the influence of religion be removed from the minds of men," Thompson declared, "civil laws will be found utterly ineffectual for the preservation of order in society, and universal anarchy must ensue." (pp. 31–32)

65. *Conference Minutes (1798)*, I, 428–29. For a discussion by an Irish Methodist of the atrocities committed by ʻPopish Rebels" and their republican allies in Ireland, see *An Extract of a Letter from A Gentleman in Ireland to Mr William Thompson* (London, 1798), *passim.*

66. John Stephens, *Christian Patriotism* (Rotherham: Plumbe, 1810), pp. 20–21, 26. Stephens observed that whenever Methodist preachers "yielded to the fatal dereliction" of "the delirium of Jacobinism," they had "been driven from a connection to which they were a disgrace." (pp. iii–iv) In a burst of pietist patriotism, Stephens intoned: "If I forget thee O Britain, let my right hand forget her cunning." (p. 9)

67. See *Monthly Review,* N.S., V (1791), 356–59. In its obituary article, the *Gentleman's Magazine* proclaimed Wesley's "personal influence" as "greater

than, perhaps, that of any other private gentleman in any country," and rejoiced that because of this, and because "John Wesley was a strenuous advocate for monarchy," all Wesley's followers in America were firmly loyal," while "those of Mr. Whitefield declared in favor of independence." See *Gentleman's Magazine*, LXI, 283.

68. Thomas Taylor, *Britannia's Mercies, and her Duty* (Leeds, 1799), pp. 29–30.

69. John Pawson, *The Prophet's Advice to the People of God in the Time of Danger* (Leeds: E. Baines, 1801), pp. 11, 18–19, 22–24. Pawson warned that "many eyes are upon the people of God, and if any of them were to make a false step, it would be greatly magnified, and turn to the reproach of the whole body." (p. 17)

70. Joseph Sutcliffe, *A Review of Methodism* (York: Wilson and Spence, 1805), pp. 37–38.

71. Religion, this writer concluded, apparently forgetting the history of the preceding century, made for stability and loyalty: "a general dereliction of religious principle . . . preceded the French Revolution," and "similar causes tend in their nature to produce similar effects." Careful Observer, *Strictures on Methodism*, pp. 77–78, 85, 108–9, 112.

72. Anon., *Considerations on the Alliance Between Christianity & Commerce, Applied to the Present State of this Country* (London: Cadell & Davies, 1806).

73. Anon., *A Few Words on the Increase of Methodism* (London: Miles and Hunter, 1810), pp. 9–10, 17–18, 21.

74. *Ibid.,* pp. 22–23.

75. Careful Observer, *Strictures on Methodism*, p. 112.

76. Moore, *Fear God: Honour the King,* pp. 20–23.

77. Benjamin Rhodes, *A Discourse on Civil Government and Religious Liberty; also The Duties of Subjects to their Sovereign etc.* (Birmingham: J. Belcher, 1796), pp. 7–8.

78. Thomas Roberts, *Christian Loyalty* (Bristol: R. Edwards, 1802), pp. 5–6, 9, 27–30.

79. Cursitor, *Letter to the Lord Bishop of Lincoln,* pp. 11, 20–21, 24–25.

80. See Maldwyn Edwards, *After Wesley; A Study of the Social and Political Influence of Methodism in the Middle Period (1791–1849)* (London: Epworth Press, 1948), pp. 75–78. For Sidmouth's efforts, temporarily successful, to persuade prominent Methodist leaders, including Adam Clarke, of the usefulness of such legislation, see letters of Adam Clarke to George Marsden, 14 March 1810, 29 April 1811, 6 May 1811, 13 May 1811. Clarke Papers. M.C.A.

81. *Parliamentary Debates,* House of Lords, XIX (9 May 1811), 1128–34.

82. *Mr. Redhead Yorke's Weekly Political Review,* May 25, 1811, pp. 353–54; see also pp. 355 ff. Cobbett, who had described Methodism as Jacobin over a decade earlier in his *Anti-Jacobin Review,* wrote, in 1811, as a convert to Jacobinism, and denounced the Methodists as enemies to change. The Methodists—in which category, Cobbett apparently included the Evangelical members of the Establishment—were "the main prop of the PITT system," and "under the garb of sanctity, they have been aiding and abetting in all the worst things that have been done in the last twenty years." "My great dislike to them," he continued, "is grounded in their politics, which are the very worst in the country"; "as a body I know of none so decidedly hostile to public liberty." It was not, then, because the Methodists were promoting revolution, but because they were props of the existing system, that Cobbett confessed that "I do

not want to see their numbers increase," and he, consequently, was ready to urge the government to defend the Establishment by suppressing the Methodists. *Cobbett's Weekly Political Register,* May 25, 1811, pp. 1283–84, 1293.

83. *A Narrative of the Proceedings of the General Committee of the People Called Methodists, Late in Connexion with the Rev. John Wesley; Of Protestant Dissenters, and other Friends to Religious Liberty, Respecting the Bill, Introduced into the House of Lords, by Lord Viscount Sidmouth* etc. (London: For Methodist Preaching Houses, 1811), pp. 13–15.

84. *Resolutions of the Methodist Ministers of the Manchester District, Assembled at Liverpool, May 23, 1811, on the subject of a Bill Introduced into Parliament by the Rt. Hon. Lord Viscount Sidmouth* etc. (Liverpool: Kaye, 1811), pp. 3–4.

85. *Parliamentary Debates,* House of Lords, XX (17 May 1811), 196–98.

86. *Parliamentary Debates,* House of Lords, XX (21 May 1811), 233–55. See Thomas Roberts, *The Outcasts Delivered* etc. (Camarthen: Harris, 1811), with its grateful dedication to Lord Erskine for opposing Sidmouth's Bill.

87. See, for example, *Mr. Redhead Yorke's Weekly Review,* May 25, 1811, pp. 358–59.

88. *Conference Minutes (1812),* III, 308–09.

89. *Parliamentary Debates,* House of Lords, XXIII (2 June 1812), 318–19.

90. *Parliamentary Debates,* House of Lords, XXIII (3 July 1812), 887–92.

91. *Parliamentary Debates,* House of Lords, XXIII (23 July 1812), 1191–93.

92. *Parliamentary Debates,* House of Commons, XXIII (21 July 1812), 1108–9.

93. *Conference Minutes* (1812), III, 313–14.

94. *Address of the Preachers Assembled at the Sixty-Ninth Annual Conference* (n.p.: Conference Office, 1812), pp. 1, 2. For a further expression of Methodist gratitude, see *Conference Minutes (1813),* III, 393.

95. Phileleutherus, *A Defence of the British Constitution, Against the Attacks of Civis, Upon the Methodists and Dissenters* etc. (London, 1813), p. 22.

96. John Hughes, *A Plea for Religious Liberty; Or a Vindication of the Methodists* (Macclesfield, 1813), pp. iv–v, 8–9.

97. Joseph Sutcliffe, *The Divine Mission of the People Called Methodists, to Revive and Spread Religion* (London: T. Blanshard, 1814), pp. 28–29, 30–31.

98. Anon., *An Address to the Common Sense and Understanding of Every Protestant, Evidently Shewing and Proving the Impiety, Folly, and Fanaticism, of the Sect Called Methodists* (London: Causton, 1813), p. 14.

99. See, for example, W. M. Heald, Vicar of Bristol, *A Letter; With an Address, Expostulatory and Admonitory, to the Stewards, Leaders, and Members of the Methodist Society at Bristol* (Leeds, 1813), p. 21 and *passim*.

100. Ward, *A Brief Statement of Facts,* p. 82.

101. See Currie, *Methodism Divided,* p. 32; see also Ward, "The Religion of the People," in Cuming and Baker, eds., *Popular Belief and Practice,* p. 247, where Bunting is quoted as having described the progress of Methodism in the West Riding of Yorkshire in 1813 as "more swift than solid; more extensive than deep, more in the increase of numbers, than in diffusion of . . . piety."

102. See Townsend, Workman, Eayrs, eds., *New History of Methodism,* pp. 481–598; also, Wearmouth, *Methodism and Working-Class Movements, passim.*

103. Jackson, *Recollections,* pp. 172 f. One writer has observed that "the choice in the end was between the Wesleyan chapel and the Radical club. See P. Stigant, "Wesleyan Methodism and Working-Class Radicalism in the North, 1792–1821," *Northern History,* VI (1971), 116.

104. See Watson, *Works,* VIII, pp. 330 ff.

105. Broadsheet headed "To the Societies in the Connexion Established by the late Rev. John Wesley, A.M.," 12 November 1819, and signed Charles Atmore, Chairman, and Thomas Blanshard, Secretary, to the Committee on Religious Privileges.

106. John Stephens, *The Mutual Relations, Claims, and Duties of the Rich and the Poor* (Manchester: J. Roberts, 1819), pp. iii–vi, 10–15, 17, 19, 21–23, 25–40.

107. Letter from John Stephens, at Manchester, to Jabez Bunting, in London, February 1, 1821. Stephens Papers. M.C.A.

108. Watson, *Works,* VIII, 360.

109. As late as 1827, a former Methodist preacher who had become a Catholic, revived the view of Methodism that had been so prevalent twenty years earlier, and warned all to remember the deeds of Puritans, Covenanters, and French philosophers, and to "beware of the teeth of Methodism!!!" He also cast into doubt the Methodist picture of themselves as "the humble servants of the government" when he observed their activities "when their interests appear to them to be in danger," as "in the case of Lord Sidmouth's bill, as well as in the riots of Lord George Gordon." J. A. Mason, *An Earnest Appeal to the People Called Methodists and to the Nation at Large* (London: W. E. Andrews, 1827), pp. 6, 8, 37 f., 46.

110. Anon., *The Patriot; A Tale, Illustrating the Pernicious Effects of Bad Principles on the lower orders of Society* (London: T. Cordeux, 1821), pp. 13 f.

111. Watson, *Works,* VII, 514.

112. Jackson, *Recollections,* pp. 154, 195 f.

113. See Maldwyn Edwards, *Adam Clarke* (London: Epworth Press, 1942), pp. 11–12, 19–20, 24, 29, 34 ff., 38.

114. Adam Clarke, *The Origin and End of Civil Government* (London: J. & T. Clarke, 1822), pp. 9–10, 19, 24, 33–36. See also Adam Clarke, *The Rights of God and Caesar: A Discourse on Matt. xxii 15–21* (London: Blanshard, 1821).

115. *The Annual Address of the Conference to the Methodist Societies in Great Britain. . . . August 1820* (London: Blanshard, 1820), pp. 3 ff. This address was also written by Richard Watson. Watson wrote the Annual Addresses of 1819, 1820, 1821, 1824, and 1825.

116. *The Annual Address of the Conference to the Methodist Societies in Great Britain. . . . August 1822* (London: T. Cordeux, 1822), p. 10.

117. *The Annual Address of the Conference to the Methodist Societies in Great Britain. . . . August 1831* (London: John Mason, 1831), p. 8.

118. *The Annual Address of the Conference to the Methodist Societies in Great Britain. . . . August 1832* (London: John Mason, 1832), p. 7.

119. *Conference Minutes* (1833), VII, 305 ff.

120. *Conference Minutes* (1834), VII, 426 f.

121. *Conference Minutes* (1836), VIII, 96.

122. See, for example, on the Methodist side, James Etchells, *A Mirror for Intolerance or Methodism Illustrated and Defended* (Daventry: Blanchard, 1819). J. B. Holroyd, *The Doctrines of the Methodists Stated and Defended* (Alnwick: M. Smith, 1822); and Abraham Scott, *Calvinistic Election Unscriptural, and Incapable of a Rational Defence; A Reply to a Review in the Evangelical Magazine* (Sheffield: J. Blackwell, 1824).

123. See, for example, the republication of Philalethes [T. Taylor], *A Sol-*

emn *Caution Against the Ten Horns of Calvinism* (Leeds: J. Nichols, 1816); a further edition of the original tract of 1779 was to appear in 1819. A reprinting of a tract by Toplady was countered by Tacitus, *A Brief Vindication of Evangelical Methodism In Reply to 'A Caveat Against Unsound Doctrines,' published in the Last Century by the Rev. Augustus Toplady, and Now Reprinted and Circulated in the Town of Preston* (Preston: T. Hill, 1817).

124. See, for example, Edward Hare, *A Caveat Against Antinomianism* (Leeds: Cullingworth, 1816), and *A Second Caveat Against Antinomianism* (Leeds: J. Nichols, 1817); also Robert Woods, *The Discrepancy of Bigotry and Equity Displayed* (Sheffield, 1819).

125. See, for example, A Layman, *Modern Methodism Unmasked* (London: Baldwin & Cradock, 1830), p. 58.

126. See, for example, the following sermons preached on the death of George III: Samuel Woolmer, *A Sermon . . . Intended as a Sacred Memorial of his late most excellent majesty king George the Third* (Hull: W. Ross, 1820); and David McNicoll, *Divine Providence Illustrated in the Ordination of Political Government* (London: Whittaker, 1820). McNicoll quoted at length from Burke's *Reflections* (p. 40), and also from his *Regicide Peace* (p. 44).

127. For example, William Stewart, *Vindication of the Methodists Respecting Personal and Social Character* (Dublin: J. Jones, 1822), p. 56.

128. See R. Polwhele, ed., *The Enthusiasm of Methodists and Papists Considered: by Bishop Lavington* (London: Whittaker et al., 1820), pp. cclxviii, cclxx–cclxxv.

129. See R. Polwhele. *A Letter to the Right Rev. the Lord Bishop of Exeter . . . Examining the Distinctive Characters of the Calvinists and Arminian Sectarists; and proposing to his Lordship a Scheme of Coalition between the Wesleyans and the Church of England* (Truro: E. Heard, 1833). Also see A Member of the Wesleyan Methodist Congregations, *Union is Strength* (Manchester: C. Ambery, 1834); and Thomas Jackson, *The Church and the Methodists* (London: John Mason, 1834). Jackson's tract rejected the pleas of Dissenters that Methodists join them in opposition to the Established Church not only because of the "unflinching loyalty" of the Methodists, but also because "the blaspheming disciples of Paine and Carlisle" were "especially anxious to get rid of the Church." (pp. 19, 50, 54) The ostensible cause for the expulsion of J. R. Stephens in the early thirties was his participation in the activities of the Church Separation Society.

130. A Methodist of the Old School, *Methodism in 1821; With Recollections of Primitive Methodism* (London: W. Whittemore, 1821), p. 17.

131. William Hatton, *Methodist Remembrances Comprising a Contrast Between the Original and Present State of Methodism and the Methodists* (Birmingham, 1833), pp. 5–8.

132. Methodist of Old School, *Methodism in 1821*, pp. 26 f.

133. Humphry Sandwith, *A Reply to Lord John Russel's* (sic) *Animadversions on Wesleyan Methodism* (London: J. Mason. 1830), p 65.

134. "It cannot be doubted," Vevers wrote, "that the writings of Voltaire and his associates, were one of the chief causes of the French Revolution," and that the people of England, "by their ignorance of the principles of morals and religion," were "peculiarly susceptible of the influence of infidelity;" however, "it was during this eventful period, that Methodism was founded and organised, and brought into full and efficient operation." "Who can compute the consequences, which might have resulted from the wide diffusion of the principles of infidelity, and the unwearied exertions of its promoters in England, if it

had not been for the still wider diffusion of Methodism," Vevers declared. William Vevers, *An Essay on the National Importance of Methodism* (London: J. Mason, 1831), pp. 74–77, 91 f., 94, 109.

135. Simeon Woodhouse, *The Moral Influence and National Importance of Methodism* (London: J. Mason, 1839).

136. Edmund Grindrod, *Wesleyan Methodism Viewed in Retrospect* (London: J. Mason, 1839), pp. 16–17, 20–21.

137. Rev. William Arthur, *The French Revolution of 1848* (London: W. Jones, 1849), pp. 278 f.

138. John Pawson to Thomas Benson, 25 November 1797. Pawson Papers. M.C.A.

139. Stephens, *Mutual Relations . . . of the Rich and the Poor*, p. 27.

VI / "PRACTICAL ARMINIANISM" AND ENGLAND'S WORLD-MISSION

1. George Eliot, *Adam Bede* (London: C. H. Kelly, n.d.), pp. 28, 39, 104, 124, 218.

2. See discussion in Bernard Semmel, *The Governor Eyre Controversy* (London: Macgibbon & Kee, 1962), pp. 19–20, 102–120, and *passim*.

3. James Hutton, *A Letter to a Friend in Which Some Account is Given of the Brethren's Society for the Furtherance of the Gospel Among the Heathen* (London, 1769), pp. 4–7, 10.

4. Benjamin La Trobe, writing in 1771, observed that "the white people from false political principles, dreaded the conversion of the Negroes to Christianity." These whites soon discovered that, as "the Proprietors of the Estates acknowledge," their slaves, "since they have believed in Jesus, are become faithful, obedient, and diligent." The "Magistrates themselves," La Trobe concluded, "have more than once declared, that the baptized Negroes are a greater security to them than their forts." Benj. La Trobe, *A Succinct View of the Missions Established Among the Heathen By the Church of the Brethren* (London: Lewis, 1771), pp. 9, 16–17. La Trobe and Hutton guided Moravian efforts in the eighteenth century to raise money for missionary activity. See B. La Trobe, James Hutton, and John Wollin, *An Address from the Brethren's Society for the Furtherance of the Gospel Among the Heathen* (n.p., 1781 [?]).

5. See *Instructions for the Members of the Unitas Fratrium Who Minister in the Gospel Among the Heathen* (London: Brethren's Society for the Furtherance of the Gospel Among the Heathen, 1784), pp. 44–45, 47.

6. Beilby [Porteus], Bishop of London, *A Letter to the Clergy of the West-Indian Islands* (n.p., 1788), pp. 4, 6.

7. See Rev. Charles Hole, *The Early History of the Church Missionary Society for Africa and the East to the End of A.D. 1814* (London: Church Missionary Society, 1896), p. 632.

8. Melville Horne, *Letters on Missions; Addressed to the Protestant Ministers of the British Churches* (Bristol: Bulgin and Rosser, 1794), pp. vii–viii, 21 f., 60 f., 97, 43, 53, 108, 98, 118, 31, 36 f.

9. A Methodist, writing in 1806, pointed to the "unexampled zeal and usefulness" of Methodist missionaries, the "beneficial effects of their instruction, in a political point of view"; "for notwithstanding that christianized slaves are convinced that slavery is in no degree either sanctioned, or encouraged, but is contrary to the spirit of Christianity, they become conscientiously obedient to

their unfeeling and less civilized holders." See C. Hulbert, *Candid Strictures on Several Passages in a Recent Publication* etc. (Shrewsbury: T. Wood, 1806), pp. 14–15. Hulbert also pointed to the good effects of Methodism upon "the dark and lawless tinners of Cornwall," "the brutal ferocious colliers of Kingswood and Newcastle," and the English "rustic." (p. 16)

10. Bradburn, *Evil of Encouraging the Slave Trade*, pp. 2, 6, 10–16, 18–19, 24. In disputing the view that abstention from rum and sugar, as a means of undermining slavery, "would avail nothing, unless they refuse Cotton also," Bradburn, rather disingenuously argued, that this was an "absolute falsehood" since "nearly three fourths of the Cotton which is manufactured in England," came not from the British West Indies, but "from Foreigners." (p. 23) The pamphlet, after all, was published at Manchester!

11. "An Arminian" [T. Jackson], *A Letter to the Rev. John Cockin* (Leeds: J. Nichols, 1814), pp. 20, 22–23.

12. T. Jackson, *A Second Letter to the Rev. John Cockin* (Leeds: J. Nichols, 1814), p. 38.

13. John Cockin, *A Valedictory Letter to the Rev. T. Jackson, Containing A Reply to the Remarks In His Second Letter* (Huddersfield, 1815), pp. 46, 47 f.

14. W. Hutton, *A Reply to the Rev. John Cockin, Occasioned by His Severe Reflections on An Extract from the Address of the Methodist Missionary Society for the Halifax District* (Leeds: J. Capes, 1815), pp. 6, 14–16.

15. Jackson, *Second Letter*, p. 38. The difficulties of determining who was a true Calvinist and who a true Arminian can be seen in T. Jackson, *A Third Letter to the Rev. John Cockin, Containing A Reply to His Valedictory Letter* (Leeds: J. Nichols, 1815), *passim*.

16. A Missionary, *Lines on the Much Lamented Death of the Rev. Thomas Coke, L.L.D.* etc. (London, 1815), pp. 20, 17–18. See also Samuel Woolner, *The Servant of the Lord; A Sermon Occasioned by the Death of the Late Rev. T. Coke, L.L.D.* (London: Conference Office, 1815); Thomas Roberts, *The Burning and Shining Light. A Sermon Occasioned by the Death of the Rev. Thomas Coke, L.L.D.* (Bath: Meyler and Son, 1815); and it was "as a Missionary, perhaps . . . never [to] be surpassed to the end of the world," that Coke was eulogized in Samuel Warren, *A Sermon . . . On the Occasion of the Death of the Late Rev. Thos. Coke, L.L.D.* (Chester: J. Smith, 1815), p. 37.

17. See, for example, *Conference Minutes* (1797), I, 396–97.

18. *Conference Minutes* (1798), I, 431–32.

19. In 1803, for example, some £2,216 were received for Methodist missionaries, in various parts of the world: there were two missionaries for each of the stations in Barbadoes, Dominica, Newfoundland, and New Providence; three for those at St. Kitts, Jamaica, and Nova Scotia; a single preacher had been sent to each of the five stations in Guernsey, Wales, St. Bartholomews, Antigua, St. Vincents, and Gibraltar. *A Statement of the Receipts and Disbursements of the Methodist Missions in the Years 1803 and 1804* (London: R. Lomas, 1804), pp. 13–15, 19–20. Contributions grew considerably over the years. See, for example, *Conference Minutes* (1811), III, 222; and *The Annual Report of the State of the Missions* (London: Conference Office, n.d.), pp. 3, 25, 41–43, and *passim*.

20. Thomas Attentive (pseud.), *A Friendly Address to the Preacher and Principal members of the M—d—ts* (n.p., 1788), pp. 3, 6–7.

21. Joseph Sutcliffe, *A Treatise on the Universal Spread of the Gospel, The Glorious Millennium, and the Second Coming of Christ* (Doncaster, 1798), p. 6.

22. See J. Pratt, ed., *Eclectic Notes,* pp. 96–104. For the history of the C.M.S., also see *The Centenary Volume of the Church Missionary Society for Africa and the East 1799–1899* (London: Church Missionary Society, 1902); and Hole, *Early History.*

23. *Proceedings of the Church Missionary Society for Africa and the East,* I (1801), 60, 65, 69, 70, 72.

24. *Ibid.,* I (1805), 422.

25. *Ibid.,* II (1807), 161.

26. *Ibid.,* III (1811), 201, 205.

27. See Hole, *Early History, passim.*

28. See the discussion in F. K. Brown, *Fathers of the Victorians* (Cambridge: Cambridge University Press, 1959).

29. G. G. Findlay and W. W. Holdsworth, *The History of the Wesleyan Methodist Missionary Society* (London: Epworth Press, 1921), I, 37–38.

30. *Gentleman's Magazine,* LXXXII, Pt. I (July 15, 1812), Preface, iv.

31. *Ibid.,* LXXXII, Pt. II (December 31, 1812), Preface, iii.

32. *Ibid.,* LXXXIII, Pt. I (June 30, 1813), Preface, iii.

33. *Ibid.,* LXXXIII, Pt. II (December 1813), Preface, iii–iv.

34. *The Annual Register or a View of the History, Politics and Literature for the Year 1813* (London, 1814), pp. iii, v, vi.

35. *Gentleman's Magazine,* LXXXIV, Pt. I (June 1814), Preface, iii.

36. *Ibid.,* LXXXIV, Pt. II (December 31, 1814), Preface, iv.

37. *Ibid.,* LXXXV, Pt. I (June 1815), Preface, iii.

38. *Ibid.,* LXXXV, Pt. II (December 1815), Preface, iii.

39. *Ibid.,* LXXXVI, Pt. I (June 1816), Preface, iii.

40. *Proceedings of the C.M.S.,* IV (1813), 248–54.

41. *Ibid.,* V (1817), 367.

42. *Ibid.,* 1822–23, pp. 6, 23, 25.

43. Quoted in Viscountess Knutsford, *Life and Letters of Zachary Macaulay* (London: Edward Arnold, 1900), p. 342.

44. The details used in this narrative of Methodist politics may be found in T. P. Bunting, *The Life of Jabez Bunting* (London: Longmans, 1859), I, 11–12, 30–32, 36–37, 42–94, 116–17, 124–25, 145–47, 153, 287; Thomas Jackson, *Memoirs of the Life and Writings of the Rev. Richard Watson* (London: John Mason, 1890), pp. 135–40, 170–72, 180, 193–95, 274–75; George Smith, *History of Wesleyan Methodism* (London: Longmans, Green, 1872), II, 542, 546–51, 579; Vickers, *Thomas Coke,* pp. 138, 229–30, 239, 271–88, 304–6, 311–13, 341–44, 348, 352–54. Also to be noted are the Coke papers, and the Home Correspondence for 1813 in the Wesleyan Methodist Missionary Society Archives; and the Bunting, Entwistle, and Moore papers, in the Methodist Church Archives (note specific references below.) On Bunting, also see John Kent, *Jabez Bunting; The Lost Wesleyan* (London: Epworth Press, 1955).

45. Quoted in Vickers, *Thomas Coke,* p. 306.

46. For a discussion of Coke's activities, see *ibid.,* pp. 138, 239, 271–86, 341 ff., 352 f., 300 f., 304 ff., 311 ff.

47. See T. P. Bunting, *Jabez Bunting,* II, 30 f. Jabez Bunting's son observed, perhaps naively, that "it is a strong proof of the depth and earnestness of my father's thoughts on this occasion, that, in after life, he so seldom referred to the conviction [that he must go to India] to which they led him. . . . it was no common sacrifice which my father was now prepared to make."

48. Quoted in Smith, *History of Wesleyan Methodism,* II, 542; see also pp. 538–41.

49. Quoted in Jackson, *Richard Watson,* p. 140.

50. T. P. Bunting, *Jabez Bunting*, pp. 50, 47.

51. Jabez Bunting, in Leeds, to Robert Smith, in London, 28 September 1813. See also Bunting's letter to Smith, 11 October 1813. Home Correspondence. Wesley Methodist Missionary Society Archives. (In the future, W.M.M.S. Archives.)

52. Jabez Bunting, in Leeds, to Robert Smith, in London, 11 October 1813. Home Correspondence. W.M.M.S. Archives.

53. James Nichols, *A Report of the Principal Speeches delivered on the Sixth Day of October 1813, at the Formation of the Methodist Missionary Society, for the Leeds District* etc. 5th ed. (London: Simpkin & Marshall, 1840), pp. 19, 21–22, 25, 28–29, 31–35, 38–40, 42.

54. Richard Watson, "Address to the Public, By the General Committee of the Methodist Missionary Society for the Leeds District," in *The First Report of the Methodist Missionary Society for the Leeds District; MDCCCXIV* etc. (Leeds: J. Nichols, 1814), pp. 16–18. See also Richard Watson, *A Sermon Preached at Albion Street Chapel, Leeds, At the Formation of the Methodist Missionary Society for the Leeds District, October 5, 1813* (Liverpool: Kaye, 1813).

55. See Appendix to Nichols, etc., *Report of the Principal Speeches*, pp. 44–46.

56. Richard Watson, *A Sermon Preached at the Methodist Chapel, Wakefield . . . On Thursday, the Seventh Day of July*, etc. (Leeds: J. Nichols, 1814), pp. 8, 11, 13–17. Watson further observed on this occasion that no "man of thinking now fixes himself on either extreme of political opinion, and advocates either the *jus divinum* of kings, or the sovereignty of mobs," or, indeed, "looks to a vain philosophy to accomplish that which nothing but true religion can perform" (that is "to perfect the human character and banish misery from the world").

57. Quoted in Vickers, *Coke*, p. 354.

58. Jabez Bunting, in Leeds, to T. S. Swale, in Halifax, 5 November 1813. See also Bunting's letter to Swale, 29 September 1813. Jabez Bunting Papers, M.C.A.

59. Jabez Bunting, in Leeds, in a letter to a friend in Birmingham, 25 January 1815. Jabez Bunting Papers. M.C.A.

60. The *Conference Minutes* (1814), IV, 35–36, recorded that the Conference "strongly recommend the immediate establishment of a *Methodist Missionary Society* in every District in the Kingdom . . . on the general plan of those Societies, which have been formed in Yorkshire and elsewhere during the past year."

61. *Report of the Methodist Missionary Society For Leeds*, p. 11.

62. Humphrey Sandwith, Surgeon, *A Report of a Speech delivered on the 13th of January, 1814, at a Public Meeting held in the Methodist Chapel, Beverly, for the Purpose of Forming An Auxiliary Missionary Society* (Beverly, 1814), pp. 17–18.

63. *An Account of the Formation of a Methodist Missionary Society at Plymouth-Dock on Tuesday November 15, 1814* ([Plymouth] Dock: J. Johns, 1814), p. 25.

64. *A Report of the Formation of a Methodist Missionary Society for the London District* (London: T. Blanshard, City Road, 1815), pp. 25, 40.

65. David McNicoll, *On the Gospel. Or, the Substance of a Discourse delivered in Bridge-Street Chapel, Bolton, May 17th, 1815, at the Formation of the Missionary Auxiliary Society In That Town, for the Manchester District* (Manchester: Russell and Allen, 1815), pp. 29, 31.

66. *Resolutions at the Formation of the Methodist Missionary Society, of the Dublin District, On the 5th of May, 1814* (Dublin, 1814), p. 31.

67. *Report of the Methodist Missionary Society for Leeds (1814)*, p. 6.

68. *The First Report of the Methodist Missionary Society of the Sheffield District, May 16, 1815* (n.p., n.d.), pp. 4, 2.

69. *The First Report of the General Committee of the Methodist Missionary Society for Hull, York, and the Other Circuits in the York District, 12 April 1815* (Hull: Topping & Dawson, 1815 [?]), pp. 10, 6, 11.

70. Quoted in T. P. Bunting, *Jabez Bunting,* p. 58.

71. Quoted in *ibid.,* p. 55.

72. Quoted in *ibid.,* p. 56.

73. Joseph Entwistle, in Bristol, to George Marsden, in Liverpool, 16 December 1813. See also Entwistle to Jabez Bunting, at Leeds, 15 December 1814. Entwistle papers. M.C.A.

74. Quoted in Vickers, *Coke,* p. 354.

75. Quoted in T. P. Bunting, *Jabez Bunting,* pp. 77–78.

76. Henry Moore, in Liverpool, to George Marsden, in Sunderland, 10 June 1815. Henry Moore Papers. M.C.A.

77. Henry Moore, at Birmingham, to George Marsden, in London, 10 December 1816. Henry Moore Papers. M.C.A.

78. See T. P. Bunting, *Jabez Bunting,* p. 93, and *passim.*

79. Jackson, *Watson,* p. 195.

80. T. P. Bunting wrote of the new direction which his father had given Methodism: "And again,—supposing a wise and prayerful man to have forecast for the welfare of the cause at large; for a renewal of its primitive life; for the unity of the hosts of new and raw recruits who were daily crowding into its service; for the healthy development and most profitable use of that tendency to spend their force wildly and 'as one that beateth the air,' but with the certain and ceaseless aim, which the genius of Wesley impressed upon his people; —was there any plan so surely full of rich results,—as to make every Methodist Church in England the parent or the nurse of a church abroad, and to bring down upon the associated body here the blessings of the families of the whole earth? Those, I have no doubt, were some of the considerations which finally induced my father to devote himself to missionary work." T. P. Bunting, *Jabez Bunting,* p. 32.

81. Letter of Joseph Entwistle, in Bristol, to Thomas Allan, in London, 3 May 1813. Joseph Entwistle Papers. M.C.A.

82. Quoted in T. P. Bunting, *Jabez Bunting,* pp. 146–47.

83. *The Reports of the Wesleyan Methodist Missionary Society 1818–1834.* First Report, 1818, p. iv.

84. *Missionary Notices, Relating Principally to the Foreign Missions . . . Now Carried on under the Direction of the Methodist Conference,* II, No. 42, June 1819, p. 82.

85. *Ibid.,* pp. 88–89; III, No. 78, June 1822, pp. 276–77; IV, No. 90, June 1823, pp. 88–90; VI, No. 162, June 1829, pp. 89–91; VII, No. 162, June 1824, pp. 89–91, and No. 222, June 1834, p. 478.

86. *Ibid.,* IV, No. 90, June 1823, p. 89.

87. Quoted in D. Fraser, *A Letter Addressed to the Rev. Valentine Ward Occasioned by His Remarks on Dr. Clarke's Letter to the Missionary Committee* (Belper: J. Ogle, 1819), p. 10.

88. Valentine Ward, *Free and Candid Strictures on Methodism* (Aberdeen: D. Chalmers, 1818), pp. 6 ff., 9 ff.

89. Fraser, *Letter to Ward,* pp. 11, 20, 16.

VII / THE METHODIST SYNTHESIS:
LIBERALISM, ORDER, AND
NATIONAL MISSION

1. Richard Watson, trans., of Simon Episcopius, *The Labyrinth or Popish Circle, Being a Confutation of the Assumed Infallibility of the Church of Rome* (London: Simpkin & Marshall, 1826).

2. Richard Watson, *Theological Institutes: or A View of the Evidences, Doctrines, Morals, and Institutions of Christianity* (London: J. Mason, 1829), 3rd ed., I, 1; III, 286, 291–95, 303–7, 322–24.

3. Watson, *Theological Institutes*, III, 327–40.

4. Richard Watson, "On Christian Citizenship," *Works*, II, 372–82.

5. Watson, reviews in *Methodist Magazine* (1820), *Works*, VII, pp. 227–57, 264–90.

6. Richard Watson, "The Reign of God" (February 1814), *Works*, IV, 241–48, 250–51, 254.

7. *Missionary Notices*, VI, No. 174 (June 1830), 282.

8. As early as 1824, Watson, as a good Arminian, and in the characteristic manner of a later Exeter Hall, denounced the "civilized savage" who enslaved men and then, "pointing to their contrary colour and different features, finds his justification in denying them to be men." Such "civilized savages' defended themselves on the basis of "a petty philosophy," Watson declared, "which "not content, that the ape and baboon should fill the chasm which exists between the quadruped and man," declared that "the gradations of animated nature are gentle and almost imperceptible," and, insisting that "an intermediate link must be invented," placed the Negro in this position. Richard Watson, *The Religious Instruction of the Slaves In the West India Colonies Advocated and Defended; A Sermon Preached Before the Wesleyan Methodist Missionary Society . . . April 28, 1824* (London: Batterworth, 1825), pp 4–5. See also Richard Watson, *A Defence of the Wesleyan Methodist Missions in the West Indies* (London: Blanshard, 1817), pp. 161–62.

9. For example, see *The Tenth Annual Report of the Aborigines Protection Society* (London, 1847), which subscribed to the views of one of the leaders of the Society, the Quaker banker, J. J. Gurney, that a nation which behaved in a Christian manner, which would "proclaim the principles of universal peace, suffer wrong with condescension, abstain from all retaliation, return good for evil, and diligently promote the welfare of men," would "be blessed with eminent prosperity, enriched with unrestricted commerce, loaded with reciprocal benefits, and endowed for every good and wise and worthy purpose with irresistible influence over nations." (p. 29)

10. Semmel, *Governor Eyre Controversy*, pp. 108–16, and *passim*.

11. Quoted in R. I. and S. Wilberforce, *William Wilberforce*, I, p. 206.

12. *Ibid.*, I, 129–30.

13. This is the argument which pervades Brown, *Fathers of the Victorians*. Watson was to argue that God had begun this work of reformation by "forming a people for himself from among the lower classes," and thus "awakening attention," causing the work "to spread through all gradations of society till it influences men of rank, and finally reaches the cabinet." Richard Watson, "Excitements to Missionary Effort." *Works*, II, 364–65. Curiously though with Fabius Cunctator rather than the Webbs in mind, Stephen described the Evan-

gelical method of fighting for Abolition as "this Fabian policy." Sir James Stephen, "William Wilberforce," *Essays in Ecclesiastical Biography* (London: Longmans, 1849), II, 235.

14. *Thirteenth Report of the Directors of the African Institution,* 1819, p. 11.

15. *Twelfth Report of the Directors of the African Institution* (London: J. Hatchard, 1818), pp. 4–5.

16. Macaulay was the associate of Melville Horne in 1793 when Horne went as missionary to Sierra Leone. Both Horne and Macaulay were disturbed at lack of discipline of the converts of the Methodists. Macaulay concluded that Africa required missionaries of "sober yet elevated views, humble yet enlarged minds," and that "it is not among mechanics we are to look for men of this last description." Knutsford, *Macaulay,* pp. 49–51, 54, 60, 199–200. In 1813, Macaulay found himself in the vanguard of the effort to alter the charter of the East India Co. so as to permit Christian missionaries to come to India. A letter to his son, T. B. Macaulay, in 1813, telling of a meeting of the African Institution, possessed a truly imperial ring: "No sooner was Africa disposed of than Asia called for our exertions; and the very day after the meeting of the African Institution, I was obliged to take active measures for calling a meeting which should prevent the blessed light of Christianity from continuing to be shut out of Asia." *Ibid.,* p. 297.

17. [James Stephen], *The Speech of James Stephen, Esq. at the Annual Meeting of the African Institution,* 26th March, 1817 (London: J. Butterworth and J. Hatchard, 1817), pp. 8–9, 32–33, 55; also pp. 34–46.

18. T. P. Bunting, *Jabez Bunting,* I, 202–5, 212, 215.

19. The resolution declared that slavery was "in direct opposition to all the principles of natural right, and to the benign spirit of the religion of Christ," and "that, in this great crisis, when the question is, whether justice and humanity shall triumph over oppression and cruelty, or nearly a million of our fellow men, many of whom are also our fellow Christians, shall remain excluded from the rights of humanity, and the privileges of that constitution under which they are born; . . . that, in the elections now on the eve of taking place, they will give their influence and votes only to those candidates who pledge themselves to support, in Parliament, the most effectual measures for the entire abolition of slavery throughout the colonies of the British empire." *Conferences Minutes,* (1830), VI, 613–15. See also *The Annual Address of the Conference to the Methodist Societies in Great Britain.* August 1831 (London: John Mason, 1831), p. 9.

20. T. P. Bunting, *Jabez Bunting,* I, 166.

21. See the two letters to the *Manchester Times, Remarks on the Vote Given to Lord Sandon by the Rev. Jabez Bunting, at the late Liverpool Election* (Manchester: Everett & Thompson, 1833), pp. 3, 5–7, 10, 16. The writer, a defender of Bunting's position, observed: "Place Hunt, for instance, as a possible case, and Lord Sandon in opposite scales, and however reluctantly, yet the writer,—though a thorough-bred Anti-Slaveryman, would rather give the latter than the former his vote." (p. 3.)

22. T. P. Bunting, *Jabez Bunting,* I, 285–87.

23. Richard Watson to Rev. John Anderson, 16 September 1831. Watson Papers. Methodist Church Archives. Anderson, thinking himself to be following Watson's instructions, made the letter public, a course which brought an upsetting call upon Watson by Sadler, and an angry letter by Watson suggesting to Anderson that Macaulay be supported without the Methodists "gratui-

tously" attacking Sadler. Richard Watson to Rev. John Anderson, 26 September 1831. Watson Papers. Methodist Church Archives.

24. *Missionary Notes,* VI, No. 222 (June 1834), 478–84.

25. See Findlay and Holdsworth, *Wesleyan Methodist Missionary Society,* pp. 110–14.

26. See statistical table in Bailey Hillyard, *Numerical Statistics of Wesleyan Methodism,* p. 43; see Currie, *Methodism Divided,* p. 32.

27. Quoted in T. P. Bunting, *Jabez Bunting,* II, 373.

28. *The Annual Address of the Conference to the Methodist Societies in Great Britain* (August 1838) (London: J. Mason, 1838), pp. 8–13.

29. *Report of the Proceedings of a Meeting held in Ebenezer Chapel, Leeds, On Christmas Day, the 25th of December, 1817, Relative to the Establishment of a Home Mission Society in the Leeds Circuit, Connected with the Interest of the New Connexion of Methodists* (Leeds: Davies & Booth, 1818), pp. 5, 10, 11, 14, 16 f. See also the *Report of the Committee of the Home Missions, Established Amongst the Methodists of the New Connexion* (Hanley: T. Allbut, 1819).

30. See the early description of their home missions in *Some Account of the Rise and Progress of the Missions Belonging to the Arminian Bible Christians* (Stoke-Damarel, Devon: S. Thorne, 1822).

31. See Townsend et al., *New History of Methodism,* I, 549.

32. Findlay and Holdsworth, *History of the Wesleyan Methodist Missionary Society,* I, 128 ff., 137–60, 187, and *passim.*

33. E. R. Taylor, *Methodism and Politics, 1791–1851* (Cambridge: Cambridge University Press, 1935).

34. J. R. Vincent, *Pollbooks: How Victorians Voted* (Cambridge: Cambridge University Press, 1967), p. 18.

35. John Kent, *The Age of Disunity* (London: Epworth Press, 1966), pp. 126 f., 129, 141, 145.

36. Kent, indeed, depicted the Methodists as moving from, say, Peel's Conservatism to the Liberalism of Hughes and Perks, and thus as having "stayed where they were, if, indeed, they had not shifted a little to the right." John Kent, "Hugh Price Jones and the Non-Conformist Conscience," in G. V. Bennett and J. D. Walsh, eds., *Essays in Modern English Church History, In Memory of Norman Sykes* (London: A. & C. Black, 1966), pp. 199–200, 203–4. For Liberal social-imperialism, see B. Semmel, *Imperialism and Social Reform* (Cambridge: Harvard University Press, 1960), *passim.*

37. See Rev. George Cubitt, *The Power of Circumstances: Being the Seventh of a Series of Lectures Against Socialism* (London: Seeley, 1840); see also Henry Fish, *Natural Theology. . . . Containing An Exposure of the Errors of Socialism* (Bristol: N. Lomas, 1840), which spoke of socialism as a species of Antinomianism (p. 29) and denounced "the *folly of atheism,* in other words, *Socialism.*" (p. 27).

38. *The Life of Hugh Price Hughes* [by his Daughter] (London: Hodder & Stoughton, 1904), pp. 553, 556 f.; also pp. 542–74, *passim.* An admirer of Kipling's "Recessional," Hughes observed: "He owes that poem to the Methodism in him. You may smile, but it is true." (p. 562)

39. J. Wesley, "Upon Our Lord's Sermon on the Mount" (Discourse V), *Works,* V, 319–27.

40. Joseph Priestley, "Some Considerations on the State of the Poor in General" (1787), *Theological and Miscellaneous Works* (ed. by J. T. Rutt) (London, 1831), Vol. XXV, Appendix XII, pp. 315–16.

41. Careful Observer, *Strictures on Methodism*, p. 47.

42. Even this, however, was to make its appearance in the nineteenth century when a body of the Friends sought to give Quakerism a more evangelical character. Some of these became Plymouth Brethren, concerning whose views Gosse has written so well in *Father and Son*.

43. See Joseph Priestley, "An Address to the Methodists" in *Original Letters by the Rev. John Wesley etc.* (Birmingham: Pearson, 1791); Priestley suggested, somewhat ambiguously, that because of his belief in universal redemption, he even agreed with the Methodists on certain issues of free will. (pp. xxiv–xxv.)

44. Quoted in John Holloway, *A Letter to the Rev. Dr. Price. Containing a few Strictures Upon His Sermon . . . 'The Love of our Country.'* (London: J. Chalmers, 1789), pp. 10–11.

45. [R. B. Aspland], *The Rise, Progress, and Present Influence of Wesleyan Methodism* (London: British and Foreign Unitarian Association, 1831), pp. 1, 3–11, 15 f., 18 ff., 24, 26, 29, 31 f., 37–40, 42–60.

46. Holloway, *Letter to Dr. Price*, pp. 10–11, 16 f., 26–30, 31 n.

47. [Aspland], *Rise, Progress, and Present Influence of Wesleyan Methodism*, pp. 58–60.

48. For details of the movement, see Benjamin Gregory, "Methodism in the Middle of the Century," *Wesleyan Methodist Magazine* (1893), pp. 147–48; J. Edward Cooper, "The Derby Faith; the Story of a Secession," *The Methodist Recorder*, February 12, 1903, p. 11; G. B. Macdonald, *Facts Against Fiction; or a Statement of the Real Cause, Which Produced the Division Among the Wesleyan Methodists in Derby* (Derby: Pike, 1832), *passim*.

49. John Hackett, *Arminian Methodism, Miscalled 'Derby Faith'* (Derby: T. Ward, 182?), pp. 11–12, 28. Also *Minutes of Several Conversations, Between the Preachers and Representatives of the Arminian Methodist Connexion, At the Yearly Meeting, Begun in Derby, on Tuesday, June 25th, 1833* (Derby: T. Ward, 1833), p. 4. For the distressed reaction of the leaders of the Connection to the new group, see T. P. Bunting, *Bunting*, II, 273. See Macdonald, *Facts Against Fiction*, pp. 31–32; Hackett, *Arminian Methodism*, pp. 20–21. The Arminian Methodists turned for support to John Fletcher, insisting that their doctrine might be found in Fletcher's *Essay on Truth*, though without substantial grounds, for indeed, in a private letter Fletcher had specifically struck out at the very similar doctrine of eighteenth-century Sandemanianism. See letter by John Fletcher to Mr. Ley of Oxford, dated 9 May [?]. Fletcher Papers, M.C.A.

50. A Minister of Derby, *A Letter to the Rev. John Davis, Wesleyan Minister, Derby, On the Subject of the late Secession from the Society Under his Superintendence* (Derby: Pike, 1832?), pp. 6–7.

51. We must note, however, that the Arminian Methodists maintained that they adhered to the Wesleyan view of subjection to higher powers, to the King and his Government. See *Rules of the Arminian Methodist Societies, First Established in Derby, in the Year 1832* (Derby: Ward & Probstt. 183?), pp. 8–9.

52. See the discussion in J. D. Y. Peel, *Herbert Spencer; the Evolution of a Sociologist* (New York: Basic Books, 1971), pp. 36–43.

53. See, for example, Martin Schmidt, *John Wesley: A Theological Biography* (London: Epworth Press, 1962), I, 88 f., 303 f., 308 f. Also Thompson, *Making of the English Working Class*.

54. A view of Wesley as belonging to the Puritan tradition to which Goodwin and Baxter belonged may be found in R. C. Monk, *John Wesley: His*

Puritan Heritage (London: Epworth Press, 1966). See also Cell, *Rediscovery of John Wesley.*

55. See Piette, *Wesley in the Evolution of Protestantism, passim.*

56. When an Anglican clergyman, the Rev. Robert Nares, made the charge of Puritanism in 1813, a Methodist itinerant, describing the Puritans as men of "unconquerable virtue," added that "the Methodists, Sir, you highly honour by such a resemblance." Stanley, *Increase, Influence, and Stability,* pp. 9–10. Certainly the Methodists felt able to identify with the Puritanism of Richard Baxter. See, for example, the eulogy of Baxter in Thomas Rutherford, *The Christian's Walk with God. . . . Being an extract from two treatises of the Pious and Learned Mr Richard Baxter* (London: Conference Office, 1806), p. vi; also, T. Jackson, *A Third Letter to the Rev. John Cockin. Containing A Reply to His Valedictory Letter* (Leeds: J. Nichols, 1815), p. 16, and *passim.* See also T. Jackson, *Life of Richard Watson.* Yet most of the leaders of the Revival came from a High Church rather than from a Dissenting or Calvinist background. On this question, see the discussion in J. D. Walsh, "Origins of the Evangelical Revival," in Bennett and Walsh, eds., *Essays in Modern English Church History,* pp. 144, 155 ff., and *passim.* See also John Walsh, "Methodism at the End of the Eighteenth Century," in Rupert Davies and Gordon Rupp, eds., *A History of the Methodist Church in Great Britain* (London: Epworth Press, 1965), I, 290, 298, and *passim.*

56. See Careful Observer, *Strictures on Methodism,* p. 117, where Wesley is praised as "the Luther of his age." Wesley frequently saw himself in such terms. See, for example, Wesley, *Letters,* IV (April 10, 1761), 152.

57. See H. R. McAdoo [Bishop of Ossory], *The Spirit of Anglicanism,* (London: A. & C. Black, 1965), pp. v, vi, and *passim.*

58. Wesley, *Letters,* IV, 91.

59. Wesley, *Letters,* IV (November 26, 1762), 347.

60. *Gentleman's Magazine,* LXI, Pt. I (1791), 282.

61. Sir Leslie Stephen, *History of English Thought in the Eighteenth Century* (New York: Harcourt, Brace, 1962), II, 362, 368.

62. Thompson, *Making of the English Working Class,* p. 362.

63. Michael Walzer, *The Revolution of the Saints; A Study in the Origin of Radical Politics* (New York: Atheneum, 1968), pp. 1–4, 10, 13 ff., 18–21, 24 f., 28–33, 35 ff., 42, 45, 47–65, 291–95, 303–6.

64. Smollett, *Humphrey Clinker,* pp. xiii, 142–43.

65. Oliver Goldsmith, "Of Eloquence," *The Bee* (November 17, 1759), in Friedman, ed., *Collected Works,* I, 481–83.

66. There have been a number of works dealing with Wesley's work as a social reformer, as an anticipator of "socialism" and as a democrat. Among them are: J. A. Faulkner, *The Socialism of John Wesley,* 1908; J. H. Holmes, *John Wesley and the Methodist Revolt* (Toronto: Ryerson Press, 1923); R. J. Doidge, *Wesley and the Industrial Era* (London: Epworth, 1938); F. A. J. Harding, *The Social Impact of the Evangelical Revival* (London: Epworth, 1947).

67. The "rabble" Protestantism of the Protestant Association which was behind the Lord George Gordon riots of 1780 was seen by Charles Wesley, in a lengthy poem upon the subject, and to a lesser degree by John Wesley, as a product of the Reformation. Charles Wesley's lines ran:

> Less fierce the saints of Forty-one
> With 'prentices their work begun.
> And carrying on the Reformation,
> O'erturn'd at last both church and nation.

(Wesley, *Poetical Works,* VIII, p. 451.) John Wesley, while eschewing the movement, appears to have had some sympathy for the Protestant pretensions of Gordon. Wesley visited Gordon, at Gordon's request, when the riot leader was imprisoned in the Tower.

68. This is essentially the question posed by a recent historian who observed that "Methodism was easily the most highly co-ordinated body of opinion in the country, the most fervent, the most dynamic"; adding that "had it been bent on revolution in Church or State, nothing could have stopped it." J. H. Plumb, *England in the Eighteenth Century* (Baltimore: Penguin, 1965), pp. 93–94.

69. John Wesley, "A Short History of the People Called Methodists" (1781), *Works*, XIII, 313, 337.

70. Quoted in C. C. O'Brien, "Introduction," Edmund Burke, *Reflections on the Revolution in France* (Baltimore: Penguin, 1969), p. 75.

71. For Burke's unhappiness with Wesley's Toryism, see his letter to the Duke of Portland, dated 3 September 1780. "There is one Sect (if they may be so called,) behind; pretty numerous; and still more under the discipline of their Teachers than any of the rest—that is the sect of the Methodists. I am not yet quite certain what part they will take, except that negative certainty, that they will not take it for me. . . . It is near five years since Wesley carried over that set of men. to the Court, and to all the slavish doctrines of Charles the 2ds reign in their utmost extent." See J. A. Woods, ed., *The Correspondence of Edmund Burke* (Cambridge: Cambridge University Press, 1963), IV, p. 271.

72. See O'Brien, "Introduction," Burke, *Reflections*, pp. 25–26, 34–40, 51, 75.

73. See J. L. Talmon, *The Origins of Totalitarian Democracy* (New York: Praeger, 1961), pp. 1–13, 257–66, and *passim;* J. L. Talmon, *Political Messianism; The Romantic Phase* (New York: Praeger, 1960), *passim*. For a similar view of medieval chiliastic sects, see Norman Cohn, *The Pursuit of the Millennium; Revolutionary messianism in medieval and Reformation Europe and its bearing on modern totalitarian movements* (New York: Harper Torchbooks, 1961).

74. See Semmel, "Halévy, Methodism, and Revolution," in Halévy, *Birth of Methodism*, pp. 1–29.

75. See Lagarde, *L'esprit politique de la Réforme*, pp. 424, 462, 464–65. Lagarde suggested that "Le déterminisme théologique de Luther trouve sa suite logique dans l'apothéose hégelienne du fait accompli."

76. Alexis de Tocqueville, *Democracy in America* (New York: Harper & Row, 1966), pp. 271, 611, 39–40.

Selected Bibliography

―――――――

SERIALS, PERIODICALS, REPORTS,

AND

GENERAL REFERENCES

Annual Addresses of the Conferences to the Methodist Societies in Great
  Britain
Annual Register
Annual Report of the State of the Missions
Anti-Jacobin Review
Arminian Magazine (1778–1797); continued as The Methodist Magazine
  (1798–1821); continued as The Wesleyan Methodist Magazine (1822–1832).
Cobbett's Weekly Political Register
Dictionary of National Biography
Evangelical Magazine
Gentleman's Magazine
The Gospel Magazine
Minutes of the Methodist Conferences, From the First Held in London By the
  Late Rev. John Wesley, A.M. in the Year 1744. Vols. I-VIII (1744–1836).
Missionary Notices, Relating Principally to the Foreign Missions . . . Now
  Carried on under the Direction of the Methodist Conference
Monthly Review
Parliamentary Debates
Proceedings of the Church Missionary Society for Africa and the East
Proceedings of the Wesley Historical Society
Mr. Redhead Yorke's Weekly Political Review
Reports of the Directors of the African Institution

MANUSCRIPTS

Samuel Bradburn Papers. Methodist Church Archives. London.
Jabez Bunting Papers. Methodist Church Archives, and Wesleyan Methodist
  Missionary Society Archives. London.
Adam Clarke Papers. Methodist Church Archives. London.
Thomas Coke Papers. Wesleyan Methodist Missionary Society Archives. Lon-
  don.
Joseph Entwistle Papers. Methodist Church Archives. London.
J. W. Fletcher Papers. Methodist Church Archives. London.
Home Correspondence. Wesleyan Methodist Missionary Society Archives. Lon-
  don.
Henry Moore Papers. Methodist Church Archives. London.

James Nichols Papers. Methodist Church Archives. London.
John Pawson Papers. Methodist Church Archives. London.
John Stephens Papers. Methodist Church Archives. London.
Richard Watson Papers. Methodist Church Archives. London.

SERMONS, TRACTS, AND
OTHER WRITINGS OF
JOHN WESLEY

(Roman numerals refer to the volumes in *The Works of the Rev. John Wesley, A.M.* 5th ed. London: John Mason, 1860. Hereafter cited as *Works*.)

"Advice to the People Called Methodists," *Works*, VIII (1745).
"An Answer to Mr. Rowland Hill's Tract, Entitled 'Imposture Detected'," *Works*, X (1777).
"A Blow at the Root, or Christ Stabb'd in the House of His Friends," *Works*, X (1762).
"Brief Thoughts on Christian Perfection," *Works*, XI (1777).
A Calm Address to Our American Colonies. London: R. Hawes, [1775].
A Calm Address to the Inhabitants of England. London: J. Fry, 1777.
"A Caution Against Bigotry," *Works*, V.
"The Character of a Methodist," *Works*, VIII.
"A Circumcision of the Heart," *Works*, V (1733).
"A Compassionate Address to the Inhabitants of Ireland," *Works*, XI (1778).
"The Consequence Proved," *Works*, X (1771).
"The Danger of Riches," *Works*, VII.
"A Dialogue between a Predestinarian and His Friend," *Works*, X (1741).
"A Dialogue between an Antinomian and His Friend," *Works*, X (1745).
"A Dialogue between an Arminian and His Friend," *Works*, X (1745).
"The Doctrine of Absolute Predestination Stated and Asserted by the Reverend Mr A_____ T_____," *Works*, XIV (1770).
"An Estimate of the Manners of the Present Times," *Works*, XI (1782).
"Free Grace, A Sermon Preached at Bristol," *Works*, VII (1740).
"Free Thoughts on the Present State of Public Affairs," *Works*, XI (1768).
"How Far Is It the Duty of A Christian Minister to Preach Politics?" *Works*, XI (1782).
"The Life of the Rev. John Wesley," *Works*, V.
"Minutes of Several Conversations between the Rev. Mr. Wesley and others; From the Year 1744 to the Year 1789," *Works*, VIII (1791).
"National Sins and Miseries," *Works*, VII (1775).
"On Riches," *Works*, VII.
"On the Danger of Increasing Riches," *Works*, VII (1790).
"On the Death of the Rev. Mr. George Whitefield," *Works*, VI (1770).
"A Plain Account of Christian Perfection, As Believed and Taught by the Reverend Mr. John Wesley," *Works*, XI (1777).
"Predestination Calmly Considered," *Works*, X (1752).
"The Principles of Methodism," *Works*, VIII.
"The Question, What is an Arminian? Answered. By a Lover of Free Grace," *Works*, X (1770).
"Reasons Against a Separation From the Church of England," *Works*, XIII (1758).
"Some Remarks on Mr. Hill's 'Farrago Double-Distilled,' " *Works*, X (1773).
"Remarks on the Count de Buffon's 'Natural History,' " *Works*, XIII (1782).

"Remarks Upon Mr Locke's 'Essay on Human Understanding,' " *Works*, XIII (1781).

"Salvation by Faith," *Works*, V (1738).

[A Lover of Peace]. "A Seasonable Address to the More Serious Part of the Inhabitants of Great Britain, Respecting the Unhappy Contest Between Us and Our American Brethren; With an Occasional Word Interspersed to those of a Different Complexion," *Works*, XI (1776).

"A Second Dialogue Between an Antinomian and His Friend," *Works*, X (1745).

"A Serious Address to the People of England, With Regard to the State of the Nation," *Works*, XI (1778).

"Serious Thoughts Upon the Perseverance of the Saints," *Works*, X (1751).

A Short Account of the Life and Death of the Reverend John Fletcher. London. 1786. See also. *Works*, XI.

"A Short Address to the Inhabitants of Ireland, Occasioned by some late Occurrences," *Works*, IX (1749).

"A Short History of the People Called Methodists," *Works*, XIII (1781).

Some Account of the Late Work of God in North America in a Sermon on Ezekiel 1:16. London: R. Hawes, 1778.

"Some Observations on Liberty; Occasioned by a Late Tract," *Works*, XI (1776).

"Some Remarks on 'A Defence of the Preface to the Edinburgh Edition of Aspasio Vindicated,' " *Works*, X (1766).

"Some Remarks on Mr. Hill's 'Review of All the Doctrines Taught by Mr. John Wesley,' " *Works*, X (1772).

"A Thought on Necessity," *Works*, X.

"Thoughts Concerning the Origin of Power," *Works*, XI.

"Thoughts on Salvation by Faith," *Works*, XI (1779).

Thoughts on the Imputed Righteousness of Christ. London: W. Strahan, 1762.

"Thoughts Upon God's Sovereignty," *Works*. X (1777).

"Thoughts Upon Liberty," *Works*, XI (1772).

"Thoughts Upon Methodism." *Arminian Magazine*, X (March 1787).

"Thoughts Upon Necessity," *Works*, X (1774).

"Thoughts Upon Baron Montesquieu's Spirit of the Laws," *Arminian Magazine*, IV (1781).

"Thoughts Upon Slavery," *Works*, XI (1774).

"Upon Our Lord's Sermon on the Mount," *Works*, V.

"The Use of Money," *Works*, VI.

"A Word in Season; Or, Advice to an Englishmen," *Works*, XI (1745).

"A Word to a Freeholder," *Works*, XI (1748).

"A Word to a Smuggler," *Works*, XI (1767).

PRIMARY SOURCES

Anon. *An Address to the Common Sense and Understanding of Every Protestant, Evidently Showing and Proving the Impiety, Folly, and Fanaticism, of the Sect Called Methodists*. London: Causton, 1813.

Anon. *An Address to the Lower Class of His Parishioners, on the Subject of Methodism*. Ipswich: J. Raw, 1806.

Anon. *An Alarm to Dissenters and Methodists*. London: G. Keith, 1769.

Anon. *A Chronological and Alphabetical List of all the Itinerant Methodist Preachers in the Connexion of the Late Rev. John Wesley, and With the Methodist Conference in the Year 1814*. Exeter, 1814.

Anon. *Considerations on the Alliance Between Christianity & Commerce, Applied to the Present State of this Country.* London: Cadell & Davies, 180?

Anon. *A Constitutional Answer to the Rev. Mr. John Wesley's Calm Address to the American Colonies.* London: Dilly & Almon, 1775.

Anon. *A Dialogue Between James, A Member of the Old, and Jacob, a Member of the New Connexion of Methodists.* Leeds: T. Hannam, 1797.

Anon. *An Earnest and Affectionate Address to the People Called Methodists.* London: Rivington, 1815.

Anon. *A Few Words on the Increase of Methodism.* London: Miles & Hunter, 1810.

Anon. *A Letter to a Country Gentleman, on the Subject of Methodism . . . From the Clergyman of his Parish.* Ipswich, 1805.

Anon. *Methodism Exposed: With the History and Tendency of That Sect.* London: Cradock & Joy, 1813.

Anon. *A Narrative of the Proceedings of the General Committee of the People Called Methodists. Late in Connexion with the Rev. John Wesley; Of Protestant Dissenters, and other Friends to Religious Liberty. Respecting the Bill, Introduced into the House of Lords, by Lord Viscount Sidmouth,* etc. London: For Methodist Preaching Houses, 1811.

Anon. *The Patriot; A Tale, Illustrating the Fernicious Effects of Bad Principles on the lower orders of Society.* London: T. Cordeux, 1821.

Anon. *Puritanism Revived; Or Methodism as Old as the Great Rebellion. In a Series of Letters from a Curate to his Rector.* London: Rivington, 1808.

Anon. *Some Account of the Rise and Progress of the Missions Belonging to the Arminian Bible Christians.* Stoke-Damarel, Devon: S. Thorne, 1822.

Anon. *Mr. Wesley's principles detected; or, a defence of the Preface to the Edinburgh edition of Aspasio vindicated.* Edinburgh, 1765.

Arthur, Rev. William. *The French Revolution of 1848.* London: W. Jones, 1849.

[Aspland, R. B.]. *The Rise, Progress, and Present Influence of Wesleyan Methodism.* London: British and Foreign Unitarian Association, 1831.

Attentive, Thomas [pseud.]. *A Friendly Address to the Preacher and Principal members of the M—d—ts.* n.p., 1788.

Beilby [Porteus], Bishop of London. *A Letter to the Clergy of the West-Indian Islands.* n.p., 1788.

Belsham, Thomas. *A Review of Mr. Wilberforce's Treatise.* London: J. Johnson, 1798.

Benson, Joseph. *A Defence of the Methodists in Five Letters Addressed to the Rev. Dr. Tatham.* London, 1793.

Booker, Rev. Moore. *Two Letters Concerning the Methodists.* Dublin: Kilburn, 1751.

Bradburn, Samuel. *An Address to the People Called Methodists; Concerning the Evil of Encouraging the Slave Trade.* Manchester: T. Harper, 1792.

————. *Equality* [Sermon preached at Bristol, February 28, 1794]. Bristol: Lancaster & Edwards, 1794.

————. *God Shining Forth, From Between the Cherubim.* Bolton: Garner, 1805.

————. *Memoirs of the Late Rev. Samuel Bradburn.* (E. W. Bradburn, ed.). London: R. Edwards, 1816.

————. *Methodism Set Forth and Defended in a Sermon . . . Preached at the Opening of Portland Chapel.* Bristol: Lancaster & Edwards, 1792.

Brethren's Society for the Furtherance of the Gospel Among the Heathen. *In-*

structions for the Members of the Unitas Fratrium Who Minister in the Gospel Among the Heathen. London, 1784.

Brittell, Jeremiah. *Fear God and Honour the King.* n.p., 1796.

Brooke, Henry. *The Fool of Quality; Or, the History of Henry Earl of Moreland.* With a Preface by Rev. Charles Kingsley. London: Smith, Elder, 1859.

———. *The History of Henry Earl of Moreland.* Originally written by H. Brooke, Esq. Revised and edited by the Rev. John Wesley, A. M. Plymouth: J. Bennett, 1815.

Bunting, Jabez. *Justification by Faith.* Leeds: Leak & Nichols, 1813.

———. *Memorials of the late Rev. Richard Watson: including the Funeral Sermon . . . January 18, 1833.* London: J. Mason, 1833.

Burns, William. *An Inquiry into the Moral Tendency of Methodism and Evangelical Preaching.* London: J. Johnson, 1810.

Byron, J. M. *Thoughts on the Evil of Persecution; Occasioned by the Rioting at Newent. Including A Friendly Address to the Inhabitants.* Gloucester: D. Walker, 1806.

A Careful Observer. *Strictures on Methodism.* London: R. Edwards, 1804.

Clarke, Adam. *The Origin and End of Civil Government.* London: J. & T. Clarke, 1822.

———. *The Rights of God and Caesar: A Discourse on Matt. xxii 15–21.* London: Blanshard, 1821.

Cockin, John. *A Valedictory Letter to the Rev. T. Jackson, Containing A Reply to the Remarks in His Second Letter.* Huddersfield, 1815.

Coke, Thomas. *A Series of Letters Addressed to the Methodist Connection.* London: Blanshard, 1810.

A Consistent Whig. *Considerations on the late Disturbances.* London: J. Almon, 1780.

Creighton, Rev. James. *Remarks on Some Observations of the Rev. Rowland Hill, Introduced into his 'Village Dialogues,' Concerning the Religious Principles of the Venerable and Pious John Fletcher.* London: Conference Office, 1805.

Croft, George D. D. *Thoughts Concerning the Methodists and the Established Clergy.* London: Rivington, 1795.

Crowther, Jonathan. *Christian Order: Or, Liberty Without Anarchy; Government Without Tyranny; and Every Man in his proper Place* etc. Bristol: R. Edwards, 1796.

Cubitt, Rev. George. *The Power of Circumstances: Being the Seventh of a Series of Lectures Against Socialism.* London: Seeley, 1840.

Cudworth, William. *A Defence of Theron and Aspasio* [i.e., the work by *James Hervey*] *against the objections contained in a late Treatise of* [*Robert Sandeman*] etc. London: G. Keith, 1760.

———. *A Dialogue between a Preacher of Inherent Righteousness and a Preacher of God's Righteousness . . . : Being an Answer to a Late Dialogue between an Antinomian and His Friend.* London, 1745.

———. *The Discovery of the most Dangerous Dead Faith.* London, 1747.

———. *A Second Dialogue between a Preacher of Inherent Righteousness and a Preacher of God's Righteousness.* London, 1746.

———. *To Mr. John Wesley, occasion'd by the revival of his Dialogues, in a late Treatise, called A Preservative against Unsettled Notions.* London, 1806.

Cursitor. *A Letter to the Lord Bishop of Lincoln, Respecting the 'Report from the Clergy of a District in the Diocese of Lincoln,' In Which Report the Increase of Methodism Is Considered as a Cause of the Declension of Religion.* London, 1800.

Douglas, James. *Methodism Condemned; or Priestcraft Detected*. Newcastle-on-Tyne, 1814.

Drew, Samuel. *Observations (In behalf of the Methodists) on a Pamphlet Lately Published by the Rev. R. Polwhele*. Falmouth, 1800.

Eliot, George. *Adam Bede*. London: C. H. Kelly, n.d.

Etchells, James. *A Mirror for Intolerance or Methodism Illustrated and Defended*. Daventry: Blanshard, 1819.

[Evans, Caleb]. Americanus [pseud.]. *A Letter to the Rev. Mr. John Wesley Occasioned by His Calm Address to the American Colonies*. London: Dilly, 1775.

———. *Political Sophistry Detected, Or Brief Remarks on the Rev. Mr. Fletcher's late Tract Entitled 'American Patriotism.'* Bristol: W. Pine, 1776.

———. *A Reply to the Rev. Mr. Fletcher's Vindication of Mr. Wesley's Calm Address to Our American Colonies*. Bristol: W. Pine, n.d. [1776].

Fielden, Joshua. *Religious Fasting: Its Nature Considered, and Design Stated, With Reference to the Safety and Happiness of the Nation*. Swansea, 1806.

Fish, Henry. *Natural Theology . . . Containing An Exposure of the Errors of Socialism*. Bristol: N. Lomas, 1840.

Fletcher, John. *American Patriotism Farther Confronted with Reason, Scripture, and the Constitution: Being Observations on the Dangerous Politicks Taught by the Rev. Mr. Evans, M.A. and the Rev. Dr. Price*. Shrewsbury: Eddowes, 1776.

———. *Checks to Antinomianism in a Series of Letters*. New York: Carlton & Porter, n.d.

———. *A Vindication of the Rev. Mr. Wesley's 'Calm Address to Our American Colonies'. In Some Letters to Mr. Caleb Evans*. London: R. Hawes, 1776.

Fraser, D. *A Letter Addressed to the Rev. Valentine Ward Occasioned by His Remarks on Dr. Clarke's Letter to the Missionary Committee*. Belper: J. Ogle, 1819.

A Gentleman of Northumberland, *A Compleat Answer to Mr. Wesley's Observations, Upon Dr. Price's Essay on Civil Liberty*. Newcastle: Hobson, 1776?.

Goldsmith, Oliver. *Collected Works of Oliver Goldsmith*. (A. Friedman, ed.). Oxford: Clarendon Press, 1966. 5 vols.

Grindrod, Edmund. *Wesleyan Methodism Viewed in Retrospect*. London: J. Mason, 1839.

Hackett, John. *Arminian Methodism, Miscalled 'Derby Faith.'* Derby: T. Ward, 182?

Hampson, John. *Memoirs of the late Rev. John Wesley, A.M., With a Review of His Life and Writings and a History of Methodism*. Sunderland, 1791. 3 vols.

Hare, Edward. *A Caveat Against Antinomianism*. Leeds: Cullingworth, 1816.

———. *A Letter to the Rev. Melville Horne; Occasioned by his Investigation on the Doctrines Imputed by him to Certain Methodist Preachers*. Sheffield: J. Montgomery, 1809.

———. *A Second Caveat Against Antinomianism*. Leeds: J. Nichols, 1817.

Hatton, William. *Methodist Remembrances; Comprising a Contrast Between the Original and Present State of Methodism and the Methodists*. Birmingham, 1833.

Hazlitt, William. *The Complete Works of William Hazlitt*. (P. P. Howe, ed.) London: J. M. Dent. 1930–1931. 15 vols.

Heald, W. M. Vicar of Bristol. *A Letter; With an Address, Expostulatory and*

Admonitory, to the Stewards, Leaders, and Members of the Methodist Society at Bristol. Leeds, 1813.

[Hervey, James]. *Mr. Wesley's principles detected; or, a defence of the Preface to the Edinburgh edition of Aspasio Vindicated; in answer to Mr. Kershaw's Earnest Appeal,* etc. Edinburgh, 1765.

Hill, Sir Richard. *An Apology for Brotherly Love . . . With a Vindication of Such Parts of Mr Wilberforce's Practical View As Have Been Objected to by Mr Daubeny, in his . . . Guide to the Church.* London, 1798.

————. *Conversations between Richard Hill, Esq.; the Rev. Mr. Madan, and the Superior of a Convent of English Benedictine monks at Paris,* etc. London, 1772.

————. *Daubenism Confuted, and Martin Luther Vindicated.* London, 1800.

————. *Five Letters to . . . Mr Fletcher relative to the Vindication of the . . . minutes . . . of John Wesley.* n.p., 1772.

————. *A Lash at Enthusiasm etc.* n.p., 1792.

————. *Logica Wesleiensis: Or, the Farrago double distilled.* London: Dilly, 1773.

————. *A Review of all the Doctrines Taught by the Rev. J. Wesley; Containing a Full and Particular Answer to a Book, Entitled, "A Second Check to Antinomianism"* etc. London, 1772.

————. *The Tables Turned, A Letter to the Author of a Pamphlet, Entitled Observations on the Election of Members for the Borough of Ludlow In the Year 1780.* Shrewsbury: T. Wood, 1782.

————. *Three Letters written by R. Hill, Esq. to the Rev. J. Fletcher, . . . in the year 1773. Setting forth Mr. Hill's Reasons for declining any further controversy relative to Mr. Wesley's principles.* Shrewsbury, 1775?.

Hill, Rowland. *A Full Answer to the Rev. J. Wesley's Remarks Upon a late Pamphlet, Published in Defence of the Character of the Rev. Mr. Whitefield and Others.* Bristol, 1777.

————. *Imposture detected & the dead vindicated.* London, 1777.

Hill, W. Methodist Preacher. *The Sectaries Defended and the Church Not Endangered. An Answer to the Charge Delivered by the Rev. Robert Nares,* etc. Chester, 1813.

Holloway, John. *A Letter to the Rev. Dr. Price. Containing a few Strictures Upon His Sermon . . . 'The Love of our Country.'* London: J. Chalmers, 1789.

Holroyd, J. B. *The Doctrines of the Methodists Stated and Defended.* Alnwick: M. Smith, 1822.

Horne, Melville. *An Investigation of the Definition of Justifying Faith . . . Held by Dr. Coke, and other Methodist Preachers.* London: Longmans et al., 1809.

————. *Letters on Missions; Addressed to the Protestant Ministers of the British Churches.* Bristol: Bulgin & Rosser, 1794.

Hughes, John. *A Plea for Religious Liberty; Or a Vindication of the Methodists.* Macclesfield, 1813.

Hulbert, C. *Candid Strictures on Several Passages in a Recent Publication* etc. Shrewsbury: T. Wood, 1806.

Hume, David. *The Philosophical Works of David Hume.* (T. H. Green & T. H. Grose, eds.). London, 1882, 4 vols.

Huntingford, G. I. Bishop of Gloucester. *A Charge Delivered to the Clergy of the Diocese of Gloucester.* London: Cadell & Davies, 1807.

Hutton, James. *A Letter to a Friend in Which Some Account is Given of the Brethren's Society for the Furtherance of the Gospel Among the Heathen.* London, 1769.

Hutton, W. *A Reply to the Rev. John Cockin, Occasioned by His Severe Reflections on An Extract from the Address of the Methodist Missionary Society for the Halifax District.* Leeds: J. Capes, 1815.

Jackson, Thomas. *The Church and the Methodists.* London: J. Mason, 1834.

———. [An Arminian]. *A Letter to the Rev. John Cockin.* Leeds: J. Nichols, 1814.

———. *Recollections of My Own Life and Times.* London: Wesleyan Conference Office, 1878.

———. *A Second Letter to the Rev. John Cockin.* Leeds: J. Nichols, 1814.

———. *A Third Reply to the Rev. John Cockin, Containing A Reply to His Valedictory Letter.* Leeds: J. Nichols, 1815.

Jones, Rev. James. *Moral Freedom and Divine Benevolence; A Letter Addressed to the Rev. Jabez Bunting, M.A., President of the Methodist Conference.* Margate: R. Osborne, 1829.

Kilham, Alexander. *An Account of the Trial of Alexander Kilham, Methodist Preacher, Before the General Conference in London: On the 26th, 27th, and 28th of July, 1796.* Leeds: Binns & Brown, 1796.

———. *Appeal to the Methodist Societies of the Alnwick Circuit.* n.p., 1796.

———. *A Candid Examination, of the London Methodistical Bull.* Alnwick: J. Catnach, 1796.

———. *A Defence of the Account Published by Alexander Kilham on His Trial Before the London Conference.* [16 December, 1796]. Leeds: Binns & Brown, 1796.

———. [Paul & Silas, pseud.] *An Earnest Address to the Preachers Assembled in Conference.* n.p., 1795.

———. *The Progress of Liberty, Amongst the People Called Methodists.* Alnwick: J. Catnach, 1795.

———. *A Short Account of the Trial of Alex. Kilham, At a Special District Meeting, Held at Newcastle, On the 18th, 19th, & 20th, of February 1796.* Alnwick: J. Catnach, 1796.

La Trobe, B., Hutton, J., and Wollin, W. *An Address from the Brethren's Society for the Furtherance of the Gospel Among the Heathen.* n.p., 1781?.

La Trobe, B. *A Succinct View of the Missions Established Among the Heathen By the Church of the Brethren.* London: Lewis, 1771.

Lavington, George, Bishop of Exeter. *The Enthusiasm of Methodists and Papists Compared.* London: Knapton, 1749 & 1751. Another edition, edited by R. Polwhele. London: Whittaker et al., 1820.

A Layman. *Letters to William Wilberforce on the Doctrine of Hereditary Depravity.* London: J. Johnson, 1806.

A Layman. *Modern Methodism Unmasked.* London: Baldwin & Cradock, 1830.

Macdonald, G. B. *Facts Against Fiction; or a Statement of the Real Cause, Which Produced the Division Among the Wesleyan Methodists in Derby.* Derby: Pike, 1832.

McNicoll, David. *Divine Providence Illustrated in the Ordination of Political Government.* London: Whittaker, 1820.

———. *On the Gospel. Or, the Substance of a Discourse delivered in Bridge-Street Chapel, Bolton, May 17, 1815, at the Formation of the Missionary Auxiliary Society in That Town, for the Manchester District.* Manchester: Russell & Allen, 1815.

Mason, J. A. *An Earnest Appeal to the People Called Methodists and to the Nation at Large*. London: W. E. Andrews, 1827.

Mason, William. *The Absolute and Indispensable Duty of Christians, in this Critical Juncture*. London: Pasham, 1776.

———. *Axe Laid to the Root of Antinomian Licentiousness*. N.p., n.d.

A Member of the Church of England. *Hints for the Security of the Established Church Humbly Addressed to His Grace the Archbishop of Canterbury*. London: J. Hatchard, 1806.

A Member of the Old Methodist Society. *An Exposition of the Proceedings of the Old Methodist Conference With Reflections on the Nature and Tendency of its System of Government* etc. Manchester: G. Innes, 1815. 2nd edition.

A Member of the Wesleyan Methodist Congregations. *Union is Strength*. Manchester: C. Ambery, 1834.

A Methodist of the Old School. *Methodism in 1821; With Recollections of Primitive Methodism*. London: W. Whittemore, 1821.

A Minister of Derby. *A Letter to the Rev. John Davis, Wesleyan Minister, Derby, On the Subject of the late Secession from the Society Under his Superintendence*. Derby: Pike, 1832.

A Missionary. *Lines on the Much Lamented Death of the Rev. Thomas Coke, L.L.D., etc.* London, 1815.

Moore, Henry. *Fear God; Honour the King*. London: G. Paramore. 1794.

Nichols, James. *Calvinism and Arminianism Compared*. London, 1824.

———. *A Report of the Principal Speeches delivered on the Sixth Day of October 1813, at the Formation of the Methodist Missionary Society, for the Leeds District*, etc. London: Simpkin & Marshall, 1840. 5th edition.

———. *The Works of Arminius*. Translated by J. Nichols. London, 1825.

Olivers, Thomas. *Defence of Methodism: Delivered . . . in a public debate . . . held in London . . . 1785, on the following question, Have the Methodists done most good or evil?* etc. Leeds, 1818.

———. *A Full Defence of the Rev. John Wesley. In Answer to . . . the Rev. Caleb Evans*. London, 1776.

———. *A Letter to the Reverend Mr. Toplady*. London, 1770.

———. *A Rod for a Reviler: Or A Full Answer to Mr. Rowland Hill's Letter Entitled Imposture Detected, and the Dead Vindicated*. London: J. Fry, 1777.

———. *A Scourge to Calumny, in Two Parts, Inscribed to Richard Hill, Esq.* London: R. Hawes, 1774.

Pawson, John. *A Chronological Catalogue of all the Travelling Preachers Now in the Methodist Connexion*. Liverpool, 1795.

———. *The Prophet's Advice to the People of God in the Time of Danger*. Leeds: E. Baines, 1801.

Perronet, Charles. *Leviathan or the Crooked Serpent; Being an Antinomian Creed, Taken from Richard Hill, Esq.* n.p., 1773.

Phileleutherus. *A Defence of the British Constitution, Against the Attacks of Civis, Upon the Methodists and Dissenters etc.* London, 1813.

Polwhele, R. *A Letter to the Right Rev. the Lord Bishop of Exeter . . . Examining the Distinctive Characters of the Calvinists and Arminian Sectarists; and proposing to his Lordship a Scheme of Coalition between the Wesleyans and the Church of England*. Truro: E. Heard, 1833.

Pratt, Josiah H., ed. *Eclectic Notes, or Notes of discussions on religious topics, at the meetings of the Eclectic Society, 1798–1814*. London: J. Nisbet, 1865.

Priestley, Joseph. "An Address to the Methodists," in *Original Letters by the Rev. John Wesley,* etc. (J. Priestley, ed.) Birmingham: Pearson, 1791.

———. *The Theological and Miscellaneous Works of Joseph Priestley.* (J. T. Rutt, ed.) London, 1831, 25 vols.

———. *Writings on Philosophy, Science, and Politics.* (J. A. Passmire, ed). New York: Collier Books, 1965.

Relly, James. *Antichrist resisted; in a reply to a pamphlet, written by W. Mason, intitled: Antinomian Heresy exploded.* London, 1761.

Rhodes, Benjamin. *A Discourse on Civil Government and Religious Liberty; also The Duties of Subjects to their Sovereign* etc. Birmingham: J. Belcher, 1796.

Roberts, Thomas. *The Burning and Shining Light. A Sermon Occasioned by the Death of the Rev. Thomas Coke, L.L.D.* Bath: Meyler & Son, 1815.

———. *Christian Loyalty; A Sermon Delivered at the Methodist Chapel, King Street, Bristol, June 1, 1802.* Bristol: R. Edwards, 1802.

———. *The Outcasts Delivered,* etc. Camarthen: Harris, 1811.

Rutherford, Thomas. *The Christian's Walk with God . . . Being an extract from two treatises of the Pious and Learned Mr Richard Baxter.* London: Conference Office, 1806.

———. *The Voice of the Rod.* London: R. Edwards, 1803.

S., T. [pseud.] *A Cool Reply to a Calm Address, Lately Published by Mr. John Wesley.* London: J. Plummer, 1775.

Sadler, Michael. *An Apology for the Methodists; Being a Copy of a Letter to the Rev. H. Stokes.* Birmingham, n.d. 2nd edition. 1st edition, 1797.

Sandwith, Humphrey. *A Reply to Lord John Russel's* (sic) *Animadversions on Wesleyan Methodism.* London: J. Mason, 1830.

———. *A Report of a Speech delivered on the 13th of January, 1814, at a Public Meeting held in the Methodist Chapel, Beverly, for the Purpose of Forming an Auxiliary Missionary Society.* Beverly, 1814.

Scott, Abraham. *Calvinistic Election Unscriptural, and Incapable of a Rational Defence; A Reply to a Review in the Evangelical Magazine.* Sheffield: J. Blackwell, 1824.

Sellon, Walter. *An Answer to 'Aspasio Vindicated,' in Eleven Letters.* London, 1767.

———. *Church of England Vindicated from the Charge of Predestination.* London, 1771.

———. *A Defence of God's Sovereignty against the impious and horrible aspersions cast upon it by Elisha Cole, in his Practical Treatise on that subject.* London, 1814. 2 vols.

Smith, Charles. *A Short Essay on the Corn Trade, and the Corn Laws . . . First printed in 1758.* London, 1766.

Smollett, T. *The History of England from the Revolution to the Death of George the Second.* London: Cadell, 1791. 5 vols.

Stanley, Jacob. *The Increase, Influence, and Stability, of Unestablished Religion, No Cause of Alarm to Established Christians.* Wednesbury: J. Booth, 1813.

Stephen, James. *The Speech of James Stephen, Esq. at the Annual Meeting of the African Institution, 26th March, 1817.* London: J. Butterworth & J. Hatchard, 1817.

Stephens, John. *Christian Patriotism.* Rotherham: Plumbe, 1810.

———. *The Mutual Relations, Claims, and Duties of the Rich and the Poor.* Manchester: J. Roberts, 1819.

————. *The Privileges, Sins, Dangers, and Duties of Britons.* Edinburgh: Chapman, 1803.

————. *The Signs of the Times. A Sermon Preached In the Methodist Chapel, Colchester; On the 18th of June, 1797.* London: Chapman, 1797.

Stewart, William. *Vindication of the Methodists Respecting Personal and Social Character.* Dublin: J. Jones, 1822.

Sutcliffe, Joseph. *The Divine Mission of the People Called Methodists, to Revive and Spread Religion.* London: T. Blanshard, 1814.

————. *A Review of Methodism.* York: Wilson & Spence, 1805.

————. *A Treatise on the Universal Spread of the Gospel, The Glorious Millennium, and the Second Coming of Christ.* Doncaster, 1798.

Tacitus. *A Brief Vindication of Evangelical Methodism in Reply to 'A Caveat Against Unsound Doctrines,' published in the Last Century by the Rev. Augustus Toplady, and Now Reprinted and Circulated in the Town of Preston.* Preston: T. Hill, 1817.

Taylor, Thomas. *An Answer to the First Part of the Age of Reason.* Printed in 1794. Manchester, 1796.

————. *Britannia's Mercies, and her Duty; Considered in Two Discourses delivered in the Methodist Chapel, at Halifax . . . November 29, 1798.* Leeds, 1799.

———— [Philalethes]. *A Solemn Caution Against the Ten Horns of Calvinism.* Leeds: J. Nichols, 1816.

————. *The World Turn'd Upside-down.* Leeds: J. Bowling, 1784.

Thompson, T. *French Philosophy; Or, A Short Account of the Principles and Conduct of the French Infidels.* London, 1803. 3rd edition.

Thorn, W. *Serious Advice to the Servants, of the Methodist Society, of the Circuit of Leeds.* Leeds, 1796.

Toplady, A. M. *Historic Proof of the Doctrinal Calvinism of the Church of England.* London, 1774. 2 vols.

————. *The Works of Augustus M. Toplady.* London: Baynes & Son, 1825. 6 vols.

A Trustee and Layman. *An Apology for the Methodists of the New Connexion* etc. Hanley: Conference Office, 1815.

Tucker, Josiah. *A Brief History of the Principles of Methodism, Wherein the Rise and Progress, together with the causes of the several Variations, Divisions, and Present inconsistencies of this sect are attempted to be traced out, and accounted for.* Oxford: James Fletcher, 1742.

————. *Letter to the Rev. Dr. Kippis.* Gloucester Raikes, 1773.

Vevers, William. *An Essay on the National Importance of Methodism.* London: J. Mason, 1831.

Vidler, William. *A Letter to Samuel Bradburn and all the Preachers in the Methodist Connection.* Tottenham, 1796.

Vipond, W. *The Doctrines, Discipline and Mode of Worship of the Methodists.* Canterbury, 1807.

[Warburton], William, Lord Bishop of Gloucester. *The Doctrine of Grace: Or, the Office and Operations of the Holy Spirit Vindicated from the Insults of Infidelity, and the Abuses of Fanaticism: With Some Thoughts (humbly Offered to the Consideration of the Established Clergy regarding the right method of defending Religion against the attacks of either Party).* London: A. Millar, 1763. 2nd edition.

Ward, Valentine. *A Brief Statement of Facts, Designed for the Information of those Who from Good Motives Enquire 'What are these Methodists.'* Leeds: James Nichols, 1815.

————. *Free and Candid Strictures on Methodism.* Aberdeen: D. Chalmers, 1818.

Warren, Samuel. *A Sermon . . . On the Occasion of the Death of the Late Rev. Thos. Coke, L.L.D.* Chester: J. Smith, 1815.

[Watson, Richard]. "Address to the Public, By the General Committee of the Methodist Missionary Society for the Leeds District," in *The First Report of the Methodist Missionary Society for the Leeds District; MDCCCXIV* etc. Leeds: J. Nichols, 1814.

————. *A Defence of the Wesleyan Methodist Missions in the West Indies.* London: Blanshard, 1817.

————. *The Life of the Rev. John Wesley, A.M.* London: Wesleyan-Methodist Book Room, 1831.

————. *The Religious Instruction of the Slaves in the West India Colonies Advocated and Defended; A Sermon Preached Before the Wesleyan Methodist Missionary Society . . . April 28, 1824.* London: Batterworth, 1825.

————. *A Sermon Preached at Albion Street Chapel, Leeds, At the Formation of the Methodist Missionary Society for the Leeds District, October 6, 1813.* Liverpool: Kaye, 1813.

————. *A Sermon Preached at the Methodist Chapel, Wakefield . . . On Thursday, the Seventh Day of July,* etc. Leeds: J. Nichols, 1814.

————. *Theological Institutes: or A View of the Evidences, Doctrines, Morals, and Institutions of Christianity.* 3rd ed. London: J. Mason, 1829.

————. *The Works of the Rev. Richard Watson.* 8th ed. London: Wesleyan Conference Office, 1865.

Wesley, Charles. *The Journal of the Rev. Charles Wesley, M.A.* London: Culley, 1909.

Wesley, John. *A Concise Ecclesiastical History from the Birth of Christ to the Beginning of the Present Century.* 4 vols. London, 1781.

————. *A Concise History of England from the Earliest Times to the death of George II.* 4 vols. London: R. Hawes, 1776.

————. *The Journal of John Wesley.* (N. Curnock, ed.). London: Epworth Press, 1909–1916. 8 vols.

————. *The Letters of John Wesley.* (J. Telford, ed.). 8 vols. London: Epworth Press, 1931.

———— and Charles. *The Poetical Works of John and Charles Wesley.* 13 vols. London: Wesleyan Methodist Conference Office, 1869.

————. *The Works of the Rev. John Wesley, A.M.* 14 vols. London: John Mason, 1860. 5th edition.

Whitefield, George. *An Alarm in Zion . . . on the alarm of Invasion written . . . in 1756.* London, 1803.

————. *Britain's Mercies and Britain's Duty . . . Occasioned by the Suppression of the late Unnatural Rebellion.* Boston, 1746.

Wilberforce, William. *A Practical View of the Prevailing Religious System of Professed Christians in the Higher and Middle Classes in This Country, Contrasted with Real Christianity.* London: Cadell, 1797.

————. *Private Papers of William Wilberforce.* (A.M. Wilberforce, ed.). London: T. Fisher Unwin, 1897.

Williams, Thomas. *A Vindication of the Calvinistic Doctrines of Human Depravity etc. . . . in a Series of Letters to the Rev. T. Belsham: Occasioned by His 'Review of Mr. Wilberforce's Treatise.'* London: A. Parns, 1799.

Wood, Thomas. *Essays on Civil Government and Subjection and Obedience.* Wigan: Lyon, 1796.

————. *Victory and Death.* Huddersfield: T. Smart, 1804.

Woodhouse, Simeon. *The Moral Influence and National Importance of Methodism*. London: J. Mason, 1839.

Woods, Robert. *The Discrepancy of Bigotry and Equity Displayed*. Sheffield, 1819.

Woolner, Samuel. *A Sermon . . . Intended as a Sacred Memorial of his late most excellent majesty king George the Third*. Hull: W. Ross, 1820.

―――. *The Servant of the Lord; A Sermon Occasioned by the Death of the Late Rev. T. Coke, L.L.D.* London: Conference Office, 1815.

SECONDARY SOURCES

Abbey, C. J., and Overton, J. H. *The English Church in the Eighteenth Century*. 2 vols. London: Longmans, 1878.

Andrews, Stuart. "John Wesley and the Age of Reason." *History Today* XIX (January 1969): 25–32.

―――. *Methodism and Society*. London: Longmans, 1970.

Ashley, W. J. "An Economist on Calvinism, Arminianism, Puritanism." *Proceedings of the Wesley Historical Society* XVI (1927): 32–34.

Baker, E. W. *A Herald of the Evangelical Revival; a Critical Inquiry into the Relation of William Law to John Wesley and the Beginnings of Methodism*. London: Epworth Press, 1948.

Baker, F. "Methodism and the '45 Rebellion." *London Quarterly and Holborn Review* 172 (October 1947): 325–33.

Baker, Frank. *John Wesley and the Church of England*. Nashville: Abingdon Press, 1970.

Behrens, C. B. A. *The Ancien Regime*. New York: Harcourt, Brace & World, 1967.

Bennett, G. V., and Walsh, John D., eds. *Essays in Modern English Church History. In Memory of Norman Sykes*. London: A. & C. Black, 1966.

Blanshard, T. W. *The Life of Samuel Bradburn; the Methodist Demosthenes*. London: E. Stock, 1871.

Bowmer, J. C. "Early Methodism and the Quakers." *Religion in Life* XXIII, No. 3 (1954): 418–29.

Bready, J. W. *England: Before and After Wesley*. New York: Harper, 1938.

Bridgen, T. E. "Methodism and Jacobinism at the Dawn of the Nineteenth Century." *Proceedings of the Wesley Historical Society* III, Pt. 1 (1901): 3–9.

Brown, F. K. *Fathers of the Victorians*. Cambridge: Cambridge University Press, 1959.

Brunschvicg, L. "Elie Halévy (1870–1937)." *Revue de Métaphysique et de Morale* XLIV, No. 4 (October 1937): 679–92.

Bunting, T. P. *The Life of Jabez Bunting*. vol. I, London: Longmans, 1859; vol. II, London: T. Woolmer, 1887.

Cannon, W. R. *The Theology of John Wesley with Special Reference to the Doctrine of Justification*. New York: Abingdon-Cokesbury Press, 1946.

Cell, G. C. "Influence of Religion upon its Subjects as Economic Agents." *Methodist Review* CVII (May 1924): 380–400.

―――. *The Rediscovery of John Wesley*. New York: Holt, 1935.

Chamberlayne, John H. "From *Sect* to *Church* in British Methodism." *British Journal of Sociology* XV (1964): 139–49.

Church, L. F. *The Early Methodist People*. London: Epworth Press, 1948.

―――. *More About the Early Methodist People*. London: Epworth Press, 1949.

Church Missionary Society. *The Centenary Volume of the Church Missionary Society for Africa and the East 1799–1899*. London, 1902.

Cobb, R. C. "The English Jacobins and the French Revolution." Reprinted in P. Amann, ed., *The Eighteenth Century Revolution: French or Western*. Boston: D. C. Heath, 1963.

Cobban, Alfred. "The Age of the Democratic Revolution." *History* XLV (1960): 234–39.

————. *The Myth of the French Revolution*. London: H. K. Lewis, 1955.

Cohn, Norman. *The Pursuit of the Millennium: Revolutionary Messianism in Medieval and Reformation Europe and Its Bearing on Modern Totalitarian Movements*. New York: Harper Torchbooks, 1961.

Colie, R. L. *Light and Enlightenment; A Study of the Cambridge Platonists and the Dutch Arminians*. Cambridge: Cambridge University Press, 1957.

Cox, L. G. *John Wesley's Concept of Perfection*. Kansas City, Mo.: Beacon Hill Press, 1968.

Currie, Robert. *Methodism Divided: A Study in the Sociology of Ecumenicalism*. London: Faber and Faber, 1968.

Davies, R. E. *Methodism*. London: Epworth Press, 1963.

Davies, R., and Rupp, G., eds. *A History of the Methodist Church in Great Britain*. London: Epworth Press, 1965.

De Jong, J. A. *As the Waters Cover the Sea; Millennial Expectations in the Rise of Anglo-American Missions 1640–1810*. Amsterdam: Kok, 1970.

Dicey, A. V. *Lectures on the Relation between Law and Public Opinion in England during the Nineteenth Century*. London: Macmillan, 1914.

Dimond, Sidney. *The Psychology of the Methodist Revival; An Empirical and Descriptive Study*. Oxford: Oxford University Press, 1926.

Doidge, R. J. *Wesley and the Industrial Era*. London: Epworth Press, 1938.

Dollimore, A. A. *George Whitefield; The Life and Times of the Great Evangelist of the Eighteenth Century Revival*. London: Banner of Truth Trust, 1970.

Doughty, W. L. *John Wesley, Preacher*. London: Epworth Press, 1955.

Dunn, John. *The Political Thought of John Locke: An Historical Account of the Argument of the 'Two Treatises of Government.'* London: Cambridge University Press, 1969.

Edwards, Maldwyn. *Adam Clarke*. London: Epworth Press, 1942.

————. *After Wesley; A Study of the Social and Political Influence of Methodism in the Middle Period (1791–1849)*. London: Epworth Press, 1948.

————. "John Wesley." Chapter II in *A History of the Methodist Churches in Great Britain*. London: Epworth Press, 37–79.

————. *John Wesley and the Eighteenth Century; A Study of His Social and Political Influence*. London: Epworth Press, 1955.

————. "Years of Unrest: 1790–1800." *London Quarterly Review* 166 (October 1941): 451–58; 167 (January 1942): 84–93.

Elliott, Charles M. "The Ideology of Economic Growth: A Case Study." In E. L. Jones and G. E. Mingay, eds., *Land, Labour, and Population in the Industrial Revolution. Essays Presented to J. D. Chambers*. New York: Barnes and Noble, 1967.

Etheridge, J. W. *Life of the Rev. Adam Clarke*. New York: Carlton & Porter, 1859.

Evans, R. W. "Relations of George Whitefield and Howell Harris, Fathers of Calvinistic Methodism." *Church History* XXX (June 1961): 179–90.

Fanon, F. *The Wretched of the Earth*. New York: Grove Press, 1966.

Faulkner, J. A. *The Socialism of John Wesley.* London: C. H. Kelly, 1908.

Findlay, G. G., and Holdsworth, W. W. *The History of the Wesleyan Methodist Missionary Society.* London: Epworth Press, 1921.

Flew, R. Newton. *The Idea of Perfection in Christian Theology.* Oxford: Oxford University Press, 1934.

Gill, F. C. *Charles Wesley, The First Methodist.* London: Lutterworth Press, 1964.

de la Gorce, Agnes. *Wesley, Maître d'un Peuple (1703–1791).* Paris: Albin Michel, 1940.

Green, J. B. *John Wesley and William Law.* London: Epworth Press, 1945.

Green, R. *Anti-Methodist Publications Issued During the Eighteenth Century.* London: C. H. Kelly, 1902.

Green, V. H. H. *The Young Mr. Wesley: a Study of John Wesley and Oxford.* New York: St. Martin's Press, 1961.

Guizot, F. *A Popular History of England.* 4 vols. Boston, 1876.

Halévy, E. *England in 1815.* London: E. Benn, 1949.

———. "La Naissance du Méthodisme en Angleterre." *Revue de Paris* (August 1 and 15, 1906): 519–39, 841–67. Translated as *The Birth of Methodism,* by Bernard Semmel. Chicago and London: University of Chicago Press, 1971.

Hammond, J. L. and B. *The Town Labourer, 1760–1832.* London: Longmans, Green, 1918.

Harding, F. A. J. *The Social Impact of the Evangelical Revival.* London: Epworth Press, 1947.

Harrison, A. W. "Why the Eighteenth Century Dreaded Methodist Enthusiasm," in *Proceedings of the Wesley Historical Society* XVIII (1931): 40–42.

Harrison, J. F. C. *Quest for a New Moral World.* New York: Scribner's, 1969.

Haywood, C. R. "Was John Wesley a Political Economist?" *Church History* XXXIII (1964): 314–21.

Heimert, Alan. *Religion and the American Mind; From the Great Awakening to the Revolution.* Cambridge, Mass.: Harvard University Press, 1966.

Henry, L. "The Population of France in the Eighteenth Century," in D. V. Glass and D. E. C. Eversley, eds., *Population in History; Essays in Historical Demography.* Chicago: Aldine Publishing Company, 1965.

Himmelfarb, G. *Victorian Minds.* New York: Alfred A. Knopf, 1968.

Hobhouse, S. *William Law and Eighteenth Century Quakerism.* London: Allen, 1927.

Hobsbawm, E. J. *Labouring Men: Studies in the History of Labour.* New York: Basic Books, 1964.

———. *Primitive Rebels.* New York: W. W. Norton, 1965.

Hodgson, Rev. Robert. *The Life of the Right Reverend Beilby Porteus, D.D., Late Bishop of London.* London: Cadell and Davies, 1811.

Hole, Rev. Charles. *The Early History of the Church Missionary Society for Africa and the East to the End of A.D. 1814.* London: Church Missionary Society, 1896.

Holmes, J. H. *John Wesley and the Methodist Revolt.* Toronto: Ryerson Press, 1923.

Huehns, G. *Antinomianism in English History.* London: Cresset Press, 1951.

Hughes, Dorothea P. *The Life of Hugh Price Hughes.* [By his Daughter]. London: Hodder & Stoughton, 1904.

Jackson, Thomas. *The Life of John Goodwin.* London: Longmans, Hurst, Rees, etc., 1822.

————. *Life of Charles Wesley*. New York: Lane & Sandford, 1842.
————. *Memoirs of the Life and Writings of the Rev. Richard Watson*. London: John Mason, 1890.
Jones, Morgan H. *The Trevecka Letters, or the Unpublished MSS. Correspondence of Howell Harris and His Contemporaries*. London, 1932.
Kent, J. H. S. "M. Elie Halévy on Methodism," *Proceedings of the Wesley Historical Society*. XXXIV, Pt. 8 (December 1964) and XXIX, Pt. 4 (December 1953).
————. *The Age of Disunity*. London: Epworth Press, 1966.
————. *Jabez Bunting; The Last Wesleyan*. London: Epworth Press, 1955.
Kiernan, V. "Evangelicalism and the French Revolution." *Past and Present* I (1952): 44–56.
Kingdon, R. M. "Laissez-faire or Government Control: A Problem for John Wesley." *Church History* XXVI (December 1957): 342–54.
Knox, R. A. *Enthusiasm; A Chapter in the History of Religion, with Special Reference to the Seventeenth and Eighteenth Centuries*. New York: Oxford University Press, 1950.
Knutsford, Viscountess. *Life and Letters of Zachary Macaulay*. London: Edward Arnold, 1900.
de Lagarde, Georges. *Recherches sur l'esprit politique de la Réforme*. Paris: Auguste Picard, 1926.
Lamont, William. *Godly Rule*. London: Macmillan, 1970.
Lawson, A. B. *John Wesley and the Christian Ministry: The Sources and Development of His Opinions and Practice*. London: S.P.C.K., 1963.
Lawton, George. "Matthew Bramble, Tom Paine, and John Wesley. *Proceedings of the Wesley Historical Society* XXXIII, Pt. 2 (June 1961): 41–45.
Lecky, W. E. H. *A History of England in the Eighteenth Century*. 8 vols. London: Longmans, Green, 1878.
Lee, Umphrey. *The Historical Backgrounds of Early Methodist Enthusiasm*. New York: Columbia University Press, 1931.
————. *John Wesley and Modern Religion*. Nashville: Cokesbury Press, 1936.
Léger, Augustin. *L'Angleterre religieuse et les origines du Méthodisme au XVIIIᵉ siècle; la jeunesse de Wesley*. Paris: Hachette, 1910.
Lelièvre, M. *John Wesley: His Life and Work*. London: C. H. Kelly, 1900.
Lindström, Harald. *Wesley and Sanctification: A Study in the Doctrine of Salvation*. Upsala, 1946.
Lunn, A. *John Wesley*. New York: Dial, 1929.
Lyles, A. M. *Methodism Mocked; The Satiric Reaction to Methodism in the Eighteenth Century*. London: Epworth Press, 1960.
McAdoo, H. R., Bishop of Ossory. *The Spirit of Anglicanism: A Survey of Anglican Theological Method*. London: A. & C. Black, 1965.
MacArthur, K. W. *The Economic Ethics of John Wesley*. New York: Abingdon Press, 1936.
Mannoni, O. *Prospero and Caliban; The Psychology of Colonization*. New York: Frederick A. Praeger, 1956.
Martin, D. A. "The Denomination." *British Journal of Sociology* XIII (1962): 1–14.
Meacham, Standish. "The Evangelical Inheritance." *Journal of British Studies* III (1963): 88–104.
Monk, R. C. *John Wesley: His Puritan Heritage*. London: Epworth Press, 1966.
Moore, H. *Life of John Wesley*. 2 vols. New York: Bangs and Emory, 1824–1825.

Outler, A. C., ed. *John Wesley; A Representative Collection of His Writings*. New York: Oxford University Press, 1964.

Overton, J. H. *The Evangelical Revival in the Eighteenth Century*. London: Longmans, 1886.

————. *William Law, Nonjuror and Mystic*. London: Longmans, 1881.

————. *John Wesley*. London: Methuen, 1891.

————, and Relton, F. *The English Church, from the Accession of George 1 to the End of the Eighteenth Century (1714–1800)*. London: Macmillan, 1906.

Palmer, R. R. *The Age of the Democratic Revolution*. 2 vols. Princeton: Princeton University Press, 1959.

Parsons, T., and Shils, E. A. *Toward a General Theory of Action*. Cambridge, Mass.: Harvard University Press, 1962.

Peel, J. D. Y. *Herbert Spencer; the Evolution of a Sociologist*. New York: Basic Books, 1971.

Perkin, Harold. *The Origins of Modern English Society, 1780–1880*. London: Routledge & Kegan Paul, 1969.

Piette, Maximin. *John Wesley in the Evolution of Protestantism*. New York: Sheed and Ward, 1937.

Pinson, K. S. *Pietism as a Factor in the Rise of German Nationalism*. New York: Columbia University Press, 1934.

de Rémusat, Charles. *L'Angleterre au dix-huitième siècle*. Paris: Didier, 1856. 2 vols.

————. *De la Réforme et du Protestantisme*. Paris, 1854

Robbins, Caroline. *The Eighteenth Century Commonwealthman*. Cambridge Mass.: Harvard University Press, 1959.

Rupp, E. G. *Methodism in Relation to the Protestant Tradition* London: Epworth, 1954.

————. *Principalities and Powers; Studies in the Christian Conflict in History*. London: Epworth Press, 1965.

Rutt, J. T. "The Wesleys—An Attempt to Account for Their High Church Principles." *Proceedings of the Wesley Historica. Society* XI (1918): 40–42.

Sangster, W. E. *The Path of Perfection, An Examination and Restatement of John Wesley's Doctrine of Christian Perfection*. London: Hodder and Stoughton, 1943.

Schmidt, Martin. *John Wesley: A Theological Biography*. London: Epworth Press, 1962.

Semmel, B. "Elie Halévy, Methodism, and Revolution," introduction to Elie Halévy, *The Birth of Methodism in England*. Chicago: University of Chicago Press, 1971.

————. *The Governor Eyre Controversy*. London Macgibbon & Kee, 1962.

————. *Imperialism and Social Reform*. Cambridge: Harvard University Press, 1960.

————. "The Issue of 'Race' in the British Reaction to the Morant Bay Uprising of 1865," *Caribbean Studies*. II (October 1962): 3–15.

————. *The Rise of Free Trade Imperialism*. Cambridge: Cambridge University Press, 1970.

Seymour, Aaron C. H. *The Life and Times of Selina, Countess of Huntingdon*. 2 vols. London: W. E. Painter, 1844.

Shaw, Thomas. *A History of Cornish Methodism*. Truro: Barton, 1967.

Sherwin, Oscar. *John Wesley, Friend of the People*. New York: Twayne, 1961.

Simon, J. S. *John Wesley and the Methodist Societies*. London: Epworth Press, 1923.

―――――. *John Wesley and the Advance of Methodism*. London: Epworth Press, 1925.

Smith, George. *History of Wesleyan Methodism*. London: Longmans, Green, 1866, 1872.

Smith, Preserved. *The Enlightenment, 1687–1776*. (Vol. II of *A History of Modern Culture*). New York: Collier Books, 1962.

Soloway, R. A. *Prelates and People; Ecclesiastical Social Thought in England, 1783–1852*. London: Routledge & Kegan Paul, 1969.

Soman, Alfred. "Arminianism in France. The D'Huisseau Incident." *Journal of the History of Ideas* XXVIII, No. 4 (October–December 1967): 597–600.

Southey, Robert. *The Life of Wesley; and the Rise and Progress of Methodism*. 2 vols. London: Longmans, 1820.

Starkey, L. M. *The Work of the Holy Spirit: A Study in Wesleyan Theology*. New York: Abingdon Press, 1962.

Stephen, Sir James. "William Wilberforce." Vol. II, *Essays in Ecclesiastical Biography*. London: Longmans, 1849.

Stephen, Sir Leslie. *History of English Thought in the Eighteenth Century*. 2 vols. London: Smith, Elder, 1902.

Stephenson, G. J. *Methodist Worthies; Characteristic Sketches of Methodist Preachers of the Several Denominations*. London: T. C. Jack, 1884.

Stigant, P. "Wesleyan Methodism and Working-Class Radicalism in the North, 1792–1821." *Northern History* VI (1971): 98–116.

Stromberg, Roland. *Religious Liberalism in Eighteenth Century England*. 1951.

Sweet, William Warren. "John Wesley, Tory." *Methodist Quarterly Review* LXXI, No. 2 (April 1922): 255–68.

Sykes, Norman. *Church and State in England in the Eighteenth Century*. Cambridge: Cambridge University Press, 1934.

―――――. *The English Religious Tradition*. London: SCM Press, 1953.

―――――. *From Sheldon to Secker; Aspects of English Church History, 1660–1768*. Cambridge: Cambridge University Press, 1959.

Taine, H. A. *The Ancien Regime*. New York: Henry Holt, 1896.

―――――. *History of English Literature*. 4 vols. Edinburgh, 1874.

―――――. *Notes on England*. Fair Lawn, N.J.: Essential Books, 1958.

Talmon, J. L. *The Origins of Totalitarian Democracy*. New York: Praeger, 1961.

―――――. *Political Messianism; the Romantic Phase*. New York: Praeger, 1960.

Talon, Henri. *William Law: A Study in Literary Craftsmanship*. London: Rockliff, 1948.

Taylor, E. R. *Methodism and Politics, 1791–1815*. Cambridge: Cambridge University Press, 1935.

Telford, John. *The Life of Wesley*. New York: Eaton & Mains, n.d. [ca. 1911].

Tholfsen, T. R. "The Intellectual Origins of Mid-Victorian Stability." *Political Science Quarterly* LXXXVI (1971): 57–91.

Thompson, D. D. *John Wesley as a Social Reformer*. New York and Cincinnati, 1898.

Thompson, E. P. *The Making of the English Working Class*. New York: Pantheon Books, 1964.

―――――. "The Moral Economy of the English Crowd in the Eighteenth Century." *Past and Present*, No. 50 (February 1971): 76–136.

de Tocqueville, Alexis. *Democracy in America*. New York: Harper & Row, 1966.

————. *The Old Regime and the French Revolution*. Garden City, N.Y.: Anchor Books, 1955.

Toon, Peter. *The Emergence of Hyper-Calvinism in English Nonconformity, 1689–1765*. London: The Olive Tree, 1968.

Towlson, C. W. *Moravian and Methodist: Relationships and Influences in the Eighteenth Century*. London: Epworth Press, 1957.

Townsend, W. J., Workman, H. B., and Eayrs, George, eds. *A New History of Methodism*. 2 vols. London: Hodder and Stoughton, 1919.

Trevor-Roper, Hugh. *The Crisis of the Seventeenth Century: Religion, the Reformation and Social Change*. New York: Harper & Row, 1968.

Troeltsch, E. *The Social Teaching of the Christian Churches*. 2 vols. New York: Harper, 1960.

Turner, E. E. "John Wesley and Mysticism." *Methodist Review* CXIII (January 1930): 16–31.

Turner, G. A. *The Vision Which Transforms: Is Christian Perfection Scriptural?* Kansas City, Mo.: Beacon Hill Press, 1964.

Tyerman, Rev. L. *The Life and Times of the Rev. John Wesley, M.A., Founder of the Methodists*. 3 vols. London, 1890.

————. *The Oxford Methodists*. New York: Harper, 1873.

————. *Wesley's Designated Successor: The Life, Letters, and Literary Labour of the Rev. John William Fletcher*. New York: Philips and Hunt, 1883.

Vickers, John. *Thomas Coke: An Apostle of Methodism*. London: Epworth Press, 1969.

Vincent, J. R. *Pollbooks: How Victorians Voted*. Cambridge: Cambridge University Press, 1967.

Walsh, John D. "Methodism at the End of the Eighteenth Century." In *A History of the Methodist Church in Great Britain*. Edited by Davies, Rupp. London: Epworth Press, 1965.

————. "Origins of the Evangelical Revival." In *Essays in Modern English Church History. In Memory of Norman Sykes*. Edited by Bennett and Walsh. London: A. & C. Black, 1966.

————. "Methodism and the Mob in the Eighteenth Century." In *Popular Belief and Practice*. Edited by G. J. Cuming and D. Baker. Cambridge: Cambridge University Press, 1972.

Walzer, Michael. "Puritanism as a Revolutionary Ideology." *History and Theory* III, No. 1:59–90.

————. *The Revolution of the Saints: A Study in the Origin of Radical Politics*. New York: Atheneum, 1968.

Ward, W. R. "The Religion of the People and the Problem of Control, 1790–1830." In *Popular Belief and Practice*. Edited by G. J. Cuming and D. Baker. Cambridge: Cambridge University Press, 1972.

Warner, W. J. *The Wesleyan Movement in the Industrial Revolution*. London: Longmans, Green, 1930.

Warnock, Mary. Introduction to J. S. Mill, *Utilitarianism, On Liberty, Essay on Bentham*. New York: World, 1962. pp. 14–15.

Wearmouth, R. F. *Methodism and the Common People of the Eighteenth Century*. London: Epworth Press, 1945.

————. *Methodism and the Working-Class Movements of England, 1800–1850*. London: Epworth Press, 1937.

Weber, Max. *From Max Weber: Essays in Sociology*. Translated and edited by H. H. Gerth and C. W. Mills. New York: Oxford University Press, 1946.

Weinstein, F., and Platt, G. M. *The Wish to Be Free: Society, Psyche, and Value Change*. Berkeley: University of California Press, 1969.

Whitehead, John. *The Life of the Rev. John Wesley*. Philadelphia: Stockton, 1845.

Whitney, A. P. *The Basis of Opposition to Methodism in England in the Eighteenth Century*. New York: New York University Press, 1951.

Wilberforce, R. I. and S. *The Life of William Wilberforce*. 5 vols. London: John Murray, 1838.

Williams, C. W. *John Wesley's Theology Today*. New York: Abingdon Press, 1960.

Wilson, D. D. *Many Waters Cannot Quench: A Study of Sufferings of Eighteenth Century Methodism and their Significance for John Wesley and the First Methodists*. London: Epworth Press, 1969.

Wood, A. S. *The Inextinguishable Blaze: Spiritual Renewal and Advance in the Eighteenth Century*. London: Paternoster Press, 1960.

Yates, A. S. *The Doctrine of Assurance with Special Reference to John Wesley*. London: Epworth Press, 1952.

Index